Sacred Rhetoric

THE FAIRLEIGH DICKINSON UNIVERSITY PRESS SERIES IN COMMUNICATION STUDIES

General Editor: Gary Radford, Department of Communication Studies, Fairleigh Dickinson University, Madison, New Jersey.

The Fairleigh Dickinson University Press Series in Communication Studies publishes scholarly works in communication theory, practice, history, and culture.

On the Web at http://www.fdu.edu/fdupress
Recent Publications in Communication Studies

David M. Barbee and Brent C. Sleasman, *Sacred Rhetoric: Discourses in Identity and Meaning* (2024)
Corey Anton, *How Non-being Haunts Being: On Possibilities, Morality, and Death Acceptance* (2020)
Özüm Üçok-Sayrak, *Aesthetic Ecology of Communication Ethics: Existential Rootedness* (2019)
Jennifer Biedendorf, *Cosmopolitanism and the Development of the International Criminal Court: Non-Governmental Organizations' Advocacy and Transnational Human Rights* (2019)
Kate Dunsmore, *Discourse of Reciprocity* (2019)
Paul Matthew St. Pierre, *Cinematography of Carl Theodor Dreyer: Performative Camerawork, Transgressing the Frame* (2018)
Michelle Scollo and Trudy Milburn (eds.), *Engaging and Transforming Global Communication through Cultural Discourse Analysis: A Tribute to Donal Carbaugh* (2018)
Isaac E. Catt, *Embodiment in the Semiotic Matrix: Communicology in Peirce, Dewey, Bateson, and Bourdieu* (2017)
Craig T. Maier, *Communicating Catholicism: Rhetoric, Ecclesial Leadership, and the Future of the American Roman Catholic Diocese* (2016)
Paul Matthew St. Pierre, *Cinematography in the Weimar Republic: Lola-Lola, Dirty Singles, and the Men Who Shot Them* (2016)
Anastacia Kurylo and Tatyana Dumov (eds.), *Social Networking: Redefining Communication in the Digital Age* (2016)

Sacred Rhetoric

Discourses in Identity and Meaning

Edited by

David M. Barbee
Brent C. Sleasman

FAIRLEIGH DICKINSON UNIVERSITY PRESS
Vancouver • Madison • Teaneck • Wroxton

Published by Fairleigh Dickinson University Press
Copublished by The Rowman & Littlefield Publishing Group, Inc.
4501 Forbes Boulevard, Suite 200, Lanham, Maryland 20706
www.rowman.com

86-90 Paul Street, London EC2A 4NE, United Kingdom

Copyright © 2024 by The Rowman & Littlefield Publishing Group, Inc.

All rights reserved. No part of this book may be reproduced in any form or by any electronic or mechanical means, including information storage and retrieval systems, without written permission from the publisher, except by a reviewer who may quote passages in a review.

Fairleigh Dickinson University Press gratefully acknowledges the support received for scholarly publishing from the Friends of FDU Press.

British Library Cataloguing in Publication Information Available

Library of Congress Cataloging-in-Publication Data

Names: Barbee, David M., 1978– editor. | Sleasman, Brent C., editor.
Title: Sacred rhetoric : discourses in identity and meaning / edited by David Barbee, Brent C. Sleasman.
Description: Vancouver ; Madison : Fairleigh Dickinson University Press, 2024. | Series: The fairleigh dickinson university press series in communication studies | Includes bibliographical references and index. | Summary: "The collective essays in Sacred Rhetoric dissect the manner in which religious actors or religious themes inform various layers of cultural discourse to foster discussion based upon a greater awareness of the issues at stake and contribute to ongoing discourse about identity and meaning."—Provided by publisher.
Identifiers: LCCN 2023049599 (print) | LCCN 2023049600 (ebook) | ISBN 9781683933489 (cloth) | ISBN 9781683933496 (epub)
Subjects: LCSH: Rhetoric—Religious aspects. | Language and languages—Religious aspects.
Classification: LCC BL65.L2 S15 2024 (print) | LCC BL65.L2 (ebook) | DDC 201/.6808—dc23/eng/20240117
LC record available at https://lccn.loc.gov/2023049599
LC ebook record available at https://lccn.loc.gov/2023049600

∞™ The paper used in this publication meets the minimum requirements of American National Standard for Information Sciences—Permanence of Paper for Printed Library Materials, ANSI/NISO Z39.48-1992.

Contents

Introduction   vii
  David M. Barbee

Chapter 1: Temporal Light and Shadows: The Rhetoric of the Sacred   1
  Ronald C. Arnett

Chapter 2: The Sacred as Rhetoric: Contextualized Story
Performances in Ancient Delphi   17
  Corey Hackworth

Chapter 3: The Music Never Stops: Some Grateful Dead in the
American Mystical Tradition   45
  Aaron K. Kerr

Chapter 4: Unashamedly Just: Doctrine of Justification by Grace
through Faith as Anti-Shame Rhetoric   77
  Sang-Il Kim

Chapter 5: Walker Percy's Rhetoric of the Sacred: Signposts in the
Strange Land of Triadic Communication   101
  Michael R. Kearney

Chapter 6: Pastoral Preaching: Prophetic and Priestly Rhetoric in
Congregational Leadership   131
  Steven Tramel Gaines

Chapter 7: Sex, Purity, and Community in First-Century
Corinth: Paul's Disciplinary Directive in 1 Corinthians
5:3–5, Its Meaning, Anticipated Outcome, and Contemporary
Applicability   151
  James P. Sweeney

Chapter 8: Joy and Mercy: The Heart of Pope Francis's Rhetoric of
   Restoration and Reform   185
   Dũng Q. Trần

Chapter 9: Leaning into Death: A Philosophy of Equanimity   221
   Annette M. Holba

Index   239

About the Editors and Contributors   243

Introduction

David M. Barbee

What exactly *is* "sacred rhetoric?" For many readers, the conjunction of the terms likely solicits connotations of preaching or some other act of public religious speech. That is a reasonable conclusion to reach. A quick internet search for "sacred rhetoric" may yield a nineteenth-century homiletical instructional manual, a more contemporary exploration of preaching practice, or a study of seventeenth-century English adaptation and development of classical rhetoric as found in treatises on rhetoric and preaching manuals.[1] Although this is a natural and perhaps even unavoidable conclusion to reach, it does represent a radical diminution of the potential for academic analysis of the concept. "Sacred rhetoric" certainly covers homiletics, but it is also conceptually plastic enough to stretch over a much wider territory. An examination of the terms will elucidate the possibilities for further engagement as well as the themes of the essays in this initial inquiry.

Rhetoric is perhaps an easier entrée point insofar as there are standard canonical definitions of the term. In his work on rhetoric, Aristotle succinctly defines it "as the faculty of observing in any given case the available means of persuasion . . . as the power of observing the means of persuasion on almost any subject presented to us."[2] The philosopher asserted that, like dialectics, rhetoric transcends the boundaries of the sciences and so serves as a kind of universal method that everyone could employ in evaluating or constructing arguments.[3] The pseudo-Ciceronian *Ad Herennium* delimits rhetoric to the theory of public speaking while also clearly delineating three specific forms of rhetoric related to the tasks of the public speaker. The anonymous author states that the "epideictic kind is devoted to the praise or censure of some specific person. The deliberative consists in the discussion of policy and embraces persuasion and dissuasion. The judicial is based on legal controversy, and comprises criminal prosecution or civil suit, and defence."[4] Classical rhetoric hits a zenith with the Ciceronian corpus. It influences Christianity, at least in part because of the rhetorical training of luminary figures such as Augustine. The tradition survives through the medieval period and into the Renaissance period, though it is often depicted as a narrative of decline before a period of rejuvenation, particularly marked by interest in Cicero.[5] This story need not distract us here.

In some ways, Aristotle's definition of rhetoric foreshadows twentieth-century developments in the philosophy of language and the application of rhetoric. The advent of analytic philosophy and the accompanying "linguistic turn" marks a sharpening focus on language in its attempt to describe reality. Richard Rorty, one of the initial torchbearers of the movement, described "linguistic philosophy" as "the view that philosophical problems are problems which may be solved (or dissolved) either by reforming language, or by understanding more about the language we presently use."[6] Among other cornerstones, the movement is founded upon the work of Ludwig Wittgenstein. The initial soundings are voiced in his earlier *Tractatus Logico-Philosophicus*, but in his *Philosophical Investigations*, Wittgenstein comments,

> We must do away with all *explanation*, and description alone must take its place. And this description gets its light, that is to say its purpose, from the philosophical problems. These are, of course, not empirical problems; they are solved, rather, by looking into the workings of our language, and that in such a way as to make us recognize these workings *in despite of* an urge to misunderstand them. The problems are solved, not by reporting new experience, but by arranging what we have always known. Philosophy is a battle against the bewitchment of our intelligence by means of our language.[7]

Language becomes a method for doing philosophy, a kind of first philosophy, with the recognition that language is inherently a symbolic system designed to convey meaning.

The "linguistic turn" presages and develops alongside a revitalization in the study of rhetoric in the last decades of the twentieth century. The so-called new rhetorics or "rhetorical turn" dissents from the classical tradition to some degree but shows affinities with the concerns in the "linguistic turn." I. A. Richards, for example, describes rhetoric as "a study of misunderstanding and its remedies."[8] Dilip Gaonkar helpfully enumerates three ways the movement evolves as it shifts from a disparate body of ideas into a more cohesive and constructive movement. First, Gaonkar observes that "as a pedagogical practice, rhetoric is no longer viewed as a merely technical discipline for imparting communicative skills. It is now seen as the medium *par excellence* for molding the human personality."[9] In this way, rhetoric is intended both to shape eloquent speech and create citizens made for community. Second, the scope of rhetoric is further broadened as it shifts from being "a discursive instrument of politics into that which is constitutive of politic discourse. This transformation is mediated through a certain equation between rhetoric, politics, and ideology."[10] In what likely seems an obvious point now, rhetoric draws attention to the equation of discourse as inherently ideological and ideology as laden with symbols and serves to unmask biases within discursive structures. Third, pushing back against a tradition hostile to rhetoric as viewed as something alien and artificial while limited to literary expression in either written or oral form, advocates of the "rhetorical turn" all "deny that tropes and figures are artificial creations of the schoolmaster's classificatory mania. They point out that tropes and figures are a common feature of 'ordinary' language rather than the special feature of 'literary' language."[11] This has the effect of normalizing and naturalizing rhetoric as a common human expression. All of this repositions rhetoric as a metadiscipline that can be deployed across all formats of human communication and discourse.

Much of the foregoing is drawn together in semiotics. Umberto Eco identifies the scope of a general semiotics as "the whole of the human signifying activity—languages—and languages are what constitutes human beings as such, that is, as semiotic animals. It studies and describes languages through languages. By studying the human signifying activity it influences its course. A general semiotics transforms, for the very fact of its theoretical claim, its own object."[12] Semiotics generally pivots around the concepts of the signifier, the sign, and the signified. As Roland Barthes explains it, "The sign is a (two-faced) slice of sonority, visuality, etc. The *signification* can be conceived as a process; it is the act which binds the signifier and the signified, an act whose product is the sign."[13] The meaning of a sign, whatever it is, results as the product of the process of signification; there is nothing inherent in a cow that makes us call it a cow. Yet, a connection has been forged between the sign "cow" and our concept of "cow." This is the act of signification. Meaning here is only relative to the context of agreed upon signs. Systems of meaning can then be constructed. This is, more or less, what constitutes language as a value structure.[14]

Note the flexibility of the nature of the sign in Barthes's definition. It can be something spoken, seen, or delivered through any other mode of communication. This opens the possibility of conceptualizing society as a constellation of signs. Barthes himself applies this technique to food, clothes, and furniture in *Elements of Semiology*.[15] This, though, is only a window into his much more extensive treatment in *Mythologies*, in which a wrestling match, steak, and a Billy Graham crusade, among other topics, are all dismantled semiotically to reveal the manner in which culture functions similar to language insofar as both are relative and historically conditioned.[16] Barthes's methodology is fairly amenable to that of scholars in other discipline of social sciences. The anthropologist Clifford Geertz, for example, states that the "concept of culture I espouse . . . is essentially a semiotic one. Believing, with Max Weber, that man is an animal suspended in webs of significance he himself has spun, I take culture to be those webs of significance he himself has spun, I take culture to be those webs, and the analysis of it to be therefore not an experimental science in search of law but an interpretive one in search of meaning."[17] For Geertz, the heart of interpretive anthropology is unraveling those webs in the form of cultural symbols to discover their underlying meaning. Sociologists Peter Berger and Thomas Luckmann identify language as the force behind the construction of "immense edifices of symbolic representations that appear to tower over the reality of everyday life like gigantic presences from another world."[18] These "symbolic universes," as Berger and Luckmann call them, erected by society provide order and meaning for an individual situated therein. Seen in this light, culture is the end product of rhetorical discourse as signs are created and assigned meaning. This is a point seized upon by postmodern thinkers such as Jean-François Lyotard.[19]

If that is a sufficient account of the function and nature of rhetoric in the process of cultural formation, we can then turn our attention to the sacred part of sacred rhetoric. At the inception of modern comparative religious studies lies the idea of the sacred as defined by Rudolf Otto. Otto intends his definition of the sacred to cut across all theistic traditions. He begins by carving out the category of *numen*, an ineffable state or awareness of the absolute holiness and goodness of God.[20] Alternatively, Otto employs the phrase *mysterium tremendum et fascinans* (a fearful and fascinating mystery). This is a composite concept intended to convey the awful majesty, the wholly otherness of the divine, marked by a sense of curious fascination as well.[21] Otto's account proved to be highly influential and directly influenced some of the chief architects of comparative religious studies such as Mircea Eliade. In fact, Eliade explicitly invokes Otto at the outset of *The Sacred and the Profane* to define the "sacred" as simply the opposite of the profane.[22] For Eliade, the sacred does manifest itself in various forms he calls hierophanies, ranging from a stone or a tree in traditional religions to the incarnation of God in Jesus in Christianity.[23]

It is this instantiation that helps to explain the solidification of religion as a category. Religion has proved to be a notoriously difficult concept to define.[24] Ninian Smart, a scholar who also shows some indebtedness to Otto, enumerates no less than seven different dimensions of religion, noting that each tradition will place a greater or lesser weight on each dimension:

1. *Ritual.* A dimension that involves religious activities such as sacraments, worship, meditation, healing ritual practices, etcetera.

2. *Doctrinal or philosophical.* This dimension has to do with the key teachings of a tradition, typically understood to justify or explain ritual practices.
3. *Mythic or narrative.* This consists of the stories embedded within religious traditions, such as one might fit in the New Testament gospels about Jesus or the Mahāparinibbāṇa Sutta consisting of the last days of Gautama Buddha's life.
4. *Experiential or emotional.* Otto's influence is felt here as this is the dimension relevant to the experience of *numen*, whether one finds it in conversion or a mystical ecstatic vision.
5. *Ethical or legal.* Religious traditions typically obligate some kind of behavioral change to adherents and provide guidelines for conduct. Obvious examples include the Torah in Judaism and sharia in Islam.
6. *Organizational or social.* This dimension takes into account the social incorporation of a religion within society, describing hierarchical structures or the designation of religious experts in priests or imams.
7. *Material or artistic.* Running alongside the structure of a religion is the expression of religion in material realities, including icons within strands of Christianity or a Zoroastrian fire temple.[25]

By comparison, Bruce Lincoln proposes a more modest four domains, which similarly allows for flexibility in application to divergent religious traditions and covers familiar territory:

1. *Discourse.* Discourse becomes religious when it is both authoritative and transcendent, insofar as it is based on just such a source. Discourses, consisting of propositions or narratives, "position themselves as truths to be interpreted, but never ignored or rejected."
2. *Practices.* This domain covers both ritual practice as well as ethical for Lincoln, bringing discourse into operation. The discourse provides the motivation for the practice and thereby legitimizes it as religious in nature.
3. *Community.* Community life centers around and is galvanized by the discourse and practices. The prior two domains foster communal boundaries and contribute to a shared affinity over and against outsiders; when there is internal dissent, disagreements refer to how to understand the discourse or how to perform practices, not whether they are valid.
4. *Institution.* Community life all but demands a regulatory body that oversees correct interpretation of the discourse and application of the discourse in appropriate practices. The goal of the institution is to faithfully reproduce the discourse and practices, thereby preserving the

community through established structures. Authoritative structures vary widely from a hierarchical church to more decentralized traditions.[26]

Given the complex and comprehensive definition of religion that Smart and Lincoln offer, one might ultimately prefer Paul Tillich's definition of religion simply as "that which is ultimate, infinite, unconditional in man's spiritual life. Religion, in the largest and most basic sense of the word, is ultimate concern."[27]

Both Smart and Lincoln draw our attention to the sociological dimension of religion. In fact, Geertz defines a religion as "(1) a system of symbols which acts to (2) establish powerful, pervasive, and long-lasting moods and motivations in men by (3) formulating conceptions of a general order of existence and (4) clothing these conceptions with such an aura of factuality that (5) the moods and motivations seem uniquely realistic."[28] Geertz's definition is too expansive to work through here. It is sufficient to conclude, as Geertz does, that the anthropological study of religions involves, first, an analysis of symbols within a religious culture; and second, connection of these symbols to social-structural and psychological processes.[29]

Peter Berger strikes similar chords when he writes that "religion has played a strategic part in the human enterprise of world-building. Religion implies the farthest reach of man's self-externalization, of his infusion of reality with his own meanings. Religion implies that human order is projected into the totality of being. Put differently, religion is the audacious attempt to conceive of the entire universe as being humanly significant."[30] Invoking language reminiscent of Otto, Berger views religion as the establishment of a sacred cosmos in which the sacred permeates the created order, pointing humans to a transcendent reality.[31] Bearing in mind Talal Asad's criticism of an anthropological approach as inevitably Procrustean in nature and observing that an adherent to a religious tradition would not likely see religion as *only* or even *primarily* in sociological terms absent a confession of some kind of belief in transcendence, some value still remains in reading religion through these analytic lenses.[32]

Assuming a modest acceptance of the foregoing accounts of religion that Geertz and Berger advance along with the definitions that Smart and Lincoln offer, the discursive nature of religion can be seen. Working within the Christian tradition, George Lindbeck draws upon Geertz and Wittgenstein, among others, in developing what he calls a "cultural-linguistic" view of doctrine. According to this schema as Lindbeck describes it, the "function of church doctrines that becomes more prominent in this perspective is their use, not as expressive symbols or as truth claims, but as communally authoritative rules of discourse, attitude, and action."[33] In his account, religions "are seen as comprehensive interpretive schemes, usually embodied in myths or narratives and heavily ritualized, which structure human experience and understanding of self and world."[34]

Lindbeck distinguishes between three kinds of truth: categorial, ontological, and intrasystematic. The first is analogous to a kind of grammar for "construing reality, expressing experience, and ordering life."[35] This may, in fact, correspond to ontological truth as rightly used and corresponds to ultimate reality.[36] Intrasystematic truth is simply the measure of internal coherence within a given system of religion, though intrasystematic truth may not be ontologically true.[37] Lindbeck's work illustrates the potential for discourse analysis in unfolding the many layers of meaning within a religion. That he has an eye on interreligious dialogue is suggestive. Marcus Moberg argues that the use of discourse analysis is an urgent matter in religious studies that will advance the field.[38]

If we recall the prior account of cultural as rhetorical in nature, there is a sense in which one can say the same of religion. In fact, Kenneth Burke maintains that the

> subject of religion falls under the head of *rhetoric* in the sense that rhetoric is the art of *persuasion*, and religious cosmogonies, in the last analysis, as exceptionally thoroughgoing modes of persuasion. To persuade men towards certain acts, religions would form the kinds of attitude which prepare men for such acts. And in order to plead for such attitudes as persuasively as possible, the religious always ground their exhortations (to themselves and others) in statements of the widest and deepest possible scope, concerning the authorship of men's motives.[39]

It is entirely possible that Burke is overstating his case here, but it is nonetheless true that religions borrow from rhetorical traditions and are, in turn, shaped by rhetoric. The history of Christianity is shot through with rhetoricians who have framed the message of their faith by employing rhetoric.[40] Christianity is hardly alone. One can find rhetoric deployed in Zen Buddhism as well as Muslim sources.[41] It might even be true that Yahweh of the Hebrew Bible was a kind of rhetorician.[42]

Given the common language of culture and religion, the potential is great for fruitful exchange under the rubric sacred rhetoric. Sacred rhetoric might ultimately be defined as a consideration of discourses of religion, both as it is depicted in various media formats and how religious practitioners discuss issues within confessional communities, including the depiction of religion and religious issues in popular media, philosophies of religious language, and the discussion or presentation of ethical/philosophical debates in popular media and within religious communities. Richard Kearney's anatheism, understood as "an invitation to revisit what might be termed a primary scene of religion: the encounter with a radical Stranger who we choose, or don't choose, to call God," draws our attention to the way the sacred inhabits cultural forms in our midst.[43] It should come as no surprise that the sacred emerges in literature, art, music, and film.[44] Even baseball and amusement parks could be construed as having sacred dimensions.[45]

Another more meaningful locus of interaction is in the construction of personal identity. If both culture and religion offer meaning, both inevitably shape a sense of personhood through how worth is assigned. In his magisterial study of modern anthropology, Charles Taylor identifies three distinct axes that inform moral thinking about the self, particularly in relation to others. These are "our sense of respect for and obligation to others, and our understandings of what makes a full life," along with "the range of notions concerned with dignity."[46]

At the core of modern anthropology, Taylor finds a "sense that human life is to be respected and that the prohibitions and obligations that this imposes on us are among the most weighty and serious in our lives." This idea of respect, though, is "peculiarly modern" and involves "a salient place for freedom and self-control, places a high priority on avoiding suffering, and sees productive activity and family life as central to our well-being."[47] But, the degree to which respect is understood to be culturally subjective, rather than rooted in an objective metaphysical reality, is the degree to which the framework provides by the axes begins to dissolve and that is the degree to which a sense of meaning and identity is lost. This gives rise to what Taylor sees as a uniquely modern preoccupation in the fear that life may actually be meaningless.[48] Modernity lacks what Taylor calls a "constitutive good" that serves both as a moral source and an object to be loved, thereby empowering us to love the good.[49] Taylor ultimately concludes that a retrieval of "Judaeo-Christian theism (however terrible the record of its adherents in history), and in its central promise of a divine affirmation of the human" can cure the self-mutilation delivered through the agency of purely secular anthropologies.[50]

Critical theorists have offered up a variety of options for articulating the formation of human identity. Michel Foucault practically revels in the deconstruction of modern anthropology, insofar as it both banishes dogmatism and facilitates the renewal of philosophy.[51] For Foucault, human nature is bound together with philosophy of language, particularly a kind of discourse. The problem of finitude entails that a human is a "strange empirico-transcendental doublet"; that is, in Foucault's estimation, humans are both sources of transcendental representation and constructed by empirical representation.[52] This is why he can conclude that the "only thing we know at the moment, in all certainty, is that in Western culture the being of man and the being of language have never, at any time, been able to coexist and to articulate themselves one upon the other.[53]

Paul Ricoeur offers a contrasting account. Ricoeur shares in Foucault's rejection of a kind of essentialism as an answer to defining human nature but seeks to rehabilitate the idea of personhood from the incoherence that results from assigning competing descriptions to an individual.[54] He finds a solution in what he calls "narrative identity." He comments, "Our own existence cannot be separated from the account we can give of ourselves. It is in telling our own stories that we give ourselves an identity. We recognize ourselves in the stories we tell about ourselves."[55] It is narrative that binds together the dialectical components of identity, sameness (*idem*-identity) and selfhood (*ipse*-identity) through the formation of a character that provides a stable core of identity, even while allowing for change.[56]

Jacques Lacan's mirror stage theory provides another alternative for the construction of the self in critical theory. Lacan's appropriation of Freud posits that an infant's encounter of his or her *imago* in a mirror constitutes a gestalt, an ideal-I, toward which one strives, even though one surpasses the mirror stage at a young age. The self is shaped out of a dialect between the inner, speculative I and the outer, social I for Lacan. The formation and maturation of the individual is, therefore, contingent upon external social conditions in Lacan, as one assumes an identity through social engagement. Naturally, this can give rise to misconstruals of the self, though the ideal-I formed in the mirror stage serves as a bulwark against misformations and can also be addressed through psychoanalysis.[57] The approaches to postmodern anthropology could go on and on for quite some time. Each of the critical thinkers briefly canvassed here offers different perspectives on the question of human identity and formation, though each assumes that an ontological definition is no longer tenable and instead emphasize the formation of the self through other means.

Religious traditions propose various solutions to the basic question of human nature as well. "It is clear that there are a number of variant positions that can be taken of the place of human life in the universe, and it seems that every possible position has been filled by some world-view," Keith Ward observes. "Since these views span the whole spectrum of possibilities, it would be absurd to say that they all really agree."[58]

While running the risk of overgeneralization, one might say that religious traditions often communicate a kind of ambivalence regarding human nature in simultaneously affirming the goodness of human nature and positing a deficiency. It is the tension between the two that tends to serve as a catalyst and provides direction for religious behavior. Although theologians in each tradition disagree over what the term means, the Judeo-Christian doctrine belief in human creation in the image of God according to Genesis 1:26–27 upholds the essential goodness of human nature and serves as a basis for ethics.[59] Perhaps unsurprisingly, similar views can be found in Islam.

In Quran 30:30, the passage implies at the very least that all human beings have a *fitra*, or an inclination, toward Allah, though not everyone realizes it. Humans are created as *khala'if*, Allah's representatives on Earth according to Quran 6:165, an interpretation of human nature compatible with some readings of the passage in Genesis. There is a sense in which some Eastern religions share this sense of optimism about human nature. One might think most generally about the non-dualist Advaita Vedānta school within Hinduism and its all-inclusive view of reality in which everything participates in Brahman.[60] Certain passages in the *Tao Te Ching* evidence a similar kind of panentheism that extends to include human nature.[61] Ward's caution is well heeded at this point in that although these traditions maintain a positive view of human nature as in touch with the divine, each tradition articulates different anthropological discourses that distinguish one from the other.

The same holds true when one considers religious anthropology from the opposite perspective. It is typically this more negative assessment that triggers views on salvation, liberation, or other such constructs. The most radical position in this trajectory is found within Buddhism in the teaching of anattā or anātman, the belief that there is no such thing as an essential, permanent self. In the *Visuddhimagga*, it is written that "when we come to examine the elements of being one by one, we discover that in the absolute sense there is no living entity there to form a basis for such figments as 'I am' or 'I'; in other words, that in the absolute sense there is only name and form."[62] The thing we call human nature is only a collection of five impermanent *skandhas* that amount to attachment to the material world.

More moderate views identify a kind of deficient or corruption in human nature. This can take different forms and, consequently, alter the understanding of personal identity. The doctrine of original sin found predominantly in Western Christianity posits a basic kind of corruption to human creation in the image of God. These two contrasting ideas are held in creative dynamic tension in Martin Luther's belief in Christians as *simul justus et peccator*, simultaneously sinful and just. Other traditions retain a positive view of human personhood in the present life, even while realizing that development of one kind or another is required. Self-cultivation is central to Confucianism, for example, and the difference between a *junzi* (a gentleman) and a *xiaoren* (a small or petty person) is practice.[63] These more sobering accounts of human nature give rise to practices of asceticism and mysticism that seek to reshape the self and transcend traditions.

Socially, this outlook can manifest in hostility toward or distancing from those who stand outside the tradition, particularly among exclusivist religious traditions. Part of Judaism's self-definition, for example, comes through a contrast with *goy*, or non-Jews.[64] Interpreting Islam on this point is obviously more controversial and relevant in the modern world. While Islam does distinguish between *dhimmis*, Jews and Christians as people of the book, and adherents to other religious traditions, this does not always guarantee that *dhimmis* are regarded as equals with Muslims.[65] Insofar as Christianity provides the context for colonialism, it contributes to what Antonio Gramsci has described as a subaltern, those who are disenfranchised within a society.[66] Gramsci's concept can be and has been applied to the caste system in Hinduism, with a focus on the plight of the *dalit* in Indian culture.[67] In the extreme, this process of dehumanizing can contribute to the formation of an apocalyptic worldview that justifies the use of religious violence insofar as it places an adherent within the context of a cosmic war against the forces of evil and endows such actions with divine blessing. This worldview forms the basis for the development of cults and sects across religious traditions.[68] To be fair, religious traditions often have internal resources to defuse the process of dehumanization. One might point toward the Bartolomé de las Casas's passionate defense of the indigenous peoples of the Americas over and against his coreligionist colonizers precisely on the grounds that the native inhabitants are human and, therefore, reflect the image of God.[69] That there is dissent within traditions is a function of internal discourses among adherents within an architecture of communal doctrinal or ideological beliefs.

In an alluringly titled essay, Jürgen Habermas notes "the defeatism lurking within" modern reason and calls for a secular engagement with faith traditions to compensate for what he seems to think is a gaping lacuna modern society.[70] Although this is a bit of a departure from Habermas's earlier views, it is consistent with later developments in his career. Just a few years prior, Habermas commended on openness to cognitive content from religion, including semantic content, provided such content can be detached from claims of revelation, on the grounds that "the regenerative power of the metaphysical heritage is supposed in this way to compensate for a *lack* in modernity."[71] Habermas might be overly optimistic in his hope for a meaningful dialogue between religious traditions and secular ideologies in modern society.[72]

If there is any hope for religion to accept Habermas's invitation to a seat at the table in the public sphere, it is up to sacred rhetoric to unmask the discourses latent within religious traditions and place them in dialogue with larger cultural semiotic structures. One cannot understand religious dispositions toward gender identity, race, and other issues related to personal identity without first locating them within larger doctrinal discourses. This is an area where religion may have much to contribute to the conversation. The same is true on a myriad of other issues in which religion and culture collide over matters of meaning and value.

NOTES

1. Robert L. Dabney, *Sacred Rhetoric; Or, A Course of Lectures on Preaching* (New York: Anson D. F. Randolph, 1870); Michael Pasquarello III, *Sacred Rhetoric: Preaching as a Theological and Pastoral Practice of the Church* (Eugene, OR: Wipf and Stock, 2005); and Debora K. Shuger, *Sacred Rhetoric: The Christian Grand Style in the English Renaissance* (Princeton, NJ: Princeton University Press, 1988), respectively.
2. Aristotle, *Rhetoric*, in *The Complete Works of Aristotle*, ed. Jonathan Barnes, 2 vols. (Princeton, NJ: Princeton University Press, 1984), I.2.27–33.
3. Aristotle, *Rhetoric*, in *The Complete Works of Aristotle*, I.1.1–6.
4. Pseudo-Cicero, *Rhetorica ad Herennium*, trans. Henry Caplan, Loeb Classical Library (Cambridge: Harvard University Press, 1964), I.II.2.
5. See George A. Kennedy, *Classical Rhetoric and Its Christian and Secular Tradition from Ancient to Modern Times*, 2nd ed. (Chapel Hill: University of North Carolina Press, 1999), 183–258; and Virginia Cox and John Ward, ed., *The Rhetoric of Cicero in its Medieval and Early Renaissance Commentary Tradition* (Leiden: Brill, 2018).
6. Richard M. Rorty, "Introduction: Metaphysical Difficulties of Linguistic Philosophy," in *The Linguistic Turn: Essays in Philosophical Method; with Two Retrospective Essays*, ed. Richard M. Rorty, 2nd ed. (Chicago: University of Chicago Press, 1992), 3.
7. Ludwig Wittgenstein, *Philosophical Investigations*, trans. G. E. M. Anscombe (Oxford: Blackwell Publishing, 2001), 40.
8. I. A. Richards, *The Philosophy of Rhetoric* (London: Oxford University Press, 1936), 3.
9. Dilip Parameshwar Gaonkar, "The Revival of Rhetoric, the New Rhetoric, and the Rhetorical Turn: Some Distinctions," *Informal Logic* 15 (1993): 59.
10. Gaonkar, "The Revival of Rhetoric, the New Rhetoric, and the Rhetorical Turn," 59.
11. Gaonkar, "The Revival of Rhetoric, the New Rhetoric, and the Rhetorical Turn," 60.
12. Umberto Eco, *Semiotics and the Philosophy of Language* (Bloomington: Indiana University Press, 1986), 12.
13. Roland Barthes, *Elements of Semiology*, trans. Annette Lavers and Colin Smith (New York: Hill & Wang, 1973), 48.
14. Barthes, *Elements of Semiology*, 14.
15. Barthes, *Elements of Semiology*, 25–29.
16. Roland Barthes, *Mythologies*, trans. Richard Howard and Annette Lavers (New York: Hill & Wang, 2012), 3–14, 83–85, and 109–12, for Barthes's analysis of these specific examples.
17. Clifford Geertz, *The Interpretation of Cultures* (New York: Basic Books, 1973), 5.
18. Peter L. Berger and Thomas Luckmann, *The Social Construction of Reality: A Treatise in the Sociology of Knowledge* (New York: Anchor Books, 1967), 40.

19. Jean-François Lyotard, *The Postmodern Condition: A Report on Knowledge*, trans. Geoff Bennington and Brian Massumi (Minneapolis: University of Minnesota Press, 1984), 9–17.

20. Rudolf Otto, *The Idea of the Holy*, trans. John W. Harvey (Oxford: Oxford University Press, 1950), 5–7.

21. Otto, *The Idea of the Holy*, 12–40.

22. Mircea Eliade, *The Sacred and the Profane: The Nature of Religion*, trans. Willard R. Trask (New York: Harcourt, 1987), 10.

23. Eliade, *The Sacred and the Profane*, 11.

24. In part, the challenge lies in identifying religion as a discrete area of study that transcends the world in the style of Eliade as opposed to something that exists within and reflects specific historic-social contexts. The other part of the dilemma is in developing an essential definition that is not biased toward one tradition or another and is adequately large enough to cover all religions without being too vague. As such, the question is both foundational and methodologically important, unleashing a number of fine studies. See Russell T. McCutcheon, *Manufacturing Religion: The Discourse of Sui Generis Religion and the Politics of Nostalgia* (Oxford: Oxford University Press, 1997); and Tomoko Masuzawa, *The Invention of World Religions: Or, How European Universalism Was Preserved in the Language of Pluralism* (Chicago: University of Chicago Press, 2005).

25. Ninian Smart, *Dimensions of the Sacred: An Anatomy of the World's Beliefs* (Berkeley: University of California Press, 1996), 10–11.

26. Bruce Lincoln, *Holy Terrors: Thinking about Religion after September 11*, 2nd ed. (Chicago: University of Chicago Press, 2006), 5–7.

27. Paul Tillich, *Theology of Culture*, ed. Robert C. Kimball (Oxford: Oxford University Press, 1959), 7–8.

28. Geertz, *The Interpretation of Cultures*, 90.

29. Geertz, *The Interpretation of Cultures*, 125.

30. Peter L. Berger, *The Sacred Canopy: Elements of a Sociological Theory of Religion* (New York: Anchor Books, 1990), 27–28. John Bowker critiques Berger's notion of projection as essentially Freudian. But this is likely an inevitable position given Berger's commitment to methodological atheism. See John Bowker, *The Sense of God: Sociological, Anthropological, and Psychological Approaches to the Origin of the Sense of God* (Oxford: Oneworld, 1995), 31–43.

31. Berger, *The Sacred Canopy*, 25–26.

32. See Talal Asad's appraisal of Geertz in *Genealogies of Religion: Discipline and Reasons of Power in Christianity and Islam* (Baltimore: Johns Hopkins University Press, 1993), 29.

33. George A. Lindbeck, *The Nature of Doctrine: Religion and Theology in a Postliberal Age*, 25th anniversary edition (Louisville, KY: Westminster John Knox Press, 2009), 4.

34. Lindbeck, *The Nature of Doctrine*, 18.

35. Lindbeck, *The Nature of Doctrine*, 33–34.

36. Lindbeck, *The Nature of Doctrine*, 38.

37. Lindbeck, *The Nature of Doctrine*, 50.

38. Marcus Moberg, "First-, Second-, and Third-level Discourse Analytic Approaches in the Study of Religion: Moving from Meta-theoretical Reflection to Implementation in Practice," *Religion* 43 (2013): 4–25.

39. Kenneth Burke, *The Rhetoric of Religion: Studies in Logology* (Berkeley: University of California Press, 1970), v.

40. See Robert H. Woods Jr. and Naaman K. Wood, eds., *Words and Witnesses: Communication Studies in Christian Thought from Athanasius to Desmond Tutu* (Peabody, MA: Hendrickson, 2018).

41. See Christoph Anderl, ed., *Zen Buddhist Rhetoric in China, Korea, and Japan* (Leiden: Brill, 2011); and Uwe Vagelpohl, *Aristotle's Rhetoric in the East: The Syriac and Arabic Translation and Commentary Tradition* (Leiden: Brill, 2008), respectively.

42. See Phillip Arrington, *Eloquence Divine: In Search of God's Rhetoric* (Eugene, OR: Cascade Books, 2017).

43. Richard Kearney, *Anatheism: Returning to God after God* (New York: Columbia University Press, 2010), 7.

44. See Richard Kearney and Matthew Clemente, ed., *The Art of Anatheism* (London: Rowman & Littlefield, 2018).

45. See John Sexton, Thomas Oliphant, and Peter J. Schwartz, *Baseball as a Road to God: Seeing beyond the Game* (New York: Gotham Books, 2014); and Crispin Paine, *Gods and Rollercoasters: Religion in Theme Parks Worldwide* (London: Bloomsbury Academic, 2019), respectively.

46. Charles Taylor, *Sources of the Self: The Making of Modern Identity* (Cambridge, MA: Harvard University Press, 1989), 15.

47. Taylor, *Sources of the Self*, 14.

48. Taylor, *Sources of the Self*, 18.

49. Taylor, *Sources of the Self*, 92–93.

50. Taylor, *Sources of the Self*, 521.

51. Michel Foucault, *The Order of Things: An Archaeology of the Human Sciences*, trans. Alan Sheridan (New York: Vintage Books, 1994), 340–43.

52. Foucault, *The Order of Things*, 318.

53. Foucault, *The Order of Things*, 339.

54. See Paul Ricoeur, *Oneself as Another*, trans. Kathleen Blamey (Chicago: University of Chicago Press, 1992), 27–39.

55. Paul Ricoeur, "History as Narrative and Practice," *Philosophy Today* 29 (1985): 214.

56. Ricoeur, *Oneself as Another*, 113–68.

57. See Jacques Lacan, *Écrits*, trans. Bruce Fink (New York: Norton, 2006), 75–81.

58. Keith Ward, *Religion and Human Nature* (Oxford: Clarendon Press, 1998), 324.

59. On the latter point, see Genesis 9:6 where murder is prohibited on the grounds that the victim is a bearer of the image of God.

60. See Anantanand Rambachan, *The Advaita Worldview: God, World, and Humanity* (Albany: State University of New York Press, 2006).

61. Lao Tzu, *Tao Te Ching*, trans. Gia-fu Feng and Jane English (New York: Vintage Books, 1997), chaps. 6 and 34, for example. See also Joseph A. Magno, *The Spiritual Philosophy of the Tao Te Ching* (Chicago: Pendragon, 2004), 17–26.

62. Charles W. Eliot, ed., *Sacred Writings*, 2 vols. (New York: P. F. Collier & Son, 1910), 657.
63. Confucius, *The Analects of Confucius*, trans. Arthur Whaley (New York: Vintage Books, 1989), 17.2.
64. See Adi Ophir and Ishay Rosen-Zvi, *Goy: Israel's Others and the Birth of the Gentile* (Oxford: Oxford University Press, 2018).
65. See the essay and documents in Bat Ye'or, *The Dhimmi: Jews and Christians under Islam*, trans. David Maisel, Paul Fenton, and David Littman (Rutherford, NJ: Fairleigh Dickinson University Press, 1985); and Yohanan Friedmann, *Tolerance and Coercion in Islam: Interfaith Relations in the Muslim Tradition* (Cambridge: Cambridge University Press, 2003).
66. See Antonio Gramsci, *Selections from the Prison Notebooks*, ed. Quintin Hoare and Geoffrey Nowell Smith (New York: International Publishers, 1971), 52–55.
67. See Manu Bhagavan and Anne Feldhaus, eds., *Claiming Power from Below* (Oxford: Oxford University Press, 2009).
68. See Mark Juergensmeyer, *Terror in the Mind of God: The Global Rise of Religious Violence*, 4th ed. (Oakland: University of California Press, 2017); and Catherine Wessinger, *How the Millennium Comes Violently: From Jonestown to Heaven's Gate* (New York: Seven Bridges Press, 2000) among many fine studies on religion and violence.
69. See Bartolomé de las Casas, *In Defense of the Indians*, trans. Stafford Poole (Dekalb: Northern Illinois University Press, 1974).
70. Jürgen Habermas, "An Awareness of What is Missing," in Jürgen Habermas et al., *An Awareness of What is Missing*, trans. Ciaran Cronin (Cambridge: Polity Press, 2010), 18.
71. Jürgen Habermas, *Between Naturalism and Religion*, trans. Ciaran Cronin (Cambridge: Polity Press, 2008), 245–46. Italics in the original.
72. See Maeve Cooke, "Salvaging and Secularizing the Semantic Contents of Religion: The Limitations of Habermas's Postmetaphysical Proposal," *International Journal for Philosophy of Religion* 60 (2006): 187–207, for a criticism of Habermas's suggestion.

BIBLIOGRAPHY

Anderl, Christoph, ed. *Zen Buddhist Rhetoric in China, Korea, and Japan*. Leiden: Brill, 2011.
Aristotle. *Rhetoric*. In *The Complete Works of Aristotle*, edited by Jonathan Barnes. 2 vols. Princeton, NJ: Princeton University Press, 1984.
Arrington, Phillip. *Eloquence Divine: In Search of God's Rhetoric*. Eugene, OR: Cascade Books, 2017.
Asad, Talal. *Genealogies of Religion: Discipline and Reasons of Power in Christianity and Islam*. Baltimore: Johns Hopkins University Press, 1993.
Barthes, Roland. *Elements of Semiology*. Translated by Annette Lavers and Colin Smith. New York: Hill & Wang, 1973.

———. *Mythologies*. Translated by Richard Howard and Annette Lavers. New York: Hill & Wang, 2012.
Berger, Peter L. *The Sacred Canopy: Elements of a Sociological Theory of Religion*. New York: Anchor Books, 1990.
Berger, Peter L., and Thomas Luckmann. *The Social Construction of Reality: A Treatise in the Sociology of Knowledge*. New York: Anchor Books, 1967.
Bhagavan, Manu, and Anne Feldhaus, eds. *Claiming Power from Below*. Oxford: Oxford University Press, 2009.
Bowker, John. *The Sense of God: Sociological, Anthropological, and Psychological Approaches to the Origin of the Sense of God*. Oxford: Oneworld, 1995.
Burke, Kenneth. *The Rhetoric of Religion: Studies in Logology*. Berkeley: University of California Press, 1970.
Confucius. *The Analects of Confucius*. Translated by Arthur Whaley. New York: Vintage Books, 1989.
Cooke, Maeve. "Salvaging and Secularizing the Semantic Contents of Religion: The Limitations of Habermas's Postmetaphysical Proposal." *International Journal for Philosophy of Religion* 60 (2006): 187–207.
Cox, Virginia, and John Ward, ed. *The Rhetoric of Cicero in its Medieval and Early Renaissance Commentary Tradition*. Leiden: Brill, 2018.
Dabney, Robert L. *Sacred Rhetoric; Or, A Course of Lectures on Preaching*. New York: Anson D. F. Randolph, 1870.
De las Casas, Bartolomé. *In Defense of the Indians*. Translated by Stafford Poole. Dekalb: Northern Illinois University Press, 1974.
Eco, Umberto. *Semiotics and the Philosophy of Language*. Bloomington: Indiana University Press, 1986.
Eliade, Mircea. *The Sacred and the Profane: The Nature of Religion*. Translated by Willard R. Trask. New York: Harcourt, 1987.
Eliot, Charles W., ed. *Sacred Writings*. 2 vols. New York: P. F. Collier & Son, 1910.
Foucault, Michel. *The Order of Things: An Archaeology of the Human Sciences*. Translated by Alan Sheridan. New York: Vintage Books, 1994.
Friedmann, Yohanan. *Tolerance and Coercion in Islam: Interfaith Relations in the Muslim Tradition*. Cambridge: Cambridge University Press, 2003.
Gaonkar, Dilip Parameshwar. "The Revival of Rhetoric, the New Rhetoric, and the Rhetorical Turn: Some Distinctions." *Informal Logic* 15 (1993): 53–64.
Geertz, Clifford. *The Interpretation of Cultures*. New York: Basic Books, 1973.
Gramsci, Antonio. *Selections from the Prison Notebooks*. Edited by Quintin Hoare and Geoffrey Nowell Smith. New York: International Publishers, 1971.
Habermas, Jürgen. "An Awareness of What is Missing." In Jürgen Habermas et al., *An Awareness of What Is Missing*. Translated by Ciaran Cronin, 15–24. Cambridge: Polity Press, 2010.
———. *Between Naturalism and Religion*. Translated by Ciaran Cronin. Cambridge: Polity Press, 2008.
Juergensmeyer, Mark. *Terror in the Mind of God: The Global Rise of Religious Violence*, 4th ed. Oakland: University of California Press, 2017.

Kearney, Richard. *Anatheism: Returning to God after God*. New York: Columbia University Press, 2010.
Kearney, Richard, and Matthew Clemente, eds. *The Art of Anatheism*. London: Rowman & Littlefield, 2018.
Kennedy, George A. *Classical Rhetoric and Its Christian and Secular Tradition from Ancient to Modern Times*, 2nd ed. Chapel Hill: University of North Carolina Press, 1999.
Lacan, Jacques. *Écrits*. Translated by Bruce Fink. New York: Norton, 2006.
Lincoln, Bruce. *Holy Terrors: Thinking about Religion after September 11*, 2nd ed. Chicago: University of Chicago Press, 2006.
Lindbeck, George A. *The Nature of Doctrine: Religion and Theology in a Postliberal Age*, 25th anniversary edition. Louisville, KY: Westminster John Knox Press, 2009.
Lyotard, Jean-François. *The Postmodern Condition: A Report on Knowledge*. Translated by Geoff Bennington and Brian Massumi. Minneapolis: University of Minnesota Press, 1984.
Magno, Joseph A. *The Spiritual Philosophy of the Tao Te Ching*. Chicago: Pendragon, 2004.
Masuzawa, Tomoko. *The Invention of World Religions: Or, How European Universalism Was Preserved in the Language of Pluralism*. Chicago: University of Chicago Press, 2005.
McCutcheon, Russell T. *Manufacturing Religion: The Discourse of* Sui Generis *Religion and the Politics of Nostalgia*. Oxford: Oxford University Press, 1997.
Moberg, Marcus. "First-, Second-, and Third-level Discourse Analytic Approaches in the Study of Religion: Moving from Meta-theoretical Reflection to Implementation in Practice." *Religion* 43 (2013): 4–25.
Ophir, Adi, and Ishay Rosen-Zvi. *Goy: Israel's Others and the Birth of the Gentile*. Oxford: Oxford University Press, 2018.
Otto, Rudolf. *The Idea of the Holy*. Translated by John W. Harvey. Oxford: Oxford University Press, 1950.
Paine, Crispin. *Gods and Rollercoasters: Religion in Theme Parks Worldwide*. London: Bloomsbury Academic, 2019.
Pasquarello, Michael, III. *Sacred Rhetoric: Preaching as a Theological and Pastoral Practice of the Church*. Eugene, OR: Wipf and Stock, 2005.
Pseudo-Cicero. *Rhetorica ad Herennium*. Translated by Henry Caplan. Loeb Classical Library. Cambridge, MA: Harvard University Press, 1964.
Rambachan, Anantanand. *The Advaita Worldview: God, World, and Humanity*. Albany: State University of New York Press, 2006.
Richards, I. A. *The Philosophy of Rhetoric*. London: Oxford University Press, 1936.
Ricoeur, Paul. "History as Narrative and Practice," *Philosophy Today* 29 (1985): 213–22.
———. *Oneself as Another*. Translated by Kathleen Blamey. Chicago: University of Chicago Press, 1992.
Rorty, Richard M. "Introduction: Metaphysical Difficulties of Linguistic Philosophy." In *The Linguistic Turn: Essays in Philosophical Method; with Two Retrospective*

Essays, edited by Richard M. Rorty, 2nd ed., 1–39. Chicago: University of Chicago Press, 1992.

Sexton, John, Thomas Oliphant, and Peter J. Schwartz. *Baseball as a Road to God: Seeing Beyond the Game*. New York: Gotham Books, 2014.

Shuger, Debora K. *Sacred Rhetoric: The Christian Grand Style in the English Renaissance*. Princeton, NJ: Princeton University Press, 1988.

Smart, Ninian. *Dimensions of the Sacred: An Anatomy of the World's Beliefs*. Berkeley: University of California Press, 1996.

Taylor, Charles. *Sources of the Self: The Making of Modern Identity*. Cambridge, MA: Harvard University Press, 1989.

Tillich, Paul. *Theology of Culture*. Edited by Robert C. Kimball. Oxford: Oxford University Press, 1959.

Tzu, Lao. *Tao Te Ching*. Translated by Gia-fu Feng and Jane English. New York: Vintage Books, 1997.

Vagelpohl, Uwe. *Aristotle's Rhetoric in the East: The Syriac and Arabic Translation and Commentary Tradition*. Leiden: Brill, 2008.

Ward, Keith. *Religion and Human Nature*. Oxford: Clarendon Press, 1998.

Wessinger, Catherine. *How the Millennium Comes Violently: From Jonestown to Heaven's Gate*. New York: Seven Bridges Press, 2000.

Wittgenstein, Ludwig. *Philosophical Investigations*. Translated by G. E. M. Anscombe. Oxford: Blackwell, 2001.

Woods, Robert H., Jr., and Naaman K. Wood, eds. *Words and Witnesses: Communication Studies in Christian Thought from Athanasius to Desmond Tutu*. Peabody, MA: Hendrickson, 2018.

Ye'or, Bat. *The Dhimmi: Jews and Christians under Islam*. Translated by David Maisel, Paul Fenton, and David Littman. Rutherford, NJ: Fairleigh Dickinson University Press, 1985.

Chapter 1

Temporal Light and Shadows
The Rhetoric of the Sacred

Ronald C. Arnett

The realm of the sacred seems increasingly smaller in everyday life, lessening opportunities for imagination in a place and moment capable of reminding us of the profoundly meaningful. Such an assertion propels the insights of a number of contemporary scholars, lamenting the social direction of the West, such as Robert Bellah et al. (1985/2008), Christopher Lasch (1991), Charles Taylor (2007), Neil Postman (1985/2006), Robert D. Putnam (2000), and Jacques Ellul (1986/2011). In addition to a scholarly call to reclaim sacred space observations, such a reality is visible in changes transforming space within my own lifetime, announcing the veracity of a cultural trend—diminishing sacred spaces and moments. In my experience, this era uniquely publicizes the necessity to invite sacred moments and places through preservation, renovation, and innovation (Arnett 1999).

During my lifetime, I have witnessed decline in church attendance (Pew Research 2015), attacks on library funding (American Library Association 2012), challenges to public common places (Standing 2016), ongoing hostility toward the liberal arts (Deb 2017), and confusion between a calling and a career (Fritz 2013). We live in an era of consistent public erosion of support for places and activities that support the sacred. Yet, at the same time, all of us perceive individual people who hallow the everyday, reminding us that life, itself, is sacred. Such persons testify to the sacredness of everyday living with others; such people act as lamp holders for the sacred. The performative importance of lamp holders is underscored in *Communication Ethics in Dark Times: Hannah Arendt's Rhetoric of Warning and Hope*:

> Lamp holders give us hope in existence—not false optimism but rather tenacious hope and courage. The figures discussed in *Men in Dark Times* met life on its own terms, in the darkness, providing a corrective to the social world gone awry and illuminating holy sparks. To know such a person in a moment of despair is to witness hope before one's own eyes. Lamp holders are not drawn by humanistic heroism but by the light claiming them, demanding that they hold it up for others to see. As a derivative creature called by the light, one then acts within a Jewish call—"If not me, then whom?" (Arnett 2013, 118)

Those who shed light upon scared places, persons, ideas, and acts have one characteristic in common—they do not emphasize themselves; they point to something greater and more meaningful than themselves. Lamp holders engage an imagination that meets existence on its own terms, which is the initial foundation for those celebrating the sacred.

In hopes of illuminating the importance of the sacred more thoroughly, I turn to Paul Ricoeur's (1995) understanding of the sacred. Ricoeur's insights gather around one basic existential fact: one must understand the value and significance of the ambiguous. Within the obscure dwells signs living within the shadows of the inarticulate, giving them an unexpected power that suggests places, ideas, and people who live unceremoniously within the sacred. I am drawn to Ricoeur's conception of the sacred in that he does not conflate it with the notion of the holy. Ricoeur did not follow the path of Jacques Ellul (Fasching 2008; Ellul 1975), who situated the sacred within experiences nourished by myth and ritual. For Ricoeur, one must understand the singular task of the holy; it is capable of disrupting all, including the authority of the sacred. The creative application of Ricoeur's work begins with recognition of places and moments of sacred access, giving a secular world an opportunity to turn toward meaning.

Ricoeur (1995) situated the sacred between the realms of the known and the simultaneously "not yet" envisioned. For Ricoeur, the sacred often goes missed due to a refusal to attend to the inarticulate on the one hand and the unduly articulate on the other hand. The sacred emerges beyond our control and grasp, dwelling in places that are both articulate and inarticulate, clear and ambiguous. For Ricoeur (1995), the sacred implies a direction composed of enough obscured vision that one is less likely to stumble into the abyss of undue self-righteous confidence. Perhaps, Ricoeur's wariness with self-righteous confidence bonded his friendship with Emmanuel Levinas and permitted the two to join Pope John Paul II in multiple moments of reflection and discussion (Arnett 2017).

The sacred disrupts a secular world obsessed with increasing "use value." Ricoeur proclaims the importance of rhetoric attentive to the sacred, engaged in thoughtful responsiveness to existence. Ricoeur's (1995) *Figuring the*

Sacred: Religion, Narrative, and Imagination is a call for reflection upon the significant. I contend that his book of twenty-five years ago is more relevant today than when it first entered public conversation. In the time since the printing of his volume on the sacred, we have witnessed an era bent on destroying sacred places and acts capable of sustaining beleaguered souls. The power of the sacred resides with its ability to highlight the revelatory importance of existence. Ricoeur's perspective on the sacred in his 1995 work consists of a compilation of essays, which outline questions about the sacred without reifying place and moments within existence. Each essay reads as a suggestive horizon, intentionally avoiding a precise definition of the sacred. Ricoeur recognizes that ambiguity invokes interpretive responses capable of providing a performative impressionist picture of the sacred in action.

The profundity of Ricoeur's understanding of the sacred finds illumination in book reviews that articulate the interpretive power of his scholarly labor. A noteworthy review emanates from one of the premier Old Testament scholars, Walter Brueggemann (1996). He reminds readers of the interplay of imagination, narrative, and religion, which situates Ricoeur's scholarly corpus. Brueggemann's stress on Ricoeur's use of the term "figuring" elucidates a modern problem driven by the desire to possess rather than engage a world via the ambiguous, artistic, and delicate. The sacred dwells in meetings of the profound that linger within shadows of signification and resist imposition of undue clarity. Imagination, narrative, and religion reside within a region of the fuzzy and the often hesitant, giving rise to a vernacular alien to claims of intimate knowledge capable of offering assurance via certainty and perceived accuracy.

The sacred routinely dwells outside the empirical and the calculable; it resides within a phenomenological reality that fuels its power and vitality through meaning that resists reification. Such a perspective is akin to Levinas's stress on testimony, which he characterized as a plea that acts as a cry for ethics and concern for the Other. Such action counters a self-absorbed society. The meaningfully inarticulate is the "saying" power of the sacred, void of statements of faultless conviction (Arnett 2017). The sacred lives within shadows and rests beyond the outskirts of normative expectation, acting in a manner anathema to undue confidence fueled by self-righteous declaration. The celebration of direction without a guarantee is central to Ricoeur and registers with the faith perspective of Brueggemann (1996). Such cooperative alliance of Brueggemann and Ricoeur led Brueggemann to suggest that Ricoeur's scholarship calls forth from the reader acts of affirmation, not criticism. Serious engagement with everyday life within the shadows and speechless nature of the sacredness demands that we attend to that which goes almost eclipsed and little seen by far too many. The needs of the wounded, the suffering, and the forgotten linger within the shades of modern life. Brueggemann (1996) understood Ricoeur's sacred as a "defense against carelessness, indifference, glibness, and trivialization" (98). He understood that Ricoeur's portrait of the sacred is an invitation to acknowledge genuine light bursting forth from margins of existence, ever resistant to acts of possession and imposition upon an Other.

Peter Fink (1996) continued admiration of Ricoeur's story about the sacred. As a Jesuit scholar and reader, Fink unites faith and interpretation with questions of radical evil, death, and dismissal of others, which necessitate interpretive rejoinders capable of constituting an "authentic human identity" situated within sacred spaces (546). Fink, like Brueggemann, affirmed Ricoeur's willingness to engage the sacred within dim light, permitting genuine insight to emerge in the midst of darkness. Fink understood Ricoeur as taking us into a journey that begins with a basic assertion: "there is no easy road into his world, no privileged or logical place to begin" (547). One commences where one is, recognizing the power of a faith narrative in our sociality together. The sacred lives everyway and, when reified, nowhere.

In addition, Dan R. Stiver (1998) recognized Ricoeur's work as a hermeneutics of testimony that embraces a wise faith composed of ambiguity and determined contribution to others. Ricoeur's sacred bridge building between love and justice is essential in this historical moment as he resisted a precise template for action. Following this emphasis, Jim Fodor (1998) accentuates Ricoeur's teleology of naming that resides within the dialectic of incompleteness and direction. Fodor stated that Ricoeur's understanding of radical evil pivots on the fact that no unity of contraries works to temper the extreme of evil. Radical evil embraces a single direction, rushing blindly forward with unquestioning certainty.

Dennis Sansom (1998) resumes the emphasis on the sacred void of undue lucidity. He outlined the historical importance of Charles Reagan's book on Ricoeur's life and ideas, which underscores Ricoeur's commitment to narrative and his aversion to indiscriminate use of deconstruction. In discussion of Ricoeur's understanding of the sacred, Sansom highlights Friedrich Schleiermacher's contention that faith remains ultimately dependent upon the sacred. Samson cautions readers against both reflective and unreflective efforts to desacralize the world. A narrative theology keeps before us the importance of the meaningful. In the meeting of religious texts, one finds meaning that shapes one's identity through engagement with the particularity of a text interrogated by distinctive, unique, and authentic questions. Interpretive meeting of questions brought to the text invite revelatory insight. From such encounters, one discerns sacred directions, which are ever infused with doubt that repels self-righteous warrants of undisputed clarity of conviction.

In the reviews of Ricoeur's work on the sacred, a consistent theme emerges—one cannot possess the sacred; it abides in revelatory spaces. In addition to Ricoeur, Mark I. Wallace, the editor of *Figuring the Sacred: Religion, Narrative, and Imagination*, is largely responsible for the consistency of this perspective. Wallace was instrumental in compiling twenty-one representative articles on this theme; together, they compose Ricoeur's (1995) comprehension of the sacred. Wallace's (1995) introduction to this collection furnishes a unifying frame for the essays. He centers Ricoeur on questions of mediation and conversation, a dialogue between and among persons, texts, artifacts, and art. Ricoeur's work assumes the basic question, "Who am I?" This fundamental question, uttered by Augustine (trans., 1960) in his *Confessions*, emerges from existential responses that acknowledge and grapple with the ambiguity of the sacred (Book X). Interpretive meeting of a text permits revelatory identity to take shape from and within such encounters. Wallace emphasized that Ricoeur's use of the term *denizen* is suggestive of a world void of the empowerment of symbols and myth that gives rise to human consciousness. There is no symbolic shortcut to finding direction and gaining identity of selfhood that claims narrative ground of direction and a rooted sense of self. Identity transpires in the hermeneutic turn of person and text, which transpires within a performative interpretive act, a fusion of horizons.

What we bring to a given text enhances what we discover; interpretive meeting opens insights to the revelatory, the sacred, from the interplay of text and interpreter. This meeting renders new insights that continue to shape the identity of the interpreter. For such revelatory acumen to transpire, one must walk between two extremes: taking the text seriously and admitting the wisdom of Jürgen Habermas—"systematic distortions" can cloud the meaning of a text (Ricoeur 1995, 10). The narrow ridge between these interpretive extremes suggests an existential interpretive reality: there is no shortcut to distinguishing a particular focus, and in so doing, one discovers that a complete self-understanding always eludes each one of us. Interpretive engagement in search of the sacred requires sorting through the reality of competing narratives. In this historical moment, no entity such as a single narrative is capable of guiding each action with performative perfection, and its pursuit gives rise to radical evil. Narrative identity comes from the acknowledgment of multiple stories, each laden with practices that demand of us action that pulls us in diverse and, at times, opposing directions. A narrative composed of the unity of contraries of stories and practices calls us forth into action that tempers the desire for absolute certainty.

As the sacred emerges, it resists efforts to impose itself upon others; such is one of the reasons Ricoeur found profundity in the insights of Levinas. Both Ricoeur and Levinas understood biblical stories as revelatory invitations.

The sacred lives within existential vitality of a given text where authentic questions can bring forth revelatory implications. Self-identity emerges from a call that includes question and text. Self-identity commences from the external, which then reconstitutes internal meaning. Narratives invite us into a world of differing meaning; in the clashing and combining of signification, they offer novel understanding and unexpected meaning, which invokes the unexpected. This attentiveness to exteriority further attracts Ricoeur to the perceptions of Levinas. Ricoeur's (1995) only lament is an admission of difference between the two men on the role of narrative in housing the sacred, with Ricoeur on the side of narrative and Levinas articulating the sacred as an a priori, not in need of narrative support. Both scholars, however, concurred that whatever the formation of the sacred, it repels reification and is not equitable with a statue, monument, building, person, or institution alone. The sacred arises through a dialogic spirit that appears via response; such action elevates the interpreter and invites revelatory meaning beyond a concrete moment. The sacred invites a temporal transcendence, reminding one that the biblical faith is an interpretive reality of language and meaning that elevates human understanding and meaning. Ricoeur situates the sacred within a phenomenological lodging, eschewing an empirical house composed of the desire to solidify and codify the sacred into the realm of possession, which curtails its revelatory capability.

Ricoeur offered a description of a phenomenology of the sacred, which included five traits. The first attribute of the sacred is the revelatory, from which one senses the "awesome" and "overwhelming" nature of existence situated within an irrational awareness (49). The second trait of the sacred is recognition of its form; the sacred points to something other than itself (49–50). The third characteristic of the sacred acknowledges its nonlinguistic heart, which remains at its core (50–51). The fourth feature of the sacred is recognition of the profundity of experience (52–54). The fifth trait of the sacred consists of an ambiguous logic of meaning that situates existential understanding (54–55). This understanding of the sacred comes from a gathering process akin to what Charles Sanders Peirce called "abduction." Peirce described abduction as "a method of forming a general prediction without any positive assurance that it will succeed either in the special case or usually, its justification being that it is the only possible hope of regulating our future conduct rationally, and that induction from past experience gives us strong encouragement to hope that it will be successful in the future" (Peirce 1998, 299).

Ricoeur framed a sacred phenomenology that manifested, announced, and revealed a hermeneutic of proclamation that articulated, clarified, and suggested what matters without reliance on a myth of pure precision. The sacred has renewing power capable of guiding and propelling proclamation, as long as possession of a single vision of accuracy and correctness goes restrained. The revelatory of the sacred ceases when proclamation demands more than an ambiguous reality composed of temporal tiny glances of the sacred. Even the term *revelation* begins to obscure the power of the sacred when expectation turns from acknowledgment of its presence to possessive demand for its routine appearance.

Possession is the house of evil as humans become impatient with meaning that is inscrutable and inarticulate (Arnett 2017, 157–74). The task of philosophy is to sort out the forms of the sacred—when necessary, unmasking evil masquerading as the sacred. Ricoeur (1995) aligns his analysis of evil with Immanuel Kant (75–92), who warned against the rejection of the flawed. Precision invites something much more dangerous. Ricoeur contends that Kant attended to traces, marks, and invisible signification that alludes to a genuine community beyond the flawed and the visible. The hermeneutics of good and evil originates with a basic assumption: the interplay between these social extremes is a necessary and ongoing reality of human existence, making knowledge of the good possible and self-righteousness less likely.

Ricoeur's discussion of the sacred includes response to *The Star of Redemption*, written by Franz Rosenzweig (Ricoeur 1995, 93–107); Rosenzweig and his work were inspirational to the insights of Levinas. Ricoeur's entrance into discussion about Rosenzweig and his alliance with Levinas centers on the notion of the "figure." A figure has no home; it invites us into a world of reification, codification, and commodification. "Rosenzweig writes regarding Moses, who was not allowed to enter the [P]romised [L]and: 'God sealed this completed life with a kiss of his mouth. Thus does God seal and so too does man.' The reader will, of course, have recognized the birth here of the theme of the face to which Emmanuel Levinas has given so much breadth and force" (Ricoeur 1995, 97). The figure, the face, is an enigma that cannot be possessed or grasped. At best, we gather temporal glimpses of a figure or a face. What endures is not what one grasps by an audible call, but that which renders a unique and specific answer to a vague, nonspecific but ever-powerful demand to enact personal responsibility. The figure carries no code of conduct; only its ambiguous pointing to something other than itself permits genuine meaning or signification to emerge.

Ricoeur's (1995) emphasis on Levinas's understanding of testimony (108–26) continues the theme of ambiguity of the figure and the face. Testimony emanates from the face of the Other without clarity of schematization. The face of the Other acts as a testimony that commences from exteriority, calling forth an assignment of internal and personal responsibility that comes without template or a precise code of behavior. Testimony from the face of the Other demands a substitution of myself for the Other: I am responsible without certitude of answer. I am propelled only by a conviction of obligation. This testimony is an ethical Saying, a revelatory call into action, answered and performed by me alone, which then reconstitutes the knowing Said of one's own identity. The testimony of sacred begins with exteriority of pronouncement that recasts and reconstitutes the interiority of the one called into responsibility. The "I" responsible for protecting and promoting the sacred is dependent upon an ambiguous call into obligation, which when answered reorders the "I" of self-concern into an "I" of ethical action for others. One then assumes the burden of responsibility that accepts the obligation of a sacred existential reality: "if not me, then whom?" Ricoeur details testimony from persons, through an emphasis on the face of the Other and an underscoring of an exegetic meeting of the text (129–43).

Ricoeur also stresses the vital importance of the notion of origin in the history of traditions and within the structure of a given work. Ricoeur emphasizes that the history of any tradition requires understanding through a particular structure, which makes perfection of any exegesis unreachable and existentially impossible. Temporal answers of signification rest within ambiguity while simultaneously embracing the flawed with no one answer capable of offering universal interpretive assurance. For Ricoeur (1995), it is within the revelatory act of interpretation that the testimony of the sacred respites. Interpretation witnesses to a tradition, a structure of the Said that gathers an eventual hope of inviting a revelatory sense of Saying. Novel insights emerge from Saying, capable of guiding performative action in a given direction. Exegesis attends to the weight of a text, to its height, in "the interplay of structure, genesis, and intention" (Ricoeur 1995, 143). Intention within exegesis, understood phenomenologically, commences externally with no internal attribution capable of imposing ideological certainty upon the world. Direction in exegesis finds the interpreter, suggesting a temporal path of clarity. Such is the reason Martin Buber (1952/1997) insinuated that a life without direction houses the demonic (130).

Contrarily, life lived in response to a call does not impose upon the Other. Calls function as a genesis, a beginning. Genesis structures an interpretation, lending order and direction that offer a glimpse and glance of the sacred before us. Origins do not provide a long gaze; they are void of full clarity. Temporal beginnings come with partial confidence nagged continually by questions of doubt. Revelatory sacred paths of imagination do not transpire in a vacuum. Genesis structures afford contextual insight for understanding a given text and question, permitting phenomenological revelation of imagination, which resides, not in fantasy, but within genuine responses to real narrative structures that constitute directional ground under our feet. As stated earlier, Kant discussed the interplay of good and evil, contrasting fantasy with imagination. In the fantasy of ethical abstraction, one invites an evil of imposed conviction, opposed to genuine imagination tied to ambiguity of perception. The house of the good dwells in performative action that responds to the realm with ethical imagination.

Ricoeur (1995), working with the theme of imagination opposed to fantasy, details the rule-governed nature of imagination (144–66). He states that imagination functions like a narrative parable, taking us to where we are "not yet"; and like any good parable, originates with communal ties and common places. Ricoeur offers the parable of the sower as an explication of imagination at work: a sower seeds by performing labor in real soil tied to an uncertain outcome. Parables take us into intertextuality, the heart of the imaginative multiplicity composed of the known and the "not yet," the now and the might be. Imagination envisions a life that is "not yet" but is possible in response to what is. The sacred does not dwell simply in the now—it actively rests in the "not yet" of imagination that emerges in response to existence on its own terms.

Imagination is central to biblical time and the notion of kerygma; it is revelatory and emergent. Ricoeur (1995) designates biblical time as woven within narrative, law, prophecies, wisdom sayings, and hymns that generate an intertextual model able to announce meaningfulness of time line and relational history (171). The telling of stories and hymns enlivens biblical time, casting us upon narrative ground that permits a journey of a life capable of envisioning sacred space. In biblical time, stories, hymns, and ongoing discussions remind us of interiority of responsibility that is without end; it embraces no beginning and no end. An immemorial sense of time permits us to walk within a community of saints and with those "not yet" with us. Biblical time spreads the wings of its interpretive community, taking all beyond the "now" to a gathered space composed of a more inclusive welcome beyond our immediate presence.

The sacred, for Ricoeur (1995), remains ever active within the interplay of kerygma of a risen Christ, offering a narrative that puts solid possibilities under the feet of believers. For Ricoeur, the sacred offers an interpretive narrative that is alert and responsive to the revelatory while being conscious of the necessity to respond from the empirical ground before us within the spirit of the faith. Narratives lend themselves to novel positions; they house the revelatory, providing an account of origin that continues to give birth to the unexpected (181–99). The sacred dwells in relationships that give birth to kerygmatic revelation, narrative explication, and articulate Saying. These revelatory points of Saying give way to a temporal Said that, in turn, nurtures future imagination of renewed revelatory Saying that will summon new insights. Both the clarity of the Said and the holy sparks of Saying provide a people with direction that propels and shapes imaginative possibilities of hope.

A theological view of hope nourishes the sacred lives within the realm of the absurd, where death is not the final answer, and resurrection is forever possible (Ricoeur 1995, 203–16). Tony Campolo (1984/2008) announces such hope when recounting S. M. Lockridge's famous line, "It's Friday, but Sunday's comin.'" The task of a sacred philosophy is the navigation of moments before Friday and after Sunday, helping us to do our best to discern direction when hope is less clear. The sacred does not live in clarity of pristine philosophy; it dwells in waiting space between Friday and Sunday. The naming of God in the Old Testament begins with a sacred admission; God goes unnamed. The Old Testament's emphasis on Yahweh, as an ineffable name, functions as a sign of ongoing deliverance beyond our possession. The unutterable naming of God is an invitation to poetry, which refuses to reify an answer in one's own image. The prophecies of faith dwell within a hope that delivers, indicating a direction that opens the way without claiming undue direct assurance from God. Such ambiguity limits violence that seeks to possess God as one demands that God abide by one's own image. Such a faith is false in that its sole purpose is to function as a caretaker of one's own desires. Contrarily, one finds in the Lord's Prayer a reminder of whose world we live within:

> Our Father in Heaven,
> hallowed be your name,
> your kingdom come,
> your will be done,
> on earth as it is in heaven.
> Give us today our daily bread.
> And forgive us our debts,
> as we also have forgiven our debtors.
> And lead us not into temptation,
> but deliver us from the evil one. (Matthew 6:9–13; NIV)

Ambiguity of the sacred lives within the phrase "Thy will be done." The ultimate form of naming begins with recognition that there is a power greater and more sacred than the possessive clarity of my own demands.

Recognition of power, meaning, and significance of direction beyond me nourishes the ground of a sacred narrative theology that houses the hallowed. Such a theology in everyday life consists of prophecies, wisdom, hymns, and committee meetings; collectively, they announce a historic truth, a confessional presupposition of an "I" of faith responding to a narrative call. The "me" that finds identity in the "I" of faith dwells within a sacred narrative of characters, episodes, events, and activities that tell and retell a basic existential fact of the faith: life does not begin with me; it originates with the call of the faith and a community of saints.

Ambiguity within the sacred is present in the question of evil. For instance, if one begins with the assumption that God is good, then how does one understand evil philosophically and theologically? Ricoeur (1995) unmasks this question and rejects repetitive acts of blame and lament that he labels as attempts to escape suffering through various forms of Gnosticism and denial of the body and its contact with empirical experiences of everyday life. The danger of melancholy and prolonged mourning does not permit understanding and experience of God's will; such self-focused reflection moves us closer to Hannah Arendt's (1963/2006) "banality of evil," where the naming of extreme commonness resides. Countering the banality of evil commences with eschewing jargon situated within unreflective repetitiveness. Such is the reason that Ricoeur names God with the performative language of ambiguous direction, not as an absolute that one commands and owns. Responding to God as reflective of ambiguity of direction reminds us of a good beyond us. Evil inhabits a space constituted by an effort to grasp an absolute good. Evil resides wherever and whenever the focus rests on me alone and wherever and whenever I seek to possess. Evil dwells in places where suffering consumes and melancholy derails performative action. Each of us, in a dark moment, finds life lingering within an abyss without direction and hope. A sacred answer remains within a hope that lingers within shadows that can unexpectedly pluck us from a sense of "existential homelessness" (Arnett 1994).

The reality of ambiguous hope lives in stories such as the following familiar tale. A fellow was stuck on a rooftop in a flood, which caused him to pray to God for help. Soon, a man in a rowboat came by and shouted to the man on the roof, "Jump in; I can save you." The stranded fellow shouted back, "No, it is OK; I am praying to God, and he is going to save me," so the rowboat went on. Then, a man in a motorboat came by, shouting, "Jump in; I can save you." To this, the stranded man said, "No thanks, I'm praying to God, and he's going to save me; I have faith," so the motorboat went on. Then, a helicopter came by, and the pilot shouted down "Grab the rope; I will lift you to safety." To this, the stranded man, once again, replied, "No thanks, I am praying to God, and he will save me; I have faith," so the helicopter reluctantly flew away. Soon, the water rose above the rooftop, and the man drowned and went to Heaven. Then, he was able to discuss this situation with God. At this point, he explained, "I had faith in you, and you did not save me; you let me drown, and I do not understand why." To this, God replied, "I sent you a rowboat, a motorboat, and a helicopter—what more did you expect?" (Schwartz 1996, 110). The banality of evil dwells in our reified expectations about what we contend should be the reality before us; it lives in existence otherwise from attentiveness to the revelatory. God's sacred voice speaks in the midst of ambiguity, noise, clatter, and without our approval.

The call of faith points to what Ricoeur (1995) calls a "summoned subject" (262–75), who experiences life within the call of conscience awakened by ambiguity, vagueness, glimpses, glances, and unexpected visitors. Without answering a summons in the form of a call of conscience, the sacred goes disregarded. In the words of Levinas, when we think we have grasped the sacred and own it, our sense of self-righteousness misses the sacred and disavows its power. Sacred narrative power within the logic of faith lives in the performative action of the doing of a Christian narrative that enlarges the world and one's field of inquiry and responsibility. Such a narrative resists the temptation to plant a flag in the name of God, even as one witnesses to miracles announced by the temporal Said of a named God.

I contend that a summoned subject is more at home in a postmodern world of narrative and virtue contention than in a world of modern efficiency and universal assurance. Postmodernity, in the eyes of many Christians, is a moral cul-de-sac, a mistaken point of view. However, it is better understood as sacred ambiguity; postmodernity is recognition of narrative ground void of clear precision, the space of and for the sacred. Postmodernity consists of multiple petite narratives vying for attention with each guided by a basic presupposition: the author, the speaker, is not the center of sacred rhetoric. We live in an ambiguous space closer to what we term postmodernity. This lack of precision propels sacred narratives, calling us into a world that demands responsibility from us and resists our narcissistic demands placed upon existence. Modernity, on the other hand, demands that we alter and change the world before us with the ambiguity of postmodernity recognizing that we are narrative creatures embedded within existence. Postmodernity acknowledges sacred narratives that question the West's love of an originative "I" that seeks to impose, rather than respond. Postmodernity understands a basic presupposition of the faith: "For whoever wants to save their life will lose it, but whoever loses their life for me will find it" (Matthew 16:25, NIV). The faith calls each one of us into an embedded life, not for an "I" that attempts to use the faith, but a faith that calls us out and directs a derivative "I." Ricoeur (1995) accepted an embedded understanding of the faith, which continues to call upon God in the cry of the Psalms, evoking our responsibility.

The embedded life of a person of faith has a promise without precise clarity. It is a life without direction, without great lucidity, and with joy found even in the midst of suffering and lament. Memories composed of deep, dark places of sadness cannot eclipse sacred sparks that can uplift one to enact the golden rule: tending to others as oneself, giving to others with abundance without measure (Arnett 2016). Without measure does not suggest more than one could ever desire; the definition rests with God, not me. For example, sometimes the abundance is more akin to emptiness that calls us forth into action. I penned the following story of a man following a rainbow to discover and uncover a pot of gold. When the man is disappointed after finding an empty pot, an older gentleman tells him, "Go back one more time. But this time look carefully, not with the eyes of greed, but with prayer of finding direction." Upon a second glance, the young man finds an old, yellowed piece of paper with the following message: "Your task is not to find a pot of gold, but to help fill this kettle. For some significance is given by birth, but for most, including you and me, [one finds] meaningful significance . . . in service to the other" (Arnett and Arneson 1999, 136–37). More often than we might wish, it seems that God simply empties the pot of gold, requiring us to find abundance among its lack, despite its presence. In a space filled without, ambiguous direction finds possible paths in hope propelled by the sacred.

Performative, pastoral acts embedded within the story of the faith witness to a sacred narrative that offers identity and sustains us with temporal courage. Moving us to action of the faith discerns an answer to Augustine's (trans., 1960) existential question, "Who am I?" (Book X). Responses to a sacred narrative discover oneself anew as a summoned subject constituted by a derivative "I"—called, found, and compelled by responsibility without clarity of correct action in a specific instant. In such moments, our prayers seek glimpses, not possession, of the sacred as it separates the "me" of faith from the "me" of cynical self-righteous demands. The sacred continually reminds me that the world is not here to conform to my wishes.

A sacred narrative unites love and justice (Ricoeur 1995, 315–29). Love is a powerful term; and when aligned with justice, not the secular demand of liking, the sacred finds a temporal home. To be a just parent is to love when you do not like. To be a just friend is to love when you do not like. To be a just spouse is to love when you do not like. To be a person of faith is to love when you do not like. Such tasks often seem greater than human abilities, and they are. Such is the importance of the sacred power of the narrative of the faith. It permits one to find a way in and through the absurd to a home one cannot possess. The sacred does not run from power; it houses it within the bounds of love. As Martin Luther King Jr. (1998) stated, "What is needed is a realization that power without love is reckless and abusive and that love without power is sentimental and anemic. Power at its best is love implementing the demands of justice. Justice at its best is love correcting everything that stands against love" (324–25). The powerful interplay of love and justice keeps us from falling into the abyss of likability evaluated by my needs alone, as well as the temptation of self-righteousness.

The sacred dwells when and where we do not expect to discover its presence. Its rhetoric and power live despite us and pull us onward; the sacred story of the faith is the spirit that gives life. Martin Buber, as a world-renowned

Jewish theologian and philosopher, wrote about a significant encounter tied to possession of God, in this case a negative encapsulation. Buber was writing an introduction to one of his books, just a few short years after the Holocaust, while resting at another man's home. The person naturally asked Buber what he was doing as he witnessed Buber writing. The response from Buber was that he was writing an introduction to his latest book. The man then asked Buber to read the introduction, which Buber did with repetitive references to the name of God in the introduction. The gentleman providing housing for Buber listened attentively as his eyes began to glow with anger. He then screamed at Buber and demanded that Buber stop using the name of God. He reminded Buber of all the Holocaust evil that had transpired under the use of God's name. Buber's retort was short: just because people defile the name of God, one must never forget that its power remains.[1]

The sacred narrative of the faith lives despite abuse that seeks to eclipse its power. The sacred breathes despite violence, stupidity, and banality of use. The sacred narrative of the faith survives despite our eagerness to embrace self-righteousness. The sacred dwells in shadows where controllers of existence seek to impose upon God's Earth, failing to recognize the power of the sacred. Yet, there are those, even in an era that questions and wonders about the sacred and claims it is no more, who somehow and someway find the courage and strength to answer unexpected knocking of the sacred on their doors. The sacred narrative of the faith calls us to take help from all and any of God's Earth, seeking shelter long before water rises to the rooftop. Moreover, when we are safe, we can then kiss the dry ground, hitting our knees in thankful prayer, "Thank you, God—that was a close one," and in thanks one goes back to work as a sacred task of service. Indeed, the rejoinder of faith generates practices responsive to a sacred narrative. We then pivot and return to work for and in God's world; such is the reward of a good and faithful servant responding to a sacred rhetoric: no false assurance and direction, just a call to responsibility, an obligation without end.

NOTES

1. For more information regarding Buber's response to the Holocaust, see Arnett (1986, 41–42).

REFERENCES

American Library Association. 2012. *Public Library Funding Landscape*. Public Library Funding & Technology Access Study 2011–2012. http://www.ala.org

/research/sites/ala.org.research/files/content/initiatives/plftas/2011_2012/plftas12_funding%20landscape.pdf.
Arendt, Hannah. 2006. *Eichmann in Jerusalem: A Report on the Banality of Evil.* New York: Penguin. Original work published 1963.
Arnett, Ronald C. 1986. *Communication and Community: Implications of Martin Buber's Dialogue.* Carbondale: Southern Illinois University Press.
———. 1994. "Existential Homelessness: A Contemporary Case for Dialogue." In *The Reach of Dialogue: Confirmation, Voice and Community*, edited by Rob Anderson, Kenneth Cissna, and Ronald C. Arnett, 229–246. Cresskill, NJ: Hampton Press, 1994.
———. 1999. "Metaphorical Guidance: Administration as Building and Renovation." *Journal of Educational Administration* 37: 80–89.
———. 2013. *Communication Ethics in Dark Times: Hannah Arendt's Rhetoric of Warning and Hope.* Carbondale: Southern Illinois University Press.
———. 2016. "An Immemorial Obligation: Countering the Eclipse of the Other." *Journal of Communication and Religion* 39, no. 2: 7–21.
———. 2017. *Levinas's Rhetorical Demand: The Unending Obligation of Communication Ethics.* Carbondale: Southern Illinois University Press.
Arnett, Ronald C., and Pat Arneson. 1999. *Dialogic Civility in a Cynical Age: Community, Hope, and Interpersonal Relationship.* Albany: State University of New York Press.
Augustine. *The Confessions of St. Augustine.* Translated by John K. Ryan. Garden City, NJ: Image Books, 1960.
Bellah, Robert N., et al. 2008. *Habits of the Heart: Individualism and Commitment in American Life.* Berkeley: University of California Press. Original work published 1985.
Brueggemann, Walter. 1996. Review of *Figuring the Sacred: Religion, Narrative, and Imagination*, by Paul Ricoeur. *Theology Today* 53, no. 1: 95–98.
Buber, Martin. 1997. *Good and Evil: Two Interpretations.* Upper Saddle River, NJ: Prentice Hall. Original work published 1952.
Campolo, Tony. 2008. *It's Friday, but Sunday's Comin'.* Bakersfield, CA: Thomas Nelson. Original work published 1984.
Deb, Sopan. March 15, 2017. "Trump Proposes Eliminating the Arts and Humanities Endowments." *New York Times.* https://www.nytimes.com/2017/03/15/arts/nea-neh-endowments-trump.html.
Ellul, Jacques. 1975. *The New Demons.* Translated by C. Edward Hopkin. New York: Seabury.
———. 2011. *The Subversion of Christianity.* Translated by Geoffrey W. Bromiley. Eugene, OR: Wipf & Stock. Original work published 1986.
Fasching, Darrell J. 2008. "Authority and Religious Experience." In *The Blackwell Companion to Religious Ethics*, edited by W. Schweiker, 61–68. Hoboken, NJ: Wiley.
Fink, Peter E. 1996. Review of *Figuring the Sacred: Religion, Narrative, and Imagination*, by Paul Ricoeur. *Theological Studies* 57, no. 3: 545–47.

Fodor, Jim. 1998. Review of *Figuring the Sacred: Religion, Narrative, and Imagination*, by Paul Ricoeur. *Pro Ecclesia* 7, no. 3: 371–72.

Fritz, Janie M. Harden. 2013. *Professional Civility: Communicative Virtue at Work*. New York: Peter Lang.

King, Martin Luther, Jr. 1998. *The Autobiography of Martin Luther King, Jr.* Edited by Carson Clayborne. New York: Warner Books.

Lasch, Christopher. 1991. *The True and Only Heaven: Progress and Its Critics*. New York: Norton.

Peirce, Charles S. 1998. *The Essential Peirce: Selected Philosophical Writings*, edited by the Peirce Edition Project. Bloomington: Indiana University Press.

Pew Research Center. November 3, 2015. "US Public Becoming Less Religious." http://www.pewforum.org/2015/11/03/u-s-public-becoming-less-religious/.

Postman, Neil. 2006. *Amusing Ourselves to Death: Public Discourse in the Age of Show Business*. New York: Penguin. Original work published 1985.

Putnam, Robert. 2000. *Bowling Alone: The Collapse and Revival of American Community*. New York: Simon & Schuster.

Ricoeur, Paul. 1995. *Figuring the Sacred: Religion, Narrative, and Imagination*. Edited by Martin I. Wallace. Translated by S. Pellauer. Minneapolis, MN: Augsburg Fortress.

Sansom, Dennis. 1998. Review of *Figuring the Sacred: Religion, Narrative, and Imagination*, by Paul Ricoeur. *Perspectives in Religious Studies* 25, no. 4: 399–404.

Schwartz, Dannel I. 1996. *Finding Joy: A Practical Spiritual Guide to Happiness*. Woodstock, VT: Jewish Lights Publishing.

Standing, Guy. 2016. *The Corruption of Capitalism: Why Rentiers Thrive and Work Does Not Pay*. London: Biteback Publishing.

Stiver, Dan R. 1998. Review of *Figuring the Sacred: Religion, Narrative, and Imagination*, by Paul Ricoeur. *Review and Expositor* 95: 609–10.

Taylor, Charles. 2007. *A Secular Age*. Cambridge, MA: Harvard University Press.

Wallace, Mark I. 1995. "Introduction." In *Figuring the Sacred: Religion, Narrative, and Imagination* by Paul Ricoeur, edited by Mark I. Wallace. Translated by S. Pellauer. Minneapolis, MN: Augsburg Fortress.

Chapter 2

The Sacred as Rhetoric

Contextualized Story Performances in Ancient Delphi

Corey Hackworth

INTRODUCTION

There were no sermons in ancient Greece. The modern habit of associating textual exegesis with religious ritual derives from the great monotheisms of Judaism, Christianity, and Islam.[1] There were no preachers, no evangelists, and no sacred scriptures.[2] The central ritual of sacrifice, followed by communal (yet circumscribed) consumption, rarely demanded prescribed speech acts, although prayers were common, and dining, we might expect, involved a considerable degree of free conversation.[3] The moments preceding sacrifice, in contrast, were characterized by a proscription of speech—a demand for *euphemia*, a word that we more often than not translate as "silence."[4] We must turn to the larger ritual context to find what may profitably be described as *sacred rhetoric*—rather than looking to expository teachings or special language accompanying ritual action, we must broaden our gaze and set aside modern categories and assumptions.

To the amateur enthusiast of ancient Greek religion, the most visible remains are often exciting, impressive, and, therefore, significant: architectural artifacts are easily mistaken as sacred spaces, graphic portrayals of deities lend themselves to mischaracterizations as sacred embodiments of the divine, and surviving literary texts are taken (regardless of provenance) as singular, normative, and (after being subjected to procrustean bricolage) taken as representative of orthodox thought.[5] All of this must be set aside. More important to the ancient Greeks was the sanctuary (the *temenos*), and the *definitions* that it embodied, articulated, and sustained. These definitions can be considered profitably by means of two conceptual maps: a) *Inside/Outside*, and b) *Relationships*.[6] Both of these concepts are aspects of the Greek idea of *kosmos*; pursuing better understanding, these matters will directly illuminate the matter of *sacred rhetoric* among the ancient Greeks.[7] Rhetoric precedes and goes beyond words: context both permits and defines language usage that is located *within*. Various elements that independently would lack any explicit significance may collectively exert an implicit rhetorical force. Time, setting, narrative, and historical-literary associations made possible by a shared cultural knowledge permit the "full experience" to communicate more persuasively and effectively than we might expect. In this chapter, I hope to show how Greeks might employ the performance of traditional mythological narrative so as to speak powerfully to a current political moment.

DEFINING INSIDE/OUTSIDE

At its most basic level, the *temenos* was a well-defined geographical region with a clearly articulated "ownership" by one or more divinities. This carefully delineated territory might include one or more house-like structures (*naos*) but could also include more functional additions such as dining halls, storage (*thesauros*), theaters, and even racetracks. The god or goddess had a claim to the interior space and most things within (refuse and junk were buried rather than removed)—the chief exception being the people who entered. Even in this exclusion, strict control was exercised over who might enter, under which conditions, and the host deity wielded a protective custody over those within, particularly those who had successfully petitioned for succor.[8] For an individual to practice the cult required that he or she have access to the *temenos*; entry and/or participation might be permitted or denied for various reasons: ethnicity, citizenship, gender, crime (sacred or civic), profession, recent exposure to birth or death, membership in a particular "tribe" (familial) or "club" (social/voluntary), and so forth.[9] Identity and social status were closely associated with cult participation and sanctuary access. Sanctuaries were explicitly defined spaces, with a defined ownership and clientele. As communal spaces, they concomitantly represented, constituted, and were used by defined communities. The identity of any given individual was, to a large degree, reflected by the "tangle" of cultic communities in which they participated, and most changes in identity were accomplished through participation in cultic community.[10] With respect to sacred rhetoric, it is important to realize the high degree of social control exercised over who might be located *within* such a space, the prerequisite for speaking or hearing words. This complex weave of inside/outside produced a relational tapestry, which leads us to the second "map."[11]

DEFINING RELATIONSHIPS

There is an inherently tautological relationship between Greek perspectives on the *kosmos* of society and nature, and the *kosmos* of sanctuary cult.[12] Rather than attempt to analyze the causality of the arrangement, it is more productive to consider how it thickened the perceived and desired orderliness of reality. The interior organization of any given sanctuary might be essentially haphazard, the unplanned product of the lay of the land and history (with the exception that temple structures were consistently, but not always, oriented with the "front" facing the East and the sunrise). On the other hand, the location of the sanctuary itself has been convincingly shown to be anything but accidental.[13] There are always exceptions when dealing with a culture spanning thousands of miles and a thousand years, but sanctuaries consistently tended to appear in one of two places: *center* and *edge*. We find sanctuaries, for the most part, in the following sorts of locations: the center of the *polis*, the edge of the *polis*, the edge of inhabited regions, shorelines, riverbanks, dramatically elevated points, and geographically distant points to which varied neighboring communities must all travel. These two labels are, moreover, somewhat ambivalent, in that a liminal location is itself a kind of center by nature of its *betweenness*—that which divides is also the place where two (or more) sides meet. Perspective is contingent upon the need of the observer. This concept is depicted again and again in graphic portrayals of sacrifice; the altar stands between mortals and the divine. That which divides is the very point at which it is possible to negotiate relationship and (re)union. Edges and centers provide a mobile series of boundaries and sets within which to practice inclusion, exclusion, and definition. The manipulation, or ownership, of these boundaries, sets, and definitions constituted a form of rhetoric, made authoritative by their sacred nature. Very real rhetorical implications not only were associated with *who* spoke and listened, but indeed with *where* this was accomplished. Sanctuaries were tightly controlled (and often contested) performative spaces that were *located* in a significant manner.

Sanctuaries might be associated with only a single god or goddess, but they could also be spaces shared by a society of divinities (e.g., muses or nymphs); alternatively, one deity might host one or more others (e.g., we often find Apollo and Athena together, or Apollo, his sister Artemis, and their mother Leto, together—the Delian triad).[14] These "group" cults are particularly interesting because they highlight the fact that any given cult emphasized a particular, rather than general, aspect of divine power and interest (Apollo and Artemis suggest initiation, whereas Apollo and Athena resonate with sociopolitical concerns). This is a difficult concept for a modern reader to grasp: there was a clear continuity between the persons of Apollo or Athena as they were worshipped in differing *poleis*, yet fundamental differences are manifest, not only between varying ethnic groups, but geopolitical groupings, and even within the same *polis*.[15] The most visible difference presents itself through *epithet*—the divine names occurred with significant descriptive adjectives that localized and particularized. Consider Apollo at the Delphic Oracle (*Pythios*), on the slopes of Mt. Parnassos above (*Lykeios*), or in Sparta (*Karneios*);[16] even between various cults of Athena in Athens—*Polias, Nike, and Parthenos* on the Acropolis, *Skiras* at the port of Phaleron, *Areia* at the temple of Ares, and *Paionia* in a portico near the gate to the Kerameikos burial ground.[17] Different aspects may have been ritually emphasized in the same sanctuary at specific festivals. Deities, cults, and aspects interacted somewhat kaleidoscopically—and the eye of the beholder (the participant) was engaged in the process. The great diversity of available cult meant that some choice was involved in what to emphasize, and how—intentional or not—selectivity shapes message and its rhetorical effect. With respect to cult, Greek personal identity might be fairly described as *Balkanized* by unique "tangles" of ritually defined communities.

Space, time, and social groupings contextually determined the identity of the divinity and the particular way of apprehending the god or goddess at a specific moment and locality; *kosmic* definition arises from context but also defines that context. This is significant, as action, image, and speech (only very loosely regulated) allowed for affirmation or renegotiation of these matters. Greek gods or goddesses could not be all things to all people, but they could be different things to different people, or even the same people, provided that the relational contexts of space or time differed. Much like vocabulary, where the meaning of any given word is determined by its context but also determines the meaning of that context, so, too, sanctuary cult reflected and defined the communities that participated in it.[18] The power to augment or neglect the practice of cult carried significant political capital.[19] With respect to sacred rhetoric, it is important to realize the level of social complexity woven into matters of who spoke and listened, where, when, and about what.

Sanctuaries (location, owners, participants) embodied and defined *kosmos*, an intrinsically structured concept. As such, it can be somewhat surprising to realize just how varied and flexible the practice of Greek religion could be. This is true particularly with respect to mythical narrative, which is where we must turn now to further pursue the matter of sacred rhetoric. Words did play a role, but it has been important to argue for their second-order status, as expression *within*. To understand words, we must read contexts first. To understand both, it will be helpful to briefly consider the notion of *canon*.

RESTRICTION AS INSPIRATION

To scholars of modern religions, the notion of *canon* is familiar, and a great bulk of scholarship over the past two centuries has hotly contested matters of origins, stability, content, value, and authority. Researchers are acutely aware that they run the risk of being entangled in defensive or antagonistic strategies. The matter is not quite so self-evident in studies of ancient Greek religion for the very simple reason that the Greeks had no texts that were sacred in the modern sense. Yes, they had the words of Homer and Hesiod, but neither of these texts was normative for belief or practice, and the textual traditions were spectacularly divergent—we easily forget how dependent we are on the best comparative guesses of Alexandrian textual critics for our modern editions (texts in use before the Hellenistic period might differ significantly).[20] And yet, a seeming obsession remains with locating the *ur*-text for any given myth that parallels the intense source criticism we see in biblical studies. From *whence* a particular "set" of sacred texts comes indeed has great bearing on religious practice and thought that founds and grounds itself in those texts, as modern religions do, but the reality is that the text in use has far more bearing on practice and thought. Regardless, ancient Greece is a markedly different milieu, as neither original form nor function mattered much, and innovation was encouraged.[21]

J. Z. Smith has suggested a fresh way of looking at certain kinds of religious practice.[22] Rather than concerning ourselves with the historical appurtenance of a given text or set of texts, the nature of what sort of authority such a limited collection might possess, or even the very interesting question of *why* such a thing as canon might exist or be valued, he proposed that we ought, instead, to consider the unexpected *creative* and *elaborative* force that flourishes within tightly regulated circumscriptions. The *possible* uses of something (or readings of any canonical text) are as plural and varied as the individuals and communities who constitute its users. Some functions only become possible as new contexts arise over time—latent affordances become obvious, and older perspectives are easily forgotten or make room for new elaborations.[23] Exegesis is only possible with a fixed text, but exegesis itself is far from static or canonical—history demonstrates that canonical texts or practices tend to remain stable, whereas exegesis, interpretation, application, and such tend to flourish, exhibiting great diversity over time.

This perspective obviously holds true for sacred texts. There are only so many scriptures in the Christian *Bible*, but surely not every possible exegetical sermon has yet been preached? The meaning of any single verse is surely not infinite, but the possible *usages* have been demonstrated historically to be numerous. For my purposes, the nature of *canon* is inseparable from *sacred rhetoric*. Any number of possible rhetorical statements can be made, but *that which is sacred is grounded in the notion of stricture and fixity*. It seeks not to persuade but to reveal incarnate truth—how the world *is* or what it *must* become. Canon impinges upon sacred rhetoric in several ways, not just with respect to traditional texts:

- of all manners of speaking—*this* way
- of all topics—*this* topic
- of all contexts—*this* context
- of all aims and uses—these *many* potentials, afforded despite stricture (religion, art, entertainment, history, and politics)

Sacred rhetoric occurs within circumscribed performative spaces. Although it may appear to suffer from a reduction of access to all possible materials, that limitation produces surfaces of constraint—within, in reaction to, and upon which, one may freely elaborate—or rather, one is inspired, even compelled, to elaborate. Reduction engenders ingenuity and innovation.[24]

GREEK CANON

The Greeks not only had no authoritative textual canon comparable to today's monotheisms, but they had no canonical or normative *version* of any given myth. Yet these narratives served to historicize the establishment of cult, were regularly performed within cultic settings, and were deemed pleasing to both divine and mortal audiences. Much has been written on their literary merit and the ways in which they might serve as political propaganda, but little attention is given to the fact that they were the product of canon rather than the canon itself—a very *limited set of narratives* existed, but they appeared in nearly limitless variation.[25] Each performance *was* canonical as a sacred utterance, when considered as a singular moment, yet each new performance should also be considered as exegesis of prior cultural memory, earlier literary artifact, and the ever important expectations of the audience. Rather than the model of *original→copy/variation*, it is more useful to resort to thinking in terms of *paradigms*. Through this lens, we find that each telling of a myth is a recognizable expression of that which is canon, but it is not directly comparable to any a priori fixed standard (it has intertextual relationships with prior retellings, but it is not to be considered a genetically evolved or devolved descendant). As Giorgio Agamben has written:

a paradigm entails a movement that goes from singularity to singularity and, without ever leaving singularity, transforms every singular case into an *exemplar* of a general rule that can never be stated a priori.

the paradigm is never already given, but is generated and produced . . . by "placing alongside," "conjoining together," and above all by "showing" and "exposing" . . . The paradigmatic relation does not merely occur between sensible objects or between these objects and a general rule; it occurs instead between a singularity (which thus becomes a paradigm) and its exposition (its intelligibility).[26]

Greek myth was *kosmic* in nature, *paradigmatic* of reality: the universe, social customs, people groups, and specific cults. It was limited by the fact that sanctuary cult was central to its performance.[27]

Greek myths were traditional tales, stories that are not coincidental with a single textual manifestation and thus have no author or normative form of expression.[28] Myths changed, continuously, partly due to matters of aesthetics and competition/competence, but also on account of cultural relevance. Fritz Graf provides a succinct definition: "A myth makes a valid statement about the origins of the world, of society and of its institutions, about the gods and their relationship with mortals, in short, about everything on which human existence depends. If conditions change, a myth, if it is to survive, must change with them."[29] Any given expression, or telling, of a myth was contextualized. A successful contextualization appeared to be *true*—to make a valid statement. What is fascinating about Greek myth, however, is the way in which change and continuity negotiated to present these authoritative statements about the nature and organization of the *kosmos*. The same limited set of tales, easily familiar to an audience, was manipulated, refreshed, and restated in an endlessly creative series of retellings that were at once aesthetically pleasing in freshly contemporary ways and paradigmatic throughout centuries of sociopolitical turbulence and change.[30]

PART II
APOLLO, ATHENS, AND THE BARBARIANS
THE DELPHIC PAEANS

In the summer of 1893, the French discovered two late second century BCE hymns to Apollo while excavating at Delphi.[31] Attributed to Athenaios and Limenios, best arguments assign performances to the Athenian celebration of the *Pythaïdes* in 128/7 BCE, or possibly separately in the 128/7 and 106/5 festivals. Earliest evidence suggests that the *Pythaïdes* had originally been celebrated by at least the fourth century BCE and already may have long been traditional by this point. Athens would send a sacred embassy (*theoria*) overland, escorted by civic officials, bearing first fruits and, possibly, a tripod with which to bring back fire from Apollo's sacred hearth. This seems to have commemorated the fetching of pure fire from Apollo's sacred hearth from which to rekindle the civic hearth in Athens, after the polluting sack by the Persians in 480 BCE. The practice ended at some unknown date but was restored by Athens in the mid-second century BCE. Through Roman intervention in the early and mid-second century, power dynamics shifted dramatically in Greece, and Athens took advantage of their alliance with Rome as spaces opened in the Greek political landscape. Following the defeat of the Macedonians in the 60s, they gained full control of Delos and its sanctuary. Soon after, with Attalid influence in check, the Achaean league defeated, and finally, the total destruction of Corinth in the 40s, the Athenians began to exert influence over the reorganized Delphic Amphictyony. Not a competitive military force at this time, the Athenians leveraged their cultural capital, emphasizing their antiquity and authority in cultic matters—already exercising absolute control over the Delian Apollo cult, they began to expend significant financial resources on the newly restored *Pythaïdes* at Delphi. The festival would be celebrated four times (in 138/7, 128/7, 106/5, and 98/7 BCE) before its final cancellation, after Athens fell to Sulla in 86 BCE.[32] The performance schedule of 128 BCE included a large chorus, singing a freshly composed hymn in praise of the god. We have numerous inscriptions detailing the event, suggesting that as many as three hundred to five hundred people may have traveled from Athens to participate, presenting an extensive program of musical and theatrical performance, in addition to sacrifice.[33]

The hymns differ aesthetically, but they follow a common thematic structure. Most significant here are strikingly similar doublets that I argue are intended to be *paradigmatic*, using the sacred (mythical canon) to interpret reality (*kosmos*) as a kind of rhetoric: each hymn describes Apollo's mythical acquisition of the Delphic oracle through combat with a *drakōn* (snake) and then immediately incorporates reference to Apollo's intervention on his sanctuary's behalf against the Gallic invasion of 279/8 BCE. A real historical event was imbricated into a traditional mythic form, juxtaposed with *the* Delphic Apollo tale, and the comparative effort is clear. The rhetorical power of myth is to *realize* (i.e., to make *real*) a particular *vision* of history—past, present, and future. The audience is meant to *know* that the god *possesses* his sanctuary, and that this fact has, and will bring, mutual benefit to his allies. All of this is accomplished within a strictly limited and defined space for performative enunciation (*canon*).

DRAKŌNS AND BARBARIANS

Athenaios's short, rapid text offers us a traditional and vivid description of Apollo slaying his nemesis with arrows, which is followed immediately by a description of an unholy warband of invading Gauls. The lines that follow the doublet are sadly far too fragmentary to even conjecture restoration, but comparison with Limenios's hymn suggests that a prayer would have been offered for the prosperity and security of Athens, Delphi, and their Roman allies.[34]

]πᾶσι θνατοῖοις προφαίνει[20
[τρ]ίποδα μαντεῖειον ὡς ειει[21
[φρ]ουούρειει δράκων, ὅτε τε [22
]ηησας αἰόλον ἑλικτὰν [23
]συυρίγμαθ' ιἱεὶς ἀθῶπε[υτ' 24
]δὲ Γαλατᾶαν ἄρης[25
]ν ἐπέρaaσ' ἀσέπτ[ῶς 26

] to all mortals bring to light [
prophetic tripod, as/when you took [
the drakōn guarding, when you [
] twisting coil [
] hisses you shot, implacable [
] and the Galatian Ares [
] piercing through, unholy [

At Delphi, and in these hymns, the tripod most certainly represents the oracle, but dedicatory habits at Delphi reveal that tripods also stood as symbols of victory and dominance.[35] At Delphi, the object is not only Apollo's prize, but it is also his trophy; and when Athenaios invokes the famous mythical episode, he does so in a historical context deeply aware of struggles between political entities over control of the sanctuary.[36]

The companion text, by Limenios, deriving from either the same or the subsequent celebration of the festival, reveals that Athenaios's clever use of history was well enough received to become, perhaps, a normative tradition for the festival.[37] His text is more prolix, and so more details survive, despite significant damage to the stone.[38]

ὃς ἔχειεις τρίποδα βαῖν' ἐπὶ θ(ε)οστιβ[έα τaάνδε Π]αρναασ- 22
σίαν δειράδα φιλένθεον. Ἀμφὶ πλόκ[αμον σὺ δ'οἴ]νῶῳ [πα] 23
δάφνας κλάδον πλεξάμενος ἀἀπ[λέτους 24
ἀἀμβρόται χειρὶ σύρων, ἄναξ Γ[ᾶς 25

κόραι. ---- Ἀλλὰ Λαατοῦς ἐρατογ[λέφαρε   26
]μ παῖδα Γᾷ[ας] τ' ἔπεφνες ἰοῖς ο[27
πόθον ἔσχε μᾳτρὸς [28
θῆηρ' ἃ κατέκτ[α]ς ος[29
[σ]υύριγμ' ἀπ' ε[   ]ων[30
ἐπ]εφρούρει[εις] δὲ Γᾶα[ς   ὁ βάρ-]   31
βαρος ἄρης ὅτε [τε]ὸμ μαντόσυ [νον   πολυκυ-]   32
θὲς λη(ι)ζόμενος ὤλεθ' ὑγρᾶι χι[όνος   33

*you who hold the tripod, come upon this god-trodden, god-loved,
Parnassian ridge!
with laurel shoot woven about your wine-ruddy locks,
you were dragging immense [rocks] with your immortal hand,
Lord, . . . of Earth [   ] daughters
but, son of lovely-eyed Leto, you slew the child of Earth with arrows . . .
he had desire for mother . . .
the wild beast which you killed who . . .
hisses from . . .
and guarding . . . Earth . . .
the Barbarian Ares, when your oracular . . .
plundering, destroyed by wet snow*

Again, we see reference to possession of the tripod, combat with a beast, followed by defeat of historical invaders. Although the hymns are wildly different from an aesthetic perspective, it is clear that the two texts share a significant structural template.[39] A great deal could be said about the vocabulary employed in these texts, particularly with reference to the prior guardian of the oracular tripod. There is extreme variance throughout the many surviving accounts in terms of nouns,[40] adjectives,[41] and gender.[42] Moreover, there is variance as to whether the change in ownership was violent or peaceful, whether there *was* a prior owner, and what age Apollo was when he took control.[43] It remains paradigmatic, however, that for mortals, for the historical period, the Delphic sanctuary and its oracle belonged to *Apollo*.

Although scholars who concern themselves with establishing *ur*-texts for tales argue over the originality, and social implications, of the violent form of the narrative, it holds true that for several centuries (including the second century BCE) the Archer God versus *Drakōn* narrative was preferred.[44] One of the ways by which we can know this, aside from the preponderance of textual and graphic evidence, is a certain musical competition held regularly within the Delphic sanctuary.

PYTHIKOS NOMOS

The mythographer Hyginus claims that Apollo founded the Pythian Games after he slew the *drakōn*, and Pausanias tells us that in 586 BCE, after the first Sacred War, the new Amphictyony rebooted the Pythian Games in a manner self-consciously imitative of, but not identical to, the Olympian Games.[45] Strabo offers details, including that the original competition of *kitharoedes* performing a *paean* for the god was supplemented by the addition of instrumental competitions.[46] Most importantly for my purposes, *aulos* players competed with a certain composition named the *nomos Pythikos*, a musical representation of Apollo's famous duel with the *drakōn*.[47]

Strabo tells that there were five prescribed segments, each movement depicting a separate scene in the well-known narrative: *prelude, onset/testing, contest, victory celebration,* and the *death* of the *drakōn*.[48] Much later, Pollux described the event in his *Onomasticon* with slightly different terms: *testing/examining* the location, *challenging/summoning* the *drakōn, fighting* the *drakōn, revealing* the victory/death, *dancing* the victory dance.[49] Much can be said about the specific vocabularies and what they might reveal about the music itself.[50] What is clear, however, is that there was at any given time a *canonical* structure to competition, within which competitive innovation and creativity were expected and demanded, keyed to the tastes of an immediate audience. Apollo's destruction of the *drakōn* followed a familiar model, immediately recognizable to the audience, even when words were absent. The variations of each performance or telling would be tightly circumscribed by the need to be recognizable, and yet both competitive context and extant literary and graphic remains convincingly demonstrate that artistic "exegesis" of the paradigm/canon could be quite varied.

It was *familiar, recognizable,* and occurred in a specific place (Delphi, et al.) at a specific time (the Pythian games, the Pythaïdes, et al.)—it was the product of *canon*, was enacted within a *context*, and was recognizably paradigmatic. The intense familiarity of this mythical paradigm allowed Athenaios and Limenios to evoke and invoke the entire myth without needing to resort to full narration. The rhetoric of this sacred tale was well-known: Apollo is victor, here in his sanctuary, where he was victorious. The immediate juxtaposition of a historical event supposedly involving the god is an example of sacred rhetoric.

Brennus the Barbarian: Galatian Ares

In the early third century BCE, Greece faced a devastating Gallic invasion. After early military success in Thrace, the massed force of invaders split into smaller groups: one large contingent under the leadership of a man named Brennus managed to decisively defeat the Greek defenders at Thermopylae, and in 278, marched to plunder Apollo's famous oracle.[51] One ancient source put the outsider forces at something like sixty-five thousand, against a mere four thousand defenders.[52] One imagines that the numbers were inflated for dramatic effect, somewhat like Herodotus's accounts of Persians drinking rivers dry, but then, our source tells us that this was but a fraction of a total invasion force of some three hundred thousand. Accurate or not, it seems meant to represent a substantial, but believable, invasion force. They were crushed (pun intended) when part of the mountain, Parnassos, fell on them. Later Delphic "orthodoxy" claimed that Apollo had personally intervened to protect his sanctuary, having promised the aid of his own presence, as well as the "white maidens." The god had instructed the Delphians not to remove their food and drink from the nearby town, and the invaders gorged themselves, attacking while drunk.[53] Portents were observed: thunder, lightning, earthquakes, ghosts of heroes, and so forth. Most pertinent to the Delphic hymns, it was claimed that a freezing snowstorm mixed with hail occurred, which some writers chose to consider as the promised "white maidens." Others claimed that the priests saw Athena and Artemis manifest at Apollo's temple in a divine epiphany, rushing off with him to join in the battle. Then, as the priests ran to bring this news to the front lines, an earthquake occurred, causing a large chunk of the mountain to fall away, crushing the invaders and causing them to flee.[54] What is exciting about the inclusion of this historical episode in the Delphic hymns is that the repulsion of Brennus is already paradigmatic in its own right—history, at least according to the way the Greeks told it, had repeated itself.

THE PERSIANS

In August of 480 BCE, almost exactly two centuries earlier, King Leonidas and his three hundred Spartans were famously defeated at Thermopylae; the Persians swept throughout central Greece. Xerxes led the main force, intending to burn Athens to the ground while (according to Herodotus and some other ancient writers) a smaller contingent was sent to acquire the treasures of Delphi.[55] There is some disagreement among scholars as to whether the Persians would have, or did in fact, try to loot Delphi, but the Greeks preferred to believe they did.[56]

In response to a formal inquiry of the oracle, the locals left the sacred wealth undisturbed, as opposed to concealing or evacuating it.[57] The god had declared himself *sufficient* to take care of his own matters.[58] The people, however, either left town or went into hiding, save for sixty-men and the god's prophet who stayed to keep an eye on things. As the *barbaroi*[59] came near (and this is the word that Herodotus uses repeatedly), the sacred weapons stored within the temple supposedly appeared outside on the ground of their own accord. The most significant moment, however, occurred as the Persians reached the sanctuary of Athena *Pronaos*. At this moment, it was said that a loud shout and war cry was heard, lightning fell from the sky, and two large pieces of Mount Parnassos broke away and fell upon the Persians. The Persian troops understandably retreated in a panic, and Herodotus reports that the Delphians pursued and killed quite a few. Both Persian and Delphic accounts supposedly claimed that the pursuit was joined by two heavily armed beings of gigantic stature, whom the Delphians thought were Phylacus and Autonoüs, who received local hero cult.[60]

METAPHOR

Herodotus often employs individual episodes as *synecdoche*, that is, part-for-the-whole. Whatever meaning or pattern of cause and effect he discerns in history, he believes that it can be seen on the scales of individuals and empires, single battles and entire campaigns. There are a variety of ways to treat the relationship of part and whole; Hayden White wrote extensively on the matter, suggesting that historians tend to choose between various master tropes when emplotting historical narratives.[61]

> the facts do not speak for themselves, but . . . the historian speaks for them, speaks on their behalf, and fashions the fragments of the past into a whole whose integrity is—its *re*presentation—a purely discursive one. Novelists might be dealing only with imaginary events whereas historians are dealing with real ones, but the process of fusing events, whether imaginary or real, into a comprehensible totality capable of serving as the *object* of representation is a poetic process.[62]

> A historical interpretation, like a poetic fiction, can be said to appeal to its readers as a plausible representation of the world by virtue of its implicit appeal to those "pre-generic plot-structure" or archetypal story-forms that define the modalities of a given culture's literary endowment.[63]

The rhetorical function of history has been persuasively presented and forcefully interrogated in recent decades; what remains is to effectively dissolve the barrier between poetry/fiction/myth and historical depictions of reality to better understand the *use* of these things. Rather than being reductionist, or illustrative, synecdoche offers a qualitative representation of the whole—it is *paradigmatic* in the most essential and fundamental way. In other words, understanding this one episode *is the same as* understanding the whole narrative. For Herodotus, that means that success tends to encourage foolishness and overreach, which produces downfall. It is one thing to sack Greek cities. To plunder Delphi is something else. This is not very controversial. What is interesting, however, is the way in which these very *familiar* texts and events are woven together as a rhetorical statement by Athenaios, one repeated by Limenios—rhetorical statements that weave history into sacred storytelling, elevating the discourse, I believe, to the level of *sacred rhetoric*. The mythical moment when Apollo slays his nemesis, and the familiar and patterned way in which he defends his sanctuary, crash together as a synecdoche in these paeans. The mythical paradigm resonates with the historical one, merging into a single rhetorical image, incarnating (making real) *kosmic* truth before the eyes of the observers.

CONTEXTUALIZING THE RHETORIC

A bit earlier in his poem, Athenaios describes Athens, or rather Attica, as ἄθραυστον, that is, *unbroken*—but Athens *was* broken by the Persians. That was why they sent a *theoria* to Delphi after the war, to retrieve clean fire for the acropolis sanctuary, which occasioned the founding of the original Pythaïdes, which these new celebrations in the second century look back upon. But Athens, while sacked and burned, was saved, so they claimed, by the oracular advice to trust in the wooden wall of their navy. In the intervening centuries, Athens was most certainly broken as a political force—by the Spartans, the Macedonians, the Aetolians, and so forth—but never destroyed (unlike Corinth and Thebes). Now leveraging their cultural capital, and once more regional influence, in control of Delos, and throwing their weight around at Delphi—Athens is back, baby! Athenaios and Limenios weave a triumphant and ascendant Athens into this familiar pattern of divine triumph, this repeated historical event, where Apollo wins, and therefore, so does Athens. They are living the mythical paradigm. The *canon* that gives rise to these performances, that is expressed by the poetic retelling of the sacred tale, is expressly linked with historical episodes that reveal that *kosmos* is incarnational. The rhetorical use of the sacred is a declarative statement of what is meant to be experienced as *fact*.

HISTORICIZING MYTH—MYTHOLOGIZING REALITY

It is impossible to know if the Athenians and other Greeks honestly believed in the historical accuracy of Apollonian myths. Certainly, later writers such as the intellectual Plutarch were open to the idea that certain stories were fantastical, whereas others were distortions of less astonishing historical persons and events, but he himself appears to have believed in the efficacy of the oracle, served as a priest at Delphi, and believed in the reality of divine agents.[64] The Greeks consistently treated myth as a kind of history, or at least something to be historicized. Herodotus carefully incorporated the tales of Europa and Helen into his prologue (albeit with the fantastical elements stripped out), and even cynical Thucydides allowed that the Trojan War really did occur. The most skeptical Euhemerists took great effort to permit that the names of gods and demigods were, in fact, those of ancient culture heroes grown fantastical through centuries of renarration. It is likely that images of *kosmic* conflict such as that between Apollo and the *drakōn*, in addition to wars with centaurs, giants, and Amazons, were far too useful, symbolically, to bother debunking—the struggle between civilization and barbarianism was self-evidently true on a politically necessary level.[65] Rather than concern ourselves with matters of *accuracy*, it is more useful to approach myth as history with a view toward *veracity*—while they might squabble over or question factual details, Greeks seem to have happily accepted mythological narrative as generically *true*.

In a pair of articles, Sarah Iles Johnston has argued that narrative performance in a ritual context serves to momentarily enchant the audience, bringing the worlds of myth and history close together, just as the sacrificial altar and meal bring human and divine communities together. The power of this enchantment is underappreciated by our modern ways of storytelling.[66] Unlike our own practices, all Greek myths belong to the same story universe, or what we might call a mega-text. That is, all the characters, events, and locations featured in Greek myths are capable of engaging in crossovers, and they *do*. Johnston refers to this somewhat unexpected practice as a kind of *hyper-seriality*.[67] Each story and each telling contributes to and becomes part of the material available to later narrators. Conflict tends to either get ironed out, "ret-conned," or ignored, and a subset of privileged texts and authors are invoked as referees when too much conflict arises. Greek storytelling limits itself to a single story world. This by itself would be fascinating enough, but it is only a short step to realize that this hyper-seriality is, in fact, a foundational assumption and practice for historiographical texts—both our own and the Greeks'.

This matter goes further for them, however, as there was a fundamental connectivity between what we would consider two separate categories of hyper-serialized narratives: myth and history. These realms are conjoined for the Greeks. The Greek historians historicized their myths. Not only did they seem to believe that they described some sort of actual distant past—they wrote them into the introductory parts of their more contemporary histories. Athenaios and Limenios have done the opposite, writing history into their myths—the authors, performers, and audiences intentionally step over the dividing line and fuse divine myth and human history in a stronger way—history and myth do more than meet, they mingle—they mutually guarantee the validity of each other, revealing that each is paradigmatic of the whole.

Apollo's victory is good for mortals, all mortals—the oracle was accessible to all. The restoration of the *Pythaïdes* by Athens occurs as a public display of the *polis*'s newly regained influence at Delphi. As with snakes and gods, so between various mortal political powers as well. Athens' (and Rome's) "*liberation*" of Delphi could be understood in a similar light. The reference to the Gauls and their failure can surely be read with more recent triumphs in mind. Sadly, sacred rhetoric is not always successful in its incarnational efforts. Athens would fall to Sulla in 86 BCE, and the *Pythaïdes* festival was canceled for good. In 84 BCE northern barbarians would invade Delphi, this time successfully, causing damage to sanctuary and temple, looting what treasure remained, and extinguishing Apollo's sacred hearth.

Sacred rhetoric, for the Greeks, did not just evoke the mythical past, or even visualize the historical past, but it demanded that those present view themselves and their own time as belonging to this continuous mythical narrative. They were *living* the myth.

NOTES

1. It has been argued that myth served an exegetical function for Roman cult, existing on the margins of the ritual process, serving simultaneously as a pleasing thing (like a beautiful statue) to the divinity as well as commentary on canonical *action*. Its dual function was interpretive and aesthetic. Cf. John Scheid, "Cults, Myths, and Politics at the Beginning of the Empire," in *Roman Religion*, ed. Clifford Ando (Edinburgh: Edinburgh University Press, 2003), 117–38. It was useful and beneficial but hardly necessary; texts were the exegesis of canonical action, not of other texts.

2. Moses Finley offers an excellent, but brief, summary of the way in which ancient Greek religion differed from modern monotheistic categories, cf. "Foreword," in *Greek Religion and Society*, ed. P. E. Easterling and J. V. Muir (Cambridge; New York: Cambridge University Press, 1985), xvii–xx. This is generically true, but it must be acknowledged that Greek religion (if that is even a valid category) was diverse both geographically and chronologically. Philosophical schools and mystery

cults, especially in the Roman period, raise obvious problems. I speak largely to *polis* and domestic religion. It is also true that rhetoric was immensely popular among the Greeks, and that myths and gods found use in these speeches. Cf. Terry Papillion, "Rhetoric, Art, and Myth: Isocrates and Busiris," in *The Orator in Action and Theory in Greece and Rome: Essays in Honor of George A. Kennedy*, ed. Cecil W. Wooten (Leiden; Boston: Brill, 2001), 73–93. I distinguish, however, between the use of the sacred *in* rhetoric, and *sacred rhetoric*. Greek religion was imbricated throughout social life (e.g., there would be a sacrifice before important political meetings), but certain arenas were more intensely religious, and it is there that I focus.

3. Prayer has convincingly been treated as rhetorical speech, but it would be unwise to make overly strong comparisons between ancient and modern practices. Cf. Fritz Graf, "Prayer in Magic and Religious Ritual," in *Magika Hiera: Ancient Greek Magic and Religion*, ed. Christopher A. Faraone and Dirk Obbink (New York: Oxford University Press, 1991), 188–97; Jan N. Bremmer, "Greek Normative Sacrifice," in *A Companion to Greek Religion*, ed. Daniel Ogden (Malden, MA: Blackwell, 2007), 132–44. Prayer and song were important components of Greek cult, and they certainly had rhetorical form and effect; Cf. Laurent Pernot, "The Rhetoric of Religion," *Rhetorica: A Journal of the History of Rhetoric* 24, no. 3 (August 2006): 235–54. The Second Sophistic period, eccentrics such as Aelius Aristides, and collections such as the Dionsiac Hymns are not reliable guides to earlier, normative, Greek practice. Fundamentally, words must be understood as second-order phenomena for Greek religion (unlike Christianity), and the concept of rhetoric must be freed from an overly formalist attachment to words.

4. *Euphemia* was typically defined as "words of good omen" (the prefix *eu*- being positive, the stem *phēm*- having to do with speech); often enforced though use of *aulos*—silence marked by noise, broken by actual silence at the moment the victim was slain, followed by the *ololuge*, the ritual shrieking of the women who are present.

5. Any attempt to accurately describe something as broad and varied as Greek culture or Greek religion will be subject to this problem, but we can do better with respect to generic practice, and we can refrain from speaking in absolutes.

6. Neither of these categories is "Greek," but they are useful as external lenses. The Greek word *temenos* seems to derive from the root for *cutting*, indicating that consecrated land was sharply demarcated, separated from ordinary usage. Foucault famously said, "knowledge is not made for understanding; it is made for cutting." We may take this inversely to mean that "cutting" is meant to suggest knowledge, and therefore understanding. By considering how the "cuts" were made in ancient Greece, we can make guesses as to which definitions they felt were important. Cf. Michel Foucault, "Nietzsche, Genealogy, History," in *The Foucault Reader*, ed. Paul Rabinow (New York: Pantheon Books, 1984), 76–100. The "cuts" determine what can be known, thought, and said.

7. The Sicilian *rhetor* Gorgias of Leontini began his famous "Encomium of Helen" by addressing the matter of *kosmos* as it might manifest in varying contexts: populated cities, beautiful bodies, wise souls, virtuous actions, and true words. In other words, each circumstance as it might be *best* or *praiseworthy*. The reality is that life

is experienced as a markedly different sort of thing—Clifford Geertz has argued that religion is, in part, a response to the chaos (the opposite of *kosmos*) that threatens to emerge when mere mortals discover the limits of intellectual interpretability, physical endurance, and moral clarity. Religion may not always provide answers (although sometimes it does), but it does offer the means of *coping*; "Religion as a Cultural System," in *The Interpretation of Cultures: Selected Essays* (London: Hutchinson, 1975), 100.

8. Cf. Ulrich Sinn, "Greek Sanctuaries as Places of Refuge," in *Oxford Readings in Greek Religion*, ed. Richard Buxton (Oxford; New York: Oxford University Press, 2000), 155–79.

9. The role of *miasma*, or "pollution" for sanctuary access is often underappreciated. Although significant crimes might very well prevent an individual from participating in cult, the most frequent occurrences of the concept (times of birth and death) temporarily exclude the individual from the larger social grouping but simultaneously express an intense sense of him or her *belonging* to the immediate household or extended family group. Cf. Andreas Bendlin, "Purity and Pollution," in *A Companion to Greek Religion*, ed. Daniel Ogden (Malden, MA: Blackwell, 2007), 178–89. Unlike most popular religious groups today, one did not "shop" according to personal tastes in spirituality, nor did one convert from/to different cults and communities. Voluntary and/or inclusive cults existed (e.g., the so-called mysteries, various Pan-Hellenic festivals, as well as the oracles), but these were the exceptions rather than the rule.

10. Cf. Nanno Marinatos, "Striding across Boundaries: Hermes and Aphrodite as Gods of Initiation," in *Initiation in Ancient Greek Rituals and Narratives: New Critical Perspectives*, ed. David B. Dodd and Christopher A. Farone (London; New York: Routledge, 2003), 130–52; Sarah Hitch, "From Birth to Death: Life-Change Rituals," in *The Oxford Handbook of Ancient Greek Religion*, ed. Esther Eidinow and Julia Kindt (Oxford: Oxford University Press, 2015), 521–36.

11. The seminal essays on community through cult are Christiane Sourvinou-Inwood, "What Is *Polis* Religion," in *Oxford Readings in Greek Religion*, ed. Richard Buxton (Oxford; New York: Oxford University Press, 2000), 13–37; Christiane Sourvinou-Inwood, "Further Aspects of *Polis* Religion," in *Oxford Readings in Greek Religion*, ed. Richard Buxton (Oxford; New York: Oxford University Press, 2000), 38–55. The *polis* religion theory has proven *too* useful, and has therefore invited substantial criticism; cf. Julia Kindt, *Rethinking Greek Religion* (Cambridge: Cambridge University Press, 2012). Although Greek religion has to do with community, we should avoid "always" and "only" characterizations of this function as it tends to privilege certain types of data over others and consciously impose an interpretive framework upon a lived reality that was unconsciously organized and accepted without necessarily being "understood."

12. Reality and the cultic "map," which represents, reinforces, and enables description/interpretation of said reality, exist in a complex relationship. It was popularized in the study of religion by Jonathan Z. Smith in *Map Is Not Territory: Studies in the History of Religions* (Chicago: University of Chicago Press, 1993). The distinction between map and territory was put quite succinctly, in a manner pertinent to the topic at hand, by Alfred Korzybski: "A map *is not* the territory it represents, but, if correct,

it has a *similar structure* to the territory, which accounts for its usefulness . . . . If we reflect upon our languages, we find that at best they must be considered *only as maps*. A word *is not* the object it represents; and languages exhibit also this peculiar self-reflexiveness, that we can analyze languages by linguist means." Korzybski suggests that we need a map of the map, and a map of the map of the map. *Science and Sanity: An Introduction to Non-Aristotelian Systems and General Semantics* (New York: International Non-Aristotelian Library Publishing Co.; Lancaster, PA: Science Press, distributors, 1933), 58.

13. François de Polignac, "Mediation, Competition, and Sovereignty: The Evolution of Rural Sanctuaries in Geometric Greece," in *Placing the Gods: Sanctuaries and Sacred Space in Ancient Greece*, ed. Susan E. Alcock and Robin Osborne (Oxford: Clarendon Press; New York: Oxford University Press, 1994), 3–18. For an introduction to what might be found *inside* sanctuaries, and how it was generally used, cf. John Pedley, *Sanctuaries and the Sacred in the Ancient Greek World* (New York: Cambridge University Press, 2005).

14. This is comparable to the social organization of mortal cult communities, as they might be quite limited, quite open, or have a limited community hosting a broad audience. The concept of ownership can be complicated, as many sanctuaries were shared by more than one deity. One was typically considered to be the "host," but some sites such as Delphi not only seem to have had more than one *temenos* (e.g., the adjacent site of Athena *pronaos*) but also had a seasonal rotation wherein Apollo and Dionysos exchanged dominance. In other cases, we find clustered groups (typically without proper names) such as the *Semnai Theai* or the nymphs. The sanctuary might be extensive enough to "rent" land for agricultural purposes. For an accessible historical description of the early development of Delphi and Olympia (two important Pan-Hellenic sanctuaries), revealing the complexity behind later organizational schemes, cf. Catherine Morgan, *Athletes and Oracles: The Transformation of Olympia and Delphi in the Eighth Century BC* (Cambridge; New York: Cambridge University Press, 1990).

15. Some Greeks operated under the assumption that all people everywhere worshipped the same gods but knew them differently and by different names. Cf. Herodotus, *Histories* 2.4.2; he claims that the Egyptians were the first to discover and practice the worship of the twelve (Olympians).

16. For *Apollo Lykeios,* cf. Lewis Farnell, *The Cults of the Greek States*, five vols. (Oxford: Clarendon Press, 1896–1909), vol. 4, 113–23; Pausanias, *Description of Greece* 10.14.8; for *Apollo Karneios* cf. Farnell, vol. 4, 131–36; Callimachos, *Hymn to Apollo*, 72–73; Pausanias 3.13.3–4.

17. For *Athena Skiras*, cf. Lewis Farnell, *The Cults of the Greek States*, five vols. (Oxford: Clarendon Press, 1896–1909), vol. 1, 291–92; Pausanias, *Description of Greece* 1.1.4, 1.36.4; for *Athena Aeria*, cf. Farnell, vol. 1, 309; Pausanias 1.28.5; for *Athena Paionia*, cf. Farnell, vol. 1, 317; Pausanias 1.2.5. For a detailed discussion of Athenian cult in general, cf. Robert Parker, *Polytheism and Society at Athens* (Oxford; New York: Oxford University Press, 2005).

18. Jean Pierre Vernant suggested that the gods might be thought of as "vocabulary" expressed in a sort of divine "grammar" articulating *kosmos*—the significant

insight here being the understanding that the semantic force of a deity was subject to context: sanctuary, festival, and above, relationships with other divinities. "Thus their religion and their pantheon can be seen to be a system of classification, a particular way of ordering and conceptualizing the universe, distinguishing between multiple types of force and power operating within it. So in this sense I would suggest that a pantheon, as an organized system implying definite relations between the various gods, is a kind of language, a particular way of apprehending reality and expressing it in symbolic terms." "The Society of the Gods," in *Myth and Society in Ancient Greece*, trans. Janet Lloyd (New York: Zone Books; Cambridge, MA: Distributed by the MIT Press, 1988), 94.

19. For example, Athens took great pride in its "stewardship" of the Eleusinian mysteries, a Pan-Hellenic cult that advertised Athenian prestige, in part, by requiring participants to ritually process *from* the heart of Athens to the sanctuary in Eleusis.

20. Very large quantities of lines were purged from the *Iliad* and the *Odyssey*. There is no compelling evidence that any of these poets' texts were ever used for, or determined, regular cult practice beyond public recitation during festivals such as the Panathenaea.

21. "For all its weight of tradition (not less evident in ancient Greek religion than in other religions), Greek religion remains fundamentally improvisatory." John Gould, "On Making Sense of Greek Religion," in *Greek Religion and Society*, ed. P. E. Easterling and J. V. Muir (Cambridge; New York: Cambridge University Press, 1985), 7.

22. Jonathan Z. Smith, "Sacred Persistence: Toward a Redescription of Canon," in *Imagining Religion: From Babylon to Jonestown* (Chicago: University of Chicago Press, 1982), 36–52.

23. On *affordances* and the matter of Greek myth, cf. Sarah Iles Johnston, "A New Web for Arachne," in *Antike Mythen: Medien, Transformationen und Konstruktionen*, ed. Christine Walde and Ueli Dill (Berlin; New York: Walter de Gruyter, 2009), 1–20. Foundational works on affordances include James Gibson, "The Theory of Affordances," in *Perceiving, Acting, and Knowing: Toward an Ecological Psychology*, ed. Robert Shaw and John Bransford (Hillsdale, NJ: Lawrence Erlbaum Associates; New York: distributed by the Halsted Press Division, Wiley, 1977), pt. 3; James Gibson, *The Ecological Approach to Visual Perception* (Boston: Houghton Mifflin, 1979); Maurizio Bettini, *Nascere: Storie di Donne, Donnole, Madri ed Eroi* (Torino: G. Einaudi, 1998). Gibson coined the term as a psychological description of the sum of all "action possibilities" lying latent in a particular object or environment. Bettini and Johnston employed the concept to discuss the mental operations belonging to culture. It is a tremendously useful concept when considering *canons*.

24. One might say that all great art seems to arise in this way. Music with its limited set of pitches, cooking with a culturally limited set of ingredients, poetry with set meter and rhyme schemes—in fact, the haiku seems to me to be all the more profound for its extreme limitations, with every sound, shade of meaning, and pause having been polished to a high luster.

25. Rather than seeing a telling of a myth as an effort to dogmatize, to produce a normative sacred text, I prefer to see the *event* of telling the myth as an *enactment* of canon (proper and limited place, theme, structure, speaker/audience, time, etc.).

26. Giorgio Agamben, *The Signature of All Things: On Method*, trans. Luca D'Isanto and Kevin Attell (New York: Zone Books; Cambridge, MA: distributed by the MIT Press, 2009), 22, 33.

27. Myth did appear in symposiastic poetry and philosophical discourse, but this is something different from sacred rhetoric. Theater was cultic in context, performed during festivals, within sacred precincts, but due to its somewhat unique status as a genre, it was able not only to function as a paradigm, but it was able to make paradigm visible by showing it in inversion or distress. One may easily see how things *ought* to be when one is confronted by things that are disturbingly "off."

28. Based on the definition offered by Fritz Graf, *Greek Mythology: An Introduction*, trans Thomas Marier (Baltimore: Johns Hopkins University Press, 1993), 1–8.

29. Graf, *Greek Mythology* (1993), 3. There are as many definitions and theories of myth as there are those who study them. Graf's definition is a good definition, in my view, because even while it addresses the matter of change over time, it stays focused on *use* over origins. For a different perspective, more biological and evolutionary in nature, cf. Walter Burkert, *Structure and History in Greek Mythology and Ritual* (Berkeley: University of California Press, 1979).

30. This was a trait fundamental to Greek oral poetry, especially as found in the epic tradition, which produced the oldest literary tellings of these myths. Recognition was always in dialogue with innovation. Making changes in the story was part of the art form. Cf. Bruno Gentili, *Poetry and Its Public in Ancient Greece: From Homer to the Fifth Century*, trans. with an introduction, A. Thomas Cole (Baltimore: Johns Hopkins University Press, 1988), 3–23.

31. Once monumentalized on the south wall of the Athenian treasury at Delphi, they have received little to no attention beyond epigraphical studies and theoretical analyses of the accompanying musical notation (the longest and oldest extant Greek musical scores in existence!). Cf. Annie Bélis, *Les Deux Hymnes Delphiques à Apollon: Étude Épigraphique et Musicale, Corpus des Inscriptions de Delphes*, vol. 3 (Paris: Boccard, 1992); Egert Pöhlmann and Martin L. West, *Documents of Ancient Greek Music: The Extant Melodies and Fragments Edited and Transcribed with Commentary* (Oxford: Clarendon Press, 2001), 62–73; William Furley and Jan Maarten Bremer, *Greek Hymns: Selected Cult Songs from the Archaic to the Hellenistic Period*, two vols. (Tübingen: Mohr Siebeck, 2001), vol. 1, 129–38; vol. 2, 84–100; Théophile Homolle, ed., *Fouilles de Delphes, Tome III: Epigraphy*, vol. 2 (Paris: De Boccard, 1909–1985), no. 137 = Delphic Inventory nos. 517, 526, 494, 499 = frag. B, A, 3, 4 as cited in some earlier sources (mounted in plaster for display in Room 8 of the Archaeological Museum of Delphi). For an extended summary of arguments on dating, cf. Stephan Schröder, "Zwei Überlegungen zu den Liedern vom Athenerschatzhaus in Delphi," *Zeitschrift für Papyrologie und Epigraphik* 128 (1999): 65–75.

32. Originally, it was celebrated on an irregular basis, in years when lightning was observed in accordance with an oracle. On the early festival, cf. Isaeus, *On the Estate of Apollodorus* 7.27; Strabo, *Geography* 9.2.11; Wilhelm Dittenberger, ed., *Sylloge Inscriptionum Graecarum*, vol. 3 (Leipzig: S. Hirzelium, 1920), 296. On the festival and discussion of sources, cf. Gaston Colin, *Le Culte d'Apollon Pythien à Athènes* (Paris: A. Fontemoing, 1905), 19–21; Axel Boëthius, *Die Pythaïs: Studien*

zur Geschichte der Verbindungen zwishen Athen und Delphi (Uppsala: Almquist and Wiksells, 1918), 13ff; Georges Daux, *Delphes au IIe et au Ier Siecle: Depuis l'Abaissement de l'Etolie Jusqu'à la Paix Romaine, 191–31 av. JC* (Paris: E. de Boccard, 1936), 521ff, 579ff, and 708ff; Robert Parker, *Polytheism and Society at Athens* (Oxford; New York: Oxford University Press, 2005), 83–87, especially his discussion of *Syll*3 696, 697–99, 771, 728, and so on; Michael Scott, *Delphi: A History of the Center of the Ancient World* (Princeton, NJ: Princeton University Press, 2014), 194, especially notes 37–40. Extensive inscriptional evidence exists for the second-century celebrations, offering exceptional detail: for example, in 128/7, The Pythaïdes of Dionysios, there are at least eight lists of participants, five decrees, as well as the two epigraphical hymns. The festival of 106/5 appears to have been the largest, with records indicating a *theoria* of three hundred to five hundred people.

33. Théophile Homolle, ed., *Fouilles de Delphes, Tome III: Epigraphy*, vol. 2 (Paris: De Boccard, 1909–1985), no. 47.

34. I provide Annie Bélis's sober edition for both texts, from *Les Deux Hymnes Delphiques à Apollon: Étude Épigraphique et Musicale, Corpus des Inscriptions de Delphes*, vol. 3 (Paris: Boccard, 1992). Other editions are embellished with fanciful reconstructions; cf. William Furley and Jan Maarten Bremer, *Greek Hymns: Selected Cult Songs from the Archaic to the Hellenistic Period*, two vols. (Tübingen: Mohr Siebeck, 2001); Egert Pöhlmann and Martin L. West, *Documents of Ancient Greek Music: The Extant Melodies and Fragments Edited and Transcribed with Commentary* (Oxford: Clarendon Press, 2001). Translation is my own.

35. Cf. Michael Scott, *Delphi and Olympia: The Spatial Politics of Panhellenism in the Archaic and Classical Periods* (Cambridge, UK; New York: Cambridge University Press, 2010), 75–91. Scott notes in detail how the dedication patterns at Delphi by various city-states are consistently political in nature and often are meant to commemorate victory in battle (e.g., the Persian Wars), with tripods becoming de rigueur for poleis, when it had been mostly associated with individuals and athletics in earlier centuries.

36. Michael Scott, *Delphi: A History of the Center of the Ancient World* (Princeton, NJ: Princeton University Press, 2014), 183–202.

37. It is possible that Athenaios is not the first to do this, but there is no evidence to indicate otherwise.

38. Greek edition is that of Annie Bélis, *Les Deux Hymnes Delphiques à Apollon: Étude Épigraphique et Musicale, Corpus des Inscriptions de Delphes*, vol. 3 (Paris: Boccard, 1992). Translation is my own.

39. In fact, the remainder of the hymns also appear to have the same overall sequence and thematic content, more or less.

40. For example, τέρας, δράκαινα, πῆμα, πέλωρ: *Homeric Hymn to Apollo*, 300, 302–4, 374; Euripides, *Iphigeneia among the Taurians*, 1245–48: δράκων, τέρας; Callimachos, *Hymn to Apollo* 100–101: θήρ, ὄφις; Callimachos, *Hymn to Delos*, 91–93: θηρίον, ὄφις; Apollonios of Rhodes, *Argonautica* 2.706: Δελφύνη; and so forth.

41. For example, ζατρεφέα, μεγάλην, ἄγριον, δαφοινόν: *Homeric Hymn to Apollo*, 302–4; Euripides, *Iphigeneia among the Taurians*, 1245–48: ποικιλόνωτος, οἰνωπός,

δάφναι, πελώριον; Callimachos, *Hymn to Apollo*, 100–101: δαιμόνιος, αἰνὸς; Callimachos, *Hymn to Delos*, 91–93: μέγας, αἰνογένειον; Apollonios of Rhodes, *Argonautica* 2.706: πελώριον; and so forth.

42. For example, Female: *Homeric Hymn to Apollo*, 300. Masculine: Euripides, *Iphigeneia among the Taurians*, 1245–48; Callimachos, *Hymn to Apollo*, 100–101; Callimachos, *Hymn to Delos*, 91–93. The Scholiast on *Apollonios of Rhodes, Argonautica* (vetera) p. 182, line 1 (2.706) and line 16 (2.711) commented that both Leandrios and Callimachos referred to a *male* guardian, named Delphynes, but that Callimachos elsewhere said that *she* was a *drakaina*, and Leandrios also elsewhere does the same.

43. Some versions present him being a small child! For comprehensive summary, cf. Joseph Fontenrose, *Python: A Study of Delphi Myth and Its Origins* (Berkeley: University of California Press, 1959); Calvert Watkins, *How to Kill a Dragon: Aspects of Indo-European Poetics* (New York: Oxford University Press, 1995); Daniel Ogden, *Drakōn: Dragon Myth and Serpent Cult in the Greek and Roman Worlds* (Oxford, UK: Oxford University Press, 2013)—these works go into great depth on this mythical episode, but go beyond the Apollo frame and address comparable tales throughout Greek (and beyond) myth. For scholarly debate, cf. Christiane Sourvinou-Inwood, "Myth as History: The Previous Owners of the Delphic Oracle," in *Interpretations of Greek Mythology*, ed. Jan Bremmer (London: Croom Helm, 1987), 215–41; François Quantin, "Gaia Oraculaire: Tradition et Réalités," *Mètis: Anthropologie des Mondes Grecs Anciens* 7, no. 1 (January 1992): 177–99; Jenny Strauss Clay, *The Politics of Olympus: Form and Meaning in the Major Homeric Hymns* (Princeton, NJ: Princeton University Press, 1989), 17–94; Polyxeni Strolonga, "The Foundation of the Oracle at Delphi in the *Homeric Hymn to Apollo*," *Greek, Roman, and Byzantine Studies* 51, no. 4: 529–51.

44. Whether or not this dyadic conflict is original to Apollo is less important than the fact that this narrative *made sense* to Greeks. We see something similar in various accounts of Cadmos's founding and the struggle between Zeus and Typhoon. The linking of *drakōn* with barbarians appears at the end of Euripides's *Bacchae*, where Cadmos and his wife are cursed by Dionysos (who also received cult at Delphi) to become serpents until the time when they would lead a host of barbarians against Apollo's sanctuary. The triangulation suggests that this antagonistic pairing underlies Greek thinking about *kosmos*.

45. Hyginus, *Fabulae* 140. Pausanias, *Description of Greece* 10.7.2–3. It is possible that games and musical contests had occurred from an earlier date. Pseudo-Plutarch, *On Music* 4, 1132e claimed that Terpander won four consecutive times in the mid-seventh century BCE. (The *Parian Marble =IG* XII.5, 34.49b has his floruit circa 645/4.) There is a strong parallel to Athens's "reboot" of the *Pythaïdes* in the second century. Shifts in politics were often matched by "redefining" sanctuary activities.

46. Strabo, *Geography*, 9.3.10.

47. The musical competitions were just as prestigious as the athletic events. Pindar's twelfth *Pythian Ode* was composed in honor of Midas of Acraga, who won the auletic competitions in the year 490 BCE. He would have played his take on the *pythikos nomos* along with the *polykephalos nomos* as part of the musical

program. Egert Pöhlmann, "'Pythikos' and 'Polykephalos Nomos': Compulsory and Optional Exercise in the Pythian Contest." In *Poetry, Music, and Contests in Ancient Greece: Proceedings of the 4th International Meeting of MOISA (Lecce 2010)*, ed. D. Castaldo, F. G. Giannachi, and A. Manieri (Galtina: Congedo, 2012), 271–84; Deborah Steiner, "The Gorgons' Lament: Auletics, Poetics, and Chorality in Pindar's *Pythian* 12," *American Journal of Philology* 134, no. 2 (2013): 173–208.

48. Strabo, *Geography*, 9.3.10. He provides definitions for each term as well: ἄγκρουσις (προοίμιον), ἄμπειρα (κατάπειρα), κατακελευσμὸς (ἀγών), ἴαμβοι and δάκτυλοι (a paired title with single definition, ἐπιπαιανισμός), and σύριγγες (ἔκλειψις).

49. Pollux, *Onomasticon*, 4.84: πεῖρα (διορᾷ), κατακελευσμὸς (προκαλεῖται), ἰαμβικὸν (μάχεται), σπονδεῖον (δηλοῖ), and καταχόρευσις (χορεύει).

50. Corey Hackworth, "Reading Athenaios' Epigraphical Hymn to Apollo: Critical Edition and Commentaries," PhD diss. (Ohio State University, 2015), 296–312.

51. Through a clever stratagem of a side sortie against the home region of the Aetolians, who left to defend their homes. Cf. Georges Nachtergael, *Les Galates en Grèce et les Sôtéria de Delphes: Recherches d'Histoire et d'Épigraphie Hellénistiques* (Bruxelles: Palais des Académies, 1977), 15–205. For ancient accounts, cf. Pausanias, *Geography*, 19.5–23.14; Polybius, *Histories* 1.6.5–6; 2.20.6; Diodorus Siculus, *Bibliotheca Historica*, 22.9.5; Cicero, *On Divination* 1.37, 81; Callimachos, *Hymn to Delos*, 173ff; Justinus, *History*, 24.8.4.

52. Justinus, *History*, 24.8.4. A composite force led by the Aetolians—other sources prefer Athenian or Boetian leadership.

53. Some claimed that their army went insane and attacked itself.

54. Not all accounts are unified—there was disagreement as to whether the sanctuary was looted before suffering catastrophe. Cf. Appian, *Illyrica*, 5. The *Sōtērion* festival at Delphi likely owes its origins to the aftermath of this event. Invitations being sent in 246/7 BCE, requesting participation in a festival the following year, in honor of Apollo and Zeus as *Sōtēr* (savior). Subsequently celebrated every four years, the event included music, poetry, athletics, and sacrifice. Cf. William Furley and Jan Maarten Bremer, *Greek Hymns: Selected Cult Songs from the Archaic to the Hellenistic Period*, two vols. (Tübingen: Mohr Siebeck, 2001), vol. 1, 132–33; Georges Nachtergael, *Les Galates en Grèce et les Sôtéria de Delphes: Recherches d'Histoire et d'Épigraphie Hellénistiques* (Bruxelles: Palais des Académies, 1977), 305.

55. Herodotus, *Histories*, 8.35–39.

56. Cf. Walter How and Joseph Wells, *A Commentary on Herodotus, with Introduction and Appendixes* (Oxford: Clarendon Press, 1912).

57. Xerxes's intention was plunder. Herodotus, *Histories*, 8.35: ὅκως συλήσαντες τὸ ἱρὸν τὸ ἐν Δελφοῖσι βασιλέϊ Ξέρξῃ ἀποδέξαιεν τὰ χρήματα.

58. Herodotus, *Histories*, 8.36: ἱκανὸς.

59. The Pan-Hellenic *openness* of Delphi extended even to foreigners, but the repeated use of *barbaroi* in this passage would seem intentional—it appears seven times in Herodotus, *Histories*, 8.35–39.

60. Herodotus, *Histories*, 8.39: Phylacus by the road above Athena Pronaos and Autonoüs near the Castalian Spring under the Hyampean Cliff.

61. Hayden White, *Metahistory: The Historical Imagination in Nineteenth-Century Europe* (Baltimore: Johns Hopkins University Press, 1979), especially the "Introduction," 1–42.
62. Hayden White, "Fictions of Factual Representation," in *Tropics of Discourse: Essays in Cultural Criticism* (Baltimore: Johns Hopkins University Press, 1978), 125.
63. Hayden White, "Interpretation in History," in *Tropics of Discourse: Essays in Cultural Criticism* (Baltimore: Johns Hopkins University Press, 1978), 58.
64. Plutarch, *On the E at Delphi, On the Obsolescence of Oracles,* and *Greek Questions* #12.
65. The conflicts were perennial favorites as temple decorations.
66. Sarah Iles Johnston, "The Greek Mythic Story World," *Arethusa* 48, no. 3 (Fall 2015): 283–311; Sarah Iles Johnston, "Narrating Myths: Story and Belief in Ancient Greece," *Arethusa* 48, no. 2 (Spring 2015): 169–215.
67. "There is no such thing as a Greek mythic character who stands completely on his or her own; he or she is always related to characters from other myths . . . . all of these figures are presented as inhabiting the same realm—a realm that is thickly crisscrossed by the relationships . . . Each story stands as the guarantor of the existential rules underlying the others and is, in turn, guaranteed by them." Sarah Iles Johnston, "The Greek Mythic Story World," *Arethusa* 48, no. 3 (Fall 2015): 283–311.

BIBLIOGRAPHY

Agamben, Giorgio. *The Signature of All Things: On Method,* translated by Luca D'Isanto and Kevin Attell. New York: Zone Books; Cambridge, MA: Distributed by the MIT Press, 2009.
Bélis, Annie. *Les Deux Hymnes Delphiques à Apollon: Étude Épigraphique et Musicale. Corpus des Inscriptions de Delphes,* vol. 3. Paris: Boccard, 1992.
Bendlin, Andreas. "Purity and Pollution." In *A Companion to Greek Religion,* edited by Daniel Ogden, 178–89. Malden, MA: Blackwell, 2007.
Bettini, Maurizio. *Nascere: Storie di Donne, Donnole, Madri ed Eroi.* Torino: G. Einaudi, 1998.
Boëthius, Axel. *Die Pythaïs: Studien zur Geschichte der Verbindungen zwishen Athen und Delphi.* Uppsala: Almquist and Wiksells, 1918.
Bremmer, Jan N. "Greek Normative Sacrifice." In *A Companion to Greek Religion,* edited by Daniel Ogden, 132–44. Malden, MA: Blackwell, 2007.
Burkert, Walter. *Structure and History in Greek Mythology and Ritual.* Berkeley: University of California Press, 1979.
de Certeau, Michel. *The Practice of Everyday Life,* translated by Steven Rendall. Berkeley: University of California Press, 1984.
Clay, Jenny Strauss. *The Politics of Olympus: Form and Meaning in the Major Homeric Hymns.* Princeton, NJ: Princeton University Press, 1989.
Colin, Gaston. *Le Culte d'Apollon Pythien à Athènes.* Paris: A. Fontemoing, 1905.

Daux, Georges. *Delphes au IIe et au Ier Siecle: Depuis l'Abaissement de l'Etolie Jusqu'à la Paix Romaine, 191–31 av. JC.* Paris: E. de Boccard, 1936.

Dittenberger, Wilhelm, editor. *Sylloge Inscriptionum Graecarum*, vol. 3. Leipzig: S. Hirzelium, 1920.

Farnell, Lewis. *The Cults of the Greek States*, five volumes. Oxford: Clarendon Press, 1896–1909.

Finley, Moses. Foreword. In *Greek Religion and Society*, edited by P. E. Easterling and J. V. Muir, xvii–xx. Cambridge; New York: Cambridge University Press, 1985.

Fontenrose, Joseph. *Python: A Study of Delphi Myth and Its Origins*. Berkeley: University of California Press, 1959.

Foucault, Michel. "Nietzsche, Genealogy, History." In *The Foucault Reader*, edited by Paul Rabinow, 76–100. New York: Pantheon, 1984.

Frost, Robert. "Mending Wall." In *North of Boston*. London: David Nutt, 1914.

Furley, William, and Jan Maarten Bremer. *Greek Hymns: Selected Cult Songs from the Archaic to the Hellenistic Period*, two volumes. Tübingen: Mohr Siebeck, 2001.

Geertz, Clifford. "Religion as a Cultural System." In *The Interpretation of Cultures: Selected Essays*, 93–135. London: Hutchinson, 1975.

Gentili, Bruno. *Poetry and Its Public in Ancient Greece: From Homer to the Fifth Century*, translated, with an introduction, by A. Thomas Cole. Baltimore: Johns Hopkins University Press, 1988.

Gibson, James. "The Theory of Affordances." In *Perceiving, Acting, and Knowing: Toward an Ecological Psychology*, edited by Robert Shaw and John Bransford, pt. 3. Hillsdale, NJ: Lawrence Erlbaum Associates; New York: distributed by the Halsted Press Division, Wiley, 1977.

———. *The Ecological Approach to Visual Perception*. Boston: Houghton Mifflin, 1979.

Gould, John. "On Making Sense of Greek Religion." In *Greek Religion and Society*, edited by P. E. Easterling and J. V. Muir, 1–33. Cambridge; New York: Cambridge University Press, 1985.

Graf, Fritz. "Prayer in Magic and Religious Ritual." In *Magika Hiera: Ancient Greek Magic and Religion*, edited by Christopher A. Faraone and Dirk Obbink, 188–97. New York: Oxford University Press, 1991.

———. *Greek Mythology: An Introduction*, translated by Thomas Marier. Baltimore: Johns Hopkins University Press, 1993.

Hackworth, Corey. "Reading Athenaios' Epigraphical Hymn to Apollo: Critical Edition and Commentaries." PhD diss., Ohio State University, 2015.

Hitch, Sarah. "From Birth to Death: Life-Change Rituals." In *The Oxford Handbook of Ancient Greek Religion*, edited by Esther Eidinow and Julia Kindt, 521–36. Oxford: Oxford University Press, 2015.

Homolle, Théophile, ed. *Fouilles de Delphes, Tome III: Epigraphy*, vol. 2. Paris: De Boccard, 1909–1985.

How, Walter, and Joseph Wells. *A Commentary on Herodotus, with Introduction and Appendixes*. Oxford: Clarendon Press, 1912.

Johnston, Sarah Iles. "A New Web for Arachne." In *Antike Mythen: Medien, Transformationen und Konstruktionen*, edited by Christine Walde and Ueli Dill, 1–20. Berlin; New York: Walter de Gruyter, 2009.

Johnston, Sarah Iles. "Narrating Myths: Story and Belief in Ancient Greece." *Arethusa* 48, no. 2 (Spring 2015): 169–215.

———. "The Greek Mythic Story World." *Arethusa* 48, no. 3 (Fall 2015): 283–311.

Kindt, Julia. *Rethinking Greek Religion*. Cambridge: Cambridge University Press, 2012.

Korzybski, Alfred. *Science and Sanity: An Introduction to Non-Aristotelian Systems and General Semantics*. New York: International Non-Aristotelian Library Publishing Co.; Lancaster, PA: Science Press, distributors, 1933.

Marinatos, Nanno. "Striding across Boundaries: Hermes and Aphrodite as Gods of Initiation." In *Initiation in Ancient Greek Rituals and Narratives: New Critical Perspectives*, edited by David B. Dodd and Christopher A. Farone, 130–52. London; New York: Routledge, 2003.

Mikalson, Jon D. *Religion in Hellenistic Athens*. Berkeley: University of California Press, 1998.

Morgan, Catherine. *Athletes and Oracles: The Transformation of Olympia and Delphi in the Eighth Century BC*. Cambridge; New York: Cambridge University Press, 1990.

Nachtergael, Georges. *Les Galates en Grèce et les Sôtéria de Delphes: Recherches d'Histoire et d'Épigraphie Hellénistiques*. Bruxelles: Palais des Académies, 1977.

Ogden, Daniel. *Drakōn: Dragon Myth and Serpent Cult in the Greek and Roman Worlds*. Oxford: Oxford University Press, 2013.

Papillion, Terry. "Rhetoric, Art, and Myth: Isocrates and Busiris." In *The Orator in Action and Theory in Greece and Rome: Essays in Honor of George A. Kennedy*, edited by Cecil W. Wooten, 73–93. Leiden; Boston: Brill, 2001.

Parker, Robert. *Miasma: Pollution and Purification in Early Greek Religion*. Oxford: Clarendon Press, 1983.

———. *Polytheism and Society at Athens*. Oxford; New York: Oxford University Press, 2005.

Pedley, John. *Sanctuaries and the Sacred in the Ancient Greek World*. New York: Cambridge University Press, 2005.

Pernot, Laurent. "The Rhetoric of Religion." *Rhetorica: A Journal of the History of Rhetoric* 24, no. 3 (August 2006): 235–54.

Pöhlmann, Egert, and Martin L.West. *Documents of Ancient Greek Music: The Extant Melodies and Fragments Edited and Transcribed with Commentary*. Oxford: Clarendon Press, 2001.

Pöhlmann, Egert. "'Pythikos' and 'Polykephalos Nomos': Compulsory and Optional Exercise in the Pythian Contest." In *Poetry, Music, and Contests in Ancient Greece: Proceedings of the 4th International Meeting of MOISA (Lecce 2010)*, edited by D. Castaldo, F. G. Giannachi, and A. Manieri, 271–84. Galtina: Congedo, 2012.

de Polignac, François. "Mediation, Competition, and Sovereignty: The Evolution of Rural Sanctuaries in Geometric Greece." In *Placing the Gods: Sanctuaries and*

Sacred Space in Ancient Greece, edited by Susan E. Alcock and Robin Osborne, 3–18. Oxford: Clarendon Press; New York: Oxford University Press, 1994.

Quantin, François. "Gaia Oraculaire: Tradition et Réalités." *Mètis: Anthropologie des Mondes Grecs Anciens* 7, no. 1 (January 1992): 177–99.

Scheid, John. "Cults, Myths, and Politics at the Beginning of the Empire." In *Roman Religion*, edited by Clifford Ando, 117–38. Edinburgh: Edinburgh University Press, 2003.

Schröder, Stephan. "Zwei Überlegungen zu den Liedern vom Athenerschatzhaus in Delphi." *Zeitschrift für Papyrologie und Epigraphik* 128 (1999): 65–75.

Scott, Michael. *Delphi and Olympia: The Spatial Politics of Panhellenism in the Archaic and Classical Periods*. Cambridge, UK; New York: Cambridge University Press, 2010.

———. *Delphi: A History of the Center of the Ancient World*. Princeton, NJ: Princeton University Press, 2014.

Sinn, Ulrich. "Greek Sanctuaries as Places of Refuge." In *Oxford Readings in Greek Religion*, edited by Richard Buxton, 155–79. Oxford; New York: Oxford University Press, 2000.

Smith, Jonathan Z. "Sacred Persistence: Toward a Redescription of Canon." In *Imagining Religion: From Babylon to Jonestown*, 36–52. Chicago: University of Chicago Press, 1982.

———. *Map Is Not Territory: Studies in the History of Religions*. Chicago: University of Chicago Press, 1993.

Sourvinou-Inwood, Christiane. "Myth as History: The Previous Owners of the Delphic Oracle." In *Interpretations of Greek Mythology*, edited by Jan Bremmer, 215–41. London: Croom Helm, 1987.

———. "Further Aspects of *Polis* Religion." In *Oxford Readings in Greek Religion*, edited by Richard Buxton, 38–55. Oxford; New York: Oxford University Press, 2000.

———. "What is *Polis* Religion." In *Oxford Readings in Greek Religion*, edited by Richard Buxton, 13–37. Oxford; New York: Oxford University Press, 2000.

Steiner, Deborah. "The Gorgons' Lament: Auletics, Poetics, and Chorality in Pindar's Pythian 12." *American Journal of Philology* 134, no. 2 (2013): 173–208.

Strolonga, Polyxeni. "The Foundation of the Oracle at Delphi in the *Homeric Hymn to Apollo*." *Greek, Roman, and Byzantine Studies* 51, no. 4: 529–51.

Vernant, Jean Pierre. "The Society of the Gods." In *Myth and Society in Ancient Greece*, translated by Janet Lloyd, 92–109. New York: Zone Books; Cambridge, MA: Distributed by the MIT Press, 1988.

Watkins, Calvert. *How to Kill a Dragon: Aspects of Indo-European Poetics*. New York: Oxford University Press, 1995.

White, Hayden. "Fictions of Factual Representation." In *Tropics of Discourse: Essays in Cultural Criticism*, 121–34. Baltimore: Johns Hopkins University Press, 1978.

———. "Interpretation in History." In *Tropics of Discourse: Essays in Cultural Criticism*, 51–80. Baltimore: Johns Hopkins University Press, 1978.

———. *Metahistory: The Historical Imagination in Nineteenth-Century Europe*. Baltimore: Johns Hopkins University Press, 1979.

Chapter 3

The Music Never Stops

Some Grateful Dead in the American Mystical Tradition

Aaron K. Kerr

THE MUSIC PLAYS THE BAND

James Cone's (1936–2018) 1972 book *The Spirituals and the Blues* opened up a conversation about the mystical meaning of the music of resistance and importantly, the relationship between the sacred and secular in the popular imagination. Since then, literature has poured forth, interrogating the artistic truth of rock 'n' roll, once a subversive and politically resistant idiom, a medium that brought the white middle and upper classes into the "mud, the blood, and the beer"[1] of the United States. Cornel West's consideration of the spirituals, Marvin Gaye, bebop and rap, and Tom Beaudoin's exploration of music's cultural and theological significance provide insight and creativity to the question of the meaning of popular music.[2]

A band whose tenure has spanned decades and maintained its outsider status is the Grateful Dead. For more than fifty years, the Grateful Dead has consistently worked at two fundamental aspects of the Western cultural tradition that communicate the sacred: music and storytelling. Because of this unyielding dedication to these arts, the legacy we explore here is rich with meaning. An analysis of the band's name alone would fill many pages.[3] Stories told often become stories lived, making it difficult to separate the texts we live by with the context of existence; this is true especially of the Grateful Dead phenomena, because the stories they told through their art were embodied and configured in both the band and their fans. For example, the song "The

Music Never Stopped" is self-referential and told from the vantage point of a Deadhead (a fan) who says:

> Like Jehovah's favorite choir
> Well they're setting us on Fire![4]

God's "choir" sets people ablaze, the fire of the Holy Spirit. "The Music Never Stopped" is a parable not of the Grateful Dead, though they certainly actualized the tale. It is a parable of music itself as sublime power; the band doesn't play music, "music plays the band." It is music that moves us, surrounds us, transcends and amends us. The story of music, art, and religion has a very particular American tone, full of the echoes of diverse linguistic, ethnic, and religious realities. The Grateful Dead have been working very hard at expanding the chambers of those echoes and enlightening thousands of people about what America sounds like in lament and celebration, elegy, and doxology. The Grateful Dead is an inquiry into American cacophonies, an inquiry of the shape and texture of America's most distinctive artistic idiom, rock 'n' roll. But what is music? Or what is it about music that integrates our experience? The sound that trips our fancy, that individuates us by our twenty-century preferences, could be experienced in a way that frees us from commodified existence rather than binds us to the consumerist paradigm.

When we hear the music of Led Zeppelin or The Who used to market cars, perhaps we do not think about what music is, though you can bet that the Cadillac marketing team has. When we are in our cars, and we turn up Tom Petty or Beyoncé, we are not inclined to become analytical about the sounds that surround. When we sing a hymn or "Take Me Out to the Ball Game," it is unlikely that we probe the very medium of our participation. Yet that is what the Grateful Dead invite us to do, because in bassist's Phil Lesh's mind, the Dead have staked their lives on "searching for the sound."[5] Searching sound is a perpetual encounter with our finitude becausee in doing so, we become aware of our powers of perception and the fleeting nature of the perceived. As Walter Ong reminds us, "sound exists only as it is going out of existence."[6] Music is the feeble attempt to capture and artistically iterate sound, but it is all *hevel*, as Ecclesiastes reminds us.[7] The Grateful Dead convene a consistent search: for beauty, experience, even truth. That primary search undergirds the secondary one, which is to interrogate American experience through music. Since the Grateful Dead have this as their mode, if we want to appreciate the story of music and the sacred, we would do well to appreciate what music does and how that doing addresses a fundamental human need.

THE SOUNDS THAT SURROUND THE WHOLE EARTH

Arthur Schopenhauer (1788–1860) has an intriguing aesthetic philosophy that offers some of the "what" in the question, what is music? In his time, Schopenhauer boldly critiqued the *philosopher as celebrity* presumptions of European academia and clearly rejected the idea that philosophy should be written to commence a career or convey honor upon its agent; doing that kind of philosophy only compromises the search for truth.[8] And to found one's life as a mere philosophical minion for a religion, or for some other established philosophical school, misses the point as well. Both of his critiques of professional philosophy are a response to how his thought was received in the narrow life world of European academia. And his uncompromising attention to the essence of philosophy is mirrored in the Grateful Dead's insistence upon the state of their project, that it remain consistent with the essential musical form, untied from the compulsive compromises of the Top 40 *Billboard* charts, advertisements, and the celebrity that drove their contemporaries. This fact of self-chosen outsider status to chase the one provocation is a recurring theme in art, religion, and philosophy, and the Grateful Dead are perhaps the most exemplary and popular musical outsiders of our time. Schopenhauer's aesthetics is the brave relief to what has come to be perceived as his dour pessimism; and when we examine his theory of music, we are led into a way to understand something of what music might entail.

First, he suggests that music stands above the other arts for its capacity to express *universally* what otherwise could never be expressed. For Schopenhauer, music is the most sublime of the arts because it represents not only the human will and all the emotions that swim in that stream but, importantly, music *represents the world* in all its fullness. In his philosophy of music, Schopenhauer proposes that the mineral, plant, animal kingdom, and humanity are represented in the bass, tenor, alto, and soprano parts of musical structure, respectively.[9] The bass's tonal distance from the tenor-soprano is analogous to inorganic nature's removal from human existence. "Now this is analogous to the fact that all the bodies and organizations of nature must be regarded as having come into existence through the gradual development out of the mass of the planet. This is both their supporter and their source, and the high notes have the same relation to the ground bass."[10]

Music is a representation of inorganic and organic nature in all its diversity. In Schopenhauer's analogy, the soprano melody gets its tonal substrate from the bass, even though the bass tone is very far removed in terms of scale. The soprano takes the melody and, in doing so, it *represents* human consciousness reflecting about the relations of the rest of material existence, mineral, vegetable, animal, as well as its own interpretive capacities. What this tells us about music is that it is an expression of the whole of the world, the rational, nonrational, and irrational dimensions, and it is offered as a corroboration of the expanse of existence, not merely the catharsis of human emotion. For Schopenhauer, "music, unlike other arts, is not a copy of ideas, but a copy of the will itself."[11] That is, music is an expression of the pre-reflective or, as Schopenhauer puts it in terms of human cognition "for man," music becomes "the immediate knowledge of the inner nature of the world unknown by his faculty of reason."[12] Participation in music, therefore, is a participation in the perennial intuitions, the intellectual underlings that give birth to discourse and meaning. Because music is a copy of the will itself it plots reality as in the dark, all the while conveying a universal experience of what is felt on a fundamental level of humanity.

Through music, humanity explores metaphysical relations, broadening our navel-gazing propensity, moving from being to becoming and back again. Art is not merely a tool to work out small and incorrigible personal issues, as so much art has become in global capitalism, as if the point of art is to define *oneself*. Today, music is consumed, and that consumption identifies me as a certain kind of consumer. From Schopenhauer's perspective, music is more explicitly an exploration of the broader reality in which one is found. In this view, music is the primary medium through which contemplative knowing is born. Yet, his reflection on the melody, on the role of the soprano to copy and express human longing and suffering, gives his view a traditional focus as well. Schopenhauer affirms in a new and naturalistic way the teaching of both Plato and Aristotle that music copies *human* passion and emotion.[13]

But more, Schopenhauer's riff on this teaching is that the melody is consonant with what cannot "speak" for itself (minerals, plants, animals) and can represent all of being, inorganic and organic. The melody (soprano) takes turns and leaps and slows and speeds to convey our common experience of exploration, sadness, and contentment. The Grateful Dead's "Dark-Star" exemplifies this sonic exploration of the whole of reality.[14] The lyrics take up perhaps two minutes of the music, so that the sound exploration may last more than thirty minutes. In Cleveland, Ohio, on December 6, 1973, "Dark-Star" was forty-three minutes of sonic exploration of a variety of themes. Tom Constanten, who played with the Grateful Dead in the years 1968–1970, has said, "Dark Star is going on all the time. It's going on right now. You don't begin it so much as you enter into it. You don't end it so much as leave it."[15] This would certainly affirm Schopenhauer's theory, but also it may intimate something of the sentiment of "The Music Never Stopped" that seems to give music a more eternal ring.

In December 1973 in Cleveland, the Dead went from this sonic exploration to their joyous "Eyes of the World," the sentiments of which Schopenhauer would certainly appreciate: that the perceiving subject is the eyes of the world; indeed, the person is the interpreter of all reality and the "song that the morning brings."[16] Music corroborates what cannot be said but is felt viscerally by humanity. In the symphony of being, humanity takes the melody and can do no other. Schopenhauer had in mind the musical scores of composers who put down on paper their representations. For the Grateful Dead the representation is always live, transitory, and improvisatory. In that way, their long and arduous American touring history becomes a representation of the places where they played. If outdoors, they may enter into songs that they would not if they were in an indoor venue. If places are referenced in the lyrics and they play there, it is likely the song will be played. Also, Schopenhauer is focused solely on *the what* of music, not the why. In fact, he is impatient with speculative philosophy, which only serves to mystify and distract us from the world at hand.[17]

But the existential ache of *why* persists throughout history; and music soothes, if not addresses, the oppressive bitterness of suffering and evil. Because American culture was born in an intense religious context, those cultural artifacts will always surface in the popular imagination. Schopenhauer's analogy may give some obscure explanation of the fact that "the music played the band," but it does not give us a way into another question, why music? Why does music "set us on fire?"

Schopenhauer's premise of immanence, namely, that the arranged furniture of music is drawn from the material world alone, exemplifies modernity's prevailing ideology. But long before and after Schopenhauer's insightful idealism, music has been and is the sound genuine community makes when it gathers. To take a rather mundane example, the seventh inning stretch in baseball is a case in point, as is the National Anthem at most sporting events.

But more refined and intimate expressions are found in the Western religions: Islam calls the community to prayer through song, Christianity's work is done through liturgical and hymnic music, and Judaism's Shabbat service is "musicful." Listening to music and singing together create a tone for a community through which vulnerability, celebration, and lament come naturally. Music and song deeply humanize us and lift the thin veil of pretension. As we know from the Hebrew Scriptures, music makes the walls come down.[18] Why music? It is a question that moves us from metaphysics to value, from idealism to daily existence. From a Western theological perspective, music unifies and humanizes, calling together the fragmented and broken populace. Why music? Because it both calls us to and sustains the work that is community. This essay's prelude about music's meaning will accompany what follows, and we can hear the story of the Grateful Dead accompanied by Schopenhauer's "what" and religion's "why" in three movements. Music implies the whole of reality; music intones a mode of faith and reason; music gathers into communities of authenticity.

RES PUBLICA: MUSIC AS IDIOM OF CONTEMPLATION AND ACTION

First, music is a holistic expression, and the Grateful Dead exemplify something of Schopenhauer's sense that music expresses all of Being, not just human being. On that score, certainly music's capacity to copy both feelings and sounds is important. Grateful Dead are exceptional in their capacity for the *onomatopoeic*—this is true not only in the way guitars are made to sound like trumpets, or drums carry melodies, but the way the whole band can sound like a freight train, a swinging pendulum, or what it sounds like to be moving on water, or the activity of a workshop, or being in a particular place, like a bay or a wharf. The sound takes you there, as it were.[19]

Second, music is what copies human emotion in the most transparent way. To put it in terms of reason, through music, first-order reason recognizes itself in the aggregations of tone, timbre, pitch, rhythm, harmony, discord. Second-order reason, that of discourse, is then able to interrogate what Schopenhauer has called "the inner nature of the world." This mimetic dimension in music brings us to imagine worlds beyond ourselves. Christian mystical awareness has been expressed in two distinct traditions: the apophatic and the kataphatic. These are ancient ways of speaking of the sacred. The apophatic, or the *via negativa*, speaks of the sacred by saying what it is not. In this, there is an acknowledgment that the more we bring language to bear on ultimate things, the more our language fails. The kataphatic begins from the revelation and affirms doctrinal truths: God, Christ, Church. The apophatic disposes us to intellectual humility, a strategy to reduce dogmatic pretension. But the kataphatic must be given its due in order that we have a way to revealed truth, which, at its best, also limits intellectual and gnostic pretensions—the singular insights of cults and fanatics, for example. The Dead's lyrics and sounds certainly promote the apophatic, as does secular mysticism generally. But it all can become rather vapid without some affirmation about the truth to which experience points.[20] Kataphatic affirmations offer dialectical and conversational entry points by which to measure religious experience. An implication for poetry could be that, measured by kataphatic truth, free verse may become an exercise in self-indulgence or self-chosen isolation and subjectivity. Both song and lyrical form resist such relativisms. In the popular song "Ripple," for example, there is form in both the music and lyrical structure. And this form gives us a sense that even though we can barely surmise the meaning of the mystery of existence, at least we can share together this uncommon sense of things. Yet there is a source, a fountain, that makes it all possible. Music and song mitigate individualist art and dogmatic and isolated insights. Sound gathers and presents a possible intersubjective moment. The third verse of "Ripple":

> Let it be known there is a fountain
> That was not made by the hands of men

The apophatic—knowing by way of this darkness and obscurity—can have music as its medium and catalyst. What is music but the simultaneity of obscurity and clarity? This is a theme in many Grateful Dead songs, including "Dark-Star," but perhaps the most famous lyric is from "Playing in the Band":

> Some folks trust in reason others trust in might
> I don't trust in nothing but I know it come out right[21]

The particular instantiation of such trust is when the band enters together jazzlike through the improvisational darkness, knowing some resolute sound will come out on the other end. Playing at life, how many of us know by not knowing? By not trusting in the score of our lives written by someone or something else, yet knowing that some resolution will come to a thousand moments of discord. Creative tension amid conventions is evidence of the birth of freedom.

Third, the reason music "sets us on fire" is that it brings humanity together to peel away the layers of posturing, pretending, and self-serving presumption. These are burned away through sound, song, and movement, the catalysts for authentic encounter. A holistic expression that corroborates reality calling us to community: this is music. And for fifty years, the Grateful Dead environment has preserved the genuine possibility of a broad mimetic, community. The event of the Grateful Dead has taken place in a particular context, and perhaps their awareness of the signs of the times and their acute historical consciousness help us understand some of their story.

ODES TO ELECTRICITY: THE CIRCUITRY OF SECULAR MYSTICISM

One significant angle of American history is innovation and technological change. By 1940, 78 percent of American households had electric light. Twenty-eight years earlier, only 16 percent had had electricity. The change was due to the consistent lowering of the cost of electricity. It had an impact on how time and work were structured. The lightbulb, not light, became the symbol for intelligent ideas, and the Victrola was replaced by the record player. The rural farm population was the holdout community, quite naturally because work was contingent upon circadian light, not generated light. In 1940 only 16 percent of farms had electric light.[22]

This gradual change of life's hue brought a contrastive element to light in American culture, the tension that produced rock 'n' roll. Even though "Johnny B. Goode" lived in "a cabin made of earth and wood," and "he never learned to read and write so well," he could still play guitar "like he was ringing a bell."[23] In addition to electricity's television, which Neil Postman viewed as a subtle attack on the literacy necessary for informed democracy, we could add rock 'n' roll.[24] Music itself became electrified, and the experimentation with sound's electric enhancement enticed anyone who could strum three chords to dream of the possibility that he could make music.

Electricity became a metaphor, too. Electric experimentation was transferred over into psychedelic experience as LSD converted the brain's energies into electric openings of perception. Thomas Wolfe's *The Electric Kool-Aid Acid Test* narrates the eccentric motifs of Ken Kesey's Merry Pranksters as they traversed the United States and held acid tests, experiments of human being at which the Grateful Dead provided the musical accompaniment. Kesey's influence on guitarist Bob Weir was rooted in friendship. In 1982, Weir said of Kesey, "He's a maniac, he's also a genius, he's also got more heart and soul than any ten of your average people put together . . . read one of his books, they're great, he's a great writer and every part as great a human being, as far as I'm concerned."[25]

Kesey's narrative experimentalism in his fiction, and particularly, *One Flew over the Cuckoo's Nest*, evinces that American anti-authoritarianism with a robust intelligence and humor. Kesey's acid "tests" were a phantasmagorical and farcical exploration of the original "tests" of the drug undertaken first by the CIA to determine the possible use of LSD in military operations.[26] Both author Ken Kesey, who had worked at a mental institution, and Grateful Dead lyricist Robert Hunter got paid to be the subjects of these early tests. The West Coast LSD scene carried a different tone than Harvard University Professor Timothy Leary's more serious and studied—one could say, more public—articulation of the benefits of psychedelic experience. On the West Coast it was all about having fun, exploring, and moving away from any semblance of conventional ethos, rather enjoying not having to explain why people should "tune in."

As early as 1963, the prominent comparative religion scholar in the United States, Huston Smith, had argued that the psychedelic experience was akin to mystical experience; his argument compared phenomenological evidence of both mystics and those who had taken mescalin or LSD. As Smith shows clearly, it is difficult to surmise whether the description of religious experience was induced by the disposition of a disciplined ascetic or a drug-induced novice, because the firsthand descriptions of both express such authentic pronouncements of metaphysical insight.[27] Music plays the band, in part, because the band had been opened to the vast expanse of existence through LSD. It is enough here to report the fact that the Grateful Dead (including their primary lyricists) and thousands of their fans became practiced in the experience of "the trip," and that trip was infused, enhanced, and set very often in an environment of sound and celebration. Plenty of artists from the sixties, Sly and the Family Stone, the Beatles, Jefferson Airplane, Pink Floyd, Rolling Stones, and a host of others sing of the benefits of the psychedelic experience. It is important to consider the cultural soup the Grateful Dead found themselves in that pursued the psychedelic experience from a particular vantage point vis-a-vis the dominant culture.

Then, too, it is important to acknowledge that somewhere in the early seventies, some in the band report refraining from LSD altogether.[28] Though they stopped taking acid, they maintained a lifestyle and embodied the stories their songs expressed; and these values were derived from a particular edge of American society. It was the beat culture of Cassady, Kerouac, Ferlinghetti, and Ginsberg. Of these, Neal Cassady is the least literary but the most robust in terms of life itself being the canvas of experimentation. This inheritance of life as art—or living as the most profound and effective form of art—informed from the start the Grateful Dead phenomenon.

1968: BEING BEAT AMONG THE DEAD

The beat movement actively sought to resist the dominant culture's obsessions with modernity's trophies: conformity, war, technocracy, and suburbanization. It was purportedly a self-conscious religious movement as well, at least for Allen Ginsberg and Jack Kerouac.[29] Kerouac and Cassady found each other at Columbia. They became fast friends, in part because of their outsider status and their sense of being "beat." As in *beat down*, and *beatific*. Kerouac certainly amassed a lifetime of being "beat," mostly by his alcoholism. And Cassady seemed to articulate creatively the beatific fact of just being alive. They inspired one another and traveled cross-country together, an experience that generated Kerouac's best-known work, *On the Road*, and the book's large character Dean Moriarty, fashioned after Cassady. Both had been in jail, and Cassady would later become the bus driver for Kesey's Merry Pranksters.[30] That is how the Grateful Dead connected with Neal Cassady. Lead guitarist Jerry Garcia gives testimony to Cassady's "incredible mind, physical comedy" and importantly, living as art.[31] Rhythm guitarist Bob Weir wrote a stanza in "The Other One" about Cassady, describing Cassady's invitation to join him in this life-as-art mélange of experience. "Cassidy."

The practices of the beats: spontaneity, improvisation, mobility, writing and speaking at the rawer edges of reason—these are a few of the American virtues the beats amplified, and the Grateful Dead lived into them to great aplomb. The beats' medium was human language. Poets, writers, and commentators, they practiced literature in a way that disregarded literary convention, speaking directly to the inner consternation of the American underground and poor. This subversion and sense of alienation from the mainstream was shared by Trappist monk Thomas Merton as well. Angus Stuart and others place Merton as a precursor to the beats. In the forties at Columbia, Ginsberg, Kerouac, and Ferlinghetti were all taught by Mark Van Doren, the influential Columbia University English professor who had also taught Merton a few years before. Merton, the bohemian turned Trappist monk, appreciated much of the beat ethos, certainly because he recognized their countercultural form. Stuart has suggested that Merton's affinity with the beats was because "he was a monk, and a monk for Merton was one who had given up everything, stripped of all external support, of any reliance on wealth, owing nothing to the conformist demands or the corrupted values of society."[32]

Stuart then quotes Kerouac: "Everything belongs to me because I am poor." A generational zeitgeist, but more significantly, a material and spiritual poverty demonstrates a parallel between Merton, Cassady, and Kerouac in particular. Neal Cassady led a double life, and his second wife, Carolyn Cassady (his first marriage was annulled, a Catholic necessity) shares a different side of the man. According to Carolyn Cassady, by the time Neal took up with Kesey and the Pranksters, his goal of self-improvement and his brilliance had been compromised by his divorce and the loss of his job. Carolyn Cassady suggests that with the Pranksters he was on a trajectory of self-destruction, a line he traversed to San Miguel, where he died on February 4, 1968. Carolyn Cassady intimates that the autopsy was inconclusive, and that he did not die of "exposure" as the Grateful Dead lore would have it.[33]

An interesting contrast to figure the strange confluence of the sacred and secular in American mysticism is to compare Merton and Cassady. Both were abandoned by their parents, Merton's by death. Both were highly intelligent searchers, pursuing the weight of human being. Both were voracious readers, piecing together meaning in post WWII America. Both were irreverent in the sense of seeing through the self-serving pieties of mid-century assumptions. The presence and intensity of both influenced the artists, writers, and seekers who encountered them. Cassady was never able to shake his Denver upbringing, which amounted to taking care of his alcoholic father and being on his own very early in his adolescence. Merton found Catholicism and entered into its heart; Cassady remained a searcher, a man of inestimable gifts who fell into a spiral of alienation, yet beloved in the eyes of the much younger Dead counterculture. Here, the theme of that singular provocation in both art and life gives shape to the American mystical tradition. But Merton was also critical of what he called an antiestablishment movement that was a "false revolution." His 1963 comments to writer Napoleon Chow about beatniks help to confirm beat creativity and opacity:

> It also seems to me that the protest of the beatniks, while having a certain element of sincerity, is largely a delusion . . . its attempts to express compassion, only increase the delusion. Yet this can be said for them: their very formlessness may perhaps be something that is in their favor. It may perhaps enable them to reject most of the false solutions and deride the "square" propositions of the decadent liberalism around them . . . I think the beats have contributed much to the peace movement in the U.S., in their own way, and they are often quite committed to the only serious revolutionary movement we have: that for the rights of the Negro. So there are points in their favor, even though they are amorphous and often quite absurd.[34]

In a letter to Lawrence Ferlinghetti, who drove Merton to the airport the day of his departure to Asia in 1968, Merton expresses his uneasiness with what he considers to be reactionary resistance, a failure to construct a proper context for dialogue. He says:

> I want to talk to you about effective protest as distinct from a simple display of sensitivity and good will. I think we have to examine the question of genuine and deep spiritual non-cooperation, non-participation, and resistance . . . If it is just a question of standing up and saying with sincerity, candor and youthful abandon "I am against" . . . it perpetuates an illusion of free thought and free discussion which is actually very useful to those who have long since stifled all genuine freedom in this regard.

He goes on to suggest to Ferlinghetti that the Old Testament prophets were effective precisely because "they were not speaking for themselves."[35] This is the linchpin of Western mysticism, the scandal of a person speaking for God. On April 23, 1968, thirty years after Merton graduated from Columbia, Columbia University students' nonviolent takeover of the university failed. Seven hundred were arrested, and the university shut down. On May 3, just twenty-nine days after the assassination of Dr. Martin Luther King Jr., the Grateful Dead played to a gathering just outside Columbia's student union. Video of this is on YouTube; students look defeated, yet the neighborhood children and others are clearly energized. The band confounded the audience with a common Dead occurrence, the morphing of songs into a suite. The footage is of their "That's It for the Other One" into "The Eleven" into "Cryptical Envelopment."[36] The opening lyric to this suite, starting with,

Chapter 3

"That's It for the Other One," is a foreboding commentary on the recent murder of King, April 4, 1968, and definitely an ode to Cassady:

The sky was dark and faded,
Solemnly they stated, "He has to die, you know he has to die."

Lead guitarist Jerry Garcia, who wrote the words, would comment on this lyric: "Seriously I think that's an extension of my own personal symbology for 'The Man of Constant Sorrow'—the old folk song—which I always thought of as being a sort of Christ parable."

"The Eleven," titled so because of its eleven beats per bar, makes for a rollicking if mesmerizing tunnel of sound; it expresses a moving urgency, intoning an eschatological shift of emphasis in culture:

No more time to tell how
this is the season of what now.[37]

As Dr. King made clear in his "Letter from the Birmingham City Jail," at once a justification and field guide for nonviolent action and civil disobedience, nonviolence requires an intentional process of spiritual preparation he called "self-purification."[38] One wonders whether the Columbia students were a bit hasty and unprepared for being arrested, exemplifying Merton's question about "youthful abandon." To testify to the reasonableness of his mission, King explains to the white liberal clergy the rigorous concrete training required prior to engagement. Merton's refrain on the question sounds similar to King's because he states forcefully in his writings on Christian pacifism that nonviolent action demands that a person fight for the truth, a truth that is "common to him and the adversary."[39]

And drawing on the ancient argument of St. Maximus the Confessor, Merton, like King, implies that the discipline it takes to resist our "carnal desires" is the same discipline that will empower us to love our enemies, those "attacked" by the same evil that tempts us. Through love, St. Maximus the Confessor says, Jesus "fought by kindness for those who were burning with hatred towards him."[40] In addition, both Merton and King see nonviolent action as a way to create moral tension in order that dialogue becomes inevitable.[41] In December of 1968 in Thailand, Merton died from accidental electrocution while attending a meeting of Asian Benedictines and Cistercians. The beats, the Pranksters, the Dead, and perhaps even the Columbia University students embodied "free" not disciplined love.

However, with the Dead, is not music a nonviolent medium, a medium that can be the dialogue on a visceral level? At the least, we may be enticed *to listen.* Music's power to gather us into encounters with others and meaning can provide both a healthy catharsis and a heightened awareness of social aims, or just how things are. James Cone's message in *The Spirituals and the Blues* is affirmed here: we cannot dichotomize American mysticism so clearly into preconceived categories. Cone argued that black experience was one experience, and the secular blues and the sacred spirituals reveal that *one* experience. Music does that: it expresses and possibly integrates the meaning of our experience in a nonviolent expression. The Grateful Dead do hint at the pacifistic prospect in their popular "Uncle John's Band." The first verse asks if we are *kind*, the third intones incredulity at the military state of things, and the refrain is an invitation to hear and talk (Come, hear!). The first live performance was December 1969, released on the album *Workingman's Dead*, in 1970.

> Well, the first days are the hardest days, don't you worry anymore
> When life looks like easy street, there is danger at your door

Pacifists, those who are kind, must stay awake and aware to evil. Music can both effect that preparation in self-transcendence and importantly, make competent listeners out of anyone who will raise an ear. Yet, the tension between a sacred and secular mysticism remains. Music is not enough. Authentic compassion, not free love that creates "delusion," in Merton's words, takes more studied and intentional meditative practice; a more disciplined sort of training in prayer is required, the kind both King and Merton embodied through their profound commitments. But music does, as Schopenhauer saw clearly, bring to expression a gesture of a collective will. And it can also incite a healing tone, a sound balm, if you will. Undertaken on its own terms, in its own formless freedom, art only points the imagination in the direction of formal action; it cannot itself limit its figure into that action. The Grateful Dead have always placed their art, not politics, at the center of life. Music that is used by powers to sell things or ideologies amounts to our postmodern form of sophistry.[42]

For the sophists, reason and language were to be studied to persuade. Convincing another is more important than caring for the truth of the other. For corporations, Hollywood, and a propagandistic agenda, music's aesthetic power is appreciated only to garner the sale. The Grateful Dead consistently take and make music on its own terms, allowing the art, not the market or other powers, to lead the way. Music as a symbolic expression of chaos and apparent formlessness breeds that underlying recognition that all is not well. In other words, justice brings a necessary chaos yielding to a higher order and resolution. Jazz, blues, and gospel music, and particularly the Dead's musical suite in front of Columbia in 1968, exemplify these redemptive tensions. Merton's important distinction, that beatnik spirituality is missing self-sacrificial love, is one criterion by which to measure the sacred expressions of the Grateful Dead and their secular mysticism. King's mysticism, like Merton's, that of being attuned to Jesus's power of nonviolence, the living document of redemption, is derived from a tradition that is "Built to Last";[43] it cannot be unhinged from its ecclesial source.

ATTUNED TO EVIL INSINUATIONS: THE MUSIC OF BEING BEAT DOWN

In the mid-twentieth century, and perhaps today, blacks and whites were much more likely to speak together through a common love of music. That was the case with Phil McKernan, one of the first white DJ's on KDIA, a black radio station in the San Francisco Bay area. Phil McKernan was the father of Ronald "Pig-pen" McKernan, the Grateful Dead's first front man. Pig-pen was highly influenced by black music and culture, having been brought up in that community. The Grateful Dead's persistent efforts to interpret the blues tradition is due to Ron McKernan's legacy; he died at the age of twenty-seven from an autoimmune disease, which seemed to be unrelated to his heavy drinking, for which he was known.

McKernan's embodiment of rhythm and blues gave the Grateful Dead a currency with their white, middle-class audience. It is important to acknowledge the voyeuristic tendencies of rock 'n' roll among both white fans and musicians. What is forbidden in the white conventional Christian ethos is seen and heard in rock 'n' roll, Elvis Presley being the first bridge to, if not exploitation of, black idioms. Pig-pen's legitimacy as one who "talked the talk" made him a popular and charismatic figure in the Grateful Dead scene, which had both its beatnik hipness and psychedelic obscurity; but when Pig-pen got up from the organ and stood with his harmonica to sing Elmore James's "It Hurts Me Too," or Otis Redding's "Hard to Handle," the guessing was over, and the Dead brought forth what Cone has described as the combination of "art and life, poetry and experience, the symbolic and the real."[44] This sensibility expresses the alienation involved in segregation and what some would now describe as a police state. Along with Robert Hunter, McKernan wrote "Mr. Charlie." Mr. Charlie was the nomenclature for the master, the warden, or simply, "the white man." The refrain, "Mr. Charlie told me so," is a way of saying, "I really got no choice but to pull out this weapon and do the deeds, and I am not going to kill you, just hurt you, keep you in line." The song was first performed July 1971 at Yale University.

Gonna scare you up and shoot you

Mr. Charlie told me so[45]

The artistic effect is that the symbolic power of black experience is writ onto the American social fabric; thereby we learn, through interrogating the song, our own vantage point and relationship to "Mr. Charlie." American novelist and social critic James Baldwin (1924–1987) wrote the play *Blues for Mr. Charlie* as a response to the murder of Emmett Till, a fourteen-year-old brutally murdered in Mississippi by two white men in 1955. The murderers were acquitted by an all-white jury. Mr. Charlie's evil disease, Baldwin suggests, has been fed, festering in denial of Charlie's vile madness, by all Americans. Speaking of the acquitted murderer, Baldwin wrote, "What is ghastly and really almost hopeless in our racial situation now is that the crimes we have committed are so great and so unspeakable that the acceptance of this knowledge would lead, literally, to madness."[46]

The Grateful Dead's refrain, "Mr. Charlie told me so," conveys how violence as a mimetic power infects every social context with Mr. Charlie's sickness. Because of their interrogation of the American experience, the Grateful Dead are at that confluence of secular mysticism *and* an attunement to the madness that can only be discussed euphemistically. The strange is what modernity is loath to explore. To do so, one enters the grammars of the muse, and the Holy Spirit, two characters of history market capitalism is happy to ignore. America's Christianity is infused into its culture. America's subversive Christianity is most clearly articulated and embodied in black religion. Because of black gospel and blues' undeniable imprint on the DNA of rock 'n' roll, an American secular mysticism can never deny the manifestation of the Holy Spirit in the work of the music of resistance. But it is the feminine muse that initiates a distinctively secular creative freedom.[47]

THE MUSE WANTS US TO CHOOSE

Robert Hunter, the Dead poet who wrote "Dark-Star," "Playing in the Band," "Eyes of the World," "The Eleven," and "Built to Last," among many others, does not identify with any specific religion, though he would consider his experience to be intrinsically religious. He does say, "I write a lot about the soul . . . being that soul and going where that soul goes, into the abstract realms and the poetries and the music which is the domain of that place."[48] He has said that in translating Ranier Maria Rilke (1875–1926) he came into his own as a poet. Rilke, a poet who became a drifter, searching after something he may have only barely captured in words, thought of art *as* religion. Like Hunter, Rilke considered his poetry musical, and he gladly agreed when musicians sought to put his poetry to music.[49] Secular mysticism is largely artistic, Rilke's *Duino Elegies*, the poems translated by Dead lyricist Hunter, were started before WWI and finished in 1922. Rilke's self-understanding expresses the heart of secular mysticism: a love for singular artistic expression that inevitably abandons social compassion to express a unique *undergoing*. In Rilke's own words:

> Art cannot be helpful through our trying to keep and specially concerning ourselves with the distresses of others, but in so far as we bear our own distresses more passionately, give, now and then, a perhaps clearer meaning to endurance, and develop for ourselves the means of expressing the suffering within us and its conquest more precisely and clearly than is possible to those who have to apply their powers to something else.[50]

The artist undergoes reality for those who are too caught up in material conventions to express the "endurance." Modern art is religious in the sense that the artist carries intentionally the weight of existence while refusing to rely on a previous tradition to provide a spirituality proxy that would explain by rote what is undergone. Merton's and King's self-sacrificial love seems not to fit into Rilke's self-understanding. If Rilke would be concerned to corroborate *others'* suffering, then art may express more deeply the compassion Christianity assumes. But his project is self-enclosed within his "own distresses."

Born in Bohemia, Rilke represents an early representation of a "bohemian" poet and beat, rejecting every convention that may detract from experiential satiation. In Rilke's case, indulgence was for poetry and sex, not alcohol and drugs. Through his poetry and other writing, he expressed something of the nineteenth-century European avant-garde of which philosopher Friedrich Nietzsche was a part. But unlike Nietzsche, he hung absolutely no hopes on any philosophical insight, save the pursuit of poetry, which discounts no insight. Rilke's abandonment to art prefigures Robert Hunter's and the Dead's pursuits—pursuits that mark this freedom from convention that is a freedom toward who knows what. It is recognized as the freedom to follow creativity wherever it wills.

Distinct from Nietzsche's transvaluation of reason, Rilke was much more interested in receiving reality, perceiving its mystery, and articulating some semblance of its grandeur. His pursuit was unequivocal: he left university, resisted his parents' wishes that he find conventional employment, sought seemingly impossible romantic relationships, and failed at his marriage. Rilke went all the way, allowing no compromise that would unhinge his search for the sublime, and this broke him, at least in the eyes of the world. This engagement with the muse is the formulary of secular mysticism and seems to be captured in Robert Hunter's "Terrapin Station," a symphonic overview of life's mystery that was a staple of the Grateful Dead's exploratory second set.[51]

An unannounced brief interlude of American secular mysticism by way of the story of two dead Europeans is in order here; the poet Rilke and the philosopher Nietzsche. A side note about secular mysticism before I share the story: Rilke and Nietzsche are definitely secular mysticism's progenitors, but when their assumptions are adapted in a consumer culture, without their eccentric proclivities and/or intellectual brilliance, living becomes void of both reason and pathos. To put it more bluntly: Nietzsche and Rilke cannot be emulated en masse; and when a consumer culture blindly attempts to encourage all to be either artists or deconstructionists, absurdity ensues: "be a nonconformist, buy this shirt." To our point, both "Terrapin Station" and our story below figure an encounter with the muse, not the market.

SOUND OFF: SOLDIERS AND SAILORS AT IT AGAIN

Nietzsche pursued a woman by the name of Lou Andreas Salomé, a writer and scholar. When he proposed marriage, he was flatly rejected. About fifteen years later, Rilke was then taken by her mind, her beauty, and her maternal presence. Some have thought that she was a lesbian. In nineteenth-century European intellectual circles, marriage was too noble an institution to ruin with sex. Lou Salomé did marry, but then took Rilke as a lover; she really mentored him, encouraged him, made love to him, and put him in touch with the right people to further his writing career. She saw something in the poet that she did not see in Nietzsche the philosopher; that is important, for the poet can court the feminine spirit, learns it, massages it, bring out its best; then the feminine teaches the male poet about their creativity, their gifts, and how to see more holistically.

Had Rilke not had this relationship with Lou Salomé, it would be difficult to imagine that he would have developed the intellectual confidence to live the life of a writer and poet. We see here how literary output is always a relational currency, whether male or female. Nietzsche the philosopher has it all figured out: there is not obscurity; it makes no sense to surrender to the muses. Like Schopenhauer, Nietzsche is too encyclopedic in his linguistic skill to receive passively traditional things that convey timeless things. Lou Salomé helped Rilke with his Russian. No doubt the great philologist-turned-philosopher Nietzsche would never be that vulnerable with Lou Salomé. Nietzsche is a soldier of transvaluation, attacking the presumptions of Western reason, and he loses the girl; Rilke is the mystical poet, an exploring sailor, and he wins the girl, but not for long. She cannot be held and eventually informs Rilke that they can no longer share a bed; friendship? Yes.[52]

There is an intimation here of archetypical forms of the erotic, reason, intuition, fate, freedom, and creativity. "Terrapin Station (Lady with a Fan)" rehearses the question of the choice between the feminine, creative risk, and freedom versus strategic control, power, and survival. King's nonviolent strategy may bring us between these alternatives, as it gathers up both aggression and compassion in a disciplined opening to the *Prince of Peace*. At any rate the existential question is vexing for all of us: how shall we dispose ourselves in our pursuits? Shall we be the poetic lover or the strategic provider, the receptive perceiver or the articulate expert? The choice is born again and again in a Grateful Dead "show," not quite a musical performance but, rather, an artistic event that catches up all who are there to face this strange freedom. In this encounter, the muse is brought to life by participation in the music, a happening not unlike worship, which peels away our thin identities and beckons us to a life beyond ourselves, into the house of freedom. It is a choice most of the American population cannot even discern, caught as we are in a ubiquitous routine of getting and begetting the conventions of convenience, material wealth, and survival. Yet, the freedom before us is to inhabit artistic and existential abandonment and so to find love is a prevailing spirit of a Dead show that manifests itself by collective risk-taking and improvisation, both musically and spiritually.

Here is how Robert Hunter puts it in "Terrapin Station." First, we are introduced to a storyteller (Jerry Garcia), who begins his tale by invoking the spirit of creativity: "let my inspiration flow in token rhymes suggesting rhythm." As poetry works on us, we allow "let" to rest its case. Blood flows, and water flows, and "let" is the *subjunctive*, that composite of surrender and possibility, as in "let it be." *Let my inspiration flow* is an invocation: something is about to happen, even with "token rhymes" you may have heard a hundred times before. We are then invited to see that we are gathered around a fire, and the flames will grow strange shadows, "til things we have never seen, seem familiar." The shadows form a sailor, who "Loved a lady many years ago." Appearing next to the sailor is a soldier, who "came through many fights, but lost at love." Then, "a girl is standing there." She is "all that fancy paints as fair." From the fire comes the feminine, the beautiful, a call to risk. The lady throws her fan in the lion's den and asks the soldier and the sailor to retrieve it. "Which of you to gain me, tell, will risk uncertain pains of hell?" Soldiers and sailors. The soldier wins meaning and identity through calculated heroics, as part of an army, protecting the ideology of his kith and kin; the sailor adventures out, to worlds unknown, freely drifting away from secure shores and shoals to the expansive sea. At night on the sea, it is impossible to have any "sense" of place. These are two archetypes of masculinity: are men going to fight or explore? In terms of the United States, are we going to fight to preserve freedom or live freely to explore the bounds beyond convention?

Please note that Robert Hunter leaves the choice to the participants, thereby alleviating the modern tendency to forge binary identities.

The story does continue: "Sailor gave at least a try, the Soldier, being much too wise, strategy was his strength, not disaster." While we learn that the Sailor took the risk, and the Soldier did not, we participate in the contemplative sounds of whatever it is that is trying to get to Terrapin Station. We are led to the tension between persuasion and force. The quotidian rhythms of life evince a tense combination of both. Either way you lose something, but the value of love may outweigh any losses in security or survival. The story is happening there at the show, and the invitation is offered to live into it somehow: "story-teller makes no choice, soon you will not hear his voice." So, if freedom is possible, how do you embody and ennoble it? Do you use it to conquer or discover? The sailor/poet is bound in freedom to the muse. Once the risk is taken into novelty, there is no going back. What do we think, America? Does poetry trump security? We have arrived now at the way the Grateful Dead artistically preserve and authenticate the burden and blessing of a particular kind of freedom; and the sacrifice it takes to live authentically when all is bought and sold and measured by the values of power, violence, security, and consumerism. The muse draws us to choose our future.

FIFTY YEARS HENCE, ESTIMATED PROPHECIES: THE SPIRIT OF THE *DEAD* 2018

The year the Grateful Dead debuted "Terrapin Station," they also introduced "Estimated Prophet," a song by their other primary lyricist, John Perry Barlow. As I was writing the earlier part of this essay, John Perry Barlow died on February 7, 2018; one week later, a terribly distraught, alienated, and grieving teen shot seventeen of his peers at a Florida High School. Unlike 1968 at Columbia, we have absolutely no negotiation prospects with entrenched and powerful lobbies, to say nothing of some collective response to evil. The cell phone is our license for apathy; nothing impresses us, even so bloody a tragedy as happened on February 14; that story's preset pattern has just about run its course, and the inflexible media will fragment and chop us into data bits by which our consumptive preferences will be collected, unless, as Gil Scott Heron had suggested, *The Revolution Will Not Be Televised* (or texted, Instagrammed, Facebooked, or Tweeted). Slow resolutions to discord, the kind the Grateful Dead embellish artistically, are unacceptable even in the "marketplace of ideas," which can never resolve discord. If resolution came, how would corporations sell their empty anxieties?[53]

We live in an age of chronic and perpetual communicative discord. We live in echo chambers, forged by our own media preferences and automated data; the more we are on, the more the echoes shut us up in our cellular, artificial, and often superficially small worlds. A result is the inflation of the ego, driven by a composite of righteous indignation, immediacy, and certainty; through cellular existence, we are all on a bad acid trip bound to our sad subjectivities.[54]

That dynamic in consciousness is accurately conveyed and explored in John Perry Barlow's 1977 song. "Estimated Prophet" is a lumbering and somewhat ominous sounding song, yet it breaks into a mellifluous refrain, offering the sound of epiphany. The sounds represent the valleys and peaks of mystical insight chronically traversed. This emblem of fanaticism and/or mystical fervor is characterized exceptionally well by Bob Weir. His howls and singular presence as he delivers Barlow's lyrics present all too well an ego whose trip has privileged his religious insight. It is a song that satirizes that potentially destructive dogmatism; an insight unmeasured by the scales of the apophatic and kataphatic. Barlow and Weir, I think, offer this song as a sort of warning to Deadheads, in effect saying that dabbling in mystical awareness is playing with fire, and you don't want to lose touch or merely indulge your ego or even your perceived anointing. The righteous indignation is palpable when heard live. These lyrics barely give the sense expressed, as it is an indulgent performance of a fanatic's sung sermon:

> You've all been asleep, you would not believe me
> Them voices tellin' me, you will soon receive me

Note that John Perry Barlow quotes both Ezekiel and St. Paul; interestingly, the phrases from Ezekiel and St. Paul are sung by the rest of the band; they are backup lyrics, which are the voices in our estimated preacher's head:

> fire wheel burning in the air!
> way up, the middle of the air![55]

Barlow's biblical sensibilities are due to two factors: his Mormon upbringing and his degree in religion from Wesleyan University in Connecticut in 1969.

During his four years at Wesleyan, Barlow would have taken philosophy of religion, phenomenology of religion, Old and New Testaments, a semester of non-Western religion, one in ethics, two semesters of the history of Christianity or theology, and two additional selections in or related to the department.[56] The courses in scripture were titled "The Religion of the Old and New Testaments," so one can assume that the full arsenal of the ostensible "scientific study of religion" was on hand for Barlow to exegete carefully the scripture's context and impact on history and culture. Mainline Protestant biblical study in the twentieth century became a formidable weapon against all sorts of inflexible dogmatisms; and certainly quoting scripture to make one's case of mystical insight and authority may belie a preacher's egoistic fancies. This is why, perhaps, we can spot an "estimated" prophet the more he or she offers certainty to their listeners. Today, fanaticism seems commonplace, and it is a thin inference drawn from a vengeful world of media ecology, the habitat of a culture of consumers. Today, who is listening? And how might we begin to listen to a critical analysis of our ideological dogmatisms? We must look to history, nature, and culture for a start, and enter public places attuned to the Spirit's work, for the Holy Spirit is the public figure par excellence.

The Western mystical tradition begins in the Pentateuch. Barlow's biblical literacy informs another suite in the Dead repertoire, "Weather Report Suite." Interestingly, the suite has two parts; the first part was written by Eric Anderson; the second part ("Let It Grow") seems a testimony to the sacred in nature and the changing of the seasons, and importantly formal theology's stammering in the face of nature's mystery. Barlow wrote the lyrics to the second part of the suite, *Let It Grow*. The overwhelming power, intricacy, and operations of nature are expressed in Barlow's question, "What shall we say, shall we call it by name?" As if under his breath, the follow-up line is a reference to St. Thomas Aquinas, "as well to count the angels on the head of a pin."[57]

The latent anti-Thomism Barlow learned at Wesleyan notwithstanding, we are brought again to the mystical relevance of Dead inquiries. Certainly, nature, seasons, rain, and snow have their own logic quite apart from our anthropocentric, or "the Anthropocene," the awareness of which grew throughout the Grateful Dead's touring history.[58] Barlow's lyric suggests that before we pick apart and analyze nature and figure its operations, we would do well to acknowledge the sheer wonder of it all. He then connects that wonder to the Hebrew divine acclamation first heard resoundingly in the call of Moses, when he asks the voice from the burning bush, "Who shall I say is sending me to Pharaoh?" The voice says, "I am Who Am, tell them I AM sent you." I have always interpreted this as God's counterquestion, "Wouldn't you like to know?" Theology does have its place, but the contingency of human existence before nature is reduced to a listener in a storm, and through the storm we may hear the very voice of the divine:

Water bright as the sky from which it came
And the name is on the earth that takes it in

This ancient interpretation of nature through culture is a perfect pitch for music's power, its doxological induction. Acknowledging the religious impulse, "Weather Report Suite" lifts the thousands within earshot into the Name above every name. Humanity stands silently in the rain.

> And listen to the thunder shout
> I AM I AM I AM IAM[59]

In 1982, Barlow would write "My Brother Esau," a sort of post-Vietnam midrash. We are left to infer that Jacob is the narrator. Esau's murder of a "hunter, back in 1969," haunts Jacob's conscience and keeps him up at night. When Esau gets home, having failed at war, he finds Jacob waiting in his thin moral anxiety. Jacob has stayed home, and his empty lifestyle seems to have driven Esau to "skate on mirrors." This has left him "shadow boxing the Apocalypse, and wandering the land." I take that line to be a pretty good description of the post-Vietnam era, up to today. Deadheads, and the beats before them, seem to be fighting and resisting something that just doesn't punch back, yet takes them down somehow. The sixties are that ironic time when the Protestant social gospel reached its most pronounced actualization in King's prophetic gospel truth, though, it was heard in discordant tones. The fading din of the bass line was Weber's Protestant ethic; the time signature was global capitalism, which had no rests inscribed for capitalism's ennobling ethic. There has been this sense since the tragic events of the late sixties: namely, that institutional religion, government, the entertainment industry, are riven with hypocrisy and forces garnered to destroy, not sustain. Barlow claims as much in his anthem for those gathered at a summer concert, those who are the passengers, "wandering the land" with the Grateful Dead. The song "Passenger," like Barlow's "The Music Never Stopped," affirms that what one is experiencing in a Grateful Dead show is really "the only game in town."[60]

A reference to the nineteenth and early twentieth-century gambling culture of the American West, a Dead show is the only place one can really feel alive, taking an empowering risk beyond the superficial consumerism of conventional existence. In this way, the Grateful Dead perpetuate and epitomize that transgressive place of music and freedom, bequeathing to new American bands an open invitation to live into their particular edginess. In other words, authentic music of resistance stimulates the American adventure that has not been compromised by the forces of the market and its insinuations of superficiality. Even though "people were saying, the whole world is burning," being a part of the dancing frenzy and celebration of a show turns us "Upside out, or inside down." There *is* a place in American culture for egalitarian moments of encounter when the music undresses the sordid artifice of American triumphalism.

THE DEAD BANTER ON: THE FESTIVAL

"The only game in town" carries a distinctive public aura of festivity. The Grateful Dead concert is not entered as a spectacle but a work—a work in which the audience has a particular role. It is an exemplification of what Hans-Georg Gadamer has called a festival. A festival is an environment in which the art is produced through the play, improvisation, and participation of both band and audience, and in that participation, says Gadamer, participants no longer see themselves as cellular competitors for goods or consumers of an experience but, rather, in our shared interest of "what the artwork brings forth" we shed our identities to express the discovered core of our beings.[61] Dancing tends to do that, as does authentic worship. Stage banter is an aspect of the festival atmosphere. Bob Weir is the band member who usually explains to the participants what might be going on with the instruments or sound system, why something has seemed to go awry. Of course, it seems that it is a common occurrence that technical things at a Dead show go awry. One knows it is a work, and not a spectacle, when this happens because the audience does not seem to care; they rather revel in these chance accidents. On New Year's Eve 1976, the band's show was broadcasted live on the radio, KSAN. After a rough opening song, Bob Weir banters:

> Now just imagine our surprise that some of our equipment wasn't working exactly correctly . . . but our crack equipment crew is right on the spot and I think it is fixed already! By the way God bless all you who had enough sense to stay home tonight and listen to the radio. . . . and Lord have mercy on us crazies down here.[62]

Being present and being a part cannot compare to listening at home. Here we have a 1976 rut that has become a widening chasm in American experience. Those in the comfort of their homes, listening to internet, radio, TV, digital device, are blessed in their comforts but really have no sense of the way public experience is replete, unspun, surprising, and healing. Media ecology is a now familiar habitat and makes sense in its convenience and efficiency. But deeper timbres of ecology are missed, and we fail to embrace fundamental levels of reality. Only public encounters can induce deeper knowing. The fact that both Hunter and Barlow, along with the musicians, write songs about that festival experience is an indication that all our words and efforts to interpret this fifty-year movement become an academic exercise unless we get serious about the American experiment as *a public work*. Barlow's references to Pentecost in "The Music Never Stopped" are this indication that something sacred addresses us still; what happens at a show is that

Old men sing about their dreams
women laugh and children scream[63]

American dreams, laughter, and innocence. We end where we began, apropos because music never stops. The American empire will crumble and fall, like all the rest, but the sound of America plays on. And should we have ears to hear, we may move to the rhythms of freedom and eternity. Or, at the least, we could simply enjoy searching for the sounds of these perennial promises.

NOTES

1. The lyric is from Johnny Cash's "A Boy Named Sue," a tale about the relations between fathers and sons.

2. Cornel West, *The Cornel West Reader* (New York: Civitas, 1999), 463–84. Tom Beaudoin, ed., *Secular Music and Sacred Theology* (Collegeville, MN: Liturgical Press, 2013).

3. The name's origin, like many Grateful Dead tales, is represented as an enchanted event. In an apartment, while the group was groping for a name, Jerry Garcia opened up the dictionary, as some Christians do with the Bible, hoping for just the right Holy Spirit induced word, and there was the term, *grateful dead*, itself a genre of folklore, in which a hero comes to help the estranged bury their dead and then, alas, the estranged discover that the helper is the corpse they are trying to bury. Many of the songs, notably "Me and My Uncle" and "Jack Straw," are about the events leading up to death, and death. Then, in a death-denying culture such as ours, you have the juxtaposition of grateful and dead. This bears fruit for poetic and literary analysis, because dead can become a metaphor, as can dying, or we could analyze "dead metaphors," that is, cultural hangovers from the past that no longer evince transcendent meaning, like "Dark-Star." See footnote 14.

4. All Grateful Dead lyrics are taken from *The Complete Annotated Grateful Dead Lyrics*, ed. David Dodd (New York: Free Press, 2005), 249. The Grateful Dead "canon" contains more than 140 songs. The *Annotated Grateful Dead Lyrics* provides historical facts and some references to the Western literary canon, though this annotation stops short of commentary. The form of the text, however, is not unlike the medieval gloss, where the lyrical text is in the center of the page, and the annotations are scattered around the edges. Each song is given a birth date and some description of the degree of its appearance in the thirty-year touring history of the band. An interesting note is that this text was wrought from an online project undertaken by the editor. The book does not generate online data; the online data generates the book.

5. See bassist Phil Lesh's memoir, *Searching for the Sound: My Life with the Grateful Dead* (Boston: Little, Brown, 2005).

6. Walter Ong, *Orality and Literacy* (New York: Methuen, 1982), 32.

7. The English translation "vanity" in Ecclesiastes, "Vanity of vanity, all is vanity," does justice to the tone of the existential orientation of the text's meaning, finitude.

But scholars have suggested that the Hebraic "hevel" or wind, has an onomatopoeic role in the rendering, not unlike what we might call a scoff, or when we purse our lips and blow air through them to communicate *futility*. See James G. Williams, *The Literary Guide to the Bible*, ed. Robert Alter and Frank Kermode (Cambridge, MA: Belknap, 1987), 278.

8. Arthur Schopenhauer, *The World as Will and Representation*, vol. 1 (Indian Hills, CO: Falcon Wing, 1958), xxxi–xxxv.

9. Schopenhauer, *The World*, vol. 2, 447.

10. Schopenhauer, *The World*, vol. 1, 258.

11. Schopenhauer, *The World*, vol. 1, 257.

12. Schopenhauer, *The World*, vol. 1, 263.

13. Schopenhauer, *The World*, vol. 1, 259–60.

14. My recommendation is the first track on a released CD called *Dick's Picks Volume II*, Columbus, Ohio, 1971. In this period, they are still close to their psychedelic experiences; there is a beautiful jazz transition that is born out of more obscure sounds of chaotic and quiet forays of a minor key: like a flower, it comes up, then dies into tonal chaos.

15. *Annotated Grateful Dead Lyrics*, 52.

16. *Annotated Grateful Dead Lyrics*, 202. "Eyes of the World" also has a lyric that echoes Blaise Pascal's "The Heart has its Reasons which reason will never know." Lyricist Robert Hunter's lyric is "The heart has its seasons, its evenings and songs of its own." Pascal's fideism will appear again below in "Playing in the Band." Blaise Pascal, *Pensees* (New York: Penguin, 1995), 127.

17. Schopenhauer, *The World*, vol. 1, 273–74. Like many philosophers who come to the edge of metaphysics, Schopenhauer's frustration is perhaps an indication of what Étienne Gilson has construed as the presumption that "mind encompasses being," rather than the fact that "being encompasses mind." Music seems to me to be some evidence of the latter. A digital culture operates on the former assumption, perhaps to its peril. See Étienne Gilson, *The Unity of Philosophical Experience* (New York: Scribner, 1937), 316–17.

18. Joshua 6:1–27. God's methodology, to blow trumpets and shout, has an edifying as well as destructive capacity. Even though coopted by the military-industrial complex, the sound gun, or sonic weapons, have their origin in the sacred; music and song belongs in the armory of nonviolent "weapons." Music calls forth a kind of aggression, and the aggression can become benign, even delightful.

19. There is a rendition of "Wharf Rat" that brings to life the bay or wharf environment. Many renditions can evoke this sense, but the one at the Fillmore East, 1971, on a CD released as *Ladies and Gentleman . . . the Grateful Dead* is tremendous, art of a very high kind.

20. For a brief and informed consideration of the apophatic, see Jaroslav Pelikan, *The Melody of Theology: A Philosophical Dictionary* (Cambridge, MA: Harvard University Press, 1988), 6–8. Cf. Thomas Merton, *New Seeds of Contemplation* (New York: New Directions, 1961), 1–5, where Merton connects the question of the apophatic to the contemplative prospect, a possibility that is distinct from, but not unlike, the experience of music and poetry.

21. *Annotated Grateful Dead Lyrics*, "Playing in the Band," 148; "Ripple," 126.

22. Robert Gordon, *The Rise and Fall of American Growth: The U.S. Standard of Living since the Civil War* (Princeton, NJ: Princeton University Press, 2016), 118–22.

23. Chuck Berry's classic song "Johnny B. Goode" (1958) tells the tale: a combination of the electrification of the nation in conjunction with the railroad's invitation to sights unseen. The Grateful Dead covered this song throughout their career. In a 1971 Fillmore West show, lead guitarist Jerry Garcia announces the song by saying, "Alright folks, here's the one it's all about." https://www.youtube.com/watch?v=CNQCCKJdidk.

24. Neil Postman, *Amusing Ourselves to Death: Public Discourse in the Age of Show Business* (New York: Penguin, 1985).

25. Bob Weir interview, March 8, 1982—Ace's (Bob's studio). https://www.youtube.com/watch?v=Zc9cwllA450, accessed February 20, 2018.

26. The military industrial complex, which I assume includes the CIA, forges most of the U.S.'s technological innovations. LSD is an exemplification to the nth degree of the ethical category of "unintended consequences;" we note this with a lot of irony and a small dose of humor. For an analysis of the moral complexion of American military innovation, see my "The Use of Drones: An Argument against Optimistic Technological Determinism Featuring the Work of Albert Borgmann and an Extended Analogy." *Review of Technology and the Humanities* 34 (Fall 2015): 1–33.

27. Huston Smith, "The Religious Import of Drugs," in *Philosophical Issues: A Contemporary Introduction*, ed. James Rachels and Frank A. Tilman (Evanston, IL: Harper and Row, 1972), 494–500. Smith touches upon the literature, including the work of Aldous Huxley and William James, on the question.

28. Lesh, *Searching for the Sound*, discusses his use of LSD and then his gradual disuse. He has more than one description of trying to play his bass guitar while tripping; and a story of drummer Mickey Hart's helping him to find his way onto stage one night, because he was "not there," 147–48. Bob Weir describes his early use and his refraining in *The Other One*, a Netflix original documentary.

29. Angus Stuart, "Thomas Merton: The World in My Bloodstream," in *Grace Beats Karma: Thomas Merton and the Dharma Bums*, papers presented at the Fourth General Conference of the Thomas Merton Society of Great Britain and Ireland (2002), 95.

30. Mark Fellows, "The Apocalypse of Jack Kerouac: Meditations on the Thirtieth Anniversary of Sis Death," *Culture Wars* magazine, November 1999, http://www.culturewars.com/CultureWars/1999/kerouac.html, accessed February 27, 2018.

31. Jerry Garcia interview, *The History of Rock-n-Roll*, https://www.youtube.com/watch?v=NVkkbJ_KI2Y, accessed February 4, 2018.

32. Angus Stuart, "Merton and the Beats," in *Thomas Merton: Monk on the Edge*, ed. Ross Labrie and Angus Stuart (Friesens: Thomas Merton Society of Canada, 2012), 79–97, 85.

33. Jon Allen Carrol, "For Beats Sake: An Interview with Carolyn Cassady," *Empty Mirror*, https://www.emptymirrorbooks.com/beat/carolyn-cassady-interview, accessed September 5, 2018.

34. Thomas Merton, *The Courage for Truth: Letters to Writers*, ed. Christine M. Bochen (New York: Farrar, Straus & Giroux, 1993), 170.

35. Merton, *Courage for Truth*, 268.

36. Grateful Dead, May 3, 1968, Low Library Plaza, Columbia University https://www.youtube.com/watch?v=zq8sp6WF3bQ, accessed February 4, 2018. Also, https://www.jambase.com/article/grateful-dead-at-columbia-university-in-1968; the Jambase website has the audio and video aligned. Accessed February 4, 2018.

37. *Annotated Grateful Dead Lyrics*, 42–47.

38. Martin Luther King Jr., "Letter from the Birmingham City Jail," in *A Testament of Hope: The Essential Writings and Speeches*, ed. James M. Washington (San Francisco: Harper & Row, 1986), 289–302, 290.

39. Thomas Merton, "Blessed Are the Meek: The Christian Roots of Non-Violence," in *Passion for Peace: The Social Essays*, ed. William H. Shannon (New York: Crossroad, 1997), 248–59, 249.

40. "St. Maximus the Confessor on Non-Violence" in Merton, "Blessed Are the Meek," 243.

41. King, "Letter from the Birmingham City Jail," 292; and Merton, "Blessed Are the Meek," 259.

42. Eduard Zeller, *Outlines of the History of Greek Philosophy* (London: Routledge, 1951), 75–79.

43. This is the title to a song written twenty-one years later by Dead lyricist Robert Hunter, author of *The Eleven*. It is also wrestling with how we aptly respond to time's passing and the times. "There are times when you must live with doubt and I can't help at all." The song's sweet-sounding imperative, "show me something built to last," seems to intone what Fergus Kerr has called "immortal longings." I always think the Church is built to last, or at least it has always sought to point to that which is everlasting. *Annotated Grateful Dead Lyrics*, 348. See Fergus Kerr, *Immortal Longings: Versions of Transcending Humanity* (Notre Dame, IN: Notre Dame University Press, 1997), for an examination of philosophers who exemplify an implicit movement in "transcending humanity," a veiled agenda in secular modern thought.

44. James Cone, *The Spirituals and the Blues: An Interpretation* (Maryknoll, NY: Orbis, 1991), 103.

45. *Annotated Grateful Dead Lyrics*, 156.

46. James Baldwin, *Blues for Mr. Charlie* (New York: Dial Press, 1964), xiv.

47. From a Catholic philosophical viewpoint, the experience of the muse is a spiritual experience of the Trinitarian reality; certainly the Marian dimension of Christology has a place in that experience as well. As Étienne Gilson has it, the muse experience has traditionally been aligned with Plotinian metaphysics, by which a woman's beauty is a manifestation of "heavenly Aphrodite." See Étienne Gilson, *Choir of Muses* (New York: Sheed and Ward, 1953), 25–30.

48. Steve Silberman, *Standing in the Soul: An Interview with Robert Hunter*, reprinted in the online *Annotated Grateful Dead Lyrics*, http://artsites.ucsc.edu/GDead/agdl/silber.html, accessed February 4, 2018.

49. A helpful essay on his intellectual curiosity is Siegfried Mandel's "Rilke's Readings and Impressions from Buber to Alfred Schuler," *Modern Austrian*

Literature 15, nos. 3–4 (1982): 255–75. This essay is especially illuminating in its exploration of Rilke's syncretic consciousness. "His poetry needed no hybrid grafting since it contained its own music," 259.

50. Rainer Maria Rilke, *Duino Elegies*, trans. J. B. Leishman and Stephen Spender (New York: Norton, 1939), 15.

51. A discussion of Rilke's "mysticism" and agnosticism is provided in the introduction to his most religious work, *The Book of Hours*, trans. A. L. Peck, introduction by Eudo C. Mason, (London: Hogarth, 1961). The lyrics of *Terrapin* are in *Annotated Grateful Dead Lyrics*, 261–65.

52. Donald Prater, *A Ringing Glass: The Life of Rainer Maria Rilke* (New York: Clarendon, 1986), 36–44. Confer the introduction to *The Portable Nietzsche*, ed. and trans. Walter Kaufmann (New York: Penguin, 1982), 12, where Kaufmann makes note of Lou Salomé's rejection as the time "he made his first attempt to put down his philosophy . . . in one major work: *Zarathustra*."

53. Media are the plurality of mediums through which we make meaning in culture. In the late twentieth century, philosophers of communication spent an awfully lot of time talking about the "mass media," by considering how governments, advertising, and television seemed to work together to feed the masses meanings, signs, nationalistic propaganda, and so forth. The "mass media" were seen by some as oppressive, thus the enigmatic and engaging hip-hop poem by Gil Scott Heron; https://www.youtube.com/watch?v=QnJFhuOWgXg (written long before hip-hop was a "thing"). The song is a rebellion against many things, but one thing it is about is the superficial and distracting nature of advertising communications, keeping the masses from the weight of human problems. It is somewhat ironical and certainly interesting that on YouTube, I will be forced to look at an advertisement before I listen to Gil Scott Heron, and even more interesting that I have the option of deleting the commercial once it gets going. Today, we talk about the habitat of our existence as media ecology.

54. The literature here is legion: three popular articles are Andrew Sullivan, "I Used to Be a Human Being," *New York Times Magazine*, September 19, 2016; Nicholas Carr, "Is Google Making Us Stupid?," *Atlantic Monthly*, July/August 2008; Sherry Turkle, "The Flight from Conversation," *New York Times*, April 21, 2012. These popular laments about our predicament could be supplemented by a philosophy of culture. I have appreciated very much Albert Borgmann's *Technology and the Character of Contemporary Life* (Chicago: University of Chicago Press, 1984). His analysis of the device pattern is in some way affirmed in the popular laments. He also provides alternatives, focal practices; going to see live music is a focal practice.

55. *Annotated Grateful Dead Lyrics*, 270; Ezekiel is a testimony to theophanies in a strange land. The Jewish people are in Babylon; the dry bones and their rattling as they come together by God's spiration revive the dead. The fire wheel is an "appearance" of the arc of the covenant in an exilic existence. "Way up in the middle of the air" is a version of St. Paul's directions for the Thessalonians; they are to wait for Christ to appear at the Eschaton, "with the arch-angel's call and with the sound of God's trumpet . . . the dead in Christ will rise first, then we who are alive, who are left, will be caught up in the clouds together with them to meet the Lord in the air." 1 Thessalonians 4:13–18.

56. *Wesleyan University Bulletin*, 1965–1966, 1966–1967, 1967–1968, 1968–1969; these required religion courses did not change in title or description over the four years Barlow studied at Wesleyan. The department was steeped in modern methodologies of twentieth-century Protestant theology, which means a pronounced emphasis on both social scientific and philosophical analyses of religion. There was a class on Martin Buber's thought, and notably courses on the religions of India and contemporary Hinduism, which I want to suggest that Barlow took as his electives; he would travel extensively to India later in life.

57. St. Thomas Aquinas, *Summa Theologiae*, vol. 9 (New York: McGraw-Hill, 1968), I, q. 52, a. 3. As my Thomist friend Fr. Jason Mitchell, PhD, explains it, the answer is one "not because they fill the place according to quantity, but by the application of their angelic power to the place. Furthermore, the angel (like the soul) is not contained in the place, but rather is said to contain it."

58. The question of the Anthropocene radically shifts the possible pattern of human moral agency. Categories such as "invasive species" and "native species" become meaningless in the sense that in the Anthropocene, the Earth rewards survivors. Ideas such as stewardship are contended categories. See *Religion in the Anthropocene*, ed. Celia Deane-Drummond, Sigurd Bergmann, and Markus Vogt (Eugene, OR: Cascade Books, 2017).

59. *Annotated Grateful Dead Lyrics*, 211–12.

60. *Annotated Grateful Dead Lyrics*, "My Brother Esau," 319, "Passenger," 278.

61. Hans-Georg Gadamer, *The Relevance of the Beautiful*, trans. Nicholas Walker, ed. Robert Bernasconi (Cambridge: Cambridge University Press, 1986), 39–43.

62. Weir's banter is after the first song, "Promised Land," and before the second, "Bertha." The CD set was released as *Live at the Cow Palace: New Year's Eve 1976*. Banter is not edited out of the release. A rougher copy can be found at the Grateful Dead internet archive, a part of the internet archive. Founded in 1996, this open educational resource is a member of the American Library Association.

63. *Annotated Grateful Dead Lyrics*, 249. In Acts 2:17, "In the last days, God says, I will pour out my Spirit on all people, your young men will see visions your old men will dream dreams."

BIBLIOGRAPHY

Aquinas, Thomas. *Summa Theologiae*, vol. 9. New York: McGraw-Hill, 1968.
Baldwin, James. *Blues for Mr. Charlie*. New York: Dial Press, 1964.
Beaudoin, Tom, ed. *Secular Music and Sacred Theology*. Collegeville, MN: Liturgical Press, 2013.
Borgmann, Albert. *Technology and the Character of Contemporary Life*. Chicago: University of Chicago Press, 1984.
Carr, Nicholas. "Is Google Making Us Stupid?" *Atlantic Monthly*, July–August 2008.
Carrol, John Allen. "For Beats Sake: An Interview with Carolyn Cassady." https://www.emptymirrorbooks.com/beat/carolyn-cassady-interview.

Cone, James. *The Spirituals and the Blues: An Interpretation.* Maryknoll, NY: Orbis, 1991.

Dodd, David, ed. *The Complete Annotated Grateful Dead Lyrics.* New York: Free Press, 2005.

Drummond, Celia, Sigurd Bergmann, and Marcus Vogt, eds. *Religion in the Anthropocene.* Eugene, OR: Cascade Books, 2017.

Fellows, Mark. "The Apocalypse of Jack Kerouac: Meditations on the Thirtieth Anniversary of his Death." *Culture Wars* magazine, November 1999. http://www.culturewars.com/CultureWars/1999/kerouac.html.

Gadamer, Hans-Georg. *The Relevance of the Beautiful.* Edited by Robert Bernasconi and translated by Nicholas Walker. Cambridge: Cambridge University Press, 1986.

Gilson, Etienne. *The Unity of Philosophic Experience.* New York: Scribner, 1937.

———. *Choir of Muses.* New York: Sheed and Ward, 1953.

Gordon, Robert. *The Rise and Fall of American Growth: The U.S. Standard of Living since the Civil War.* Princeton, NJ: Princeton University Press, 2016.

Heron, Gil Scott. "The Revolution Will Not Be Televised." https://www.youtube.com/watch?v=vwSRqaZGsPw.

Kerr, Aaron. "The Use of Drones: An Argument against Optimistic Technological Determinism Featuring the Work of Albert Borgmann and an Extended Analogy." *Review of Technology and the Humanities* 34 (Fall 2015): 1–33.

Kerr, Fergus. *Immortal Longings: Versions of Transcending Humanity.* Notre Dame, IN: Notre Dame University Press, 1997.

King, Martin Luther, Jr. *A Testament of Hope: The Essential Writings and Speeches.* Edited by James M. Washington. San Francisco: Harper & Row, 1986.

Lesh, Phil. *Searching for the Sound: My Life with the Grateful Dead.* Boston: Little, Brown, 2005.

Mandel, Siegfried. "Rilke's Readings and Impressions from Buber to Arthur Schuler." *Modern Austrian Literature* 15, nos. 3–4 (1982): 255–75.

Merton, Thomas. *New Seeds of Contemplation.* New York: New Directions, 1961.

———. *Courage for Truth: Letters to Writers.* Edited by Christine M. Bochen. New York: Farrar, Straus & Giroux: 1993.

———. *Passion for Peace: The Social Essays.* Edited by William H. Shannon. New York: Crossroad, 1997.

Nietzsche, Friedrich. *The Portable Nietzsche.* Edited and translated by Walter Kaufmann. New York: Penguin, 1982.

Pascal, Blaise. *Pensees.* New York: Penguin, 1995.

Pelikan, Jarsolav. *The Melody of Theology: A Philosophical Dictionary.* Cambridge, MA: Harvard University Press, 1988.

Postman, Neil. *Amusing Ourselves to Death: Public Discourse in the Age of Show Business.* New York: Penguin, 1985.

Prater, Donald. *A Ringing Glass: The Life of Rainer Maria Rilke.* New York: Clarendon, 1986.

Rilke, Rainer Maria. *Duino Elegies.* Translated by J. B. Leishman and Stephen Spender. New York: Norton, 1939.

———. *The Book of Hours.* Translated by A. L. Peck. London: Hogarth, 1961.

Schopenhauer, Arthur. *The World as Will and Representation*, vols. 1 and 2. Indian Hills, CO: Falcon Wing, 1958.

Silberman, Steve. "Standing in the Soul: An Interview with Robert Hunter." *Online Annotated Grateful Dead Lyrics*. Reprinted. http://artsites.ucsc.edu/GDead/agdl/silber.html.

Smith, Huston, "The Religious Import of Drugs." *Philosophical Issues: A Contemporary Introduction.* Edited by James Rachels and Frank A. Tilman. Evanston, IL: Harper and Row: 1972.

Stuart, Angus. "Grace Beats Karma: Thomas Merton and the Dharma Bums." *The World in My Bloodstream: Thomas Merton's Universal Embrace.* Papers from the 2002 Oakham Conference of the Thomas Merton Society of Great Britain and Ireland. Wales, UK: Three Peaks Press, 2002, 92–105.

———. "Merton and the Beats." *Thomas Merton: Monk on the Edge.* Vancouver, BC: Thomas Merton Society of Canada, 2002, 79–100.

Sullivan, Andrew. "I Used to Be a Human Being." *New York Times Magazine*, September 19, 2016.

Turkle, Sherry. "The Flight from Conversation." *New York Times*, April 21, 2012.

Wesleyan University Bulletin, 1965–1969. Middletown, CT.

West, Cornel. *The Cornel West Reader.* New York: Civitas, 1999.

Williams, James, G. "Ecclesiastes." In *The Literary Guide to the Bible*, edited by Robert Alter and Frank Kermode. Cambridge, MA: Belknap, 1987.

Zeller, Eduard. *Outlines of the History of Greek Philosophy*. London: Routledge, 1951.

Chapter 4

Unashamedly Just

Doctrine of Justification by Grace through Faith as Anti-Shame Rhetoric

Sang-Il Kim

RHETORIC OF SHAME IN AMERICAN CULTURE

In the March 2015 issue of *Christianity Today,* Andy Crouch, executive editor of the magazine, wrote a cover story article titled "The Return of Shame."[1] While the mainstream Western theology has focused on removing guilt only in its understanding of the work of Christ, thereby inadvertently (or perhaps purposefully) eclipsing the role shame plays in the emotional lives of many Westerners (including Americans) as well as Christian theological discourse vis-à-vis shame, Crouch sees the need to bring back the dynamic of shame vis-à-vis "the whole counsel of God."[2] In it, Crouch shed light on the harmful effects of shame in the lives of American teenagers because of the predominance of mobile technology, such as internet, iPhone, and social media. Quoting Chap Clark, Fuller Theological Seminary's chair of the youth, family, and culture department, Crouch explains, "it used to be that high school students would leave school and go home, and could leave that high-pressure atmosphere behind. Now, with smart-phones and tablets, kids take that social environment into their bedrooms.'[3] Innocuous as this may seem, Crouch argues that social media and mobile devices with Wi-Fi connection instill an unimaginable amount of shame into the world of teenagers. In conversation with Crouch, Kara Powell, executive director of the Fuller Youth Institute, narrates a typical scenario of shame: when she tripped and fell, "there were maybe five kids sitting in a car . . . I remember them laughing at me as I picked myself up. But that was in front of five kids, and it was over in five minutes. Today, if someone caught a moment like that on a smartphone and shared it on social media, that shame could live with the kid for the rest of high school."[4]

Intuitively, it *makes sense* why a kid felt shame in that situation, and how Facebook and smartphones are making shame more and more common. Clinically defined, shame is "an emotional response to the experiences of insignificance in one's worth as a human person."[5] In other words, shame has to do with the self's experiences of devaluation. No wonder the teenagers bombarded with mobile Wi-Fi devices are exposed more to the instances of shame than did the previous generations, whose lives were without those devices. Worse yet, this is not just limited to teenagers, but to everyone else living in twenty-first-century America, for it is not just teenagers who are "infected" with the malaise of mobile technology.[6] It might not be an overstatement that almost everyone in contemporary America is connected to the World Wide Web via a mobile device or a computer. Such environment inundated with technological devices for connection ironically fosters an optimal atmosphere for shame. Powell's comments on the mechanism of shame in such environment sheds light on why it is so: "On Facebook, others' perceptions of us are both public and relatively permanent. You post something and everybody comments on it. People tag you, people talk about you. And if no one comments, that can be just as much a source of shame."[7] Ironically enough, more connection made possible by technology results in more opportunities for shame.

Thus, scholars are increasingly coming to a consensus that shame has become one of the most prevalent emotional experiences characterizing contemporary America.[8] Below, I show how this is the case through looking at the research of Brené Brown, research professor of social work at the University of Houston, who has contributed much to shed light on the "return of shame" in American culture.

Before examining the significance of Brown's work on shame, I provide a conceptual schema that examines shame as one of the prevailing American emotional experiences as well as one of the formidable messages that American culture conveys to its constituents. My agenda in doing so is twofold. First, I aim at observing and understanding the messages of shame in American culture, particularly how and why they have become *persuasive* and *convincing* to contemporary Americans. Second, building on the first agenda, I need to critique such messages of shame in light of the doctrine of justification by grace through faith as an alternative message to them. My stance in engaging shame is not that of a detached observer but that of a biased participant who feels the full force of the destructive messages of shame in American culture.

In this light, I ask the following questions: What conceptual schema helps one observe and understand how the messages of shame have become persuasive and convincing in American culture? Not only that, what conceptual schema provides a sound platform onto which the doctrine of justification by grace through faith critiques the messages of shame in American culture and plays the role of alternative to them, with more *persuasive* and *convincing* powers?

The key to finding such conceptual schema is that the message of shame has become *persuasive* and *convincing* in American culture. What conceptual schema deals with how people are convinced and persuaded? Among other things, it is the ancient discipline of rhetoric. In fact, it is my contention that rhetoric could be a promising candidate as a conceptual schema for the work I envision here. Although rhetoric, historically speaking, has fallen into disrepute as a practice among the sophists for cunning manipulation and insidious deception of ignorant public, the renowned hermeneutic philosopher Hans-Georg Gadamer argues that originally rhetoric plays the role of enabling certain messages to *make sense* to the members in certain linguistic, cultural, social, and other communities.[9]

In other words, rhetoric has to do with not only how people process their thoughts but how their affections, feelings, and all the other components constitute their value systems toward the world. My point is that this still holds water in contemporary times. With regard to this, in his debate with Jürgen Habermas on human rationality, Gadamer criticizes Habermas's notion of an *ideal speech situation*, which refers to "a form of life which makes possible unforced universal agreement."[10] In coining *ideal speech situation*, Habermas had in mind the pure human understanding untainted by the subjective, biased elements in our rational pursuits, and rhetoric symbolizes everything that "contaminates" the pure human understanding. Thus, Habermas believed that rhetoric was at best a hindrance to our rational pursuits. In response, Gadamer refutes Habermas in favor of the inevitability (and perhaps necessity) of rhetoric in human rationality in the following.

> If rhetoric appeals to the feelings, as has long been clear, that in no way means it falls outside the realm of the reasonable [*Vernünftigen*]. Vico rightly assigns it a special value: *copia*, the abundance of viewpoints. I find it frighteningly unreal when people like Habermas ascribe to rhetoric a compulsory quality that one must reject in favor of unconstrained, rational dialogue. This is to underestimate not only the danger of the glib manipulation and incapacitation of reason but also the possibility of coming to an understanding through persuasion, on which social life depends . . . Only a narrow view of rhetoric sees it as mere technique or even a mere instrument for social manipulation. It is in truth an essential aspect of all reasonable behavior.[11]

Here, Gadamer names three qualities about rhetoric vis-à-vis hermeneutic: *contextual, practical,* and *critical.* First, as long as we are rooted in particular historical, social, and cultural locations, we cannot get out of such locations, which, according to Gadamer, enables an abundance of viewpoints through which we persuade and convince others. This is the contextual character of rhetoric according to Gadamer. Second, it is not possible to separate rhetoric from hermeneutic. Although Habermas's project was centered around the question of filtering out rhetoric to crystallize the "unconstrained, rational dialogue" (hermeneutic), Gadamer sees through the impossibility of such an enterprise, for we cannot get out of the particular locations we are in, which is precisely why rhetoric makes possible "an abundance of viewpoints" referred to above. Because such interpenetration of hermeneutics and rhetoric in human discourse always gives rise to specific practices with specific ethical and political interests, rhetoric has to pay attention to people's practices so that through rhetorical discourse people are persuaded to act in particular ways. For this reason, rhetoric cannot help being practical.[12] I will say more on this later. Last, the very possibility of "an abundance of viewpoints" that rhetoric enables helps us to envision an alternative message in response to dominant discourses. In other words, rhetoric makes possible critiquing ideological discourses. This is the critical character of rhetoric, and it is why Gadamer titled his article responding to Habermas "Rhetoric, Hermeneutics, and Ideology-Critique."[13] In light of the foregoing, then, Gadamer characterizes the universal character of rhetoric as follows.

> Rhetoric means the whole of worldly knowledge, with all its contents, that are stated in language and interpreted in a language community . . . Rhetoric included the whole area of social life, in the family and in public, in politics and law, in culture and the school, in trade and industry—in short: in all interactions of humans with one another.[14]

In other words, rhetoric encompasses every component that makes it possible for whatever messages to sound persuasive and convincing in specific communities, which is why rhetoric has great potential for not only conceptualizing the messages of shame as powerful force in American culture but also for critiquing them and providing an alternative to them. In addition, this strategy of conceptualizing the messages of shame as rhetoric creates an apt counterpart in the Christian doctrine as a particular kind of rhetoric, for which I make a case in the next section. Eventually, in the final section of this paper, I envision the doctrine of justification by grace through faith as an anti-shame rhetoric, not just disempowering the destructive forces of shame in American culture but providing a liberating alternative to them. Thus, rhetoric is arguably one of the most fitting conceptual schemas to proceed, given my twofold agenda.[15]

Having made a case for rhetoric as a conceptual schema to approaching the messages of shame, I now examine how Brené Brown has discovered the messages of shame as a powerful rhetoric, making inroads into both the private and the public lives of Americans. The importance of looking at Brown's work in this paper is neither to give a survey of nor to subscribe to her research findings on shame but to illustrate how shame has become one of the predominant emotional experiences in American life.[16] With her TED talk on shame in 2010 reaching more than thirty-four million views as of 2018, Brown has become her own brand when it comes to resisting shame and being authentic to who we are. Even so, controversy swirls around her work.[17] Thus, rather than needlessly defending or criticizing her position on shame, I limit my inquiry strictly into how Brown, an academic conducting research on shame at purely academic and clinical levels, has gained such popularity among American people and what that tells about American culture. To do this, I take two steps. First, I demonstrate that Brown understands the message of shame as a kind of rhetoric. Second, I trace Brown's research process for how she has come to see the importance of the messages of shame in American culture.

First, according to Brown, shame is "an intensely painful feeling or experience of believing we are flawed and therefore unworthy of acceptance and belonging."[18] Having understood shame as such, Brown sees the message of shame as a kind of rhetoric. Above all, this is so because Brown is deeply aware of the power of language for any kind of dehumanizing message, including that of shame. In fact, Brown reasons as follows regarding the dehumanizing power of language, to which rhetoric is a crucial means.

> Dehumanizing always starts with language, often followed by images. We see this throughout history. During the Holocaust, Nazis described Jews as *Untermenschen*—subhuman. They called Jews rats and depicted them as disease-carrying rodents in everything from military pamphlets to children's books. Hutus involved in the Rwanda genocide called Tutsis cockroaches. Indigenous people are often referred to as savages. Serbs called Bosnians aliens. Slave owners throughout history considered slaves subhuman animals.[19]

Language conveys message about who we are and who others are. Rhetoric plays a central role in conveying messages, either positive or negative. Thus, although Brown gives no clear, explicit definition of rhetoric in her work, she still acknowledges rhetoric as an important device for shaming others. For example, Brown says, "When we engage in dehumanizing *rhetoric* or promote dehumanizing images, we diminish our own humanity in the process.

When we reduce Muslim people or Mexicans to 'illegals' or police officers to pigs, it says nothing at all about the people we're attacking."[20] In other places, she argues that *rhetoric* is an important means by which shaming messages are conveyed: "Sometimes owning our pain and bearing witness to struggle means getting angry. When we deny ourselves the right to be angry, we deny our pain. There are a lot of coded shame messages in the *rhetoric* of 'Why so hostile?' 'Don't get hysterical,' 'I'm sensing so much anger!' and 'Don't take it so personally.'"[21]

In all these, even though Brown's understanding of rhetoric is less articulate and perhaps even unreflective (rhetoric as cunning manipulation and insidious deception of ignorant public) than that of Gadamer, it is evident that Brown takes rhetoric seriously as an important means by which the messages of shame are being communicated persuasively to contemporary Americans.

Second, how has Brown's research led her to see the prevalence of the message of shame in American culture? In the appendix to *Daring Greatly*, Brown explains her research journey toward discovering shame in the following four steps. First, trained in the discipline of social work, Brown confesses that she did not begin with shame. In fact, initially shame was off her research radar. Instead, "after fifteen years of social work education, I was sure of one thing: Connection is why we're here; it is what gives purpose and meaning to our lives."[22] Next, to substantiate her thesis on the importance of the theme of connection, Brown began brainstorming how to do research on it. She found that rather than doing direct research on connection, doing research on people's fear of disconnection is much more tangible and empirical, for the fear of disconnection is "the fear that something we've done or failed to do, something about who we are and where we come from, has made us unlovable and unworthy of connection."[23] This fear of disconnection manifests itself in many ways in our relationship with ourselves and others, and it is itself what Brown defines as shame.[24]

> Thus, in the third step of her research journey, she takes on shame more directly, learning that "we resolve this concern (the fear of disconnection) by understanding our vulnerabilities and cultivating empathy, courage, and compassion—what I call shame resilience."[25] As she engaged more in shame research, however, Brown encountered a problem, which is "that there's only so much you can understand about shame and scarcity. I needed another approach to get under the experiences."[26] Interestingly enough, she drew her inspiration from chemistry at this impasse. In chemistry, especially thermodynamics, if you have an element or property that is too volatile to measure, you often have to rely on *indirect measurement*. You measure the property by combining and reducing related, less volatile compounds until those relationships and manipulations reveal a measurement of your original property. My idea was to learn more about shame and scarcity by exploring what exists in their absence.[27]

In this light, in the fourth step of her journey toward discovering shame, she devised her research questions, such as "What are people feeling, doing, and thinking when shame doesn't constantly have a knife to their throats, threatening them with being unworthy of connection? How are some people living right alongside us in this culture of scarcity and still holding on to the belief that they are enough?"[28]

After interviewing 1,280 men and women for her research over a period of twelve years with the aid of more than four hundred graduate research assistants,[29] Brown concluded that shame has become one of the most dominant American cultural and emotional experiences, and it seems that she has hit right on target at the heart of American culture. Most of her books (*Daring Greatly*, *I Thought It Was Just Me*, *Rising Strong*, and *Braving Wilderness*) have been on the list of the *New York Times* bestsellers, and her TED talk on shame is one of the top five most viewed videos of all TED talks, with more than thirty-four million views.[30] In order to support Brown's research on shame, the Huffington Foundation has pledged $2 million to the University of Houston, where Brown is a research professor, to fund the Brené Brown Endowed Chair in the Graduate College of Social Work.[31]

What Brown's research and her subsequent success testify to is that the messages of shame as cultural rhetoric are powerful forces in American culture. Fortunately enough, this does not go unnoticed among Christian theologians and cultural critics. For example, Stephen Pattison, a well-known practical theologian, has published two books on shame, respectively titled *Shame: Theory, Therapy, Theology* and *Saving Face: Enfacement, Shame, Theology*.[32] Also, Stephanie N. Arel, an Andrew Mellon Fellow at the National September 11 Memorial and Museum, has recently published her doctoral dissertation as a book, *Affect Theory, Shame, and Christian Formation*, which explores how shame has harmed Christian formation and searches for ways for more shame-resilient Christian formation.[33] With the looming significance of neuroscience affecting every academic field, Curt Thompson, a psychiatrist and Christian author, has authored *The Soul of Shame: Retelling the Stories We Believe about Ourselves*, exerting a broad impact on American Christian readers.[34] This paper joins the wave of theological and interdisciplinary research on shame with the viewpoint of Christian doctrines as rhetoric. Below I make a case for Christian doctrine as a particular kind of rhetoric, followed by my arguments for the doctrine of justification by grace through faith as an anti-shame rhetoric.

Chapter 4

CHRISTIAN DOCTRINE AS RHETORIC

In response to shame as a cultural rhetoric highly influential in contemporary America, I propose Christian doctrine as rhetoric. Below I will unpack what I mean by the foregoing statement. To do that, I engage in two tasks: 1) revisit Gadamer's understanding of rhetoric given above and 2) examine whether Christian doctrine fits into such conception of rhetoric, especially the three characters of rhetoric: *contextual, practical,* and *critical*.[35]

First, in the tradition of Aristotle, from which Gadamer inherits his conception of rhetoric, rhetoric is "the faculty of discovering, in the particular case, the available means of persuasion."[36] This means, as Gadamer understood it, that rhetoric has to do with everything that makes persuasion possible, which is not just pure logic but also feelings, sentiment, and cultural context. Thus, rhetoric "means the whole of worldly knowledge, with all its contents, that are stated in language and interpreted in a language community."[37]

In this light, I have crystallized three characters of rhetoric: *contextual, practical,* and *critical*. Rhetoric is contextual because human persuasion is always rooted in the specific locations of speakers and listeners. Also, rhetoric is practical because rhetoric, with its argumentative purpose, has in mind leading a specific audience to action. Thus, rhetoric must pay close attention to the specific practices the interested audience is engaged in at specific locations. As a corollary, rhetoric is practical because such attention to people's practices has implications for specific ethical and political interests. Last, rhetoric is critical because it functions as critiquing public discourses. This was the main thrust of the debate between Gadamer and Habermas, as discussed previously. Gadamer succeeded in bringing Habermas around in this debate, as least for the ideology-critiquing function of rhetoric.

Next, I examine whether Christian doctrine deserves to be called rhetoric in its purpose and characters. Above all, Christian doctrine is, indeed, an attempt at persuading particular readers and listeners about who God is and who we are, for which such discourse will have to be *contextual, practical,* and *critical*. To make my case for the foregoing statement, I showcase the doctrine of justification by grace through faith, of which the contemporary import of the doctrine as an anti-shame rhetoric I will take pains to substantiate in the next section of this paper.

Rather than directly making a case for why the doctrine deserves to be called rhetoric, I question why the doctrine no longer holds much appeal for the contemporary audience. In other words, I contend that the current articulation of the doctrine of justification has become an outdated argument not persuasive for the contemporary audience, not because the doctrine itself is irrelevant but we have turned it into an outdated argument. Ironically, by showing that, not only will I refute the misguided conception of Christian doctrine as unchanging, eternal truth about God, but I bring to prominence the inevitability of the doctrine as rhetoric with its contextual, practical, and critical characters. My point regarding the Christian doctrine as rhetoric is this: although God's work achieved in Jesus Christ on the cross through the Holy Spirit remains the same as now as it was two thousand years ago, how we approach the event of redemption brought about by the triune God is definitely affected deeply by what our questions are, here and now, what we see as crucial, here and now, and what our contemporaries are asking, here and now. That is why the doctrinal constructions of Augustine, Luther, Calvin, and others are all different from one another, albeit such differences do not amount to the degree of metamorphosis.

According to Elsa Tamez, who approaches the doctrine of justification from a Latin American perspective, there are three common ways of understanding the doctrine: 1) forgiveness of the sinner's sins; 2) liberation from guilt by the blood of Christ on the cross; 3) reconciliation with God or being at peace with God.[38] Tamez argues that these three ways of understanding the doctrine make little sense to contemporary Latin Americans. "Forgiveness of sin is spoken of in an individual and generic sense, and reconciliation too is seen on an individual and abstract plane. Active human participation in the event of justification is denied, with no examination of the meaning of that denial."[39] The meaning of the phrase "being justified" seems not to be communicated to most Latin Americans. Worse yet, forgiveness of sins, liberation from guilt, and reconciliation with God all make the doctrine sound more like a coded message of the distant past to decipher than a persuasive argument to act on. Why is this? Tamez keenly points out that the issue of different contexts between the Protestant reformers and the Latin Americans is at stake.

> One is the transference by our Protestant evangelizers—without examining the consequences of their doing so—of a doctrine that arose in a social and political context different from ours. The other difficulty is that these echoes of the Protestant heritage from Europe and North America arrive on our continent in a garbled form, as when static interferes with a message or signal sent from one place to another.[40]

Sadly enough, according to Miroslav Volf, this is no less true for North Americans than it is for Latin Americans. The outdated context in which the doctrine was construed has become an issue for contemporary North Americans as well. What is interesting is that Volf ascribes this problem more to theologians than laypersons.

Yet for many a theologian, justification by grace is an idle doctrine. Some have abandoned it and left it to rust away on a theological junk heap; they deem it generally useless or at least unhelpful when it comes to healing even lesser social pathologies than cycles of poverty, violence, and hopelessness. Others pursue a kind of antiquarian interest in the doctrine; they examine and polish an artifact from the sixteenth century and pridefully show it to whoever may frequent their little museum. Whether rusty or polished, the doctrine of justification by grace lies there uninhabited, lifeless. A dead doctrine.[41]

In all these, it becomes evident that context is an important issue in not only understanding the doctrine of justification but also communicating it in a convincing manner. In fact, Kevin Vanhoozer nails down the contextual character of theology and doctrine as follows.

The church is always having to improvise, and it does so not out of a desire to be original but out of a desire to minister the gospel in new contexts. Contextual theology—"the attempt to understand Christian faith in terms of a particular context"—is inevitable, for the church always inhabits particular places and times.[42]

For this reason, doctrine is a *contextual* discourse aimed at persuading specific audience about who God is and who we are as members of specific communities. At the same time, taking the context into consideration ought to mean paying close attention to the specific *practices* of audience, so much so that "it takes account of an audience's assumptions and motives. These cannot be accessed in the abstract, but only through attention to concrete practices."[43]

This is also true of the doctrine of justification. In fact, another reason that the doctrine has lost its appeal to contemporary North American audiences is that its discourse has little interest in the practices of North Americans. What implications do God's justifying acts have for contemporary North American practices? What does it mean for them that God has forgiven them? What about God's being reconciled to them? If they see little of who they are and what they do in being forgiven by God or being reconciled to God, or being liberated from guilt, then the doctrine will remain, as Volf has pointed out above, "uninhabited, lifeless."[44] This is not to say that North Americans are not interested in being forgiven by God, nor in being reconciled with God, nor in being liberated from guilt. In fact, forgiving, reconciling, and liberating could be all-important practices as clues to understanding the doctrine, yet the current doctrinal formulation is not presented in culture-specific ways for a North American audience, such that the doctrine does not "take account of the audience's assumptions and motives."[45] Thus, this tells us that Christian doctrine, much less the doctrine of justification by grace through faith, is not a set of eternal, unchanging truths about God; rather, it is a rhetorical discourse that is both context-dependent and practice-attentive.

So far, I have discussed my case for Christian doctrine as rhetoric through sampling the doctrine of justification by grace through faith. I have shown that the doctrine of justification by grace through faith is neither free from context nor independent of the practices of a particular group of people. Besides, the doctrine aims at making a convincing case for who God is and who we are through God's justifying acts. All these things suggest that Christian doctrine is a kind of rhetoric.

In light of the foregoing, what kind of rhetoric is the doctrine of justification by grace through faith? The critical character of the doctrine as rhetoric comes in precisely at this point. In other words, if the doctrine is to function as rhetoric, then it must play the role of critiquing a cultural rhetoric, which in this case is the rhetoric of shame. Thus, how could the doctrine become an alternative rhetoric to the rhetoric of shame? In the remainder of this paper, I argue that the doctrine is an anti-shame rhetoric critiquing the cultural rhetoric of shame, as well as providing an alternative to it. The reason that the doctrine of justification by grace seems so irrelevant to the cultural rhetoric of shame is that the doctrine has been construed by those who did not have in mind the cultural rhetoric of shame. This calls for the need that the doctrine must be construed with the cultural rhetoric of shame in view. Thus, that is what I do below.

DOCTRINE OF JUSTIFICATION BY GRACE THROUGH FAITH AS AN ANTI-SHAME RHETORIC: UNASHAMEDLY JUST

What does it mean that the doctrine of justification by grace through faith is an anti-shame rhetoric? The key to responding to this question hangs on God's justifying acts redefining the human relationship with God and with one another. One of the significant consequences of such redefined relationship is, I argue, resilience to the messages of shame prevalent in American culture.[46] Before proceeding to my arguments, it should be noted that dealing with the whole debate surrounding the doctrine of justification goes beyond the purpose of this paper, which might be, at any rate, an overambitious task to tackle in such a short article as this one. Thus, I restrict my inquiry into making a case for the potential of the doctrine as an anti-shame rhetoric.

Having said that, I unfold my argument in the following three steps. First, I begin with the inextricable relationship between justice and justification in the biblical traditions, especially from the Hebrew Bible, for it seems to be a scholarly consensus that separating justice from justification is one of the main causes of contemporary loss of appeal in the doctrine itself.[47] Justice is an important concern for anyone living in the twenty-first century; showing how God's justice constitutes God's justifying acts, and vice versa, will open up a spacious room for bringing back the relevance of the doctrine to the interests of contemporary Americans. Second, given that shame, defined as "an emotional response to the experiences of insignificance in one's worth as a human person,"[48] is one result of a distorted and fallen relationship between God and human persons, I will argue that the doctrine of justification by grace through faith, as inherent part of God's justice will be necessarily an anti-shame rhetoric.

First, why has the doctrine of justification lost its appeal to the contemporary audience in North America? This also means that the doctrine in its current formulation can no longer fulfill its role as critical discourse to the dominant cultural rhetoric, particularly that of shame. There might be numerous answers to this question, but scholars seem to be in consensus that the loss of connection between justification and justice is one of the primary reasons for the contemporary loss of appeal in the doctrine, let alone the possibility of critiquing the dominant cultural rhetoric. Thus, for the doctrine to function as rhetoric, namely, as critical discourse to whatever cultural rhetoric is out there, the doctrine's connection to justice should be restored.

In this regard, Kathryn Tanner draws on the contribution of biblical theology to restore God's justice back to God's justification toward sinners.[49] Unlike the traditional definition of biblical theology interpreting and articulating the conceptual apparatus of the Bible within the Bible itself, Tanner's use of biblical theology actively engages and challenges the Christian traditions in light of biblical interpretation, the concern of which is oftentimes quite different from that of Christians living and working in postbiblical times.[50] Therefore, while Paul's concern in addressing God's justification has to do with "showing the way in which God's covenants extend beyond the Jews, and how God nevertheless remains faithful to the covenant promises made to them,"[51] the theological concerns of Luther and Calvin in addressing God's mercy of justification vis-à-vis justice are different not only from that of Paul but from those of each other, as follows.

> God's mercy in Jesus Christ replaces the wrath of God under the law, which follows a strict canon of justice (Luther). Or, mercy and justice are commonly kept separate: God's mercy enables us in some sense to keep the law, to be just, but God's mercy does not substantially modify the nature of that law or justice; it seems a mere condition of its fulfillment (Calvinism).[52]

In this light, Tanner understands one of the benefits of her method of biblical theology as providing "a certain slant on the content of the terms of the account—a certain slant, that is, on the character and manner of divine initiative and the nature of human transformation."[53] In other words, reflecting the biblical understanding of the dynamic of justice and justification back into the contemporary theological problematics could result in shedding a new light on the calloused topic, especially in terms of redefining the God-human as well as the human-human relationship. This is precisely because the separation of justice from justification happened through the historical contextualizing processes of the doctrine. If so, what is so different about the biblical perspective on justice vis-à-vis justification from the contemporary one?

As for this question, Tanner says three things. "First, justice and righteousness are understood in the context of relationship. Second, they are not often opposed to mercy. And third, human justice and righteousness are often supposed to be modeled on, or correspond to, God's own justice and righteousness."[54] Concerning the first point, justice and righteousness have emphasis less on judging and punishing the parties held accountable for sin and more on restoring them back to their relationships with God and with the victims. In this regard, justification is given a new slant for redefining the God-human and the human-human relationships. "To justify someone is to restore that person to his or her proper or rightful place within the relationship, and thereby it involves the restoration or reconstitution of the relationship itself. Justice is that way of life, that body of ordinances or directives, set down by Yahweh."[55] This leads to Tanner's second point of the dynamic of justice and mercy. If justice and righteousness are to be understood in relational terms, as is with justification, then God's mercy cannot be the polar opposite of justice, as is often assumed by the general public.[56] For that matter, God's justification cannot be synonymous with mercy, as it is understood in separation from justice.

> Yahweh does not break off relations with those who would make the covenant void by violating justice—those who oppress the widow and orphan. Yahweh does not break relations with them as they deserve—Yahweh is merciful. But in being merciful in this way, Yahweh remains righteous in the sense of faithful to the covenant, faithful to God's own intent to be the God of Israel . . . God's righteousness was, then, from the very beginning an act of mercy, something that was not owed.[57]

In light of Tanner's first and second points, her third point of modeling human justice after God's should not be hard to understand. In fact, Tanner puts this point concisely and cogently as follows.

> The people of God are to act towards other human beings as God acts towards them—with a comparable sort of righteousness and justice. For example, God opposed their oppression by Pharaoh, and raised them up to a new life

in fellowship with their God; so Israel is to oppose oppression in its midst and become a society in which special care is given to the dispossessed—the stranger, widow, and orphan.[58]

This becomes the basis for which the doctrine of justification goes beyond the vertical God-human relationships toward the horizontal human-human relationship. Therefore, justification is never mere forgiveness of sins, nor simple reconciliation with God, nor the individual sinner's liberation from guilt. It involves offering mercy to others in view of restoring the broken relationship with them, for this restored relationship is based on God's justice, which "means primarily that God works to eradicate human fault and restore the relations violated by it."[59]

Now, such redefined relationship in light of God's justifying acts vis-à-vis justice has enormous implication on the culture dominated by the rhetoric of shame, defined as "an emotional response to the experiences of insignificance in one's worth as a human person."

Living and breathing in such a culture, one can naturally ask, how can God's justifying grace in line with God's justice not only critique such rhetoric of shame but also envision new lives for those inundated with the messages of shame? The message of the doctrine of justification is that God has restored the status of those who deem themselves unworthy and unlovable back to become the worthy and valuable ones before God, because a God of just mercy cannot do otherwise. A natural corollary of that message is that those who call themselves God's people should do likewise to their neighbors, just as God has shown mercy to them. Thus, if fully accepted and believed, this message that God has justified the unworthy ones has tremendous potential for restoring broken relationships, at both individual and communal levels. Thus, Volf boldly proclaims that some of the first recipients of this message are those who suffer shame most: the poor and marginalized.

> Imagine that you have no job, no money, you live cut off from the rest of society in a world ruled by poverty and violence, your skin is the "wrong" color—and you have no hope that any of this will change. Around you is a society governed by the iron law of achievement. Its gilded goods are flaunted before your eyes on TV screens, and in a thousand ways society tells you every day that you are worthless because you have no achievements. You are a failure, and you know that you will continue to be a failure because there is no way to achieve tomorrow what you have not managed to achieve today. Your dignity is shattered and your soul is enveloped in the darkness of despair. But the gospel tells you that you are not defined by outside forces. It tells you that you count—even more, that you are loved unconditionally and infinitely, irrespective of anything you have achieved or failed to achieve, even that you are loved a tad bit more than those whose efforts have been crowned with success.[60]

Even so, if this message is simply proclaimed and not lived and embodied, the power of the message might be reduced to little to no impact. After all, the Christian faith is an embodied faith following the savior who came to Earth as God incarnate. Thus, Volf hastens to add the following caveat:

> Imagine now this gospel not simply proclaimed but embodied in a community that has emerged not as a "result of works" but as a community "created in Christ Jesus for good works" (Eph 2:10). Justified by sheer grace, it seeks to "justify" by grace those who are made "unjust" by society's implacable law of achievement. Imagine furthermore this community determined to infuse the wider culture, along with its political and economic institutions, with the message that it seeks to embody and proclaim. This is justification by grace, proclaimed and practiced. A dead doctrine? Hardly.[61]

It is in this regard that the doctrine as rhetoric is not just a verbal message but an embodied one whose audience is not only to listen to but to accept and trust wholeheartedly. This is why Gadamer understood, "Rhetoric means the whole of worldly knowledge, with all its contents, that are stated in language and interpreted in a language community."[62] Just as the rhetoric of shame penetrates the whole body and the whole community, the rhetoric of God's justifying acts should do the same. Thus, the importance of the communal embodiment of such a message cannot be overemphasized in that process. In brief, in addressing the cultural rhetoric of shame, the doctrine of justification not only critiques shame's work of dehumanizing others and devaluing their worthiness through God's generous justice but also provides the needed healing for such broken relationships through God's justifying mercy.

CONCLUSION

Believing the doctrine of justification by grace through faith requires understanding what it means, even if such understanding can never exhaust the full meaning of what the doctrine points to, that is, the triune God's justifying grace for humanity. In a shame-full culture such as ours, understanding the doctrine as an anti-shame rhetoric should precede believing it. This is never to say that shame exhausts either injustice or sin. Much less for that matter, the doctrine of justification does not only have to do with shame. In fact, a history of the doctrine manifestly shows that that is not the case.[63] However, in a culture dominated by a rhetoric of shame, the doctrine as rhetoric must take on the cultural context of shaming messages, people's practices of shaming one another and themselves, thereby critiquing such rhetoric and providing an alternative rhetoric to that of shame. The present article is a mere attempt to do so, and I believe that engaging contemporary cultural rhetoric with Christian doctrine as rhetoric should happen more. Ultimately, as a student of Christian formation through paying attention to the formative aspects of Christian doctrine, I hope to expand this project to other branches of doctrine, so that the church of God will "reach unity in the faith and in the knowledge of the Son of God and become mature, attaining to the whole measure of the fullness of Christ."[64]

NOTES

1. Andy Crouch, "The Return of Shame," *Christianity Today* 59, no. 2 (2015): 32–41.

2. Acts 20:27. Here, two comments are in order: 1) the nature of sin; 2) the dominance of guilt as the effect of sin in Western theological discourse. First, defining sin as separation from God, Jayson Georges lists the primary effects of sin as fear, shame, and guilt in his coauthored book with Mark D. Baker, *Ministering in Honor-Shame Cultures: Biblical Foundations and Practical Essentials* (Downers Grove, IL: IVP Academic, 2016), 19. In this regard, the effects of sin should be approached more integrally for the redemptive work of the triune God to address the human problem of sin more fully. Second, despite this urgent need to see the effects of sin more integrally, Western theology has focused on guilt only in negligence of shame and fear. Thus, it is of recent theological trend that such disproportionate focus on guilt in Western theology has been critiqued and called into question. For a historical survey of shame, see Peter N. Stearns, *Shame: A Brief History* (Urbana: University of Illinois Press, 2017). As for the specific aligning of shame with Asian culture and not a Western one, see Ruth Benedict, *The Chrysanthemum and the Sword: Patterns of Japanese Culture* (Boston: First Mariner Books, 2005). If interested in how the guilt culture had dominated Western cultural discourse, see Jean Delumeau, *Sin and Fear: The Emergence of Western Guilt Culture 13 to 18th Centuries*, trans. Eric Nicholson (New York: St. Martin's, 1990). If interested in how shame has become more and more of a Western phenomenon, see Donald Capps, *The Depleted Self: Sin in a Narcissistic Age* (Minneapolis, MN: Augsburg Press, 1993); Curt Thompson, *The Soul of Shame: Retelling the Stories We Believe about Ourselves* (Downers Grove, IL: InterVarsity Press, 2015); Robert H. Albers, *Shame: A Faith Perspective* (New York: Haworth Pastoral Press, 1995); Stephen Pattison, *Shame: Theory, Therapy, Theology* (New York: Cambridge University Press, 2000); Stephen Pattison, *Saving Face: Enfacement, Shame, Theology* (Burlington, VT: Ashgate, 2013); Paul Goodliff, *With Unveiled Face: A Pastoral and Theological Explorations of Shame* (London: Darton, Longman & Todd, 2005); Philip D. Jamieson, *The Face of Forgiveness: A Pastoral Theology of Shame and Redemption* (Downers Grove, IL: InterVarsity Press, 2016); John A. Forrester, *Grace for Shame: The Forgotten Gospel* (Toronto: Pastor's Attic Press, 2010); and Lewis B. Smedes, *Shame & Grace: Healing the Shame We Don't Deserve* (New York: HarperOne, 1993).

3. Crouch, "The Return of Shame," 34.

4. Crouch, "The Return of Shame," 34.

5. This is my own definition. However, this definition more or less contains what psychologists, neuroscientists, and theologians understand by the term. Regarding various definitions and understandings of shame, see Stephen Pattison, in *Shame: Theory, Therapy, and Theology* (New York: Cambridge University Press, 2000). Pattison enumerates nine approaches to shame from the following disciplines and perspectives: psychoanalytic approaches, self-psychology approaches, biopsychological approaches, eclectic/synthesizing approaches, sociological approaches, cultural approaches, philosophical approaches, literary approaches, and social-constructionist approaches. What all these approaches have in common when it comes to defining shame is that they acknowledge that shame has to do with the self's experiences "of indignity, of defeat, of inferiority, and of alienation" (1). Other than the definition of shame given by these approaches, the neuroscientist Curt Thompson also concurs with them in *The Soul of Shame: Retelling the Stories We Believe about Ourselves*, 24, as he provides the following definition of shame: "One way to approach its essence is to understand it as an undercurrent of sensed emotion, of which we may have either a slight or robust impression that, should we put words to it, would declare some version of *I am not enough*; *There is something wrong with me*; *I am bad*; or *I don't matter*." Given all the approaches to shame and their common definitions, it is a valid way of defining shame as "an emotional response to the self's experiences of insignificance," as I gave it here. My last caveat is that there are two kinds of shame—what I call a healthy shame and an unhealthy one. A healthy shame helps members of a particular group or society behave in an appropriate manner, while an unhealthy shame is what I focus on in this paper, of which the definition is given above, as its harmful effects are growing more and more on Western culture. For more on this, see Carl Schneider, *Shame, Exposure, and Privacy* (New York: Beacon, 1992).

6. This is neither to highlight the harms of mobile technology nor to say that there is nothing good in it. Rather, it is to examine as closely as possible a particular aspect of modern phenomenon with regard to our emotional lives. As for critically examining the full implications of mobile technology on our lives, see Pelle Snickars and Patrick Vonderau, eds. *Moving Data: The iPhone and the Future of Media* (New York: Columbia University Press, 2012); and Jose Van Dijck, *The Culture of Connectivity: A Critical History of Social Media* (New York: Oxford University Press, 2013).

7. Crouch, "The Return of Shame," 34.

8. Apart from the dominance of technological devices for connection and the resultant shame, identity-based discourse as a distinctly modern phenomenon should be paid attention to as a context for shame rearing its ugly head more powerfully than before in the West. In fact, it becomes commonsensical that identity-based discourse is what everyone does nowadays. The fault lines of such identity discourse are drawn across race and gender, to name a few. Interestingly enough, the dynamic of shame and guilt is that shame has to do with who I am (identity) whereas guilt with what I do (external act). Thus, in a culture dominated by identity discourse, it goes without saying that shame becomes one of the driving forces in it. Such is the Western and American culture; scholars agree that shame in the West can no longer be dismissed as if it were something irrelevant. For more on this, see Forrester, *Grace for Shame: The*

Forgotten Gospel, 75; and Jamieson, *The Face of Forgiveness: A Pastoral Theology of Shame and Redemption*, 58.

9. Hans-Georg Gadamer has done much work in this area of restoring the potential of rhetoric. See Hans-Georg Gadamer, "Rhetoric, Hermeneutics, and Ideology-Critique" in *Rhetoric and Hermeneutics in Our Time*, ed. Walter Jost and Michael J. Hyde, trans. G. B. Hess and R. E. Palmer (New Haven, CT: Yale University Press, 1997), 313–34. Gadamer is controversial for his understanding of the universal linguisticality of human experiences.

10. Jürgen Habermas, "The Hermeneutic Claim to Universality," in *Contemporary Hermeneutics: Hermeneutics as Method, Philosophy, and Critique*, ed. Josef Bleicher (London: Routledge and Kegan Paul, 1980), 204.

11. Hans-Georg Gadamer, *Truth and Method*, trans. W. Glen-Doepel (New York: Continuum International, 2011), 568.

12. See Hans-Georg Gadamer, *Reason in the Age of Science*, trans. Frederick G. Lawrence (Cambridge, MA: MIT Press, 1986).

13. Gadamer, "Rhetoric, Hermeneutics, and Ideology-Critique," 313–34.

14. Hans-Georg Gadamer, "Towards a Phenomenology of Ritual and Language," in *Language and Linguisticality in Gadamer's Hermeneutics*, ed. Lawrence K. Schmidt, trans. Lawrence K. Schmidt and Monika Reuss (New York: Lexington, 2000), 24.

15. In doing so, I am not necessarily saying that rhetoric is the only way to approach either the messages of shame in American culture or the doctrine of justification by grace through faith, nor am I saying that it is the best way. Rather, as far as linguistic matters go, it is one of the most influential means of shaping American culture.

16. Crouch, "The Return of Shame," 32–41.

17. Thompson, *The Soul of Shame: Retelling the Stories We Believe about Ourselves*, 10. Adam Grant, professor of management and psychology at the University of Pennsylvania, wrote an article in the *New York Times*, criticizing Brown that her advice of being authentic to resist shame leads contemporary Americans nowhere, as many of them have no criteria to live up to. See Adam Grant, "Unless You're Oprah, 'Be Yourself' Is Terrible Advice." *New York Times*, June 4, 2016. Accessed June 8, 2018. https://www.nytimes.com/2016/06/05/opinion/sunday/unless-youre-oprah-be-yourself-is-terrible-advice.html. In response, Brown wrote a rejoinder in the same newspaper. "My Response to Adam Grant's New York Times OP/Ed." *New York Times*, June 5, 2016. Accessed June 8, 2018. https://www.linkedin.com/pulse/my-response-adam-grants-new-york-times-oped-unless-youre-bren%C3%A9-brown.

18. Brené Brown, "Shame Resilience Theory: A Grounded Theory Study on Women and Shame," in *Families in Society: The Journal of Contemporary Social Services* 87 (2006): 43–52.

19. Brené Brown, *Braving the Wilderness: The Quest for True Belonging and the Courage to Stand Alone* (New York: Penguin Random House, 2017), 73.

20. Brown, *Braving the Wilderness*, 77.

21. Brown, *Braving the Wilderness*, 67.

22. Brené Brown, *Daring Greatly: How the Courage to Be Vulnerable Transforms the Way We Live, Love, Parent, and Lead* (New York: Avery, 2012), 253.

23. Brown, *Daring Greatly*, 253. One might as well be reminded of my example of iPhone and Facebook in the beginning part of this essay. Ironically enough, more connection made possible by technology results in more opportunities for shame.

24. Note that Brown's definition of shame, which I quoted above, was "an intensely painful feeling and experience of believing we are flawed and therefore unworthy of acceptance and belonging," in Brown, "Shame Resilience Theory: A Grounded Theory Study on Women and Shame," 45.

25. Brown, *Daring Greatly*, 253. Also, see Brown's article, "Shame Resilience Theory: A Grounded Theory Study on Women and Shame."

26. Brown, *Daring Greatly*, 253.

27. Brown, *Daring Greatly*, 254.

28. Brown, *Daring Greatly*, 254.

29. Brown, *Daring Greatly*, 256.

30. Brené Brown, "Shame and Empathy," Global Influence. Accessed June 8, 2018. http://www.globalinfluence.world/en/leader/brene-brown/.

31. Marisa Ramirez, "Huffington Foundation Endows Chair for Brené Brown, Social Work Researcher, Author of 'Daring Greatly.'" University of Houston News and Events, February 4, 2016. Accessed June 8, 2018. www.uh.edu/news-events/stories/2016/February/24BreneBrownEndowment.php.

32. Crouch, "The Return of Shame," 34.

33. Crouch, "The Return of Shame," 34.

34. Gadamer, "Towards a Phenomenology of Ritual and Language," 24

35. One can argue that Gadamer's conception of rhetoric is not the standard understanding of it, which makes perfect sense. However, following Gadamer's understanding of rhetoric, especially for the purpose of this paper, is not problematic because Gadamer is still one of the most reliable and authoritative figures when it comes to contemporary retrieval of rhetoric. Thus, I follow Gadamer's conception of rhetoric here.

36. David S. Cunningham, "Theology as Rhetoric," *Theological Studies* 52 (1991): 407–30.

37. Habermas, "The Hermeneutic Claim to Universality," 204.

38. Elsa Tamez, *The Amnesty of Grace: Justification by Faith from a Latin American Perspective* (Eugene, OR: Wipf & Stock, 2002), 19.

39. Tamez, *The Amnesty of Grace*, 20.

40. Tamez, *The Amnesty of Grace*, 20.

41. Mirsolav Volf, *Against the Tide: Love in a Time of Petty Dreams and Persisting Enmities* (Grand Rapids, MI: Eerdmans, 2010), 138.

42. Kevin Vanhoozer, *The Drama of Doctrine: A Canonical Linguistic Approach to Christian Theology* (Louisville, KY: Westminster John Knox Press, 2005): 128–29.

43. Cunningham, "Theology as Rhetoric," 419.

44. Habermas, "The Hermeneutic Claim to Universality," 204.

45. Cunningham, "Theology as Rhetoric," 419.

46. I use "resilience" instead of resistance or removal of shame because I align myself with Brené Brown's position on shame. Brown, having conducted qualitative research based on interviews with 1,280 participants, concludes that it is not possible

to resist or remove shame. Instead, she is teaching that we should grow into being people who are resilient to shame. See Brown, *Daring Greatly*.

47. See Dong-Chun Kim, ed., *Justification and Justice* (Seoul, Korea: New Wave Plus Publisher, 2017); Tamez, *The Amnesty of Grace*; and Nicholas Wolterstorff, *Justice in Love* (Grand Rapids, MI: Eerdmans, 2015).

48. Crouch, "The Return of Shame," 34.

49. Kathryn Tanner, "Justification and Justice in a Theology of Grace," *Theology Today* 55, no. 4 (1999): 510–23. Also, for works on the deep connection between justice and justification, see Cunningham, "Theology as Rhetoric," 419.

50. According to Tanner, biblical theology has three possible senses in its meaning. The first is whatever theologizing that engages the Bible in support of, or with reference to, the interpreter's theological position. The second is biblical theology in its traditional sense, that is, "the interpreter's constructive efforts to fill out and develop conceptually the germ of theological ideas or the evocative symbols, images, and stories, present in biblical texts." Tanner hastens to add that this second sense "amounts here to commentary on the Bible that takes the theological ends of greater conceptual articulation and coherence for its goals."

51. Tanner, "Justification and Justice in a Theology of Grace," 511.

52. Tanner, "Justification and Justice in a Theology of Grace," 513. Afterwards, Tanner elaborates more on the benefits of her biblical theology: "My procedure allows later Christian theologies to retain their own concerns while modifying them from within, so to speak, by making the use of their central terms (justification, righteousness, and justice) more biblical. One looks back to the Bible for illumination from the standpoint of someone properly working within post-biblical theologies of justification that are designed to respond to later histories of controversy."

53. Tanner, "Justification and Justice in a Theology of Grace," 512.

54. Tanner, "Justification and Justice in a Theology of Grace," 514.

55. Tanner, "Justification and Justice in a Theology of Grace," 514.

56. This assumption of God's mercy standing at the opposite of God's justice is the very occasion for the publication of Kim, *Justification and Justice*. Other than this particular book, numerous books react to this stereotypical (yet wrong) assumption about the relation between mercy and justice. See Serene Jones, *Feminist Theory and Christian Theology: Cartographies of Grace* (Minneapolis, MN: Fortress Press, 2000); and Andrea Bieler and Hans-Martin Gutmann, *Embodying Grace: Proclaiming Justification in the Real World* (Minneapolis, MN: Fortress Press, 2010).

57. Tanner, "Justification and Justice in a Theology of Grace," 515.

58. Tanner, "Justification and Justice in a Theology of Grace," 516.

59. Tanner, "Justification and Justice in a Theology of Grace," 520.

60. Volf, *Against the Tide*, 138.

61. Volf, *Against the Tide*, 139. In the book, Volf confesses that he has found a church community that embodies the spirit of the doctrine. Meeting Mark Gornik, pastor of New Song Community Church in Baltimore, Volf explains, "As he (Gornik) was explaining the blight of the inner cities, he suggested that the doctrine of justification by grace contains untapped resources for healing. He should know, I thought. For some ten years he had been living and working in Sandtown and seen transformation

taking place, one house at a time" (137). To find out more, see Mark Gornik, *To Live in Peace: Biblical Faith and the Changing Inner City* (Grand Rapids, MI: Eerdmans, 2002).

62. Gadamer, *Truth and Method*, 568.

63. For a masterful treatment of the topic, see Alister E. McGrath, *Iustitia Dei: A History of the Christian Doctrine of Justification* (New York: Cambridge University Press, 2005).

64. Ephesians 4:13.

BIBLIOGRAPHY

Albers, Robert H. *Shame: A Faith Perspective.* New York: Haworth Pastoral Press, 1995.

Baker, Mark D. *Ministering in Honor-Shame Cultures: Biblical Foundations and Practical Essentials.* Downers Grove, IL: IVP Academic, 2016.

Benedict, Ruth. *The Chrysanthemum and the Sword: Patterns of Japanese Culture.* Boston: First Mariner Books, 2005.

Bieler, Andrea, and Hans-Martin Gutmann. *Embodying Grace: Proclaiming Justification in the Real World.* Minneapolis, MN: Fortress Press, 2010.

Brown, Brené. "Shame Resilience Theory: A Grounded Theory Study on Women and Shame." *Families in Society: The Journal of Contemporary Social Services.* 87 (2006): 43–52.

———. *Daring Greatly.* New York: Avery, 2012.

———. *Braving the Wilderness: The Quest for True Belonging and the Courage to Stand Alone.* New York: Penguin Random House, 2017.

———. "My Response to Adam Grant's New York Times OP/Ed." *New York Times*, June 5, 2016. Accessed June 8, 2018. https://www.linkedin.com/pulse/my-response-adam-grants-new-york-times-oped-unless-youre-bren%C3%A9-brown.

———. "Shame and Empathy," Global Influence. Accessed June 8, 2018. http://www.globalinfluence.world/en/leader/brene-brown/.

Capps, Donald. *The Depleted Self: Sin in a Narcissistic Age.* Minneapolis, MN: Augsburg Press, 1993.

Crouch, Andy. "The Return of Shame." *Christianity Today* 59, no. 2 (2015): 32–41.

Cunningham, David S. "Theology as Rhetoric." *Theological Studies* 52 (1991): 407–30.

Delumeau, Jean. *Sin and Fear: The Emergence of Western Guilt Culture 13 to 18th Centuries.* Translated by Eric Nicholson. New York: St. Martin's, 1990.

Forrester, John A. *Grace for Shame: The Forgotten Gospel.* Toronto: Pastor's Attic Press, 2010.

Gadamer, Hans-Georg. *Reason in the Age of Science.* Translated by Frederick G. Lawrence. Cambridge, MA: MIT Press, 1986.

———. "Rhetoric, Hermeneutic, and Ideology-Critique." In *Rhetoric and Hermeneutics in our Time*, edited by Walter Jost and Michael J. Hyde, translated by G. B. Hess and R. E. Palmer, 313–34. New Haven, CT: Yale University Press, 1997.

———. "Towards a Phenomenology of Ritual and Language." In *Language and Linguisticality in Gadamer's Hermeneutics*, edited by Lawrence K. Schmidt, translated by Lawrence K. Schmidt and Monika Reuss, 19–50. New York: Lexington, 2000.

———. *Truth and Method*. Translated by W. Glen-Doepel. New York: Continuum International, 2011.

Goodliff, Paul. *With Unveiled Face: A Pastoral and Theological Explorations of Shame*. London: Darton, Longman & Todd, 2005.

Gornik, Mark. *To Live in Peace: Biblical Faith and the Changing Inner City*. Grand Rapids, MI: Eerdmans, 2002.

Grant, Adam. "Unless You're Oprah, Be Yourself Is a Terrible Advice." *New York Times*, June 4, 2016. Accessed June 8, 2018. https://www.nytimes.com/2016/06/05/opinion/sunday/unless-youre-oprah-be-yourself-is-terrible-advice.html.

Habermas, Jürgen. "The Hermeneutic Claim to Universality." In *Contemporary Hermeneutics: Hermeneutics as Method, Philosophy, and Critique*, edited by Josef Bleicher, 181–211. London: Routledge and Kegan Paul, 1980.

Jamieson, Philip D. *The Face of Forgiveness: A Pastoral Theology of Shame and Redemption*. Downers Grove, IL: InterVarsity, 2016.

Jones, Serene. *Feminist Theory and Christian Theology: Cartographies of Grace*. Minneapolis, MN: Fortress, 2000.

Kim, Dong-Chun, ed. *Justification and Justice: Only by Faith?* Seoul, Korea: New Wave Plus, 2017.

McGrath, Alister E. *Iustitia Dei: A History of the Christian Doctrine of Justification*. New York: Cambridge University Press, 2005.

Pattison, Stephen. *Shame: Theory, Therapy, Theology*. New York: Cambridge University Press, 2000.

———. *Saving Face: Enfacement, Shame, Theology*. Burlington, VT: Ashgate, 2013.

Ramirez, Marisa. "Huffington Foundation Endows Chair for Brené Brown, Social Work Researcher, Author of 'Daring Greatly.'" University of Houston News and Events, February 4, 2016. Accessed June 8, 2018. www.uh.edu/news-events/stories/2016/February/24BreneBrownEndowment.php.

Schmidt, Lawrence K. ed., *Language and Linguisticality in Gadamer's Hermeneutics*. New York: Lexington, 2000.

Schneider, Carl. *Shame, Exposure, and Privacy*. New York: Beacon, 1992.

Smedes, Lewis B. *Shame & Grace: Healing the Shame We Don't Deserve*. New York: HarperOne, 1993.

Snickars, Pelle, and Patrick Vonderau, eds. *Moving Data: The iPhone and the Future of Media*. New York: Columbia University Press, 2012.

Stearns, Peter N. *Shame: A Brief History*. Urbana: University of Illinois Press, 2017.

Tamez, Elsa. *The Amnesty of Grace: Justification by Faith from a Latin American Perspective*. Eugene, OR: Wipf & Stock, 1991.

Tanner, Kathryn. "Justification and Justice in a Theology of Grace." *Theology Today* 55, no. 4 (1999): 510–23.

Thompson, Curt. *The Soul of Shame: Retelling the Stories We Believe about Ourselves*. Downers Grove, IL: InterVarsity Press, 2015.

Van Dijck, Jose. *The Culture of Connectivity: A Critical History of Social Media*. New York: Oxford University Press, 2013.

Vanhoozer, Kevin. *The Drama of Doctrine: A Canonical Linguistic Approach to Christian Theology*. Louisville, KY: Westminster John Knox, 2005.

Volf, Miroslav. *Against the Tide: Love in a Time of Petty Dreams and Persisting Enmities*. Grand Rapids, MI: Eerdmans, 2010.

Wolterstorff, Nicholas. *Justice in Love*. Grand Rapids, MI: Eerdmans, 2011.

Yoder, Perry. *Shalom: The Bible's Word for Salvation, Justice & Peace*. Eugene, OR: Wipf & Stock, 1997.

Chapter 5

Walker Percy's Rhetoric of the Sacred

Signposts in the Strange Land of Triadic Communication

Michael R. Kearney

If you browsed a bookstore's ever-burgeoning self-help section in 1983, you might have stumbled upon an intriguing new title, *Lost in the Cosmos*, which claimed to be not just a self-help book, but—with surprising audacity—the *last* self-help book. If your curiosity led you to thumb through the pages of the volume, your incredulity would only have grown. Authored by southern American novelist Walker Percy (1916–1990), *Lost in the Cosmos* defies the genre of self-help literature. Rather than inspiring its readers, the book abrades them with impudent observations about "why it is that of all the billions and billions of strange objects in the Cosmos—novas, quasars, pulsars, black holes—you are beyond doubt the strangest."[1] Rather than proffering positive thinking, the book offers a clinical list of the malaises of the self: amnesic, fearful, misplaced, envious, bored, depressed, impoverished, and, above all, lonely.[2] And rather than prescribing a solution for these troubles, Percy merely asks his reader: *Why?* The reader, for his or her part, may be inclined to pose the same question to Percy.

Those who persevere through eighty pages of Percy's introductory self-diagnostic tests will encounter probably the most unexpected feature of his treatise: a forty-page "Semiotic Primer of the Self."[3] Percy embarks on a philosophical investigation that invokes the names of Ernst Cassirer, Charles Sanders Peirce, Ferdinand de Saussure, Susanne K. Langer, and others—all while arguing for a theory of "triadic behavior" that provides a basis for explaining the human experience of meaning.[4] If Percy's approach to pop psychology is unorthodox, his dive into dyadic and triadic models of communication is seemingly inexplicable. What does semiotics have to do with self-help? An obvious conclusion would be that *Lost in the Cosmos* represents the ramblings of a frustrated philosopher-novelist attempting to reconcile the tensions of intellectualism and creative writing. But is it possible that Percy conceals a deeper rhetorical purpose, a carefully conceived effort to address a particular exigence of the current historical moment? And if so, what might Percy's enigmatic self-help book and its emphasis on triadic behavior reveal about his view of human communication?

Amid the multitude of answers to these questions that could be and have been proposed,[5] we possess a significant clue from the author himself. In a letter to Kenneth Laine Ketner, a scholar of Charles Sanders Peirce, Percy confided that his semiotic investigations stemmed from an interest in articulating "the pillars of a Christian apologetic."[6] A devout Roman Catholic, Percy catalogs and critiques a variety of religious narratives in *Lost in the Cosmos*—including his own—yet his work reveals persistent and paradoxical interaction with the Judeo-Christian tradition. He holds it to be "preposterous" in a postmodern age, yet worthy of serious consideration.[7] His intention is apologetic and rhetorical—apologetic as he invites dialogue about faith, rhetorical as he attempts to persuade his audience. And Percy's locus of concern, as suggested by the placement of the "Semiotic Primer of the Self" near the center of *Lost in the Cosmos*, is the mysterious phenomenon of interpersonal dialogue as the medium for communicating the truths of the faith.

My purpose in this chapter is not to attempt a rhetorical analysis of *Lost in the Cosmos* but, rather, to suggest a few implications of Percy's philosophy of dialogue as it relates to religious communication in the twenty-first century. A cluster of related inquiries guides this chapter. First, I ask: What is the historical exigence that precipitated Percy's rhetorical efforts in *Lost in the Cosmos*? To address this question, I identify common themes between Percy's nonfiction and existing literature within the philosophy of communication on dialogue. However, I also discern a growing tension in dialogic studies that questions the possibility of dialogue about faith. Second, I ask: How does Percy's specific philosophy of communication speak into this dialogic tension? Although his philosophy of communication reveals indebtedness to the pragmaticism of Charles Sanders Peirce, Percy's work also offers a unique contribution that bridges the fields of semiotics and dialogue. Third, I ask: How does Percy's philosophy of dialogue identify a postmodern possibility for communicating one's faith? I identify Peirce's notion of *abduction* as a key theme in Percy's work that assists him in responding to the tension of dialogue about faith in the current historical moment. Finally, I ask: How does Percy's own literary work offer a case study of his "Christian apologetic" in action? To illumine this, I step back from Percy's triadic theory to envision his literary project as a case study of his specific rhetoric of the sacred.

SITUATING PERCY IN THE FIELD OF DIALOGUE

The French sociologist and philosopher Jacques Ellul described his historical moment as a point of crisis in which "speaking is anything at all except saying *something* to *someone*."[8] Ellul's statement captures a common concern taken up by many philosophers of the twentieth century: the fear that despite the proliferation of theorizing *about* communication, genuine communion between human beings is increasingly scarce. Heightened attention to dialogue among philosophers of communication beginning in the late twentieth century represented multiple attempts to respond to this threat. As Rob Anderson, Leslie A. Baxter, and Kenneth N. Cissna suggest in their edited book on dialogue, many advocates of dialogue share the conviction that an overemphasis on message-centered and behavioristic models of communication may hinder the possibility of true "meeting" between persons in which deep, life-changing relationships are formed.[9] In particular, surveying the loosely defined area of dialogue studies reveals three major areas in which twentieth- and twenty-first-century philosophers identify impoverishment in today's interpersonal relationships.[10] These points assist us in triangulating a possible description of "dialogue."

First, many theories of dialogue oppose modernistic views of the autonomous self. Ronald C. Arnett links a philosophy of dialogue with postmodern scholarship, which "questions our fascination or obsession with metanarrative assurance, the self, and agency."[11] Postmodernism reacts to the autonomy and self-assurance that characterized the modernism of Enlightenment philosophy. In response, postmodernism emphasizes the importance of locality, the relativity of one's own perspective, the socially constructed nature of the world, and the role of stories in shaping identity.[12] Whereas social-scientific, psychological, and behavioristic models of communication tend to represent modernist legacies, Arnett suggests that dialogue is a more appropriate way to engage the philosophy of communication in a postmodern historical moment, describing dialogue as "a humble or particular narrative standpoint engaging the Other and the historical situation."[13] Arnett particularly identifies Martin Buber (1878–1965) and Emmanuel Levinas (1906–1995) as scholars of dialogue who emphasized the responsive and derivative nature of the self in dialogue with others.

As his sardonic self-help tactics suggest, Percy shares a suspicion of philosophical and epistemological models that begin by taking the self for granted. *Lost in the Cosmos* exposes the bankruptcy of a philosophy in which "the self locates itself at the dead center of its world"—a tautological situation in which signification and communication become impossible.[14] Likewise, Percy rejects facile attempts to theorize the self while dodging questions of agency and consciousness. "Indeed," he writes, "the self may be defined as that portion of the person which cannot be encompassed by theory, not even a theory of the self."[15] Instead, Percy's "semiotic primer" describes the self as situated, particular, and constituted through one's relations with others; it is the person with whom I speak who becomes "co-namer, co-discoverer, co-sustainer of my world."[16] Percy does not deny the existence of the self; however, he rejects the modernistic assumption that the self is an unproblematic starting point.

The problematic nature of the self brings us to a second characteristic of dialogic theory: its role as an alternative to the behavioristic and psychological models of human communication that dominated the early years of the twentieth century, as mentioned in Anderson, Baxter, and Cissna's essay.[17] Dialogue embraces the irreducible complexity of the interpersonal encounter, acknowledging that humanistic psychology conceals some poorly founded generalizations about communication.[18] The Russian philosopher Mikhail Bakhtin (1895–1975), for example, rejects "formal linguistic" and "psychological" approaches to understanding while identifying the intonation of embodied dialogue as the source of meaning.[19] Buber, similarly, differentiates the irreducible complexity of the *I–Thou* encounter of interpersonal dialogue from the static abstraction of the *I–It*.[20] As Arnett emphasizes, Buber's point is not to deny the validity of monologue and technical dialogue as forms of communication but, rather, to distinguish them from the full and embodied responsiveness implicated by the "between" of the dialogic encounter.[21] A dialogic approach to human communication respects the validity of analytic and empirical traditions, yet affirms that language surpasses the explanatory power of these theories.

Percy, too, offers a consistent critique of behavioristic psychology extending from his first scholarly essay on the work of Susanne K. Langer to his posthumous collection of nonfiction.[22] By his own account in the book *The Message in the Bottle*, the behaviorist school formed the basis for Percy's first forays into philosophical questions of human communication.[23] Ultimately, however, Percy's intellectual journey led him to reject stimulus–response theories of meaning as inadequate. Like Buber, Percy retains respect for technical discourses (he calls them "dyadic" sciences) such as biology, chemistry, and medicine—studies founded on observable patterns of stimulus and response. While affirming the validity of these fields, Percy also contends that their principles are inadequate for an analysis of the human mind in dialogue with others.[24] The advent of human language, he states, is "an event different in kind from all preceding events in the Cosmos."[25] Language conceals a mystery ignored by behavioristic models of stimulus and response.

A third theme of dialogic theory relates to the rise of the technological age. The twentieth century saw unprecedented forces of urbanization, militarization, digitalization, and other forms of technological development coalescing on a massive and global scale. Anderson, Baxter, and Cissna cite several philosophers typically associated with media ecology, such as Jacques Ellul (1912–1994) and Walter Ong (1912–2003), as "proponents of dialogue" in the face of ever more mediated forms of communication.[26] Whether one favors Ellul's critical analysis of the alienation and dehumanization of a culture enthralled by "*la technique*" or Ong's more hopeful discussion of technological transformations of human consciousness, these scholars and others converge in affirming the spoken word of dialogue as the basic, irreducible means of establishing human presence in an increasingly dehumanized technological context.[27]

Here, too, we see resonances in the work of Walker Percy, who describes the bedazzlements of "the overwhelming credentials of science, the beauty and elegance of the scientific method, the triumph of modern medicine over physical ailments, and the technological transformation of the very world itself," yet also discerns a sense of profound disappointment that accompanies these technological marvels.[28] The paradox of technological development is a "radical impoverishment of human relations" that occurs alongside a booming consumer culture in a technologically mastered world.[29] Percy's outlook on technology is closer to Ellul's than to Ong's, as he discerns "the very real possibility . . . that we may destroy ourselves in the near future."[30] Percy envisions the rediscovery of loving dialogue between human beings as the only way to avert this potential catastrophe[31]—not a vague magic-bullet view of dialogue but a specific sort of dialogue about faith and matters of ultimate human concern that can allow us to grapple with the alienation of a technologized and dehumanized society, as we will see later.

The preceding discussion provides a rough idea of "dialogue" as understood within the context of interpersonal communication. Although forgoing a universal definition, Anderson, Baxter, and Cissna note that dialogue "downplays techniques of information or message transmission, concentrating instead on the extent to which human thinking, speaking, and listening can be appreciated as social and cultural intersubjective processes, rather than simply as individualistic, organism-centered acts."[32] In this summary, we can see dialogue as a possible response to the historical themes of the problematic self, the prevalence of stimulus-response communication theories, and an increasingly technological milieu. Moreover, we can perceive resonances of this approach to dialogue in *Lost in the Cosmos*, as Percy seeks to respond to the experience of life in an alienated age. However, even as the study of dialogue provides a means of situating Percy within the field of communication, his claim to be practicing apologetics problematizes this relationship. As we will see, two persistent but apparently contradictory themes emerge in the literature on dialogue, and the apologetic aim of *Lost in the Cosmos* exacerbates the tension between them.

THE DILEMMA OF DIALOGUE ABOUT FAITH

Our discussion so far has revealed multiple philosophical points of contact between and among scholars of dialogue. An additional connection is that many of the premiere twentieth-century scholars of dialogue spoke from religious narratives. Buber and Levinas, for example, explored their respective roots in Jewish religious traditions.[33] Bakhtin gave lectures on theology in the Russian Orthodox Church.[34] Ellul's background in the French Protestant tradition closely informed his understanding of dialogue in an image-based society.[35] Ong, a Jesuit priest, spoke freely about the dialogic "presence of God" in a technologically transformed world.[36] More recently, twenty-first-century scholars such as Lisbeth Lipari have incorporated Eastern religious traditions such as Buddhism into the conversation surrounding dialogue.[37] In short, much of the extant literature on dialogue is informed by richly textured interactions with various traditions of faith.

Dialogue, with its intentional movement away from empirical and positivistic models of the self, has opened the conversation surrounding faith to new insights and possibilities, some of which Arnett explores in his 2005 address to the Religious Communication Association.[38] At the same time, the case study of articulating faith in dialogue reveals a key question. Anderson, Baxter, and Cissna suggest that dialogue moves the notion of "meaning" beyond the realm of dictionary definitions and into the realm of ascertaining one's position and purpose in life through conversation with others.[39] But if the goal of dialogue is to foster openness to meaning that emerges in conversation between persons, where is the meaning located? Does the dialogue generate a new creation, or is it a means of discovering meaning that already exists? Does this meaning emerge before (in front of) the conversational partners, or behind them?

Literature on dialogue often views meaning as a new product that *emerges* from an interpersonal encounter.[40] Buber's biographer, Maurice Friedman, recalls an occasion on which Buber expressed a wish to be asked more questions. Friedman explains, "He was saying, 'If people would come to me with real questions, something would come into being between them and me that does not exist now.' . . . He does not *have* the wisdom. It literally happens, comes to be, in the between."[41] Here, the "between" of dialogue allows participants to generate a new understanding of the world that orients their relationship toward the future. Buber's work forms the basis for Arnett's conclusion that "[t]ruth is relationally bounded. It is not found in one person or in some dogmatic assertion . . . Both partners in dialogue generate the resultant communication together for good or ill."[42] Different conceptions of ethics, aesthetics, and truth emerge from dialogue, requiring openness and attentiveness on the part of the conversational participants—what Arnett, Janie M. Harden Fritz, and Leeanne M. Bell have called "a dialogic ethic" of communication.[43] Dialogue leads to an acknowledgment of each other's humanness, a reaffirmation of each other's symbolic universes, a celebration of each other's differences, and a continuing process of misunderstanding and understanding that orients interpersonal relationships in the pursuit of emerging meaning.

If dialogue concerns itself only with emerging meaning, however, the possibility of conveying faith in dialogue is called into doubt. How can a dialogic commitment to emerging meaning reconcile with a faith commitment to already existent texts, doctrines, or traditions? Religions such as Percy's Catholicism depend upon the authority of a canon or a creed for their articulation and continuation—a source of *originating meaning* that provides an identity for individuals and communities. Moreover, a traditional metaphor for the communication of such faith commitments is "apologetics"—understood as defending a particular set of religious teachings, claiming them to be objectively true and rationally compelling.[44] The rationalistic position implied by apologetics bears a suspicious resemblance to the self-assurance of modernism that scholars of dialogue have critiqued. Even as apologetics precludes the possibility of dialogue, a postmodern understanding of dialogue excludes the truth claims integral to the articulation of many religious traditions. Orthodoxy yields to the ever-shifting emergent "between." Thus, we find ourselves caught in a dilemma between the reification of a dogmatic religious position and ephemeral aura of a dialogic faith manifested only in the occasional "holy spark" that emerges between persons.[45] Is there a way to harmonize these apparently contrary positions?

Percy acknowledges that in a postmodern era, it is one thing to affirm a temporal truth that *emerges* from a specific interpersonal encounter; it is quite another to claim access to a preexisting truth or Truth that serves as the *origin* for personal life and interpersonal conversation. He frames the dilemma as "Christianity's rather insolent claim to be true, with the implication that other religions are more or less false."[46] For Percy, however, radical relativism is no less objectionable than the Cartesian rootless self. Arnett, Fritz, and Bell's frequent description of the current historical moment as "a time of narrative and virtue contention"—a time when communities struggle to agree on what constitutes the good, the true, and the beautiful—suggests that the idea of originating meaning is currently out of our reach; that even if something is "out there," it lies beyond our capacity to know and understand in community with one another.[47] Yet, Percy persists in the belief that the interpersonal discovery of originating meaning remains possible, even in a postmodern historical moment. This problematic quest is the exigence that provokes his rhetorical project in *Lost in the Cosmos*.

How does Percy's specific philosophy of communication speak to this problem of dialogue? We have already explored a few of the thematic resonances between Percy's work and a dialogic approach to the philosophy of communication; the philosophical origins of Percy's own thought clarify this connection. In particular, his interaction with the work of Charles Sanders Peirce (1839–1914) both illumines Percy's unique approach to semiotics and suggests implications for faith-related dialogue.

FROM PEIRCEAN TO PERCIAN: UNDERSTANDING PERCY'S TRIADIC THEORY

Introducing his "Semiotic Primer of the Self" in *Lost in the Cosmos*, Percy credits his conception of triadic semiotics to a variety of philosophers including Ernst Cassirer, Charles Sanders Peirce, Ferdinand de Saussure, Hans Werner, and Susanne K. Langer.[48] However, it is to Peirce most directly that Percy owes his triadic theory. Peirce distinguishes between three phenomenal qualities in human perception: iconicity, indexicality, and symbolicity.[49] Peirce calls the last of these "thirdness" or a "triadic relation," and articulates two features essential to it: (1) "[E]very genuine triadic relation involves meaning," and (2) "a triadic relation is inexpressible by means of dyadic relations alone."[50] A triadic relation binds together a symbol, an object, and an "interpretant" that mediates between them.[51] This "thirdness" separates the interpersonal experience of shared meaning from observable "dyadic"—that is, cause and effect—relationships.[52] Percy seizes upon these two principles of triadic communication to build his own philosophy of language in *Lost in the Cosmos*.[53] The intellectual lineage is so direct that Percy called himself "a thief of Peirce."[54]

Percy champions the characteristics of triadic relations with a view to defending the uniqueness of human communication in the cosmos and the impossibility of explaining it through behavioristic models.[55] In *Lost in the Cosmos*, he describes triadic communication as an "unprecedented" development in the history of the universe.[56] The interpretive capacity of humans differentiates dialogue from a mere exchange of stimuli and responses. Percy writes, "[G]iven two mammals extraordinarily similar in organic structure and genetic code, and given that one species has made the breakthrough into triadic behavior and the other has not, there is, semiotically speaking, more difference between the two than there is between the dyadic animal and the planet Saturn."[57] Triadic behavior endows humans with more than an empirically observable environment; they also possess a "world" of signification, which may include things that do not exist in one's environment (centaurs, Big Foot, détente) or may omit things that do (the galaxy M31).[58] Although ants, bees, and other creatures also communicate, Percy concludes that they do not experience *meaning*—the first major characteristic of Peirce's triadicity.[59]

The second characteristic of Peirce's triadicity is its irreducibility. Percy takes pains to distinguish his triadic theory of communication from dyadic models—and this includes dyadic models that include a third element such as "channel," "noise," or "culture" within an information-transmission framework.[60] Ogden and Richards's famous semiotic triangle is not truly "triadic," the way Percy uses the term, because the relationships it describes are "causal"—*ergo* dyadic.[61] Nor are social-scientific theories that attempt to describe dyadic interactions between three objects or individuals in "triadic" terms.[62] The consistent problem with dyadic models, as J. P. Telotte notes, is that "a binary language theory . . . tends to diminish man to the level of another reactive organism."[63] Percy, by contrast, views human experience as irreducible to animalistic behavior or mechanistic cause and effect. He sees humankind as "a creature which is ashamed of itself and which seeks cover in myriad disguises," and he believes a triadic model of communication surpasses dyadic theories in explaining our uniquely problematic existence.[64]

As anyone who has studied Peirce knows, triadicity is not as simple as these two assertions about meaning and irreducibility might suggest. What Peirce means by "thirdness" is open to continuing debate, although it is generally agreed to refer to a principle of mediation or interpretation.[65] But Peirce himself employs a perplexing variety of descriptors in pursuit of this idea of "thirdness":

> the medium or connecting bond . . . the middle . . . the means . . . the thread of life . . . [a] fork in a road . . . a straight road . . . so far as it implies passing through intermediate places . . . acceleration or the relation of three successive positions . . . velocity in so far as it is continuous.[66]

Peirce's dense aphorisms might leave a prospective student of triadic theory more muddled than ever. It is, at best, unremarkable to assert that a third *something* is behind human communication. Such "thirdness" could represent a psychological need, a cultural context, an extraverbal setting, an imaginary arbitrator, or a divine being, among a host of other possibilities. Yet where is the "third"? What is the "third"? The specific value of triadic theory for the study of dialogue remains unclear if considering only these two tenets of triadicity.

As it turns out, Percy's self-identification as "a thief of Peirce" reveals more than his indebtedness to an earlier philosopher. Percy believes that his application of Peircean semiotics differs significantly from what Peirce would have intended. In his correspondence with Peirce scholar Kenneth Laine Ketner, Percy expresses disinterest in Peirce's formal logic and distances himself from Peirce's critiques of religion. Instead, Percy admits that his focus centers on "one percent" of Peirce's theory: specifically, his distinction between dyadicity and triadicity, his preference for Scholastic realism, and the implications of these ideas for a Catholic apologetic based on "philosophical anthropology."[67] Percy reads Peirce as a forerunner of existential phenomenology and an unwitting advocate of Christian faith. Whether or not these characterizations are entirely accurate, they illuminate Percy's specific rhetorical project and bring us closer to its implications for dialogue.

Percy's reading of Peirce as an early existential phenomenologist hinges on the concept of "intersubjectivity," which features heavily in the semiotic primer of *Lost in the Cosmos*.[68] Subjectivity (recognizing oneself as a self) is predicated on the preexistence of intersubjectivity (the world being what it is for both of us). Isaac E. Catt captures this affirmation in reference to Peirce and his fellow semiologists: "[I]ndividual identity . . . is modeled from the very beginning on interpersonal communication."[69] Or, the way Percy puts it, "the self becomes itself only through a transaction of signs with other selves—and does so, moreover, without succumbing to the mindless mechanism of the behaviorists."[70] The fact that "every triad of sign-reception requires another triad of sign-utterance" means that the act of understanding is predicated on one's being addressed.[71] Thus, intersubjectivity provides a link between Peirce's semiotics and the field of dialogue—a link Percy identifies and strengthens in his work.

We see now that Percy's theory of triadic communication expands upon Peirce by interconnecting *two* triads, relating a signifier and a referent that lie between two individuals.[72] Percy's unique development of Peirce's triadic semiotics is the addition of another triad at right angles to the first. One triad concerns "your giving a name to a class of objects to make a sign, and my understanding or misunderstanding"; the other concerns "the I–you intersubjectivity of an exchange of signs."[73] J. P. Telotte helpfully distinguishes between a "first or Peircean triad," relating man to his world, and a second (dare we call it *Percian?*) triad, relating humans to humans intersubjectively.[74] The relationship between human beings presupposes a shared symbolic world, while the possibility of a symbolic world presupposes a relationship between human beings—and each is triadic. Neither "your giving a name to a class of objects to make a sign, and my understanding or misunderstanding" nor "the I–you intersubjectivity of an exchange of signs" can be explained dyadically—which reinforces the irreducibility of triadic relations.[75] Percy thus addresses a dialogic theme that is more implicit than explicit in Peirce's triadic theory: the need for interpretive communities in which humans understand themselves and their world through a language that is always already given.[76]

The foregoing discussion clarifies how Percy reads Peirce as a forerunner of existential phenomenology and appropriates him as a philosopher of dialogue. Percy's second conviction—that Peirce provides an apologetic for Christian faith via Scholastic realism—is far less evident. It is particularly problematic if one considers that Peirce maintained a complex relationship with the Scholastic philosophy of John Duns Scotus (ca. 1265–1308), whose name has been invoked to support either nominalism or realism, depending on the interpreter.[77] The debate between the two positions could be framed today as whether a real world outside our linguistic constructions exists. Without traipsing too far into the weeds of medieval Scholasticism, we can discover an affirmation of the external world in Peirce's own pragmaticism. The better question, however, is what the relationship is between words and reality. Claudine Engel-Tiercelin leans into Peirce's own ambiguity on the subject of language with her phrase "the reality of vagueness and the vagueness of the real."[78] We cannot experience the lived world except in the sign exchanges of communication and thought, yet these very sign exchanges take for granted an external world that can be known. Indeed, Engel-Tiercelin's phrase captures the mystery of language that motivated Percy's investigations into triadic theory in the first place: the multifaceted and ambiguous relationship between words and the reality they signify.

Although Percy does not engage Duns Scotus directly in *Lost in the Cosmos*, he follows Peirce's view of realism by stating that a word is somewhere between a percept and a concept; it is both particular and abstract, and at the same time neither. The word "apple" is a "quality of appleness."[79] For Percy, the world of signification is both socially constructed *and* real, and language is the fragile go-between that mediates between these two domains of reality. Triadic semiotics asserts both that "you have to point to an apple and name it for me before I know there is such a thing" and that there is "a world of apples outside ourselves."[80] Thus, meaning is double-sided; it emerges out of the dialogic encounter, yet it also exists in the already-given world outside our linguistic constructions. As we will shortly see, this bivalence of language contains the key that Percy employs to unlock the barrier between postmodern dialogue and premodern apologetics.

Even assuming that Percy's description of a triadic semiotic theory is immediately clear—which is already a dubious proposition, though he is certainly more readable than Peirce—why does it matter? Why does Percy take such pains to articulate his theory, not in the annals of semiotics, but in the pages of a book intended for a popular audience? In a 1984 interview, Percy declared that the semiotic theory articulated in *Lost in the Cosmos* represented the most important accomplishment of his life: "If I am remembered for anything a hundred years from now, it will probably be for that."[81] A surprising statement, indeed, from a man whose novel *The Moviegoer* received the National Book Award in 1962! Although Percy's lasting impact clearly is evident in the genre of American fiction, his name remains little known in the fields of communication and semiotics. Percy's essays appeared in journals of philosophy, religion, and psychiatry, but his published scholarship remains on the fringes of the communication discipline.[82] Outside the field, his work is widely referenced and analyzed for its literary themes and, somewhat less frequently, for its philosophical implications.[83] But within the field, the dialogic implications of his semiotic theory have remained largely unexplored.

Some sporadic references to Percy in communication literature bear mentioning. The 1975 collection *The Message in the Bottle*, containing many of Percy's semiotic essays, merited a thoughtful review by Robert L. Scott in *Communication Quarterly*. Scott highlighted Percy's critique of a modernist worldview as well as mentioning two particular "gifts" of Percy's philosophy: (1) a possible answer to determinism and idealism through Percy's application of Charles Sanders Peirce's notion of abduction and (2) the intersubjectivity inherent in Percy's triadic theory.[84] In 2003, Lesley A. Rex borrowed Percy's phrase "loss of the creature" from an essay in *The Message in the Bottle* to describe the impact on the communication classroom when attention to standardized testing trumps dialogue.[85] A 2012 essay by Craig E. Mattson focused on Percy's novel *The Moviegoer* to take up much the same question as described above: "[I]s it possible, in a world of fragmented moral vocabularies and multifarious histories, to share epideictic space with others?"[86] These references, though sparse, established Percy as a worthy subject of hermeneutic study.

Interestingly, Percy's ideas receive more frequent, yet still cursory, mentions in the discipline of media ecology. He appeared in Wayne Woodward's and Clifford G. Christians's respective surveys of triadic theories of mediation, although both Woodward and Christians tended to view the triad as a fundamentally cultural rather than interpersonal metaphor.[87] Corey Anton, picking up the theme of Scholastic realism, leveraged Percy's triadic theory in defense of the view that "denotative content is not reducible to its spatial/temporal embodiment."[88] To cite two other examples, Jennifer J. Cobb lifted Percy's notion of "cosmonauts in cyberspace" from *Lost in the Cosmos* to reflect on the spiritual dimension of computer simulations.[89] And Stephanie Bennett cited Percy's novel *The Moviegoer* to defend the continuing value of embodied friendships in an age of connection through social media.[90] Percy's view of language as a mediator between human beings opens up rich discussions regarding the place of other media in relating people to one another.

The discipline of semiotics reveals the deepest engagement with Percy's work. In 1976, Percy attended the first annual conference of the Semiotic Society of America with the likes of Thomas A. Sebeok, John Deely, and Umberto Eco.[91] Percy later exchanged correspondence with Sebeok and Deely, and Jean Umiker-Sebeok contacted him in 1988 to inquire about including an article on his semiotic model in the yearbook she edited with Sebeok, *The Semiotic Web*.[92] Although a full article on Percy's semiotics apparently never came to fruition, Thomas A. Sebeok discussed Percy briefly in his review essay on "Semiotics in the United States" for *The Semiotic Web 1989*. Sebeok described Percy as a leading American semiotician whose work proved "original and interesting"; he commended Percy's "fascinating critique of transformational grammar" and lamented that his semiotic theory had gone largely unnoticed.[93] Patrick Samway edited a posthumous collection of Percy's correspondence with Peirce scholar Kenneth Laine Ketner, which appeared in 1995 under the title *A Thief of Peirce*. In 1997, Jaime Nubiola conducted a fascinating study of Percy's interaction with Peirce's semiotics, published in the proceedings of the International Association for Semiotic Studies.[94] In the 2004 volume *The Cambridge Companion to Peirce*, Peter Skagestad listed Percy among Peirce's interpreters, yet emphasized the unique characteristics of Percy's triadic theory.[95] Sebeok's lament, combined with the scattered references listed here, urges renewed attention to Percy's scholarship and its possible implications for the current historical moment.

My own conclusion is that Percy's insistence upon a triadic model of human communication in *Lost in the Cosmos* springs from his larger project of rehabilitating a rhetoric of the sacred for an alienated age. Such a conclusion builds on Percy's semiotic approach to the phenomenon of dialogue and his unique addition to Peirce's theory of triadic behavior. As we have seen, Percy's own triadic theory consists of two interconnected triangles: (1) the triad of symbol, object, and interpretant; and (2) the triad of two dialogic partners and a common object that they behold together. In this existential web of semiotic triads, meaning emerges out of the dialogic encounter, comprising both "a denotative act and a coupling principle."[96] Moreover, even as meaning emerges out of this dialogic relationship, the dialogic relationship presupposes the possibility of originating meaning that waits to be discovered in the world—the sacred, if you will. To illuminate the specific relationship between semiotics and the sacred, I turn to consider Peirce's reasoning process of *abduction*, which Percy takes up elsewhere in his work.

ABDUCTION AS DIALOGIC DISCOVERY OF THE SACRED

In *Lost in the Cosmos*, Percy writes that "the origin of consciousness is the initiation of the sign-user into the world of signs by a sign-giver."[97] While dialogic scholarship highlights the emergent meaning generated by the meeting of person and person, Percy's statement also reveals another reality: such meeting and meaning are possible only because other meaning and other persons already exist in the world. Buber and Levinas describe dialogue in terms of responsiveness and responsibility.[98] Arnett expounds on this dialogic theme in terms of "ground under one's feet" that provides an identity as a "responsive ethical 'I.'"[99] The "ground" of dialogue is the realization that a human conversation has already commenced, and I have only subsequently been invited into it. An originating perspective embraces the a priori nature of all human communication.[100] The meaning already present in the human life world is what makes communication possible.

For religious traditions that affirm the existence of an eternal divine being, the notion of originating meaning offers a ready point of integration for articulating the faith. Ellul, for example, roots his understanding of the origins of dialogue in the Biblical creation account, in which God's spoken word provides the basis for humanity's response:

> This Word that created the elements and the world is the same one which, when addressed to humanity, tells us something about God and ourselves. When the Word does this it is no less creative, since it creates the heart and ear of the one it addresses, so he can hear and receive the word.[101]

As appealing as such an explanation may be, however, it remains difficult to situate the idea of religious communication within a dialogic framework. Even granting that Percy's triadic model affirms both emerging and originating sources of meaning, the two remain apparently antithetical to one another. Can we really speak of God as an "originating third" when the very concept of God emerges from human discourse? Deborah Eicher-Catt and Isaac Catt describe religion in their discussion of Peirce as "giving birth to the ideal of a divine Other—God—who stands outside the bounds of human existence yet is responsible for its ultimate creation."[102] A gap in human perception calls for the construction of a transcendent referent to fill it. At best, we can postulate a kind of *Deus absconditus*, a "vacuum" that makes dialogue possible—the kind of divine silence that provoked a multigenerational dialogue on ethics in Simon Wiesenthal's *The Sunflower*.[103] But if we can say no more than this, it seems that we have not progressed past an emerging view of the interpersonal triad at all. The concept of "originating meaning" is itself the emerging result of our philosophical discourse.

The point of contact between originating and emerging meaning lies within a third dimension of Percy's triadic model of communication—a dimension he does not define explicitly but that can be inferred from the rest of his scholarship. Strange as it may seem, there is a "third third" implicit in Percy's model, another triad that directs our attention to the *location of meaning* in the interpersonal encounter. By *meaning*, I refer to the enigmatic interpenetration of signifier and signified upon which humans build a shared understanding of the world. This third dimension of triadic communication provides the possibility of harmony between emerging and originating meaning through the cognitive process Peirce describes as *abduction*.

Peirce describes abduction as an inferential process that chooses "any one hypothesis over others which would equally explain the facts."[104] In the words of Deborah Eicher-Catt and Isaac Catt, "[a]bduction may be understood as making guesses, but all guesses are based in experience."[105] As an informal mode of reasoning, abduction precedes the logical processes of induction and deduction.[106] Percy finds fascination in Peirce's theory of abduction and in Peirce's own fascination with it.[107] In *The Message in the Bottle*, Percy writes, "No new truth can come from deduction or induction. . . . Abduction starts from facts and seeks an explanatory theory."[108] The wonder of abduction as a cognitive process is how often the thinker "usually hits on the correct hypothesis" after only a few guesses.[109] Thus, Percy identifies the process of abduction as a way to get outside the strictures of scientific reasoning. In fact, abduction is necessary even to posit a theory of triadic communication, given its irreducibility to cause-and-effect relationships. But abduction also serves to open the observer to the possibility of *new* truth—to meaning that exceeds the cognitive power of the perceiving subject. It is this openness characteristic of abduction that suggests a possible harmonization between the apparently contradictory poles of emerging and originating meaning.

In fact, abduction preserves the openness of dialogue to the possibility of preexisting meaning through its commitment to emerging meaning. The meaning that emerges in dialogue allows participants to hypothesize—*abductively*—about an originating source of meaning.[110] Eicher-Catt and Catt comment, "For Peirce, the concept of God must be logically *abducted* as a phenomenological sign process; that is, God's existence in the universe must remain a vital 'educated guess' that sustains (and nourishes) all human thought, inquiry, and experience to the end of our days."[111] The Peircean notion of abduction allows participants in interpersonal dialogue to conduct a careful and confident search, projecting the emergent meaning of their dialogue backwards in search of the *givenness* behind their lives. The search occurs in what John F. Desmond calls a "semiotic community," capturing Percy's awe that "[y]ou are also co-namer, co-discoverer, co-sustainer of my world."[112] Understood from Percy's point of view, triadic communication underscores the value of a dialogic community in cultivating openness to abductive guesses at shared sources of originating meaning.

In short, the implicit third dimension of Percy's triadic model concerns the *location* of interpersonal meaning; it is the dimension in which you and I, in symbolic dialogue with each other, not only generate new meaning in our relationship but also attempt to know something about its origin. If Percy's "Relation AC" between signifier and referent represents naming, and his "Relation BD" between Organism 1 and Organism 2 represents intersubjectivity, the third relation is that of *abduction* between emerging and originating sources of meaning.[113] This relation is what Nathan Crick and Graham D. Bodie call "a commitment to inquiry that arises as a result of doubt and a desire to arrive at a new form of belief."[114] Meaning begins with a conversation; we engage our partner in dialogue with the hope that something new will emerge. Yet, this new meaning also serves to call us back to previous conversations and contexts, back to a shared ground we did not realize we had in common. Dialogue allows us to journey forward and backward at the same time.

Now we can bring this discussion back to the questions posed at the beginning of the chapter. Percy views the dialogic phenomenon of abduction as an essential means of grappling with the alienation of the current historical moment precisely because of the current inaccessibility of originating meaning. If we accept Percy's description of the self as "being informed—'possessed,' if you like, at certain historical stages of belief and unbelief," then we must concur with him that "in an age in which the self is not informed by cosmological myths, by totemism, by belief in God . . . it must necessarily and by reason of its own semiotic nature be informed by something else."[115] Percy's diagnosis of the current plight is that "the autonomous self in a modern technological society is possessed . . . by the spirit of the erotic and the secret love of violence," setting the course of the self in an ever-downward spiral.[116] What unites the phenomena of modernistic autonomy, behaviorist models of human communication, and an unyielding commitment to technological progress is their common root in a philosophy that severs the link between the self and the *sacred* that traditionally provided its identity.

After establishing the necessity for the self to be "placed" in a semiotic framework constituted by the intersubjectivity of dialogue and the existence of a real world, Percy's "Semiotic Primer of the Self" lists a variety of the self's possible semiotic placements. Percy contrasts the mythical and religious narratives of ancient history—totemism, pantheism, and theistic-historical (the Judeo-Christian and Islamic traditions)—with the current narrative (or lack thereof) of a "post-religious technological society."[117] Traditional religious narratives, Percy contends, anchor the self in a stable and unproblematic identity. By contrast, a "post-religious technological society" shuns such frameworks as unscientific and primitive, leaving the self unplaced and orbiting between the problematic poles of total immanence and total transcendence. The outlook for preserving meaning and hope in such a world is bleak—unless one considers the rediscovery of a traditional religious mode of understanding the human self.

This, I contend, is the rhetorical goal of *Lost in the Cosmos*. Percy believes such a rediscovery is possible *in the nature of language itself*. Before we can hope to rediscover the sacred in a desacralized age, Percy concludes that we must open ourselves to the irreducible mystery of dialogue. The practice of triadic communication with another human being provides a ground from which emerging meaning can spring and, at the same time, conceals the possibility of discovering another ground beneath it: an originating Word that makes possible dialogue itself. And here, too, we find a humble, yet confident space for apologetics, preserving the possibility of sharing the faith in a postmodern age. In an era of alienation, dehumanization, and the triumph of the scientific method, we must cultivate the humility to step forward and grope for sparks of new meaning. And, Percy suggests, we must also cultivate the humility not to rule out signs that the sun is already risen behind us.

ALIENATION, FAITH, AND THE CALL TO "COME!"

This chapter began by noting that the "Semiotic Primer of the Self" occupies a puzzlingly central place in Percy's book. If we read *Lost in the Cosmos* as a defense of dialogue in an alienated age, it should be clearer why Percy devotes so much space to this semiotic investigation. What remains, however, is to recontextualize Percy's triadic semiotics within the scope of the book as a whole. Indeed, I suggest that this "semiotic primer" represents Percy's model for sharing the faith in microcosm; it offers a window into Percy's own expression of a particular rhetoric of the sacred rooted in Catholic Christianity.

The central question that guides *Lost in the Cosmos* is how to grapple with our contemporary alienation from a sense of selfhood and meaning in the world.[118] Percy's triadic semiotics is a prescription for a time of crisis. He holds nothing but contempt for trite religious answers that fail to acknowledge the severity of humanity's problem. Percy is frank enough to admit that Jews, Catholics, and Protestants tend to outdo one another in obnoxiousness. "Yet, as obnoxious as are all three, none is as murderous as the autonomous self who, believing in nothing, can fall prey to ideology and kill millions of people."[119] Percy's faith arises out of his keen awareness of human alienation; he witnesses the full spectrum of evil in the world and considers the recovery of faith to be the only way to avert disaster. His graphic descriptions of violence, rape, suicide, and nuclear meltdown on the pages of *Lost in the Cosmos* invite readers to meditate on the severity of the human condition and to share in Percy's own journey from despair to faith.

The kind of existential despair that Percy describes results from life in the absence of signs. Because Percy identifies meaning with the "third" of communication, a worldview that admits only of dyadic cause-and-effect relationships between entities is quite literally *meaning-less*. Loneliness "comes from a triadic creature, scientist, whether it be Einstein or Darwin or Sagan, who tries to explain the whole world by dyadic theory and mostly succeeds."[120] When we attempt a purely dyadic explanation of the world, we create a scenario in which "theory and consumption" are the only allowable options.[121] Theory is the domain of the scientist or philosopher who reduces human behavior to stimulus and response; consumption is the domain of the man on the street who believes the scientist. In both the transcendence of theory and the immanence of consumption, we run the risk of locking ourselves permanently inside a meaningless world.

Echoing the motif of *Deus absconditus*, Percy views the current landscape as a time when the voice of God is mute, or, at the very least, unperceived.[122] But, Percy continues to uphold the possibility of originating signs that can be discerned, even amid the ruins of a decaying culture. From a Christian perspective, Percy views the world not as a wasteland but as "a real world of real things, a world which is a sacrament and a mystery"—and each of us is "a pilgrim whose life is a searching and a finding."[123] In fact, "the incarnational and sacramental dimensions of Catholic Christianity" that shape Percy's novels also illuminate the centrality of triadic communication to his rhetorical project in *Lost in the Cosmos*.[124]

The attribute of the Catholic Christian faith that provides Percy with hope is the persistence of divine signification. Despite humanity's most ardent efforts, originative meaning continues to break through. As we wander through the ruins of a world we have declared to be meaningless, we are confronted with what Allen Pridgen calls "sacramental signs." Pridgen comments concerning Percy's work, "These sacramental signs have the power to show [individuals] a life not available in the ruins of their culture, a life hidden from them as they desperately search for daily happiness in their professional achievements and family relationships."[125] In an essay titled "Why Are You a Catholic?," Percy calls this perspective both "Semitic and semiotic."

Semitic? Semiotic? Jews and the science of signs? Yes, because in this age of the lost self, lost in the desert of theory and consumption, nothing of significance remains but signs. And only two signs are of significance in a world where all theoretical cats are gray. One is oneself and the other is the Jews. But for the self that finds itself lost in the desert of theory and consumption, there is nothing to do but set out as a pilgrim in the desert in search of a sign. In this desert, that of theory and consumption, there remains only one sign, the Jews. By "the Jews" I mean not only Israel, the exclusive people of God, but the worldwide *ecclesia* instituted by one of them, God-become-man, a Jew.[126]

Percy believes in the existence of signs and God-become-man—in the Word and the Word made flesh. Percy acknowledges the preposterousness of divine revelation in a postmodern age and affirms it cheerfully.

In *The Message in the Bottle*, Percy uses the metaphor of a castaway to describe modern humanity's predicament. The role of a castaway is twofold. First, to be a castaway means not pretending that one is at home. "The worst of all despairs is to imagine one is at home when one is really homeless."[127] If we feel as though we do not quite belong in the world, the best thing to do is to admit it. Second, "to be a castaway is to search for news from across the seas."[128] Here, "news from across the seas" is a sort of originating meaning; it purports a kind of authority that the recipient cannot directly know or verify. At the same time, a castaway can ascertain the veracity of a message if it is "relevant to his predicament as a castaway," if it is precisely the word for which the castaway has been waiting.[129] If a messenger appears with such a message, "the castaway will, by the grace of God, believe him."[130] By implication, Percy views the Christian story of redemption as "news from across the seas" that responds to humanity's existential plight. There is a call to "Come!" What is interesting, however, is the method of delivery that this gospel assumes amid technological alienation: "In such times, when everyone is saying 'Come!' when radio and television say nothing else but 'Come!' it may be that the best way to say 'Come!' is to remain silent. Sometimes silence itself is a 'Come!'"[131] Percy, like the philosophers of dialogue we have already considered, views *Deus absconditus* as an opportunity for hope.

In an interview, Percy stated that the real theme of *Lost in the Cosmos* is the "reentry option"—the possibility for the self to recover from its alienated orbit and obtain a renewed identity that provides meaning and joy in the world.[132] Of the eleven or so possible reentry options charted in *Lost in the Cosmos*, "reentry under the direct sponsorship of God" is of particular interest. Percy acknowledges that this is a preposterous, incredible, and extremely difficult option. "Yet there have existed, so I have heard, a few writers even in this day and age who have become themselves transparently before God and managed to live intact through difficult lives."[133] Percy affirms the possibility of an existential encounter with the sacred that can provide identity, stability, and meaning to one's life. And this encounter occurs not through abstract theories or categorical imperatives but, rather, through the ephemeral, fleeting, yet irreducible power of the spoken word that reminds us of a Word behind us. As long as the human race continues, and as long as individuals are willing to participate fully in communication with each other, there will always be the "possibility of one lonely person encountering another one, *really* encountering another one and perhaps even God in a way that hasn't been possible before."[134] Originating meaning emerges from incarnational encounters—with one's traveling companions along the desert roads of life, and ultimately "from the God of the Cosmos, who took pity on your ridiculous plight and entered the space and time of your insignificant planet to tell you something."[135] Gently, Percy suggests that *Deus absconditus* has already spoken and is waiting patiently for a listening ear.

In an era marked by philosophical confusion and communicative crises, Walker Percy's defense of triadic communication speaks with grave concern and resilient hope. His concern lies with the reduction of human communication to a dyadic paradigm, rendering the living word as a series of stimulus–response patterns and its bearers as organisms to be manipulated rather than beings to be understood. His hope rests in the response of the castaway—the person who, overwhelmed by the alienation of the self, turns a listening ear to the possibility of communion with others. A triadic view of human communication preserves three essential aspects of ethical dialogue: an originating ground, an emerging meaning, and the stability needed to prevent interpersonal relationships from collapsing into domination or assimilation.

Along the way, Percy acknowledges the preposterousness of the Judeo-Christian tradition. Yet, he keeps open the possibility that the increasing alienation of the self because of the scientific-technological worldview will result in the eventuality that "it is precisely this preposterous remedy, it and no other, which is specified by the preposterous predicament of the human self as its sole remedy."[136] His existential rhetoric of the sacred avoids both modernistic certainty and radical relativism. Instead, he discerns in the experience of interpersonal dialogue both the depths of human alienation and the ever-present possibility of discovering new meaning. *Lost in the Cosmos*—such as we are. But we may read the signposts and find a traveling companion, treasuring the hope that where two or three gather, something wholly Other may be amid them.

NOTES

1. Walker Percy, *Lost in the Cosmos* (New York: Farrar, Straus & Giroux, 1983).

2. Percy, *Lost in the Cosmos*, 168.
3. Percy, *Lost in the Cosmos*, 85.
4. Percy, *Lost in the Cosmos*, 95.
5. See, for example, Lewis A. Lawson and Victor A. Kramer, eds., *Conversations with Walker Percy* (Jackson: University Press of Mississippi, 1985).
6. Patrick H. Samway, ed., *A Thief of Peirce: The Letters of Kenneth Laine Ketner and Walker Percy* (Jackson: University Press of Mississippi, 1995), 130.
7. Percy, *Cosmos*, 254.
8. Jacques Ellul, *The Humiliation of the Word*, trans. Joyce Main Hanks (Grand Rapids, MI: Eerdmans, 1985), 172. Although Ellul is best known as a critic of technology, his work *The Humiliation of the Word* is an eloquent argument for the reclaiming of dialogue in a depersonalized age.
9. Rob Anderson, Leslie A. Baxter, and Kenneth N. Cissna, "Texts and Contexts of Dialogue," in *Dialogue: Theorizing Difference in Communication Studies*, ed. Rob Anderson, Leslie A. Baxter, and Kenneth N. Cissna (Thousand Oaks, CA: Sage, 2004), 1.
10. Of course, interpersonal communication is not the only context in which a dialogic approach can apply. Anderson, Baxter, and Cissna elaborate four contexts that reveal increasing attention toward dialogue: face-to-face, public, intercultural, and mediated communication. In this chapter, however, I am mostly concerned with the first of these—dialogue in the sense of one-to-one communication—with some attention to the ways that mediated communication has transformed these one-to-one relationships.
11. Ronald C. Arnett, "A Dialogic Ethic 'between' Buber and Levinas: A Responsive Ethical 'I,'" in *Dialogue: Theorizing Difference in Communication Studies*, ed. Rob Anderson, Leslie A. Baxter, and Kenneth N. Cissna (Thousand Oaks, CA: Sage, 2004), 75.
12. Anderson, Baxter, and Cissna, "Texts and Contexts of Dialogue," 10–11.
13. Arnett, "A Dialogic Ethic 'between' Buber and Levinas," 76.
14. Percy, *Cosmos*, 107.
15. Walker Percy, *Signposts in a Strange Land*, ed. Patrick Samway (New York: Farrar, Straus & Giroux, 1991), 312.
16. Percy, *Cosmos*, 101.
17. Anderson, Baxter, and Cissna, "Texts and Contexts of Dialogue," 11.
18. Ronald C. Arnett and Gordon Nakagawa, "The Assumptive Roots of Empathic Listening: A Critique," *Communication Education* 32 (1983): 370–71.
19. Mikhail Bakhtin, "Discourse in Life and Discourse in Art," in *Landmark Essays on Voice and Writing*, ed. Peter Elbow (Mahwah, NJ: Lawrence Erlbaum, 1994), 7, 9.
20. Martin Buber, *I and Thou*, trans. Ronald Gregor Smith (New York: Continuum, 2004), 51.
21. Arnett, "A Dialogic Ethic 'between' Buber and Levinas," 89.
22. Walker Percy, "Symbol as Need," *Thought: Fordham University Quarterly* 29 (1954): 381–90; Percy, *Signposts*, 271–91.
23. Walker Percy, *The Message in the Bottle* (New York: Farrar, Straus & Giroux, 1975), 30–31.

24. Percy, *Signposts*, 273.
25. Percy, *Cosmos*, 94.
26. Anderson, Baxter, and Cissna, "Texts and Contexts of Dialogue," 14.
27. Jacques Ellul, *The Technological Society*, trans. John Wilkinson (New York: Vintage, 1964), 393; Ellul, *The Humiliation of the Word*, 254; Walter Ong, *The Presence of the Word* (Minneapolis: University of Minnesota Press, 1981), 295.
28. Percy, *Cosmos*, 178–79.
29. Percy, *Signposts*, 210.
30. Percy, *Cosmos*, 188.
31. Percy, *Cosmos*, 250–51.
32. Anderson, Baxter, and Cissna, "Texts and Contexts of Dialogue," 15.
33. Arnett, "A Dialogic Ethic 'between' Buber and Levinas," 87–90.
34. Pat Arneson, ed., *Perspectives on Philosophy of Communication* (West Lafayette, IN: Purdue University Press, 2007), 248.
35. Ellul, *Humiliation of the Word*, 48.
36. Ong, *Presence of the Word*, 308.
37. Lisbeth Lipari, *Listening, Thinking, Being: Toward an Ethics of Attunement* (University Park: Pennsylvania State University Press, 2014).
38. Ronald C. Arnett, "Through a Glass, Darkly," *Journal of Communication and Religion* 29, no. 1 (2006): 1–17.
39. Anderson, Baxter, and Cissna, "Texts and Contexts of Dialogue," 6.
40. Anderson, Baxter, and Cissna, "Texts and Contexts of Dialogue," 6.
41. Maurice Friedman, *The Hidden Human Image* (New York: Dell, 1974), 283, emphasis original.
42. Ronald C. Arnett, "Martin Buber's Theopolitical Discourse of Religious Socialism," *Journal of Communication and Religion* 10, no. 2 (1987): 18–19.
43. Ronald C. Arnett, Janie M. Harden Fritz, and Leeanne M. Bell, *Communication Ethics Literacy* (Thousand Oaks, CA: Sage, 2009), 55.
44. Douglas Groothuis, *Christian Apologetics: A Comprehensive Case for Biblical Faith* (Downers Grove, IL: IVP Academic, 2011), 24.
45. Arnett, "Through a Glass, Darkly," 1.
46. Percy, *Signposts*, 419.
47. Arnett, Fritz, and Bell, *Communication Ethics Literacy*, 64.
48. Percy, *Cosmos*, 85 n.
49. Percy, *Cosmos*, 85.
50. Charles Sanders Peirce, *Philosophical Writings of Peirce*, ed. J. Buchler (Mineola, NY: Dover Publications, 1955), 91.
51. J. P. Telotte, "Charles Peirce and Walker Percy: From Semiotic to Narrative," *Southern Quarterly* 18, no. 3 (1980): 71.
52. Mats Bergman, "Experience, Purpose, and the Value of Vagueness: On C. S. Peirce's Contribution to the Philosophy of Communication," *Communication Theory* 19 (2009): 251–52.
53. Percy, *Cosmos*, 95.
54. Samway, *A Thief of Peirce*, 130.

55. Isaac E. Catt makes a similar application of Thirdness in his book *Embodiment in the Semiotic Matrix: Communicology in Peirce, Dewey, Bateson, and Bourdieu* (Madison, NJ: Fairleigh Dickinson University Press, 2017).
56. Percy, *Cosmos*, 96.
57. Percy, *Cosmos*, 96.
58. Percy, *Cosmos*, 101.
59. Percy, *Cosmos*, 99.
60. Percy, *Cosmos*, 95.
61. C. K. Ogden and I. A. Richards, *The Meaning of Meaning: A Study of the Influence of Language upon Thought and of the Science of Symbolism* (New York: Harcourt, Brace & World, 1949), 11. See also Percy, *Message*, 42; and Robert L. Scott, review of *The Message in the Bottle*, by Walker Percy, *Communication Quarterly* 24 (1976): 52.
62. Percy, *Cosmos*, 91. See, for example, Julia Scarano de Mendonça et al., "Mother–Child and Father–Child Interactional Synchrony in Dyadic and Triadic Interactions," *Sex Roles* 64 (2011): 132; Juan-Carlos Gómez, "The Ontogeny of Triadic Cooperative Interactions with Humans in an Infant Gorilla," *Interaction Studies* 11, no. 3 (2010): 353; L. Brooks Hill and John M. McGrath, "Communication within the Triadic Context: Intercultural Prospects," *Intercultural Communication Studies* 17, no. 4 (2008): 52.
63. Telotte, "Charles Peirce and Walker Percy," 67.
64. Percy, *Cosmos*, 108.
65. Ronald C. Arnett, "Communicative Ethics: The Phenomenological Sense of Semioethics," *Language & Dialogue* 7, no. 1 (2017): 82; Graham D. Bodie and Nathan Crick, "Listening, Hearing, Sensing: Three Modes of Being and the Phenomenology of Charles Sanders Peirce," *Communication Theory* 24 (2014): 112–13; Nathan Crick and Graham D. Bodie, "'I Says to Myself, Says I': Charles Sanders Peirce on the Components of Dialogue," *Communication Theory* 26 (2016): 283; Sandra E. Moriarty, "Abduction: A Theory of Visual Interpretation," *Communication Theory* 6, no. 2 (1996): 168; Peter Skagestad, "Peirce's Semeiotic Model of the Mind," in *The Cambridge Companion to Peirce*, ed. Cheryl Misak (Cambridge: Cambridge University Press, 2004), 242–44.
66. As cited in Wayne Woodward, "Triadic Communication as Transactional Participation," *Critical Studies in Mass Communication* 13 (1996): 158.
67. Samway, *A Thief of Peirce*, 130–31.
68. Percy, *Cosmos*, 97.
69. Catt, *Embodiment in the Semiotic Matrix*, 19.
70. Percy, *Cosmos*, 87 n.
71. Percy, *Cosmos*, 96.
72. Percy, *Cosmos*, 97; see also Telotte, "Charles Peirce and Walker Percy," 71.
73. Percy, *Cosmos*, 96.
74. Telotte, "Charles Peirce and Walker Percy," 73; see also Skagestad, "Peirce's Semeiotic Model of the Mind," 244.
75. Percy, *Cosmos*, 96–97.

76. Telotte, "Charles Peirce and Walker Percy," 71; Skagestad, "Peirce's Semeiotic Model of the Mind," 245.

77. For an entry into the discussion surrounding Peirce, Duns Scotus, and Scholastic realism, see Ralph J. Bastian, "The 'Scholastic' Realism of C. S. Peirce," *Philosophy and Phenomenological Research* 14, no. 2 (1953): 246–49; John F. Boler, *Charles Peirce and Scholastic Realism: A Study of Peirce's Relation to John Duns Scotus* (Seattle: University of Washington Press, 1963); Claudine Engel-Tiercelin, "Vagueness and the Unity of C. S. Peirce's Realism," *Transactions of the Charles S. Peirce Society* 28, no. 1 (1992): 51–82; Edward C. Moore, "The Scholastic Realism of C. S. Peirce," *Philosophy and Phenomenological Research* 12, no. 3 (1952): 406–17.

78. Engel-Tiercelin, "Vagueness and the Unity of C. S. Peirce's Realism," 52.

79. Percy, *Cosmos*, 102 n.

80. Percy, *Cosmos*, 102 n.

81. Walker Percy, interview by Jo Gulledge, in *Conversations with Walker Percy*, ed. Lewis A. Lawson and Victor A. Kramer (Jackson: University Press of Mississippi, 1985), 285.

82. See the Author's Note in the front matter of Percy's *The Message in the Bottle* for the titles of the journals in which Percy's articles first appeared. *The Message in the Bottle* is a compilation of these essays.

83. See, for example, John F. Desmond, *At the Crossroads: Ethical and Religious Themes in the Writings of Walker Percy* (Troy, NY: Whitston, 1997); Mary Deems Howland, *The Gift of the Other: Gabriel Marcel's Concept of Intersubjectivity in Walker Percy's Novels* (Pittsburgh: Duquesne University Press, 1989); and Allen Pridgen, *Walker Percy's Sacramental Landscapes: The Search in the Desert* (Selingsgrove, PA: Susquehanna University Press, 2000).

84. Robert L. Scott, review of *The Message in the Bottle*, by Walker Percy, *Communication Quarterly* 24 (1976): 51–52.

85. Lesley A. Rex, "Loss of the Creature: The Obscuring of Inclusivity in Classroom Discourse," *Communication Education* 52, no. 1 (2003): 30–46.

86. Craig E. Mattson, "Impossible to Say: Walker Percy's Moviegoing Epideictic in Crisis Conditions," in *Communication Ethics and Crisis: Negotiating Differences in Public and Private Spheres*, ed. S. Alyssa Groom and J. M. H. Fritz (Madison, NJ: Fairleigh Dickinson University Press), 13.

87. Wayne Woodward, "Triadic Communication as Transactional Participation," *Critical Studies in Mass Communication* 13 (1996): 158–59; Clifford G. Christians, "Technology and Triadic Theories of Mediation," in *Rethinking Media, Religion, and Culture*, ed. Stewart M. Hoover and Knut Lundby (Thousand Oaks, CA: Sage, 1997), 74–75.

88. Corey Anton, "On the Nonlinearity of Human Communication: Insatiability, Context, Form," *Atlantic Journal of Communication* 15, no. 2 (2007): 83. See also Corey Anton, *Communication Uncovered: General Semantics and Media Ecology* (Fort Worth, TX: Institute of General Semantics, 2011), 65–67.

89. Jennifer J. Cobb, "A Spiritual Experience of Cyberspace," *Technology in Society* 21 (1999): 393.

90. Stephanie Bennett, "Jacques Ellul and the Inefficiency of Friendship: Social Life and *The Technological Society*," *Explorations in Media Ecology* 15 (2016): 254.

91. Patrick H. Samway, *Walker Percy: A Life* (New York: Farrar, Straus & Giroux, 1997), 331.

92. Samway, *A Thief of Peirce*, 182.

93. Thomas A. Sebeok, "Semiotics in the United States," in *The Semiotic Web 1989*, ed. Thomas A. Sebeok and Jean Umiker-Sebeok (Berlin: Mouton de Gruyter, 1990), 305–7.

94. Jaime Nubiola, "Walker Percy and Charles S. Peirce: Abduction and Language" (paper presented at the VI International Congress of the International Association for Semiotic Studies, Guadalajara, Mexico, July 1997). This paper was later published in Spanish in the conference proceedings, but here I cite the English version.

95. Skagestad, "Peirce's Semeiotic Model of the Mind," 244–45.

96. Telotte, "Charles Peirce and Walker Percy," 72.

97. Percy, *Cosmos*, 106.

98. Martin Buber, *Between Man and Man*, trans. Ronald Gregor Smith (New York: Collier Books, 1985), 92; Emmanuel Levinas, *Ethics and Infinity: Conversations with Philippe Nemo*, trans. Richard A. Cohen (Pittsburgh, PA: Duquesne University Press, 1985), 98.

99. Arnett, "A Dialogic Ethic 'between' Buber and Levinas," 88.

100. Arnett, "Communicative Ethics," 83.

101. Ellul, *Humiliation of the Word*, 50.

102. Deborah Eicher-Catt and Isaac E. Catt, "Pierce [sic] and Cassirer, 'Life' and 'Spirit': A Communicology of Religion," *Journal of Communication and Religion* 36, no. 2 (2013): 95.

103. Arnett, "Through a Glass, Darkly," 5; Simon Wiesenthal, *The Sunflower: On the Possibilities and Limits of Forgiveness* (New York: Schocken Books, 1997), 9.

104. Peirce, *Philosophical Writings,* 151.

105. Eicher-Catt and Catt, "Communicology of Religion," 81.

106. Moriarty, "Abduction," 180–84.

107. Walker Percy, interview by Marcus Smith, in *Conversations with Walker Percy,* ed. Lewis A. Lawson and Victor A. Kramer (Jackson: University Press of Mississippi, 1985), 133–34.

108. Percy, *Message*, 321.

109. Percy, *Message*, 322.

110. Nubiola, "Walker Percy and Charles S. Peirce," 7.

111. Eicher-Catt and Catt, "Communicology of Religion," 84.

112. Desmond, *At the Crossroads*, 139; Percy, *Cosmos*, 101.

113. Percy, *Cosmos*, 97.

114. Crick and Bodie, "'I Says to Myself,'" 277.

115. Percy, *Cosmos*, 178.

116. Percy, *Cosmos*, 178.

117. Percy, *Cosmos*, 110–13.

118. Percy, *Cosmos*, 125.

119. Percy, *Cosmos*, 157.

120. Percy, interview by Jo Gulledge, 297.
121. Percy, *Signposts*, 314.
122. Percy, *Message*, 148.
123. Percy, *Signposts*, 369.
124. Percy, *Signposts*, 366.
125. Allen Pridgen, *Walker Percy's Sacramental Landscapes: The Search in the Desert* (Selingsgrove, PA: Susquehanna University Press, 2000), 23.
126. Percy, *Signposts*, 314.
127. Percy, *Message*, 144.
128. Percy, *Message*, 144.
129. Percy, *Message*, 146.
130. Percy, *Message*, 149.
131. Percy, *Message*, 148.
132. Percy, interview by Jo Gulledge, 294.
133. Percy, *Cosmos*, 157.
134. Percy, interview by Jo Gulledge, 308.
135. Percy, *Cosmos*, 78.
136. Percy, *Cosmos*, 254.

BIBLIOGRAPHY

Anderson, Rob, Leslie A. Baxter, and Kenneth N. Cissna. "Texts and Contexts of Dialogue." In *Dialogue: Theorizing Difference in Communication Studies*, edited by Rob Anderson, Leslie A. Baxter, and Kenneth N. Cissna, 1–17. Thousand Oaks, CA: Sage, 2004.

Anton, Corey. "On the Nonlinearity of Human Communication: Insatiability, Context, Form." *Atlantic Journal of Communication* 15, no. 2 (2007): 79–102.

———. *Communication Uncovered: General Semantics and Media Ecology*. Fort Worth, TX: Institute of General Semantics, 2011.

Arneson, Pat, ed. *Perspectives on Philosophy of Communication*. West Lafayette, IN: Purdue University Press, 2007.

Arnett, Ronald C. "Martin Buber's Theopolitical Discourse of Religious Socialism." *Journal of Communication and Religion* 10, no. 2 (1987): 12–23.

———. "A Dialogic Ethic 'between' Buber and Levinas: A Responsive Ethical 'I.'" In *Dialogue: Theorizing Difference in Communication Studies*, edited by Rob Anderson, Leslie A. Baxter, and Kenneth N. Cissna, 75–90. Thousand Oaks, CA: Sage, 2004.

———. "Through a Glass, Darkly." *Journal of Communication and Religion* 29, no. 1 (2006): 1–17.

———. "Communicative Ethics: The Phenomenological Sense of Semioethics." *Language & Dialogue* 7, no. 1 (2017): 80–99. doi:10.1075/ld.7.1.06arn.

Arnett, Ronald C., Janie M. Harden Fritz, and Leeanne M. Bell. *Communication Ethics Literacy: Dialogue and Difference*. Thousand Oaks, CA: Sage, 2009.

Arnett, Ronald C., and Gordon Nakagawa. "The Assumptive Roots of Empathic Listening: A Critique." *Communication Education* 32 (1983): 368–78.

Bakhtin, Mikhail. "Discourse in Life and Discourse in Art." In *Landmark Essays on Voice and Writing*, edited by Peter Elbow, 3–10. Mahwah, NJ: Lawrence Erlbaum, 1994.

Bastian, Ralph J. "The 'Scholastic' Realism of C. S. Peirce." *Philosophy and Phenomenological Research* 14, no. 2 (1953): 246–49.

Bennett, Stephanie. "Jacques Ellul and the Inefficiency of Friendship: Social Life and *The Technological Society*." *Explorations in Media Ecology* 15 (2016): 243–60. doi:10.1386/eme.15.3-4.243_1.

Bergman, Mats. "Experience, Purpose, and the Value of Vagueness: On C. S. Peirce's Contribution to the Philosophy of Communication." *Communication Theory* 19 (2009): 248–77. doi:10.1111/j.1468-2885.2009.01343.x.

Bodie, Graham D., and Nathan Crick. "Listening, Hearing, Sensing: Three Modes of Being and the Phenomenology of Charles Sanders Peirce." *Communication Theory* 24 (2014): 105–23. doi:10.1111/comt.12032.

Boler, John F. *Charles Peirce and Scholastic Realism: A Study of Peirce's Relation to John Duns Scotus*. Seattle: University of Washington Press, 1963.

Buber, Martin. *Between Man and Man*. Translated by Ronald Gregor Smith. New York: Collier Books, 1985.

———. *I and Thou*. Translated by Ronald Gregor Smith. New York: Continuum, 2004.

Catt, Isaac E. *Embodiment in the Semiotic Matrix: Communicology in Peirce, Dewey, Bateson, and Bourdieu*. Madison, NJ: Fairleigh Dickinson University Press, 2017.

Christians, Clifford G. "Technology and Triadic Theories of Mediation." In *Rethinking Media, Religion, and Culture*, edited by Stewart M. Hoover and Knut Lundby, 65–82. Thousand Oaks, CA: Sage, 1997.

Cobb, Jennifer J. "A Spiritual Experience of Cyberspace." *Technology in Society* 21 (1999): 393–407.

Crick, Nathan, and Graham D. Bodie. "'I Says to Myself, Says I': Charles Sanders Peirce on the Components of Dialogue." *Communication Theory* 26 (2016): 273–89. doi:10.1111/comt.12092.

de Mendonça, Julia Scarano, Louise Cossette, Francis F. Strayer, and France Gravel. "Mother–Child and Father–Child Interactional Synchrony in Dyadic and Triadic Interactions." *Sex Roles* 64 (2011): 132–42. doi:10.1007/s11199-010-9875-2.

Desmond, John F. *At the Crossroads: Ethical and Religions Themes in the Writings of Walker Percy*. Troy, NY: Whitston, 1997.

Eicher-Catt, Deborah, and Isaac E. Catt. "Pierce [sic] and Cassirer, 'Life' and 'Spirit': A Communicology of Religion." *Journal of Communication and Religion* 36, no. 2 (2013): 77–103.

Ellul, Jacques. *The Technological Society*. Translated by John Wilkinson. New York: Vintage, 1964.

———. *The Humiliation of the Word*. Translated by Joyce Main Hanks. Grand Rapids, MI: Eerdmans, 1985.

Engel-Tiercelin, Claudine. "Vagueness and the Unity of C. S. Peirce's Realism." *Transactions of the Charles S. Peirce Society* 28, no. 1 (1992): 51–82.

Friedman, Maurice. *The Hidden Human Image*. New York: Dell, 1974.

Gómez, Juan-Carlos. "The Ontogeny of Triadic Cooperative Interactions with Humans in an Infant Gorilla." *Interaction Studies* 11, no. 3 (2010): 353–79.

Groothuis, Douglas. *Christian Apologetics: A Comprehensive Case for Biblical Faith*. Downers Grove, IL: IVP Academic, 2011.

Hill, L. Brooks, and John M. McGrath. "Communication within the Triadic Context: Intercultural Prospects." *Intercultural Communication Studies* 17, no. 4 (2008): 52–67.

Howland, Mary Deems. *The Gift of the Other: Gabriel Marcel's Concept of Intersubjectivity in Walker Percy's Novels*. Pittsburgh, PA: Duquesne University Press, 1989.

Lawson, Lewis A., and Victor A. Kramer, eds. *Conversations with Walker Percy*. Jackson: University Press of Mississippi, 1985.

Levinas, Emmanuel. *Ethics and Infinity: Conversations with Philippe Nemo*. Translated by Richard A. Cohen. Pittsburgh, PA: Duquesne University Press, 1985.

Lipari, Lisbeth. *Listening, Thinking, Being: Toward an Ethics of Attunement*. University Park: Pennsylvania State University Press, 2014.

Mattson, Craig E. "Impossible to Say: Walker Percy's Moviegoing Epideictic in Crisis Conditions." In *Communication Ethics and Crisis: Negotiating Differences in Public and Private Spheres*, edited by S. Alyssa Groom and J. M. H. Fritz, 11–24. Madison, NJ: Fairleigh Dickinson University Press, 2012.

Moore, Edward C. "The Scholastic Realism of C. S. Peirce." *Philosophy and Phenomenological Research* 12, no. 3 (1952): 406–17.

Moriarty, Sandra E. "Abduction: A Theory of Visual Interpretation." *Communication Theory* 6, no. 2 (1996): 167–87.

Nubiola, Jaime. "Walker Percy and Charles S. Peirce: Abduction and Language." Paper presented at the VI International Congress of the International Association for Semiotic Studies, Guadalajara, Mexico, July 1997.

Ogden, C. K., and I. A. Richards. *The Meaning of Meaning: A Study of the Influence of Language upon Thought and of the Science of Symbolism*. New York: Harcourt, Brace & World, 1949.

Ong, Walter J. *The Presence of the Word: Some Prolegomena for Cultural and Religious History*. Minneapolis: University of Minnesota Press, 1981.

Peirce, Charles Sanders. *Philosophical Writings of Peirce*. Edited by Justus Buchler. Mineola, NY: Dover Publications, 1955.

Percy, Walker. "Symbol as Need." *Thought: Fordham University Quarterly* 29 (1954): 381–90.

———. *The Message in the Bottle*. New York: Farrar, Straus & Giroux, 1975.

———. *Lost in the Cosmos*. New York: Farrar, Straus & Giroux, 1983.

———. "The Reentry Option: An Interview with Walker Percy." Interview by Jo Gulledge. In *Conversations with Walker Percy*, edited by Lewis A. Lawson and Victor A. Kramer, 284–308. Jackson: University of Mississippi Press, 1985.

———. "Talking about Talking: An Interview with Walker Percy." Interview by Marcus Smith. In *Conversations with Walker Percy*, edited by Lewis A. Lawson and Victor A. Kramer, 129–45. Jackson: University of Mississippi Press, 1985.

———. *Signposts in a Strange Land*. Edited by Patrick Samway. New York: Farrar, Straus & Giroux, 1991.

Pridgen, Allen. *Walker Percy's Sacramental Landscapes: The Search in the Desert*. Selingsgrove, PA: Susquehanna University Press, 2000.

Rex, Lesley A. "Loss of the Creature: The Obscuring of Inclusivity in Classroom Discourse." *Communication Education* 52, no. 1 (2003): 30–46.

Samway, Patrick H., ed. *A Thief of Peirce: The Letters of Kenneth Laine Ketner and Walker Percy*. Jackson: University Press of Mississippi, 1995.

———. *Walker Percy: A Life*. New York: Farrar, Straus & Giroux, 1997.

Scott, Robert L. Review of *The Message in the Bottle*, by Walker Percy. *Communication Quarterly* 24 (1976): 51–52.

Sebeok, Thomas A. "Semiotics in the United States." In *The Semiotic Web 1989*, edited by Thomas A. Sebeok and Jean Umiker-Sebeok, 275–398. Berlin: Mouton de Gruyter, 1990.

Skagestad, Peter. "Peirce's Semeiotic Model of the Mind." In *The Cambridge Companion to Peirce*, edited by Cheryl Misak, 241–56. Cambridge: Cambridge University Press, 2004.

Telotte, J. P. "Charles Peirce and Walker Percy: From Semiotic to Narrative." *Southern Quarterly* 18, no. 3 (1980): 65–79.

Wiesenthal, Simon. *The Sunflower: On the Possibilities and Limits of Forgiveness*. New York: Schocken Books, 1997.

Woodward, Wayne. "Triadic Communication as Transactional Participation." *Critical Studies in Mass Communication* 13 (1996): 155–74.

Chapter 6

Pastoral Preaching

Prophetic and Priestly Rhetoric in Congregational Leadership

Steven Tramel Gaines

Half a century after the assassination of civil rights leader Martin Luther King Jr., social crises still plague his nation. Public demonstrations protest systemic inequalities, and opponents of such cries deny social problems and condemn activists' strategies. Preachers must choose how to communicate in this chaos and can learn from past preachers who spoke prophetically while not ignoring the necessity of pastoral sensitivity.

In April 1968, responding to King's assassination, John A. Scott Sr. preached a sermon, "The Mind of Christ," for the Church of Christ at White Station in Memphis. This essay claims that the sermon prophetically called for repentance and was shaped by social privilege; that the sermon reminded listeners of their privilege and challenged them to repent of their contributions to inequalities; and that Scott, despite the blunting of his prophetic rhetoric, challenged his congregation's practice of ignoring racial and economic privileges and injustices. Those claims develop through four sections. The first one provides a few details about Scott's rhetorical situation. The second overviews recent literature about prophetic rhetoric and whiteness, especially white fragility.[1] The third, using those interpretive lenses, analyzes the sermon through a close reading.[2] The final section, based on that analysis and homiletical literature, presents pastoral preaching as a combination of prophetic and priestly rhetoric. In rhetorical analysis, I must critique an artifact's elements that might seem admirable as well as those that might seem less than ideal. I do so here with utmost respect for Scott's willingness to speak prophetically when tempted to remain silent. Also, I acknowledge that we and our word choices are unavoidably influenced by our chronological and cultural locations.

SITUATION: MEMPHIS IN 1968

Most sanitation workers in 1968 Memphis were black, and their bosses were white. The workers, who labored long hours in filthy, unsafe situations with flawed equipment and inadequate pay and were not allowed in the office building to drink water or wash their hands, had complained about the conditions for about five years but had been ignored by city officials.[3] On February 1, 1968, a defective garbage compacting truck killed two workers seeking shelter from rain.[4] More than a thousand of their colleagues went on strike, and the mayor condemned the strike as illegal.[5]

King traveled to Memphis to assist the striking sanitation workers. After a few marchers damaged property during an otherwise peaceful demonstration, he encouraged his listeners to "keep the issues where they are" and explained:

> The issue is injustice. The issue is the refusal of Memphis to be fair and honest in its dealings with its public servants, who happen to be sanitation workers. Now, we've got to keep attention on that. That's always the problem with a little violence. You know what happened the other day, and the press dealt only with the window-breaking. I read the articles. They very seldom got around to mentioning the fact that one thousand, three hundred sanitation workers are on strike, and that Memphis is not being fair to them, and that Mayor Loeb is in dire need of a doctor. They didn't get around to that.[6]

King died the next day after being shot by an assassin.[7]

Journalists were not the only people remembering the violence by a few rather than the systemic injustice, the striking sanitation workers, or the city's refusal to consider their concerns. Churches also tended to perceive the recent events as random violence instead of cries of injustice. Scott challenged that perception.

LITERATURE: PROPHETIC RHETORIC AND WHITE FRAGILITY

Prophetic preaching is a subcategory of prophetic rhetoric, and scholars variously define and describe prophetic rhetoric and prophetic preaching.[8] Some discussions of prophetic preaching treat Old Testament prophetic rhetoric as a blueprint.[9] Others perceive prophetic ministry in the Old Testament as a precursor of, not a blueprint for, more recent prophetic proclamation.[10] This analysis of Scott's sermon accepts the second option because interpreting the Old Testament prophetic literature as a blueprint misses subsequent historical development of the prophetic tradition(s). Criticism of twentieth-century prophetic rhetoric requires a grounding in analysis based on more recent artifacts.

Based on his close reading of nineteenth-century discourse, Andre Johnson defines prophetic rhetoric as "discourse grounded in the sacred and rooted in a community experience that offers a critique of existing communities and traditions by charging and challenging society to live up to the ideals espoused while offering celebration and hope for a brighter future."[11] In other words, prophetic rhetoric, grounded in sacred foundations, calls for change.[12] This section further explains prophetic rhetoric by identifying its structure and responding to possible confusion. In preparation for an analysis of prophetic rhetoric by a white preacher, the section also presents whiteness and white fragility.

Prophetic rhetoric occurs in a four-part structure. "First, speakers must ground prophetic discourse in what the speaker[s] and the audience[s] deem as sacred. . . . People who adopt prophetic personas cannot do so as rugged individuals, but must root their 'prophecy' within communal traditions, beliefs and expectations."[13] The second element of the structure is "consciousness-raising through a sharing or an announcement of the real situation. . . . Thus, instead of unveiling the hidden, the prophet reveals the hidden in plain sight" to state "the obvious that others might be afraid to speak."[14] In this consciousness-raising, a prophetic communicator wants the audience to reflect on the revealed "situation with the hope of changing its ways."[15] The third part of the structure "is the charge, challenge, critique, judgment, or warning of the audience(s) . . . usually . . . by offering reinterpretations of what is sacred and casting a vision of the world not as it is, but as it could and should be."[16] Fourth "is the offer of encouragement and hope."[17] Johnson notes two kinds of hope in this kind of rhetoric. The first is "an eschatological hope . . . a hope that things will get better in some afterlife or some other spiritual transformation to some other world," and the second is "a 'pragmatic hope' . . . a more 'this-worldly' and earthly type . . . that grounds itself in the prophet's belief in the Divine to make right order in this world . . . a hope that sees a new day coming."[18]

In a previously published essay, I responded to a couple of areas of possible confusion about prophetic rhetoric.[19] First, it is sometimes assumed that prophetic rhetoric foretells coming events. Johnson's definition, however, states that prophetic rhetoric calls for change and does not mention prediction. Study of prophetic rhetoric today has roots in ancient Hebrew literature, in which prophetic communicators predicted at times, but not always.

Their focus was change, and change remains the focus in prophetic rhetoric today.[20] The second possible confusion is the presupposition that prophetic rhetoric requires a specific position or title. However, rhetoric may be prophetic even if the rhetor does not fill any official role. According to rhetoric scholar Christopher Hobson, prophetic rhetoric is "a kind of speech or writing that occurred to its practitioners as they turned to questions that arose in community life."[21] Similarly, this paper does not attempt to determine whether Scott was a prophet. Instead, it reveals ways in which he communicated in a prophetic manner.

Because the prophetic rhetoric in Scott's sermon was spoken by a white preacher in a white congregation, my analysis of that sermon draws from literature about whiteness, especially white fragility. Communication scholars Thomas Nakayama and Robert Krizek write that "the 'white' social practice of not discussing whiteness is especially disturbing."[22] Multicultural education scholar Robin DiAngelo explains:

> White people in North America live in a social environment that protects and insulates them from race-based stress. This insulated environment of racial protection builds white expectations for racial comfort while at the same time lowering the ability to tolerate racial stress, leading to what I call White Fragility. White Fragility is a state in which even a minimum amount of racial stress becomes intolerable, triggering a range of defensive moves.[23]

White fragility is a tendency to experience difficulty in tolerating discomfort related to racial conflict. This fragility can result in a denial of racial identities. Whiteness "is often invisible or taken for granted, it is rooted in social and economic privilege, and its meaning and import are highly situational."[24] White identity "is more taken-for-granted, more naturalized and normalized than other racial identities."[25] Because of that naturalization and normalization, "white hegemony permeates American political, regional, and national identity resulting in the manifestation of marginalization and hierarchy."[26] Due to white hegemony's pervasiveness, white people tend not to recognize their racial group's identity and privilege and, as such, resist communication about racial conflict. Sociologist Amanda Lewis notes the absence of a singular whiteness experienced identically by all people racialized as white.[27] In line with that observation, this essay does not attempt to force Scott's rhetoric into a preconceived model but instead seeks what his words reveal about his own experience of whiteness and his understanding of his listeners' experiences of whiteness.

ANALYSIS: A RESPONSE TO SOCIAL CRISIS

Scott's sermon quickly mentioned the historical, cultural, and geographical context in which he spoke: "The last few weeks we have, here in Memphis, undergone great upheavals. Emotions have been wrought up and tragedies of one sort or another have occurred that have had far-reaching consequences in our lives and in the lives of our fellow countrymen."[28] Memphis had experienced chaos since King's death on April 4. Riots had rocked the city. Properties had been damaged and destroyed. Interracial relations had become even more tense than they had been previously. Accusations were flying in multiple directions, and many Memphians were confused about what had happened and what would happen.

The confusion and chaos tried Scott's soul through a bewildering combination of obligation and hesitancy to speak:

> It is during times like these when one who preaches must be reminded of the tradition in which he speaks. It is the tradition of the prophets, a tradition of the apostles, to speak where one is tempted to remain silent, but it is not easy to do so. Whether it be to speak or to remain silent when people are asking questions about Christian attitudes in times that are troubled like these. It is difficult to remain silent; in fact it is impossible. . . . It's hard to speak and it's hard to remain silent.

His experience of this obligation-hesitancy dilemma had deep roots in biblical literature. Moses and Jonah had hesitated but fulfilled their obligations to speak in different ways. Immediately following the crucifixion of Jesus, his closest followers had hidden because of their hesitancy, fear, and doubt but eventually spoke. Scott grounded his rhetoric in that tradition of prophets and apostles, and he concluded that refusing to speak was infeasible. A national crisis with a Memphian center had interrupted this preacher's normal ministry, and he could not resist a frightening call to preach prophetically.

Scott anticipated objections to his prophetic call to repentance, knowing that some members of his congregation might frown or even flee in reaction to talk about race. He responded in advance to that possible resistance by anchoring his message in words of Jesus: "Whosoever shall be ashamed of me and my words, his father shall be ashamed of him in the Day of Judgment" (Mark 8:38). Despite his pastoral experience, ecclesial office, and doctoral degree, Scott drew from the credibility that his listeners assigned to Jesus. By citing Jesus, Scott indirectly told the congregation that he had chosen to respond to King's assassination because words of Jesus had convinced him to do so, not because he was trying to cause trouble based on his own opinions.

Scott also prepared his audience for the coming call for change, saying that following Jesus "means that we constantly have to be adjusting our life so that we do not drift off course." Scott illustrated that claim with a metaphor: "There is an instrument in an airplane, which will help the pilot keep on course to his destination even when the winds or other factors may blow him off his course." Then he explained:

> And so with Christian people, there are times when, due to the forces of society, due to the emotions of upheaval, due to the problems that men face from day to day, it's easy to get off course. It's easy to drift ever so slightly and never be aware of being off course. So the pilot has to keep a constant check to stay on course. . . . we need constantly to go back to the Word, constantly go back to the message of Christ and adjust our lives accordingly. Everyone who is a follower of Christ is compelled to take his position behind Christ and let Christ lead the way wherever that may go.

Scott anchored his anti-status quo sermon in the religious establishment's sacred foundations.

Although he had drawn credibility from Jesus, Scott also spoke of his own competence: "And certainly one must do this with all humility. I feel I stand on secure ground when it comes to studying the Bible and making comments and practical applications to the everyday, work-a-day world." He appealed to his congregation's assumption that a preacher should combine competent biblical interpretation and application with humility. Claiming that blend of competence and character was crucial for preparing the listeners for a message that had potential to bring accusations of sloppy exegesis and perhaps even a "holier than thou" attitude.

Following the introduction, Scott spoke of Jesus to establish a foundation for teachings in later parts of the sermon. He claimed that Jesus was a servant to all people and that he was a person of compassion. This section presented the sermon's guiding question: "Whom did Christ serve?" Scott clearly stated his method for answering the question: "I made an effort to select the passages and the lessons and the examples and the parables and the words of Christ that would give me some guidance and more detail." Instead of leaving listeners to assume that he was speaking only his own opinions, Scott added to his claim of credibility, indicating yet again that what he was about to say would be difficult for his audience to accept.

In response to the guiding question, Scott presented two answers. First, Jesus served people experiencing various diseases. Second, he served marginalized, despised outcasts. Summarizing the answers, Scott mentioned "Christ's concern for the underdog, for the poor, halt, maimed and the blind" and said, "We are told He came to preach the Gospel to the poor, to heal the broken-hearted, to deliver the captives, to set up liberty for those that were bruised . . . the lower classes in society." That statement set the stage for reflecting on the cultural situation following the assassination of a man who, because of his Christian faith, had pursued the mission of caring for people suffering poverty, pain, and various types of captivity.

Scott presented three hindrances to Christians' willingness to follow Jesus in caring for those despised by the establishment. The first was pride and its close relative, self-righteousness. Scott did not speak of pride and self-righteousness in terms only of their historical, biblical manifestations. Instead, he contemporized them, stating that, if physically present in 1968, Jesus would have spoken against those vices. The contemporizing pushed the audience to consider their own self-righteousness and pride, especially in connection to racial and economic inequalities in Memphis. In response to the vices, Scott prescribed self-denial, citing Matthew 16:24: "Whoever will come after Me . . . let him deny himself, take up his cross and follow me." Scott identified two meanings of self-denial: (1) "that we sacrifice and that we do without things" and (2) "that we deny the existence of the self and put Christ in ourselves and we no longer stand independently and so proud in our own right. But rather that we as individuals, have been put to death in Christ, in the character of Christ, and that the thinking of Christ rules in the place of the ego." Then Scott quoted Luke 1:52 and referenced Luke 20:41–47, condemning rich people who enjoyed their luxuries at the expense of people suffering poverty. His words surely led his listeners to think of King's work on behalf of sanitation workers protesting unjust wages.

The second hindrance was hypocrisy. Instead of hypocrisy in general, Scott spoke of hypocrisy in relation to self-righteousness and pride:

> These commandments are difficult to obey, "He that hath two coats, let him impart to him that hath none. He that hath meat, likewise" (Luke 3:11). What does this mean? Oh it's an easy matter to rationalize and give excuses, and say, "Lord, we don't like to face up to these issues. Our way of life is different. We don't like to face up to pride, and hypocrisy, or we don't like to have to deny ourselves in certain ways."

Scott continued:

> Another parable to influence our character: the rich man and his barns (Luke 12). The contrast here is obvious. This is a well-known parable to all concerned. After this Jesus talked about another rich man who made a great supper and the guests didn't come to the supper as he had invited them. And so the master told his servants to "Go into the streets and into the lanes and you bring in the poor and the maimed, the halt, and the blind." And they went and brought in these people. And then he said, "Well, the house is not full yet. We're going to eat the

feast, but first go into the hedge ways and into the by-paths and you bring in, as it were, dregs from society and they can eat, too."

By citing these sacred foundations, Scott spurred his listeners to think about the reign of the rich in their own city, an economic inequality that was racially created and that had produced the turmoil that had led to King's death.

The third hindrance to having compassion on "lower classes" was supremacy of one social group over another:

> Jesus, one time said those on His right hand would be saved. And those on the right hand will be those who, He said "Have seen me when I was hungry, when I was thirsty, and when I was a stranger, when I was naked, when I was sick, when I was in prison, and they attended me when I was in these conditions" (Matthew 25:35[–36]). But people fail to see Christ in the lowliest and so seek out a rationale in resisting the Gospel saying, "Lord, this doesn't apply to me." So we speak out and say, "Lord, we don't understand. When did we see you in these circumstances?" And He says "Inasmuch as you did it not unto the least of these . . . the very least . . . " Pick out the least in society then, and we'll see where we have an obligation, where we've been passing over an obligation and a responsibility. God is our Judge.

These words revealed white fragility's influence on hermeneutics and ethics. Although the term "white fragility" did not exist in 1968, the human thought and behavior the term describes were in full force. White people's discomfort in hearing, reading, and talking about racial conflict produced their refusal, or perhaps inability, to acknowledge their contributions to social inequalities. That ignorance, or ignoring, shaped the listeners' interpretation and personal application of biblical words and produced in those interpreters an assumption that the call to care for the "hungry . . . thirsty . . . stranger . . . naked . . . sick" and imprisoned did not apply to them. In response to that way of reading and living sacred texts, Scott boldly asserted that the congregation had failed to live up to "an obligation and a responsibility" to care for people in need. Scott even claimed that caring for people lacking food, clothes, belonging, and freedom was the core of Christian doctrine. By not speaking or acting in support of under-resourced Memphians, the congregation had resisted the gospel. In reminding his listeners that "God is our Judge," Scott added an eschatological dimension to his prophetic accusation that his people had abandoned a divine mandate.

Resistance to care for those considered low, according to Scott, was resistance to gospel. He quoted words of Jesus in Luke 6:24, "But woe unto you who are rich," and indicated that the listeners tended not to perceive themselves as rich. Scott countered that tendency: "We have to talk to ourselves if we are honest. We have to talk to old number one." Scott was careful not to condemn his congregation without condemning himself: "In Christ's category of the rich I have to talk to myself." The preacher and the congregation were wealthy compared to the sanitation workers for whom King had traveled to Memphis. Revealing the economic animosity between races in Memphis in 1968, Scott cited more words of Jesus:

> "Woe unto you that are full now for ye shall hunger" (Luke 6:25). "Woe unto you that laugh now, for you shall mourn and weep. Woe unto you when all men shall speak well of you, for in the same manner did their fathers speak of the false prophets. But I say unto you that hear, 'Love your enemies, do good to them that hate you'" (Matthew 5:44).

Pushing his congregation to localize their ethics of love instead of hate and of caring for the poor and hungry, Scott asked,

> Does this mean that we do it only from a distance? Does it mean that we can show concern for those of the Negro race by sending two men to Africa as missionaries and spend 11, 12, or $13,000 to reach those, but have no obligation to those in our own city or in our own block or who are working for us in our homes? . . . or in our own church building?

He indicted his audience with those words, specifying both the population and the location of his call to action. He did not speak only about an abstract love or a universalized compassion. Instead, he localized the topic, disallowing his listeners to ignore the challenge as inapplicable to them and forcing them to acknowledge, even if only privately, their participation in the current discord in Memphis and their responsibility to respond as agents of mercy:

> "Be ye merciful even as your Father is merciful." Look at the standard of mercy that Jesus gave to us. This is the standard of mercy that God had toward us and that He has toward all the world, including the garbage men of Memphis. . . . This is mercy to the inth degree and it's a deeper mercy than I have, but I will have to work for it, I have to strive for it and I have to keep that as an end and a goal in view.

Mercy was an ideal, not yet achieved by the preacher or the congregation. The sermon called them to live out their biblical commitments. With those words, the preacher again attempted to avoid accusations of being "holier than thou." He placed himself with his congregation, sharing the condemnation and challenge.

Then Scott referenced the Golden Rule, a sacred foundation that the congregation deeply knew but did not widely practice:

> All of the children in the lower grades can give you that from memory in one form or another. We can live all of our lives and fall short of the applications of this Golden Rule as Christ intended it. It's simple. It means we have to put ourselves in the other fellow's shoes. Now it's an easy [matter] to put ourselves in the shoes of those standing beside us, those that are our closest friends. It's an easy [matter] to love those who love us; it's an easy [matter] to attend to those that already have been showing an inclination to help us. But it's more difficult, isn't it, to love one's enemies. It's more difficult to put ourselves in the shoes of others—the downtrodden and the outcast—but we have to, we have to.

The white, middle-class congregation struggled to live out the Golden Rule with less-resourced Memphians who differed from the congregation's majority not only in economic status, but also in racial identity.

Recognizing the deeply connected problems of economic and racial inequality was difficult and required social awareness. Scott said, "I have neither the skill nor the knowledge to be able to determine and to explain the involvements of a situation like this. But I think that because of the very position that Christians occupy, they need to have their fingers on the pulse of society." He acknowledged that white Memphians tended to ignore cultural conflict and social inequality but needed to be more attentive.

After mentioning the widespread hatred in the nation, Scott spoke of a moral problem. Specifically, he referenced conflict about the Vietnam war: "The hawks complain that we are not killing enough Viet Cong, while doves say that we are killing the women and children and babies needlessly." Maybe his listeners noticed that he, even if unknowingly, called King a dove, a symbol of the Holy Spirit.[29]

Then Scott said three times that "something is wrong" with a form of Christianity unable to foster peace in a culture of conflict and violence. With an idealized understanding of history, he said about the closest followers of Jesus, "A long time ago only 12 men, certainly a minority in society, were able to turn the world upside down for Christ," and continued: "when there are hundreds of thousands of people who wear the name of Christ and are unable to exercise something to stop this kind of hatred that is abroad in our world, SOMETHING IS WRONG WITH THOSE [WHO] WEAR THAT NAME." Scott then said:

> The power is in the Gospel. The power is in Jesus Christ, but it gets watered down, and if we fail to bear witness and we fail to use our influence as Christians, to have our society a law-abiding society, then something is wrong. There is something dreadfully wrong with our policemen still having to wear their riot hats in the streets even after the upheaval is all over. It means that it isn't all over.

Scott nobly noted that Christians should positively influence society amid ongoing hatred, but his perception of policing was less than ideal. He neither questioned the necessity of police riot gear in a situation that had not endangered lives nor led his listeners to ask who had created the laws or for what purpose those laws had been made.[30]

Scott responded to something other than the assassination; he responded to the upheaval that had continued since the civil rights leader's death: "I can't condemn our Mayor, though he has a part to play. I can't condemn our Council, though they had a part to play, because they represent us. Each plays a part." Scott did not condemn local authorities for the upheaval, but he claimed that he and his congregation shared responsibility for the city's turmoil. He said, "We can't condemn the labor union per se, but they have a part to play also with outside leaders coming in." However, he did not address why the union needed to call in outsiders. Nevertheless, he did not let his listeners blame others for the city's chaos: "In my opinion, we have a responsibility. If we did not object, we have a responsibility, if we have not spoken out clearly and specifically. I had more than one opportunity to object and I didn't do it. And I don't mind telling you I feel, in part, guilty." Here, Scott revealed the major issue prompting his sermon, and that issue was his own guilt. His guilt arose from his failure to object to racial and economic injustice.

Shortly after that statement, however, Scott remembered the Memphis Massacre of 1866: "The north end of town and the south end of town had it out and scores of people were killed." That deracialized memory failed to note that white Memphians had slaughtered black Memphians and destroyed their property.[31] Because Scott was well educated, he may have known of the massacre's racial imbalance. His audience, however, experienced white fragility, a discomfort with discussions of racial conflict. Simultaneously, he challenged the listeners' racism and probably catered to their white fragility.

The catering did not disarm the challenge. After retelling the story of people around the year 1900, who had combatted alcoholism and prostitution with morality, Scott asserted, "But the city of churches has been washing the pot and the platter on the outside, and has left contamination on the inside." He continued, "We've cheerfully washed and garnished the sepulchers on the outside and they are gleaming white in the sun, but inwardly they are filled with dead men's bones" (Matthew 23:29). In the Memphian context, the dead men's bones were both figurative and literal. Between those two statements, Scott quoted Jeremiah 6:14 to indicate that white Christians in Memphis had claimed peace when peace had not existed; they had ignored racial and economic inequalities.

Scott's next statement confronted the practice of ignoring injustice and revealed more about the issue that primarily prompted the sermon. He challenged:

And we can deny this and deny it, but the sooner we face up to it and say "Lord, forgive us for our inactivity, for our complacency, for keeping quiet on the principles of Jesus Christ," the sooner we can go to God on our knees.

As Scott completed that statement, he mentioned the sermon's core concern: "the sooner we can go to God on our knees and ask Him to help us. That much sooner, then, we can have the guilt off our shoulders." Dealing with the preacher's and the congregation's guilt was the sermon's primary purpose.

The beginning of Scott's healing from guilt had been an experience in which the Golden Rule had come "out of the darker resources of my mind into the light of day and hit me" after he had claimed that King and other outsiders had "had no business being here." The sermon applied the Golden Rule to facilitate a similar conviction in the listeners:

Suppose my people were abused and subjugated. The only way at their disposal to show their objection and to be heard would be to march in a mass meeting. I would go to be with them. If you were those people, I would be with you. Before God, I believe I would have to admit that. I think the Golden Rule requires me to say what I would do if the situation were reversed. I'd be with you and you know that. To stand or fall I would go down with you.

Then he voiced an objection that his audience may have been thinking: "Of course, people say,—and there's a technicality here—that the strike is against the law." Although Scott did not address the formation or purpose of "the law" that had underpaid and even killed sanitation workers and then condemned them for striking, he equated those claiming the strike's illegality and the Pharisees in the New Testament:

The Pharisees were masters at quoting a law for what they wanted to do. They were masters at giving an excuse, at laying heavy burdens and laws and technicalities upon the people. So Jesus one time came to the Pharisees and said, "You are careful to tithe mint and anise and cumin, and have left undone the weightier matters of the law, justice, and mercy, and faith: but these you ought to have done and not to have left the other undone" (Matthew 23:23). I think it is analogous. I think it applies. I believe it. I may be wrong, yes, but I believe this to be true.

Here the conviction-hesitancy dilemma voiced in the sermon's introduction began to send Scott into a rhetorical swirl. His words shifted repeatedly between two views—his conviction and his audience's possible resistance to that conviction. After this "I may be wrong, yes, but I believe this to be true," he moved from speaking negatively of the Pharisees' obsession with laws to speaking negatively of riots: "There's wrong on both sides and you know

I don't uphold riots. It's wrong before God. It was a riot that took the life of Christ. No, I don't uphold riots." According to Scott's words, riots were wrong not because they were against the law but because they were contrary to God's will. That claim's data was that a riot had taken Jesus Christ's life, but the warrant was absent.[32] In other words, an explanatory bridge was missing between the claim and its evidence. Then Scott shifted again, this time from challenging privileged Memphians who had ignored racial and economic inequality to defending himself:

> I'm not presenting what could be termed by some, perhaps, a Yankee point of view. When I was a child, I can remember my mother taught me in Oklahoma in the 1930's to always use the term "colored people" when referring to the Negro race. She was from a strong southern tradition but she was a faithful sincere Christian and my father followed through and taught me respect.

Scott apparently anticipated the audience's accusation that he did not understand the South. In response to that, he reported that he had grown up in Oklahoma and had learned to respect people different from himself. Then he said, "I'm not presenting a biased sectarian viewpoint. I believe this is the attitude of Christ. So in concluding I would say we have to repent." He imagined John the Baptist and Jesus Christ preaching repentance and love in Memphis. In doing so, Scott anchored the call for change not in himself but in his community's sacred foundations, Jesus and the Bible, citing Matthew 3:8.

He continued: "it's hard to say, 'Lord, forgive me. Lord, I repent.' It's difficult, but the commands of Christ have not always been that easy." In the sermon's earlier words about hypocrisy, Scott had asked who had called Christianity easy and indicated that no one had. Here, near the sermon's end, he quoted John 6:60 about people complaining about the difficulty of a teaching by Jesus. Scott challenged that potential complaint among his listeners:

> But if we as Christians have not been made to feel uncomfortable very often in our lives, then something may be wrong with our brand of Christianity. It may mean that we are marching with the world. It may mean that the natural man has taken over. It may mean that the natural man and the world about us has influenced us to such an extent that there is no longer any difference between the Christian and the man in the world with whom he rubs elbows day by day. If we don't feel uncomfortable at times, if we don't feel a little different from the rest of society, then something may be wrong.

Then he moved away from hypothetical speech: "We're not bearing our witness properly." He cited related words from the Bible:

Jesus said "Woe be unto you when all men speak well of you." (Luke 6:26) "Except your righteousness exceed the righteousness of the Scribes and the Pharisees, ye shall in no wise enter into the Kingdom of Heaven." (Matthew 5:20) He said it again and again. "What do ye more than others?" (Matthew 5:47) He said, "Ye shall be hated of all men of the world for my sake," (Matthew 10:22) . . . Romans 12:1 "Be ye transformed by the renewing of your minds." What does it mean to be different from the world? Not to be conformed to the world, said Paul. You have got to be transformed from the world and that is by the renewing of the mind. We can't think as the world thinks. We can't think as other people in society think if we're going to follow in the steps of Christ.

Scott called his people to repent and indicated that such action, including an admission of guilt and a commitment to seek the welfare of under-resourced Memphians, might cause other white Memphians to hate them. In Scott's perspective, cooperating with racial and economic injustice was contrary to the Christian life.

The sermon ended with a prayer that functioned as a conclusion and began with a whitened history of privilege:

> OUR HEAVENLY FATHER, Thou hast been good to us in so many ways; Thou hast given us a land of plenty; Thou hast given us freedom; Thou hast kept us from persecution that many people in foreign countries endure because of their persuasion of Jesus Christ; Thou hast delivered us from the tormentors; Thou hast given us periods of comfort and ease with which we may serve Thee and we may go about our way without fear or molestation and for this, our Father, we are thankful.

Not all residents of Scott's city and nation had received "a land of plenty" or the kind of "freedom" that white Christians enjoyed. Not all had escaped persecution and torment. Not all had experienced "comfort and ease . . . without fear of molestation." Nevertheless, Scott called his audience to "call out for peace" and "love . . . tolerance and understanding." He led the congregation in asking for "the ability to apply the Golden Rule" and in asking for forgiveness and for "the fruits of repentance." Perhaps the "fruits of repentance" were healings of guilt, but the prayer continued:

> Help us to see our responsibility for our society, that we cannot stand aloof and at a distance and let the rest of the world go by without concern, without being willing to do something to help the world and contribute something to the welfare of the betterment of mankind.

Scott's prayer did not specify what should be done. Instead, he left the request vague.

The prayer powerfully concluded the sermon by asking God to "be with our Mayor, be with our Councilmen, be with our policemen, be with those in high places, give them wisdom and judgment. Help them that they may bring the strife in our city to an abrupt end." This prayer did not intercede on behalf of the under-resourced and undervalued lives suffering racial and economic injustice. The prayer did not mention the dead sanitation workers or their striking colleagues or the assassinated civil rights leader who had traveled to Memphis to speak for people to whom "those in high places" had refused to listen. In fact, the spoken purpose of the prayer's requests was "that *we* are not threatened with death, injustice, pillaging, and rioting and war."[33] The prayer ended "in the name of Jesus Christ, Who set the standard for the world" but did not call the listeners to follow Jesus by laying down their lives for people in need.

PASTORAL PREACHING

Prophetic rhetoric calls for social change, and that call is anchored in deeply treasured foundations. Scholarly literature, such as that by Andre Johnson and Christopher Hobson cited in this essay, has studied prophetic rhetoric in messages from religious leaders to governmental authorities beyond religious systems. Compared to such intersystemic communication, priestly rhetoric is intrasystemic, sustaining religious organizations. Pastoral rhetoric combines prophetic and priestly rhetoric to call for change while nurturing faith communities and, therefore, tends to be less radical and more constrained than prophetic rhetoric may be when congregational leadership is not a concern. Pastoral preaching, a subcategory of pastoral rhetoric, is rhetorical leadership of religious communities and frequently occurs in those communities' worship assemblies.

In this essay, an April 1968 sermon preached by John A. Scott Sr. in Memphis, Tennessee, has served as a case study of pastoral preaching. Responding to Martin Luther King Jr.'s assassination, the sermon prophetically called for repentance and was shaped by social privilege, reminded listeners of their privilege, challenged them to repent of their contributions to inequalities, and challenged his congregation's practice of ignoring racial and economic privileges and injustices. Although a study of such a sermon may reasonably note that white fragility limited Scott's rhetoric, something more must be observed.

In the past few years, prophetic rhetoric scholar and black church leader Andre Johnson has facilitated a social media campaign using the hashtag #WhiteChurchQuiet to challenge white evangelical churches' failure to speak publicly against systemic injustice, especially racial inequalities. I respectfully point out that prophetic rhetoric must function differently in white churches than it does in black churches. If white preachers do not consider their congregations' discomfort with discussion about racial conflict, sermons may destroy congregations instead of strengthening them. However, if white preachers use both prophetic rhetoric to call for change and priestly rhetoric to nurture congregations, the result may be pastoral rhetoric that challenges the status quo while also practicing pastoral sensitivity. Therefore, this study of Scott's sermon invites rhetorical leaders in Christian congregations and other religious communities to discern faithful prophetic-priestly combinations in difficult ministerial situations. That discernment requires at least four considerations.

Social context is the first consideration. Preachers contribute to the shaping of congregations' attitudes, beliefs, and actions; and that role of preaching in congregational formation necessitates social awareness. Marvin McMickle, a scholar of African American religion, writes, "Those who seek to speak from the Bible in the twenty-first century must do so with an awareness of the issues of poverty and economic disparity."[34] According to homiletician John McClure, "preachers are theologians, not political theorists, political philosophers, sociologists, or historians. The goal is not political harangue or a learned lecture on social policy, but the articulation of God's redemptive plan."[35] Preachers responsible enough to stay informed about social concerns may speak prophetically, preaching from sacred texts to call for change and to envision a possible future, "God's redemptive plan."

The second consideration is white fragility. It has the power to blunt prophetic rhetoric in white church leadership in situations of racial conflict and other social tension. A preacher may speak from sacred foundations (i.e., biblical stories and teachings), encouraging listeners to acknowledge social inequalities and to cease their contributions to injustices. However, the white fragility experienced by the congregation, perhaps the preacher, can lead to an idealized memory and a vague, unspecified call to action. In this way, discomfort with discussions about social inequalities may function as a rhetorical constraint, at least partially determining what and how a preacher communicates.[36]

The third consideration is the risk of prophetic rhetoric in preaching. Even constrained prophetic rhetoric can result in congregants' objections and departures, so a prophetic preacher who allows white fragility to blunt the message might still take a risky stand. According to homiletician Leonora Tubbs Tisdale, prophetic preaching "can 'get ministers in trouble' with their congregations because it often goes against societal norms, pronouncing not only grace but also God's judgment on human action or inaction."[37] Bible scholar Walter Brueggemann writes:

Prophetic preaching, undertaken by working pastors, is profoundly difficult and leaves the preacher in an ambiguous and exposed position. The task is difficult because such a preacher must at the same time "speak the truth" while maintaining a budget, a membership, and a program in a context that is often not prepared for such truthfulness.[38]

That risky stand, however, might spark valuable conversations and lead to changes in perspective, conviction, and action. Of course, the message could be stronger. It could call out leaders of oppressive governments and corrupt businesses. It could specify ways in which listeners have contributed to injustice. Such a stronger, more prophetic message might lead to more objections and more departures, increasing congregational conflict and shrinking church membership.

The fourth consideration is the prophetic-priestly combination in pastoral preaching. Sometimes a preacher chooses to say what needs to be said regardless of any threat to congregational peace or job stability, and sometimes a preacher speaks prophetically while also remaining priestly.[39] Scott chose the latter approach. He spoke boldly but not strongly enough to rip apart his congregation, even though some members left. Prophetic and priestly rhetoric coexist in pastoral rhetoric, for people "are more willing to hear difficult words about justice when they know the preacher cares about them."[40] Homiletician Ronald Allen writes about prophetic preaching as "a special subcategory of pastoral preaching whose aim is to correct some aspect of the community's life"; and homiletician Tim Sensing states, "There should be no gulf between the prophetic role of the minister and the priestly or pastoral role of the preacher."[41] In his prophetic preaching, Scott knew his people, their concerns, and what they had been discussing. He spoke as a member of the congregation, not as someone above the people. When he challenged the congregation, he challenged himself as well. When he indicted the congregation, he indicted himself, too.

This study of Scott's sermon reveals that discerning the prophetic-priestly ratio is a difficult task. It is a challenge that requires prayerful, thoughtful discernment.

NOTES

1. This essay's analysis of prophetic rhetoric builds primarily on descriptive literature found in rhetorical studies instead of prescriptive literature found in theological studies, although a few theological writings are mentioned. Further, instead of studying prophetic rhetoric in the Bible, this essay investigates prophetic preaching in Memphis in the late 1960s and reflects more generally on prophetic preaching as it

is, instead of as it should be. On the role of rhetorical analysis in the study of preaching, see Steven Tramel Gaines, "Redefining Preaching: A Beginning," *Res Rhetorica* 4, no. 3 (2017): 42.

2. Barry Brummett, *Techniques of Close Reading* (Thousand Oaks, CA: Sage, 2010).

3. Michael Honey, "Memphis Sanitation Strike," *The Tennessee Encyclopedia of History and Culture*, December 25, 2009, updated January 1, 2010, http://tennesseeencyclopedia.net/entry.php?%20rec=902. Accessed May 1, 2017. Keith D. Miller, *Martin Luther King's Biblical Epic: His Final, Great Speech* (Jackson: University Press of Mississippi, 2012), 4–5.

4. Miller, *Martin Luther King's Biblical Epic*, 5.

5. David Appleby, Allison Graham, and Steven John Ross, directors. *At the River I Stand*. California Newsreel, 1993.

6. Martin Luther King Jr., "I've Been to the Mountaintop," *American Rhetoric*, April 3, 1968, http://www.americanrhetoric.com/speeches/mlkivebeentothemountaintop.htm. Accessed January 12, 2017.

7. The details of this event are debated.

8. David Schnasa Jacobsen, "*Schola Prophetarum*: Prophetic Preaching toward a Public, Prophetic Church," *Homiletic* 34, no. 1 (2009): 12–21.

9. Ronald J. Allen, "The Relationship between the Pastoral and the Prophetic in Preaching," *Encounter* 49, no. 3 (1988): 173–89; Timothy Sensing, "A Call to Prophetic Preaching," *ResQ* 41, no. 3 (1999): 139–54.

10. Michael A. Smith, "Through Much Tribulation: Prophetic Preaching in an Age of Hopelessness," *Review and Expositor* 109 (Summer 2012): 349–63; Christopher Z. Hobson, *The Mount of Vision: African American Prophetic Tradition, 1800–1950* (New York: Oxford, 2012).

11. Andre E. Johnson, *The Forgotten Prophet: Bishop Henry McNeal Turner and the African American Prophetic Tradition* (Lanham, MD: Lexington, 2012), 7. This section's information about prophetic rhetoric is modified Steven Tramel Gaines, "No Half Savior: Jarena Lee's Autobiography as Prophetic Rhetoric," *Carolinas Communication Annual* 33 (2017): 62–76.

12. A prescriptive chapter similarly states that "the prophetic sermon disorients the status quo by addressing present issues with a Word of God so that a new orientation (reality) can be created in the lives of the people." Timothy Sensing, "Re-imagining the Future: Past Tense Words in a Present Tense World," in *Preaching the Eighth Century Prophets*, ed. David Fleer and Dave Bland (Abilene, TX: ACU Press, 2004), 122.

13. Andre E. Johnson, "'To Make the World So Damn Uncomfortable': W. E. B. Du Bois and the African American Prophetic Tradition," *Carolinas Communication Annual* 32 (2016): 19.

14. Johnson, "'To Make the World So Damn Uncomfortable.'"

15. Johnson, "'To Make the World So Damn Uncomfortable,'" 19.

16. Johnson, "'To Make the World So Damn Uncomfortable,'" 19.

17. Johnson, "'To Make the World So Damn Uncomfortable,'" 19.

18. Johnson, "'To Make the World So Damn Uncomfortable,'" 19–20. This paragraph de-italicizes some words that Johnson italicizes.

19. Gaines, "No Half Savior," 69–70.

20. For related comments about prophetic preaching, a form of prophetic rhetoric, see Leonora Tubbs Tisdale, *Prophetic Preaching: A Pastoral Approach* (Louisville, KY: Westminster John Knox, 2010).

21. Hobson, *The Mount of Vision*, 30.

22. Thomas K. Nakayama and Robert L. Krizek, "Whiteness: A Strategic Rhetoric," *Quarterly Journal of Speech* 81 (1995): 303. This section's information about whiteness and white fragility is modified from my forthcoming book chapter about John Allen Chalk's antiracist sermons in the summer of 1968.

23. Robin DiAngelo, "White Fragility," *International Journal of Critical Pedagogy* 3 (2011): 54.

24. Monica McDermott and Frank L. Samson, "White Racial and Ethnic Identity in the United States," *Annual Review of Sociology* 31 (2005): 247. Also see David R. Roediger, *Colored White: Transcending the Racial Past* (Berkeley: University of California Press, 2002), 23–24.

25. Douglas Hartmann, Joseph Gerteis, and Paul R. Croll, "An Empirical Assessment of Whiteness Theory: Hidden from How Many?" *Social Problems* 56 (2009): 407.

26. Christina Moss, "A Nation Divided: Regional Identity, National Narratives, and Senator Zell Miller in the 2004 Presidential Election," *Southern Communication Journal* 76 (2011): 78.

27. Amanda E. Lewis, "'What Group?' Studying Whites and Whiteness in the Era of 'Color-Blindness,'" *Sociological Theory* 22 (2004): 623–46.

28. All quotations of this sermon are from John A. Scott Sr., "The Mind of Christ," April 14, 1968, http://www.cocws.org/filerequest/2124. Accessed January 30, 2017.

29. In his last year, King spoke strongly against the Vietnam War. For example, read his "Beyond Vietnam" speech, presented one year before his death and accessible on multiple websites.

30. Michelle Alexander, *The New Jim Crow: Mass Incarceration in the Age of Colorblindness* (New York: New Press, 2010).

31. Steven Tramel Gaines, "Speaking Reconstruction: Moving beyond the Silence," *Memphis Massacre 1866: The Official Blog of the Memories of a Massacre: Memphis in 1866 Project*, February 22, 2016, https://blogs.memphis.edu/memphismassacre1866/2016/02/22/speaking-reconstruction-moving-beyond-the-silence/. Accessed May 1, 2017.

32. Stephen E. Toulmin, *The Uses of Argument* (Cambridge: Cambridge University Press, 1969).

33. Emphasis added.

34. Marvin A. McMickle, "Preaching in the Face of Economic Injustice," in *Just Preaching: Prophetic Voices for Economic Justice*, ed. André Resner Jr. (St. Louis, MO: Chalice, 2003), 3.

35. John S. McClure, *Preaching Words: 144 Key Terms in Homiletics* (Louisville, KY: Westminster John Knox, 2007), 118.

36. Lloyd F. Bitzer, "The Rhetorical Situation," *Philosophy and Rhetoric* 1 (1968): 8. Cf. Allison J. Tanner, "Unpacking Prophetic Preaching: The Pastor as

Cultured Actor," *Review and Expositor* 109 (Summer 2012): 433: "Pastors . . . are culturally situated social actors" who "communicate their messaged of moral exhortation through culturally available tools."

37. Tisdale, *Prophetic Preaching: A Pastoral Approach*, 3.

38. Walter Brueggemann, *The Practice of Prophetic Imagination: Preaching an Emancipating Word* (Minneapolis, MN: Fortress, 2012), 1.

39. Roderick P. Hart and Don M. Burks, "Rhetorical Sensitivity and Social Interaction," *Speech Monographs* 39, no. 2 (1972): 76. Rhetorical sensitivity in preaching may be called pastoral sensitivity; Sangyil Park, "Speaking of Hope: Prophetic Preaching," *Review and Expositor* 109 (2012): 413–27.

40. McClure, *Preaching Words*, 118.

41. Allen, "The Relationship between the Pastoral and the Prophetic in Preaching," 181; Sensing, "Re-imagining the Future: Past Tense Words in a Present Tense World," 150; cf. Park, "Speaking of Hope," 423–25. In addition to the pastoral nature of prophetic preaching, "Nobody is being 'pastoral' who is not also being 'prophetic.'" William H. Willimon, "Pastors Who Are Preachers Who Are Prophets," in Fleer and Bland, *Preaching the Eighth Century Prophets*, 19.

Chapter 7

Sex, Purity, and Community in First-Century Corinth

Paul's Disciplinary Directive in 1 Corinthians 5:3–5, Its Meaning, Anticipated Outcome, and Contemporary Applicability

James P. Sweeney

INTRODUCTION

First-century Corinth offers contemporary scholarship many avenues of study, for it was an important city geographically, historically, commercially, culturally, socially, and religiously.[1] In addition to antiquarian interests, moreover, first-century Corinth's cultural, social, and religious dynamics provide researchers with resources for comparison to contemporary Western culture.[2] In this regard, Anthony Thiselton observes:

> Research on the social world of Corinth in the era of Paul has revealed striking resonances with secular cultures of our own day: an obsessive concern about reputation and status in the eyes of others; self-promotion to win applause and to gain influence; ambition to succeed, often by manipulating networks of influence. Rhetoric was more concerned with audience-approval ratings than with truth; people valued autonomy and "rights." Such a social background places Paul's message of divine grace and the cross of Jesus Christ into the sharpest possible focus. Contrary to cultural expectations at Corinth, the cross offered not status-enhancement but an affront, a reversal of the whole value-system of non-Christian Corinth.[3]

The complex, multilayered social setting of Corinth and Paul's countercultural message were bound to collide at some point with Paul's fledgling converts and result in many pastoral challenges for him as the believing community's founder. To meet these challenges, Paul adopted and adapted the convenient Greco-Roman letter genre. The most basic rationale of this genre was its substitutionary function. Depending on circumstances, authors either could not be or chose not to be where their recipients were. Consequently, they sent letters as a substitute for personal presence (cf. 2 Cor. 10:11).[4] Letters were flexible, served different purposes, and were of various types.[5] The typical Greco-Roman letter exhibited a three-part structure: introduction, body, and closing.[6] Paul adapted this three-part structure by expanding on each of the elements to produce some of the longest attested letters from the Greco-Roman world.[7]

The content of 1 Corinthians fully exemplifies the stark nature of the collision between first-century Corinthian culture and Paul's countercultural message and his rhetorical strategy in meeting it.[8] Almost the entirety of the letter contents reflects a plethora of pastoral problems that Paul addresses, including divisions in the believing community over the status of its principal ministers (1:10–4:21), a matter of incest involving one of its members (5:1–13), lawsuits among members (6:1–11), libertine behavior (6:12–20), uncertainty regarding matters of marriage, celibacy, widowhood, separation, and divorce (7:1–24) as well as engagement, marriage, and remarriage (7:25–40), matters of whether to eat food offered to idols (8:1–11:1), uncertainty regarding the use of head coverings (11:2–16), misbehavior at the Lord's Supper (11:17–34), the right and wrong place of spiritual manifestations in larger community gatherings for worship (12:1–14:40), and inconsistency of thought with regard to the resurrection of the body (15:1–58).

The root nature of these pastoral problems has been variously explained. Earlier biblical scholarship commonly characterized them as examples of the Corinthian believers' relapse into their pre-Christian past or the result of coming under the sway of non-Pauline influences. Thiselton suggests a more plausible rationale: "It is not the case, as older modern commentators often suggest, that Christian behaviour at Corinth simply 'relapsed' into pagan habits, or was influenced unduly by new teaching. Rather, Christians' appropriation of the cross had insufficiently pervaded their attitudes."[9]

In no case is this clearer than regarding 1 Corinthians 5, where Paul issues a directive to the community regarding a member who was engaged in a form of sexual behavior—namely, incest—that violated not only the moral standards of Paul's Jewish background[10] but also Greco-Roman moral sensibilities as well. The Roman orator Cicero exhibited typical Roman disgust toward incest nearly a century earlier: "The mother-in-law marries the son-in-law, no one looking favorably on the deed, no one approving it, all foreboding a dismal end to it."[11] About a century later than Paul, Gaius, the noted Roman jurist, stated forthrightly, "I cannot marry my former mother-in-law or daughter-in-law, or my step-daughter or step-mother."[12] On the potential legal implications with respect to man and the woman recounted in 1 Cor 5:1, Bruce Winter observes, "It appears that criminal charges had not yet been instituted which, if proven at law, would have resulted in the exile of the son and his stepmother to an island together with the stripping of their assets and civil status."[13] At the time of Paul, only the father could bring criminal action during the first two months; thereafter, any citizen could bring the charge.[14]

Our attention below will be on 1 Cor 15:3–5, with focus on the context in which the directive is found, the meaning of the directive itself, the anticipated outcome of the directive, and the follow-up matter of its contemporary applicability.

SETTING THE CONTEXT OF PAUL'S DIRECTIVE IN 1 CORINTHIANS 5:3–5

Contemporary Approaches to Interpreting Biblical Texts

Contemporary biblical interpreters commonly emphasize one of three approaches to interpreting biblical texts: (1) an *author-centered* approach, with attention given to the author of the given biblical text; (2) a *text-centered* approach, with focus on the text itself; and (3) a *reader-centered* approach, where the concentration is on the contemporary reader who is believed to produce or actualize meaning. W. Randolph Tate notes that these theories relate to the *locus* (i.e., place or locality) and *actualization* of meaning (i.e., its realization in interpretive practice).[15] Tate himself, who adopts a conversational model of interpretation, describes the author, text, and reader(s) as three worlds and the praxis of interpretation as "a journey into three worlds."[16] In comparing and contrasting oral and written forms of discourse, Tate notes that in oral discourse "a speaker seeks to communicate some information to a hearer in such a way that it will be understandable. To accomplish this goal, the speaker makes primary use of language, a language which is generally shared by both parties."[17] In written discourse, by contrast, "an *author* intends to convey meaning through the *text* to a *reader*."[18] Certain rhetorical vehicles, such as sound, inflection, gestures, and the like, are not available for use. Rather, an author needs to employ literary devices to mediate his or her message to recipients via a *text*. Moreover, although "the author is not available for questioning, some aspects of the author's world are. This assumption leaves sufficient room for the role of the reader in the production of meaning. Consequently, three realities converge: author's, text's, and reader's."[19] Tate suggests that "the locus of meaning is not to be found exclusively in either world or in a marriage of any two of the worlds, but in the interplay between all three worlds. Meaning resides in the conversation between the text and reader with the world behind the text informing that conversation."[20] I agree with Tate that the three "worlds" or realities of the author, text, and reader are important features of the interpretive process. However, I disagree with him that the contemporary reader "produces" meaning. The role of the contemporary is rather to uncover intended meaning, for the text is a concrete expression of an author: in this case Paul (primarily) and Sosthenes (secondarily) (1 Cor 1:1).[21]

The Broader Literary Context of 1 Corinthians

First Corinthians, like Paul's other earlier letters,[22] was authored in the context of his apostolic mission.[23] It is, in part, Paul's response in writing to a series of oral reports he received from Corinth.[24] In addition, Paul also answers the content of a letter the Corinthians sent him, in which they requested his guidance on a number of church-related matters.[25] Although the oral reports he received and the Corinthians' letter may not exhaust the full rationale of Paul's letter,[26] they are specifically relevant here, particularly given his initial comments in 5:1.

With regard to the structure and content of letter body of 1 Corinthians, a broad consensus begins in 1:10. Three basic termini are identified as its conclusion: 15:58,[27] 16:13,[28] or 16:18.[29] Analyses of the letter body itself diverge considerably.[30] For our purposes, however, it is important to note that the content of 1 Cor 5 follows immediately after Paul's expressed concern for unity within the community (1:10) and his related reminder of its new identity as God's holy temple indwelt by the Spirit (1 Cor 3:16–17).[31] These twin concerns are evident in his address of matters of factionalism within the Corinthian church (1:11–4:21), which had been reported to him from "some from Chloe's household" (1:11). That Paul's next subject is an instance of serious sexual misconduct (5:1–13) suggests that church unity, church purity, and appropriate behavior were closely related priorities for the apostle.[32] Fee additionally calls attention to the linguistic ties between 5:1–13 and 4:14–21 (the concluding portion of 1:10–4:21), "especially (1) the 'arrogance' of 'some' (4:18–19) and the arrogance of the church in what follows (5:2, 6), and (2) the lack of 'power' among the arrogant (4:19–20) vis-à-vis the 'power of our Lord Jesus' (5:4)."[33] Malcolm, by contrast, stresses the role that 5:1–13 plays with regard to 1 Cor 5–14. He identifies the macrostructural theme of this section as "the cross applied ethically."[34]

An Overview of the Content and Argument of 1 Corinthians 5

The general thrust of Paul's argument in 1 Cor 5 appears reasonably clear. He begins by recounting an oral report circulating about a case of incest involving a member of the believing community (v. 1). The initial verb of 5:1, "[It] is . . . reported" (ἀκούεται), indicates that Paul had heard an oral report about this matter.[35] Yet, he does not spell out whether this report originated from "some from Chloe's household" (1:11)[36] or from the triumvirate of Stephanas, Fortunatus, and Achaicus (16:17).[37] He further chastises the Corinthian community both for its *attitude* (e.g., arrogance [v. 2a] and boasting [v. 6a]) and *nonaction* in connection with it (v. 2b). In vv. 3–5, the apostle delineates his verdict regarding the perpetrator's misbehavior and issues a directive he expects the community to carry out vis-à-vis the offender: namely, to deliver him over to Satan (v. 5).[38] In vv. 6–8, Paul reminds the community, by way of Jewish cultic imagery, of its need for purity in view of Christ's sacrificial death as the Passover lamb (v. 7b). They must therefore "clean out the old yeast [of malice and evil—v. 8a] so that [they] may be a new batch" (v. 7): namely, "the unleavened bread of sincerity and truth" (v. 8b). In vv. 9–10, he offers clarification regarding his previous letter where he prohibited association with sexually immoral people. This clarification implies that the Corinthians *misunderstood* the scope of the apostle's directive and consequently dismissed it (either consciously or unconsciously) as being too impractical to implement. Paul therefore clarifies his intentions in the present correspondence and spells out its implications for the community (vv. 11–12). They are not to associate with anyone who bears the name of a fellow believer (τις ἀδελφός)[39] if such a one is guilty of the kind of representative moral offenses that Paul delineates.[40] In brief, both he and the believing Corinthians have the responsibility to separate themselves from professing believers who are engaged in immoral misbehavior ("Do not even eat with such a person"—v. 11). He and they have the responsibility to pass judgment on "insiders," whereas God will judge "outsiders" (vv. 12–13a). As a consequence, the believing community is to expel the offending person (v. 13b) introduced in 5:1.

Zeroing in on Paul's Argument in 1 Corinthians 5:3–5: The Challenge of Lexis, Grammar, and Syntax

Although the broad message of 1 Cor 5 is clear enough, an examination of exegetical commentaries and standard English translations indicates that there is considerable debate as to how best to represent the lexis, grammar, and syntactical details of vv. 3–5. James Moffatt, writing in 1938, wryly observed, "In Greek these three verses [1 Cor 5:3–5] are one long complicated sentence, and the meaning is almost as obscure as the grammar."[41] Consequently, in this portion I will attempt to limit myself to the lexical, grammatical, and syntactical issues most germane for understanding Paul's directive.

1. LEXIS: Lexical matters turn on whether τῷ πνεύματι ("in/by the S/spirit") in v. 3 refers to the Holy Spirit or Paul's own spirit.[42] There are several additional lexical matters in v. 5 (all of which I will address further below): (1) Whether παραδοῦναι τὸν τοιοῦτον τῷ σατανᾷ (deliver such a person over to Satan) implies an imprecation or excommunication;[43] (2) whether εἰς ὄλεθρον (for destruction) suggests physical death, physical suffering, and/or metaphorical chastening;[44] (3) whether τῆς σαρκός (lit. "of the flesh") is a reference to the physical body and/or sinful disposition of the offender;[45] the church, or a combination, and likewise; (4) whether τὸ πνεῦμα (lit. the spirit) refers to the spirit of the offender,[46] the church,[47] or a combination of the two.[48]
2. GRAMMAR: The principal grammatical questions regarding v. 5 turn on the grammatical understanding of the prepositional phrase εἰς and the following ἵνα clause (see below).
3. SYNTAX: The syntax of this portion largely turns on how the two prepositional phrases in v. 4 (ἐν τῷ ὀνόματι τοῦ κυρίου [ἡμῶν] Ἰησοῦ[49] {"in the name of [our] Lord Jesus"}) and σὺν τῇ δυνάμει τοῦ κυρίου ἡμῶν Ἰησοῦ[50] {"with the power of our Lord Jesus"}) connect with vv. 3, 5. Given the wide number of possibilities, I will not attempt to exhaust every possible syntactical and punctuation scenario here.[51] I'll simply focus on the four most commonly represented in standard English translations and/or by recognized authorities on 1 Corinthians.

Regarding the first of the two aforementioned syntactical issues (τῷ ὀνόματι τοῦ κυρίου [ἡμῶν] Ἰησοῦ {"in the name of [our] Lord Jesus"}), four explanations are common:

a. Some translations connect the prepositional phrase with the principal verb in v. 3 (κέκρικα):[52]
   NRSV (also RSV, TNIV, NIV 2011): "I have already *pronounced judgment* [κέκρικα] [4] *in the name of the Lord Jesus* on the man who has done such a thing."[53]
b. Some additional versions connect the prepositional phrase with the genitive absolute that follows (συναχθέντων ὑμῶν {"when you are gathered"}):
   NET (also NJB, NIV, ESV, CEV): "*When you gather together* [συναχθέντων ὑμῶν] *in the name of our Lord Jesus*"[54]

c. Still other translations connect the prepositional phrase with the infinitive of v. 5 (παραδοῦναι {"to deliver over"}):

NASB 95 (also NASB, NKJV, HCSB): "*In the name of our Lord Jesus*, when you are assembled, and I with you in spirit, with the power of our Lord Jesus,[5] *I have decided to deliver* such a one to Satan"[55]

d. Although English versions do not adopt it in their texts, the margin of the NRSV connects the prepositional phrase with the offender mentioned at the end of v. 3 (τὸν οὕτως τοῦτο κατεργασάμενον {"the man who in this way has perpetrated this [act]"}):

NRSV margin: "*on the man who has done such a thing in the name of the Lord Jesus*"[56] The resultant rendering would thus be: "For though absent in body, I am present in spirit; and as if present I have already pronounced judgment[4] *on the man who has done such a thing in the name of the Lord Jesus*."

In favor of this nontraditional fourth rendering are the following two observations: (1) the word order fits quite naturally and (2) it provides a more coherent answer regarding the inappropriate attitude and nonaction of the community that Paul sanctions in vv. 2, 6a. Regarding word order, it should be noted that the prepositional phrase "in the name of the Lord" is used sparingly elsewhere in the Pauline corpus.[57] Where it is used, however, it customarily *follows* a verb or verbal it qualifies,[58] rather that introducing one that follows.[59] Although the sampling is admittedly small, the word order alone makes views 2 and 3 unlikely but does not rule out views 1 or 4. However, with regard to view 1, the main verb is more distant from the prepositional phrase, whereas with view 4, the verbal is immediately proximate. On balance, therefore, word order favors view 4 but does not rule out view 1.

This leads to a second consideration: the relationship between the content of vv. 3–5 and the arrogance (v. 2)[60] and boasting (v. 6)[61] that immediately precede and follow it. A common explanation regarding the relationship of these statements is that the community was boasting "in spite of," not "because of," the sexual misbehavior in their midst. Hence, Ciampa and Rosner observe, "It seems fairly certain that the Corinthians (v. 2 [*sic*]) were not boasting because of the immorality among them, but in spite of it."[62] But it must first be asked whether most of the Corinthian community regarded the relationship as "immorality"? Paul introduces the oral report of what *he* clearly regarded as sexual misbehavior (v. 1), sanctions the Corinthians' arrogance (v. 2a) and nonaction (v. 2b), issues a verdict of judgment (v. 3) that he expects them to carry out (vv. 4–5), and then criticizes their boasting (v. 6a). Contextually speaking, it appears more natural to associate the behavior directly with the attitude (vv. 2a, 6a) and nonaction (v. 2b) that Paul criticizes. Moreover, boasting in the Pauline corpus elsewhere always assumes a concrete basis: regardless of whether or not the basis is judged to be legitimate.⁶³ View 4 provides a coherent contextual rationale for understanding why the behavior Paul sanctions in 1 Cor 5 could have provided a convenient cloak for the Corinthians' arrogance (v. 2a), nonaction (v. 2a), and boasting (v. 6a) that Paul criticizes. The man was doing what he did in the name of the Lord, and perhaps most of the Corinthian community excused him because of it.⁶⁴

The principal obstacle against interpretation 4 is that scholars simply have trouble comprehending how a man would have claimed divine sanction for such socially offensive behavior and why it would have served as a basis of the believing community's arrogance (v. 2a), nonaction (v. 2b), and boasting (v. 6a). Gordon Fee candidly admits as much: "[I]t is fair to say that this [sc. interpretive option] would have been the normal understanding were it not for the difficulty instinctively felt with someone's [sic] doing such a thing 'in the name of the Lord Jesus.'"⁶⁵ The problem, however, is that instinctive feelings are not a sufficiently reliable guide in exegesis. And although there is no simple answer as to why a man would have claimed divine sanction for such an action and why the broader Corinthian community was willing to countenance his claim, both the grammar and context support this interpretation. Moreover, contemporary commentators tend to project a rather advanced understanding of sexual ethics on the Corinthians. Given the notorious city in which they lived,⁶⁶ their own recent past with various forms of sexual promiscuity (note 1 Cor 6:9–11), the recentness of their conversion,⁶⁷ and resultant need of pointed instruction (1 Cor 6:15–20), this assumption is perhaps more precarious than one might at first think. Murphy-O'Connor postulates that "the incestuous man had to justify himself to his friends and neighbours, who would have instinctively rejected his behaviour. It is clear from the text, however, that he not only succeeded, but did so in such a way that the community's attitude was transformed into proud approbation."⁶⁸ He further notes that the man could not have appealed to either Judaism or paganism to justify his actions because both condemned this form of behavior. He maintains that the man must have had recourse to some aspect of the new faith that governed the life of the community, which he identifies as Paul's call for his converts to be different from their neighbors.⁶⁹ However, in light of the twice-cited Corinthian slogan elsewhere, "all things are lawful for me" (πάντα μοι ἔξεστιν), which Paul both cites (1 Cor. 6:12a; 10:23a) and corrects (6:12–20 and 10:23–33), perhaps a simpler and more plausible explanation is that this incident represented an example of misapplied and hence misused "freedom."

With regard to the second prepositional phrase (σὺν τῇ δυνάμει τοῦ κυρίου ἡμῶν Ἰησοῦ ["with the power of our Lord Jesus"]), there is less disagreement. Most standard English translations and many commentators connect it as an explanatory phrase, along with καὶ τοῦ ἐμοῦ πνεύματος ("and my spirit"), with the participle in the preceding genitive absolute (συναχθέντων ὑμῶν): "When you are assembled, and my spirit is present with the power of our Lord Jesus" (1 Cor 5:4b, NRSV).[70]

THREE KEY INTERPRETIVE ISSUES IN 1 CORINTHIANS 5:5 AND THEIR BEARING ON OUR UNDERSTANDING OF PAUL'S DIRECTIVE

The Meaning of "Flesh" and "Spirit" and Their Likely Referents

A broad number of commentators and the committee members of standard English translations understand the referent of flesh and spirit in 1 Cor 5:5 to be the offender introduced in 5:1.[71] The lack of explicit pronouns in Greek, however, opens other possibilities. In a seminal article published in 1976, Karl Paul Donfried interpreted flesh and spirit in 1 Cor 5:5 in an ethical/eschatological sense. He took "the flesh" as a reference to "the works of the flesh"—that is, ungodly actions of those *within the church*—and "the spirit" as a reference to the Holy Spirit present within the congregation, which is to be saved for the Parousia.[72] In a rhetorical study of 1 Cor 5:5 previously referenced, Barth Campbell similarly maintained that flesh and spirit are generalized ways of referring to *the church*.[73] Campbell maintains that "the arguments indicate that Paul, in the proposition, has the flesh and the spirit of the church in view when he calls for the destruction of the former and the salvation of the latter."[74] Campbell thus interprets Paul's directive in 1 Cor 5:5 as "deliver such a one over to Satan for the destruction of the [church's] flesh, that the [church's] spirit may be saved in the day of the Lord." If understood in the way Campbell suggests, the focus of the expelling action would be strictly for the temporal and eschatological benefits *of the church*. This is the means by which Paul intends the church to rid itself of the "leaven" (5:6–8), as it were, an analogy to the Jewish festal complex of unleavened bread and Passover (5:7; cf. Lev 23:4–8). Paul Toseland draws on Campbell's argument and further extends its implications to the offender, too.[75] If Campbell's interpretation is correct, however, the offender is not in view in 1 Cor 5:5, other than being the object of expulsion. This would further mean that the passage Toseland draws upon for additional support of this interpretation—namely, 1 Tim 1:20—does not fit the 1 Cor 5:5 passage at all. For then 1 Tim 1:20 would move in an opposite direction from 1 Cor 5:5, because in the 1 Timothy passage Paul's handing over Hymenaeus and Alexander to Satan is for either a penal and/or a remedial purpose: namely, "that *they* may learn not to blaspheme."[76] That is not the case in 1 Cor 5:5, if one assumes Campbell's interpretation. Rather, the offender simply fades from view, and the implication of Paul's directive is strictly the temporal and eschatological benefit of the church.

Joseph Fitzmyer identifies a combination of the referents in 1 Cor 5:5. He maintains that the flesh refers to the offender and that the spirit is a reference to "God's Spirit present in the Corinthian community."[77] However, it is difficult to see how this interpretation lines up with the language of 5:5b. If one adopts Fitzmyer's viewpoint, 5:5b would, in effect, be saying "that God's Spirit present in the Christian community might be saved in the day of the Lord." This explanation leaves one wondering why God's Spirit would need eschatological salvation.

Weighed as a whole, however, there is insufficient contextual basis for taking the referent of flesh and spirit as other than the offender. "Deliver such a one to Satan for the destruction of the flesh so that the spirit may be saved" more naturally refers to the offender. Had Paul intended flesh and spirit to be other than the offender, one would expect that he would have spelled out the intended referent(s) more clearly. Therefore, it is doubtful that flesh and spirit refer respectively to the church and the Spirit (Donfried), the church (Campbell), the church, with potential implications for the offender (Toseland), or to a combination of the offender and the God's Spirit present in the Christian community (Fitzmyer). Hence, the standard interpretation adopted by most commentators and contemporary English versions—namely, that the referents flesh and spirit refer to the offender—is the most natural and, hence, plausible interpretation of the passage.

The Nature of Paul's Directive in 1 Corinthians 5:5

More debatable than the referent of flesh and spirit is whether the expression παραδοῦναι.[78] . . . τῷ σατανᾷ ("deliver/hand over/give over to Satan") implies an imprecation or excommunication and whether the prepositional εἰς ὄλεθρον ("for destruction") suggests physical death,[79] physical suffering,[80] and/or metaphorical chastening.[81]

David Smith is the most forceful recent proponent of a combination of imprecation, physical suffering, and death. He summarized the findings of his 2005 Durham doctoral dissertation on 1 Cor 5:5 as follows:

> The results of this study show that *paradounai ton toiouton tō satana eis olethron tis sarkos* is best understood within the context of an ancient common language of cursing, in which individuals are "handed over" to a malevolent power to suffer harm. In this instance, Paul envisages an exclusion curse. The errant man is ejected from the Corinthian church, and Paul anticipates that his physical

suffering and death will ensue. This disciplinary measure prevents him from sinning further. Despite suffering a curse, the man will be saved at the End.[82]

There are indeed several examples where Paul issues curses, both in Acts and his letters.[83] Moreover, the term ὄλεθρος appears twenty-four times in the LXX in the sense of "ruin, destruction"[84] and four times in the NT, all in the Pauline corpus: here and three other instances.[85] In two of these other three instances, the focus is eschatological.[86] The other could be either temporal or eschatological.[87] Although this viewpoint for which Smith argues is increasingly represented in contemporary secondary literature, however, it is not without its detractors.[88] Two points, in particular, weaken its likelihood here.

First, it should be noted that Paul does not speak simply of the destruction of the offender's life (ζωή) or body (σῶμα) in contrast to his spirit (πνεῦμα), but of his flesh (σάρξ), or as Thiselton renders it, "the fleshly,"[89] in contrast to his spirit (πνεῦμα). Given the clear contrast with spirit, it appears that σάρξ is employed in an ethical sense, as frequently elsewhere in the Pauline corpus.[90] William Barclay suggested that in an ethical sense "The flesh is what man has made himself in contrast to man as God made him. The flesh is man as he has allowed himself to become in contrast with man as God meant him to be. The flesh stands for the total effect upon man of his own sin and of the sin of his fathers and of the sin of all men who have gone before him. . . . The flesh is man as he is apart from Jesus Christ and his Spirit."[91] This imagery suggests that "[w]hat Paul was desiring . . . was the destruction of what was 'carnal' in him, so that he might be 'saved' eschatologically."[92]

Second, this view is in keeping with Pauline language elsewhere, where he uses a wide number of terms related to crucifixion and death in a metaphorical sense.[93]

- Gal 5:24 (ESV), "And those who belong to Christ Jesus *have crucified the flesh* [τὴν σάρκα ἐσταύρωσαν] with its passions and desires."
- Rom 7:5–6 (NASB 95), "*For while we were in the flesh* [ὅτε γὰρ ἦμεν ἐν τῇ σαρκί], the sinful passions, which were *aroused* by the Law, were at work in the members of our body to bear fruit for death.[6] But now we have been released from the Law, *having died to that by which we were bound* [ἀποθανόντες ἐν ᾧ κατειχόμεθα],[94] so that we serve in newness of the Spirit and not in oldness of the letter."

Paul also often uses similarly stark language of death metaphorically, particularly regarding believers' new identity in Christ:

In Assertions:

- Galatians 2:19–20 (ESV), "For through the law *I died to the law* [ἐγὼ ... νόμῳ ἀπέθανον], so that I might live to God. *I have been crucified with Christ* [Χριστῷ συνεσταύρωμαι].[20] *It is no longer I who live* [ζῶ ... οὐκέτι ἐγώ], but Christ who lives in me. And the life I now live in the flesh I live by faith in the Son of God, who loved me and gave himself for me."
- Romans 6:3–4 (ESV), "Do you not know that all of us who have been baptized into Christ Jesus *were baptized into his death* [εἰς τὸν θάνατον αὐτοῦ ἐβαπτίσθημεν]?[4] *We were buried therefore with him by baptism into death* [συνετάφημεν οὖν αὐτῷ διὰ τοῦ βαπτίσματος εἰς τὸν θάνατον], in order that, just as Christ was raised from the dead by the glory of the Father, we too might walk in newness of life."
- Romans 7:4 (NET), "So, my brothers and sisters, *you also died to the law through the body of Christ* [καὶ ὑμεῖς ἐθανατώθητε τῷ νόμῳ διὰ τοῦ σώματος τοῦ Χριστοῦ], so that you could be joined to another, to the one who was raised from the dead, to bear fruit to God."
- Romans 8:13 (ESV), "For if you live according to the flesh you will die, but if by the Spirit *you put to death the deeds of the body* [τὰς πράξεις τοῦ σώματος θανατοῦτε], you will live."
- Colossians 2:20 (ESV), "*If with Christ you died to the elemental spirits of the world* [Εἰ ἀπεθάνετε σὺν Χριστῷ ἀπὸ τῶν στοιχείων τοῦ κόσμου], why, as if you were still alive in the world, do you submit to regulations."
- Colossians 3:3 (ESV), "For *you have died* [ἀπεθάνετε], and your life is hidden with Christ in God."

In Exhortations:

- Romans 6:11 (ESV), "So you also must *consider yourselves dead to sin* [οὕτως καὶ ὑμεῖς λογίζεσθε ἑαυτοὺς [εἶναι] νεκροὺς] and alive to God in Christ Jesus."
- Colossians 3:5 (ESV), "*Put to death* [Νεκρώσατε] therefore what is earthly in you: sexual immorality, impurity, passion, evil desire, and covetousness, which is idolatry."

Given the frequently metaphorical way in which Paul uses crucifixion and death-related language, we cannot automatically assume he intends ὄλεθρος in a strictly temporal and physiological sense here. Hence, there appears to be little basis for the confidence exhibited in Conzelmann's strong assertion: "The destruction of the flesh can hardly mean anything else but death (cf. 11:30)."[95] At best, we must simply leave this question open.

The closest analogy to the act of "delivering/handing over/giving over to Satan" is found in a partially parallel passage in 1 Tim 1:19–20. There Paul singles out Hymenaeus and Alexander (1:20) from among a group of those who said to have rejected faith and a good conscience and have suffered the shipwreck of their faith (1:19).[96] Paul further observes that he has handed them "over to Satan that [ἵνα] they may learn [παιδευθῶσιν] not to blaspheme."[97] In this instance, the ἵνα clause likely expresses purpose.[98] In 1 Cor 5:5, by contrast, we find both a prepositional phrase εἰς clause ("*for* the destruction of the flesh") and a ἵνα clause. This brings us to another debated point of grammar relative to 1 Cor 5:5, which is important for understanding the anticipated outcome of Paul's directive: namely, the grammatical force of the preposition εἰς and the conjunction ἵνα. These are matters on which commentators and standard translations are at odds. We will address these grammatical issues next.

The Anticipated Outcome of Paul's Directive in 1 Corinthians 5:5

Contextually, the controlling verb of 1 Cor 5:5 is the initial infinitive of Paul's directive that the Corinthian believers execute a divine verdict on the offender: "*Deliver* such an [offender] *over* to Satan" (cf. nn. 44, 56, 81 above). Following this we have two statements, the grammatical relation of which need to be interpreted in the light of the content of Paul's directive: "*for* [εἰς] the destruction of the flesh" and "*that* [ἵνα] the spirit might be saved in the day of the Lord." Owing to the arguments of Gordon Fee, many contemporary commentators take the εἰς clause as conveying the anticipated result and the ἵνα clause as delineating the express purpose of the action.[99] Fee acknowledged in both editions of his commentary, however, that "[i]t is common to see the prepositional phrase 'for the destruction of the flesh' as expressing purpose, followed by a final purpose clause 'in order that the spirit might be saved.'"[100] A. T. Robertson, a Greek grammarian of the early twentieth century, described the ἵνα clause both as "ultimate purpose" and "goal."[101] Much more recently, too, Fitzmyer describes the εἰς (*eis*) clause ("*for* the destruction of the flesh") as the "immediate goal" and the ἵνα clause ("*so that* the Spirit may be saved") as indicating "the more remote goal."[102]

The general impression given in many contemporary standard English translations is that εἰς as indicates purpose ("for") and ἵνα indicates result ("so that"): "Hand such a one over to Satan *for* [sc. the purpose of] the destruction of the flesh, *so that* [as a result/consequence] his spirit may be saved in the Day of the Lord."[103] A couple of translations (NIV 1984 and NLT) convey the impression that the two statements are coordinate result clauses: "*so that* the sinful nature may be destroyed *and* his spirit saved on the day of the Lord"

(NIV 1984)/"*so that* his sinful nature will be destroyed *and* he himself will be saved on the day the Lord returns" (NLT). In the translations of their respective commentaries, Thiselton and Garland translate εἰς and ἵνα along the lines that Fee suggested.[104] The one contemporary English translation that does so, too, is the Lexham English Bible (LEB): "hand over such a person to Satan *for* the destruction of the flesh, *in order that* his spirit may be saved in the day of the Lord" (italics added).

However, it should be noted that εἰς + the accusative can express either purpose or result.[105] Likewise, ἵνα + the subjunctive can express purpose, result, or even purpose-result.[106] Purpose typically answers a "Why?" question, whereas result focuses on the consequence(s) of an action, which may or may not involve intention. Wallace notes that ἵνα + the subjunctive "indicates a consequence of the verbal action that is *not intended*."[107] But it should be noted, too, that he proceeds on the same page to cite the observation in Bauer's *Lexicon*, "In many cases purpose and result cannot be clearly differentiated, and hence ἵνα is used for the result that follows according to the purpose of the subj[ect] or of God. As in Semitic and Gr[eco]-Rom[an] thought, purpose and result are identical in declarations of the divine will."[108] However, when the divine will is involved, intention and consequence are not as easily separable as one might at first think, though they may be distinguishable.

In the present instance, the twofold question in relation to the divine verdict of 1 Cor 5:5a is this: "What is the immediate *intention* of having Corinthian believers deliver the offender over to Satan and what was the ultimate *goal* of this delivery?" It is here that Fitzmyer's distinction between immediate goal (εἰς) and more remote goal (ἵνα) is helpful (cf. n. 105 above). Robertson similarly suggested that the ἵνα clause indicates "ultimate purpose" and "goal." Given the context, I find it most likely that the immediate *intention* (indicated in the εἰς phrase) is "the destruction of the flesh" of the offender, whereas the *goal* of that delivery is "that [ἵνα] the spirit [of the man] might be saved in the day of the Lord." This is consistent with the most common renderings adopted in most standard English translations.

When we compare this 1 Cor 5:5 passage with the partially parallel passage in 1 Tim 1:20 noted above, where Paul observes that he handed Hymenaeus and Alexander "over to Satan that they [ἵνα] may learn not to blaspheme," the ἵνα clause likely expresses purpose (n. 109 above), though the dual notion of purpose-result is also plausible, given the verbal idea in passive subjunctive παιδευθῶσιν.[109] For elsewhere in the Pauline corpus παιδεύω is used of divine disciplining (1 Cor 11:32; 2 Cor 6:9; Tit 2:12; cf. Heb. 12:6–7, 10), with the prospect of repentance and restoration held out (cf. 2 Tim 2:25). We can summarize the similarities and differences between 1 Tim 1:20 and 1 Cor 5:5 in the following chart.

Table 7.1 Similarities and Differences between 1 Tim 1:19–20 and 1 Cor 5:3–5

The Offender(s)	Nature of the Issue	Verdict/ Action	Delivering Agent	εἰς Phrase	ἵνα Clause
Hymenaeus and Alexander	"Apostasy" (Blasphemy)	Deliverance to Satan	Paul	-	"in order to learn not to blaspheme"
An Unnamed Man	Sexual Immorality (Incest)	Deliverance to Satan	The Corinthian Community (On Command of Paul)	"for destruction of the flesh"	"that his spirit may be saved in the day of the Lord"

Table 7.2 Competing Understandings of the εἰς phrase and the ἵνα clause in 1 Cor 5:5

Grammarian/Commentator	εἰς phrase	ἵνα clause
Robertson	-	"Ultimate Purpose"/ "The Goal"
Fee	"Anticipated Result"	"Express Purpose"
Fitzmyer	"Immediate Goal"	"The More Remote Goal"

In the light of the preceding discussion, I understand Paul to be directing the believing community to expel—that is, excommunicate—the offender from the community. This parallels Paul's cultic imagery in v. 7a, "Cleanse out the old leaven that you may be a new lump, as you really are unleavened,"[110] and his concluding comment in v. 13b, which echoes Deuteronomic language: "Remove the evil person from among you."[111] The immediate *intention* (εἰς) is "the destruction of the flesh" of the offender, whereas the *goal* of this delivery is "that [ἵνα] *his spirit may be saved in the day of the Lord.*" A good many commentators, both ancient and modern, rightly see a reference here to the eschatological day of the Lord.[112] To this point in 1 Cor, the apostle has made at least three prior references to it.[113] He is clear elsewhere in his writings, moreover, that believers must "all appear before the judgment seat of Christ, so that each one may receive what is due for what he has done in the body, whether good or evil."[114] In light of this, Paul holds forth the goal of eschatological salvation for the offender.[115]

Based on the preceding discussion, what follows is my highly interpretive translation based on my understanding of the details of 1 Corinthians 5:3–5.

"For I, indeed, being absent in body but present in spirit {or: the Spirit}, have already passed verdict—as being [indeed] present [sc. in spirit {or: by the

Spirit}]—on the one who has thus committed this [offense] in the name of [our] Lord Jesus. [Consequently,] when you are gathered together, and my spirit, with the power of our Lord Jesus [is present too], [I have decided to have you] deliver such a one to Satan for the destruction of {what is} fleshly {in him}, {with the ultimate goal that} (his) spirit may be saved in the day of the Lord."

SOME BRIEF REFLECTIONS ON CONTEMPORARY APPLICABILITY OF PAUL'S APOSTOLIC DIRECTIVE

For many today, to ask a question regarding the applicability of Paul's directive in 1 Corinthians 5:3–5 for today's church is almost unthinkable. Craig L. Blomberg is probably not far from correct when he observes, "Large sections of the contemporary church virtually ignore 1 Corinthians 5 altogether."[116] The reasons for this are not easy to reduce to a simple series of bullet points, but two general comments will provide some context for the following discussion. First, the prevailing cultural attitude in the West regards correctives about sexuality as outmoded vestiges of a bygone era. In the late 1990s, the well-known and well-regarded Roman Catholic scholar Raymond Brown observed, "Today correctives about sex are often dismissed as Victorian, but that gives her Britannic majesty credit for something that goes back to the 1st century in Christianity."[117] Second, Bruce Winter observes a fundamental inconsistency in contemporary Christianity's handling of ethical matters in relation to the larger society and itself: "The ease with which the present day church often passes judgment on the ethical or structural misconduct of the outside community is at times matched only by its reluctance to take action to remedy the ethical conduct of its own members. We have reversed Paul's order of things."[118]

A passage such as this challenges contemporary Christians to rethink what the Christian church should look like. Among the constructive things the Protestant Reformers addressed in the wake of the Reformation was the subject of the marks of the Christian Church. On this matter, Martin Luther (1483–1546) and John Calvin (1509–1564) differed. For Calvin, it was where the word of God was sincerely preached and the sacraments administered according to the institution of Christ.[119] Luther, by contrast, maintained that there were seven signs, one of which was church discipline.[120] When discipline is exercised at all in today local churches and Christian denominations, it tends to be expressed in extremes: either extreme severity or extreme leniency. First Corinthians 5 calls for a more intentional and less ad hoc approach. Reflecting on it, I'd like to draw the following observations:

First, sin has a deceptive, blinding capacity: "Everyone has heard that there is sexual immorality among you. This is a type of immorality that isn't even heard of among the Gentiles—a man is having sex with his father's wife!" (1 Cor 5:1, CEV).[121]

Sin is serious business (1 Cor 5:7, "Cleanse out the old leaven that you may be a new lump"; cf. 1 Cor 15:34, "Become sober as you ought and stop sinning. For some have no knowledge of God; I say this to your shame" [NAB]).

Flagrant sin by professing believers within the believing community calls for discipline (1 Cor 5:2, "And you are inflated with pride, instead of filled with grief so that he who has committed this act might be removed from among you"; 1 Cor 5:13b, "'Purge the evil person from among you'").

Discipline encompasses penal and restorative aspects (1 Cor 5:5, "Deliver such a one to Satan for destruction of the flesh so that [his] spirit may be saved in the day of the Lord").

The eschatological goal of discipline is eschatological salvation (1 Cor 5:5b, "*so that [his] spirit may be saved in the day of the Lord.*" Cf. 1 Cor 1:18; 10:33; 15:2).

This passage also raises practical problems: Serious offenders today can avoid discipline simply by leaving and joining a new church—and be welcomed with open arms!

This calls for the need of instruction. Do both the leadership and members of local churches understand what discipline is about from a New Testament perspective?

It also calls for the development of a network of accountability with like-minded local churches in the same geographical area, so that people cannot simply run easily to another church and so avoid dealing with sinful problems in the present that they will face them when they stand before the judgment seat of Christ (cf. 2 Cor 5:10).

Mark Matson is a contemporary scholar who probes the applicability of 1 Corinthians 5 for the contemporary church. He identifies three implications that flow in three directions: the unity of the church, the church's need to protect its purity, and the interconnectedness of local expression of the church to the larger church.[122]

Although all three of Matson's points are worthy of reflection, I will confine my following comments to the first two and will subsequently offer some additional comments regarding Paul's disciplinary directive. The first relates to our prior observation that the content of 1 Cor 5 follows immediately after Paul's address of matters of factionalism in the Corinthian church (1:11–4:21), which had been reported to him from "some from Chloe's household" (1:11). The larger context of 1 Cor 1–4 reminds us that Paul discusses this serious matter of illicit sexual expression in relation to the wider context of Paul's concern for the unity of the believing community (1:10). That Paul next addresses an instance of serious sexual misconduct (5:1–13) suggests that church unity and church purity were interrelated priorities for the apostle.

In that regard, second, the content of 1 Cor 5 relates closely to Paul's earlier comments regarding the believing community's identity as God's holy temple in Corinth: "Do you not know that you are God's temple and that God's Spirit dwells in you?[17] If anyone destroys God's temple, God will destroy him. For God's temple is holy, and you are that temple" (1 Cor 3:16–17, ESV). Paul's directive is thus a reminder that the church is called to purity, and the maintaining of that purity necessarily involves church discipline. God's lofty view of the community provides rationale to Paul's directive relative to the case of incest in 1 Cor 5. It serves to highlight the high demand placed on the church as God's temple (cf. 3:16–17) to protect its standing before God and the world.[123]

In this regard, Craig L. Blomberg's comment is worthy of reflection for professing Christians: "No matter where we live then [sc. whether urban centers, suburbs, and rural areas], Christian fellowship should be a periodic retreat from and revitalization of our regular involvement with the immoral and unbelieving in our world, and not vice versa."[124] Of course, matters are never that simple. The incident in 1 Corinthians 5 is a stark reminder that professing believers and believing communities are as capable of behaving in ways that make even the broader culture blush. Contemporary scandals involving wayward televangelists and the past and once-again-present sex abuse within a major Christian denomination are troubling reminders.[125] First Corinthians 5:3–5 is an important reminder that professing believers are called to be different and act differently.[126]

NOTES

1. For source material on Corinth, particularly as related to the Apostle Paul, see especially the valuable compendium of the late Dominican priest, Jerome Murphy-O'Connor (d. 2013): *St. Paul's Corinth: Texts and Archaeology*, Good News Studies 6 (Collegeville, MN: Glazier, 1983, 2002); see also his collection of previously published essays (with updates) on various aspects of 1 Corinthians in *Keys to First Corinthians: Revisiting the Major Issues*, (Oxford: Oxford University Press, 2009) and on various aspects of 2 Corinthians in *Keys to Second Corinthians: Revisiting the Major Issues* (Oxford: Oxford University Press, 2010).

2. For a volume devoted to comparative study, focused on Greek and Roman imperials, social strata, and local religion, see Steve Friesen, Daniel N. Schowalter, James Walters, eds., *Corinth in Context: Comparative Studies on Religion and Society*, Supplements to Novum Testamentum 134 (Leiden: Brill, 2010).

For works devoted to the social world of first-century Corinth, see, among others, Gerd Theissen, *The Social Setting of Pauline Christianity: Essays on Corinth* (Philadelphia: Fortress, 1982); J. K. Chow, *Patronage and Power: A Study of Social Networks in Corinth*, Journal for the Study of the New Testament: Supplement Series

75 (Sheffield: Sheffield Academic Press, 1992); Andrew D. Clarke, *Secular and Christian Leadership in Corinth: A Socio-Historical and Exegetical Study of 1 Corinthians 1–6* (Leiden: Brill, 1993); Bruce W. Winter, *After Paul Left Corinth: The Influence of Secular Ethics and Social Change* (Grand Rapids, MI: Eerdmans, 2001); and Kar Yong Lim, *Metaphors and Social Identity Formation in Paul's Letters to the Corinthians* (Eugene, OR: Pickwick Publications, 2017).

3. Anthony C. Thiselton, "1 Corinthians," in *New Dictionary of Biblical Theology*, ed. T. Desmond Alexander and Brian S. Rosner (Downers Grove, IL: InterVarsity, 2000), 297.

4. See, *inter alia*, Harry Gamble, "Letters in the New Testament and in the Greco-Roman World," in *The Biblical World*, vol. 1, ed. John Barton (London and New York: Routledge, 2002), 196; and Stanley E. Porter, *The Apostle Paul: His Life, Thought, and Letters* (Grand Rapids, MI: Eerdmans, 2016), 140.

5. Michael F. Hull notes the flexibility of the ancient Greco-Roman letter (*Baptism on Account of the Dead [1 Cor 15:29]: An Act of Faith in the Resurrection* [Atlanta, GA: Society of Biblical Literature/Leiden: Brill, 2005], 55, 69–70). Porter describes three major purposes of ancient letters: (1) to establish and maintain relationships, (2) to provide a dialogical interchange, and (3) to provide a permanent record of some form of the interaction between the sender and receiver (*The Apostle Paul*, 140–41). Stanley K. Stowers identified six broad types of letters that were employed in the Greco-Roman world: *friendship*, for maintaining a friendship with a correspondent; *familial*, to maintain affection and relationship with relatives/the household; *praise* and *blame*, which *commended* or, alternatively, *censured* readers for given reasons or actions; *exhortation* and *advice*, which exhorted or advised recipients as to given actions or viewpoints; *mediation*, where a person made a request to another on behalf of a third party; and *accusing, apologetic, and accounting* letters, which issued accusations, offered defense, or provided accounting details related to business. *Letter Writing in Greco-Roman Antiquity*, Library of Early Christianity 5 (Philadelphia: Westminster, 1986), pt. 2.

6. John L. White, "New Testament Epistolary Literature in the Framework of Ancient Epistolography," in *Aufstieg und Niedergang der römischen Welt* II.25.2 (Berlin: de Gruyter, 1984), 1730–56.

7. See E. Randolph Richards, *Paul and First-Century Letter Writing: Secretaries, Composition and Collection* (Downers Grove, IL: InterVarsity, 2004), esp. chap. 10.

8. First Corinthians 5:9 indicates that this was not Paul's first letter. So as not to prove unduly pedantic, however, I will employ 1 (or First) Cor(inthians) in reference to it for convenience.

9. Thiselton, "1 Corinthians," in *New Dictionary of Biblical Theology*, 297. He further notes that "The cross addressed Corinth in ways which resonate with its message for today's churches."

10. See, for example, Lev 18:18; 20:11; Deut 23:1; 27:20; Mishnah, *Sanh.* 7:4. For additional texts of a Jewish background, see Matthew R. Malcolm, *The World of 1 Corinthians: An Exegetical Source Book of Literary and Visual Background* (Eugene, OR: Cascade, 2013), 60–62.

11. Cicero, *Pro Cluentio*, in *The Orations of Marcus Tullius Cicero*, vol. 2, trans. C. D. Yonge. London: George Bell & Sons, 1902. V.14 (66 BC).

12. Gaius, *Gai Institutiones or Institutes of Roman Law*, trans. Edward Poste, 4th ed. (Oxford: Clarendon Press, 1904), I.63 (AD 161).

13. See Winter, *After Paul Left Corinth*, 49.

14. Winter, *After Paul Left Corinth*, 50, with reference to W. W. Buckland, *A Text-book of Roman Law from the Time of Cicero to the Time of Ulpian*, rev. P. Stein (Oxford: Clarendon Press, 1991), 115 nn. 13–14.

15. W. Randolph Tate, *Biblical Interpretation: An Integrated Approach*, 3rd ed. (Peabody, MA: Hendrickson, 2008), 2.

16. Tate, *Biblical Interpretation*, 1–8.

17. Tate, *Biblical Interpretation*, 5.

18. Tate, *Biblical Interpretation*, 6.

19. Tate, *Biblical Interpretation*, 5.

20. Tate, *Biblical Interpretation*, 5–6.

21. That Paul is the principal author is indicated in the more than one hundred uses of the first person singular uses throughout the letter. Apart from Paul's letters, it is rare in Hellenistic letters for an author to name a coworker, scribe, or amanuensis in the salutation. Richards prefers to describe such individuals as understudies rather than associates, for Paul was clearly in charge (*Paul and First-Century Letter Writing*, 33). With regard to 1 Corinthians, Richards plausibly suggests that Paul invited Sosthenes to join him in the writing process because he knew both the church and Corinthian culture well (*Paul and First-Century Letter Writing*, 113).

22. This includes, traditionally, 1–2 Thessalonians, Galatians, 1–2 Corinthians, and Romans. Cf. Kirsopp Lake's classic study: *The Earlier Epistles of St. Paul: Their Motive and Origin*, 2nd ed. (London: Rivingtons, 1914).

23. According to 1 Corinthians 16:8 the letter was authored from Ephesus, a prominent city directly across the Aegean Sea on the west coast of Asia Minor (modern-day western Turkey). With regard to Pauline mission, see esp. Eckhard Schnabel, *Early Christian Mission*, vol. 1, *Paul and the Early Church* (Downers Grove, IL: InterVarsity, 2004), and in mildly shorter compass, Eckhard J. Schnabel, *Paul the Missionary: Realities, Strategies and Methods*, (Downers Grove, IL: InterVarsity, 2008).

24. For example, 1 Cor 1:11 ("some from Chloe's household have informed me"). Cf. 1 Cor 5:1 (discussed further below).

25. Cf. 1 Cor 7:1a, "Now concerning the matters you wrote about" (Περὶ δὲ ὧν ἐγράψατε). The triumvirate of Stephanas, Fortunatus, and Achaicus, who are mentioned in 16:17, apparently brought Paul this letter. Paul's responses to these matters—as in 7:1—are commonly signaled by the phrase "Now concerning" (Περὶ δέ): 7:25; 8:1; 11:2; 12:1; 16:1(, 12).

26. Roy E. Ciampa and Brian S. Rosner eschew reading 1 Corinthians more narrowly as Paul's response to oral and written reports regarding the problems addressed. They favor a biblical/Jewish approach to the letter, viewing it as Paul's "attempt to tell the church of God that they are part of the fulfillment of the Old Testament expectation of worldwide worship of the God of Israel, and as God's eschatological temple they must act in a manner appropriate to their pure and holy status by becoming

unified, shunning pagan vices, and glorifying God in obedience to the lordship of Jesus Christ" (*The First Letter to the Corinthians*, Pillar New Testament Commentaries, [Grand Rapids, MI: Eerdmans, 2010], 52; their italics). Their proposed approach is not at odds with acknowledging that there are explicit elements of occasion indicated at various points in the letter's content (e.g., 1:11; 5:1; 7:1).

27. So many commentators: for example, Anthony C. Thiselton, *The First Epistle to the Corinthians*, New International Greek Testament Commentary (Grand Rapids, MI: Eerdmans, 2000), vi–xii; Eckhard Schnabel, *Der erste Brief des Paulus an die Korinther*, Historisch Theologische Auslegung (Wuppertal: R. Brockhaus, 2006), 3–5; Joseph A. Fitzmyer, *First Corinthians: A New Translation with Introduction and Commentary*, Anchor Yale Bible (New Haven, CT: Yale University Press, 2008), viii–x; and Ciampa and Rosner, *First Letter*, vi–xii.

28. Gordon D. Fee, *The First Epistle to the Corinthians*, The New International Commentary on the New Testament (Grand Rapids, MI: Eerdmans, 1987; rev. ed., 2014), 825 (1987 ed.), and 913 (2014 ed.). (I will use both editions below and differentiate them as 1987 ed. and 2014 ed., respectively.) See, too, David E. Garland, *1 Corinthians*, Baker Exegetical Commentary on the New Testament (Grand Rapids, MI: Baker Academic, 2003), vii–viii.

29. So Ben Witherington III, *Conflict and Community in Corinth: A Socio-Rhetorical Commentary on 1 and 2 Corinthians* (Grand Rapids, MI: Eerdmans, 1995), vi–viii; and Raymond E. Brown, *An Introduction to the New Testament*, Anchor Bible Reference Library (New York: Doubleday, 1997), 512, 525. Brown considered 16:1–18 the body closing and 16:19–24 the conclusion of the letter, which he titled "concluding formula."

30. For a thorough, recent study of the structure of 1 Corinthians, see Matthew R. Malcolm, *Paul and the Rhetoric of Reversal in 1 Corinthians: The Impact of Paul's Gospel on his Macro-Rhetoric*, Society for New Testament Studies Monograph Series 155 (Cambridge: Cambridge University Press, 2013). See my review of this volume in *Bulletin of Biblical Research* 24, no. 4 (2014): 588–90.

31. On the function of this metaphor in the Corinthian correspondence, see Lim, "'You are God's Temple': Temple Metaphor," in his *Metaphors and Social Identity Formation in Paul's Letters to the Corinthians*, 137–58.

32. Although Fitzmyer maintains that the problem concerning Christian behavior in 5:1–13 is "unrelated" to the problem of rivalries addresses in 1:10–4:21, he nonetheless concedes that it is "one which stems from the same root cause"—namely, arrogance (*First Corinthians*, 229).

33. Fee, *First Epistle* (2014 ed.), 212.

34. Malcolm, *Paul and the Rhetoric of Reversal in 1 Corinthians*, 228–29. He divides 1 Cor 5–14 into two portions: I: sexual immorality, greed, bodies belonging to the Lord [1 Cor 5–7]; and II: self-restraint, love, participation in the one body [1 Cor 8–14]). He further identifies four rhetorical units in this section: 5:1–7:40, 8:1–11:1, 11:2–11:34, and 12:1–14:40.

35. As Winter correctly observes, "Paul himself was in no doubt that what was reported to him was correct" (*After Paul Left Corinth*, 49).

36. As Thiselton, *First Epistle*, 385, maintains.

37. Brown favors this view (*Introduction*, 517 n. 15). Fitzmyer also holds out the possibility ("perhaps") that it was those who brought Paul the Corinthians' letter to be mentioned in 1 Cor 7:1, "if different from the delegates [sc. Stephanas, Fortunatus and Achaicus]" (*First Corinthians*, 229).

38. The simplest explanation for Paul's lack of additional reference to the woman, outside of the passing reference in 5:1b, is that she was not a member of the believing community; hence, she was outside the scope of his apostolic authority (cf. 5:12a, 13b).

39. The generalized sense of τις ἀδελφός (lit. "a brother") implied in context is captured variously as "a believer" (NLT), "a Christian" (NET), and "a brother or sister" (NIV 2011; cf. similarly CEV: "'brother' or 'sister'"). The TNIV unnecessarily employed the plural "fellow believers."

40. That is, if one is "sexually immoral or greedy, an idolater or a reviler, a drunkard or a swindler" (1 Cor 5:11).

41. James Moffatt, *The First Epistle of Paul to the Corinthians*, Moffatt New Testament Commentary 7 (London: Hodder & Stoughton, 1938), 56. Fitzmyer similarly observes that the syntax of 1 Cor 5:3–5 is "quite complicated" (*First Corinthians*, 236).

42. Most standard English translations render τῷ πνεύματι as "in spirit"; the NLT, however, offers "in the Spirit." Among commentators, Fee (*First Epistle* [1987 ed.], 205; [2014 ed.], 225) and Thiselton (*First Epistle*, 384) favor a reference to the Holy Spirit. Fitzmyer, by contrast, takes issue with both Fee and Thiselton on this matter and contends that Paul employs the body/spirit contrast as "a way of emphasizing his personal interest in the community" (*First Corinthians*, 236). Ciampa and Rosner find it hard to decide between Paul's human spirit and a reference to the Holy Spirit (*First Letter*, 204–5). Gordon D. Fee, moreover, acknowledges that there is some ambiguity in the phrase and suggests the inelegant "in S/spirit" to convey the intention of "Paul's somewhat flexible language" (*God's Empowering Spirit: The Holy Spirit in the Letters of Paul* [Peabody, MA: Hendrickson, 1994], 24–26, here 25; cf. *First Epistle* [1987 ed.], 204–206; [2014 ed.], 224).

43. Standard English translations render the injunction variously: "deliver . . . to Satan" (KJV, ASV, RSV, NASB, NKJV, NASB 95, ESV), "hand over . . . to Satan" (NIV 1984, NRSV, NLT, ISV, LEB, CEV), and "turn over . . . to Satan" (NET, HCSB).

44. Standard English translations commonly employ the following translations of εἰς ὄλεθρον: "for destruction" (KJV, ASV, RSV, NASB, NKJV, NAB, NRSV, NASB 95, NET, ESV, HCSB, ISV, LEB), "to be destroyed" (NJB, NIV 1984, NLT), or "to destroy" (CEV).

45. Some standard English translations identify the referent as the offender, whether "of *his* flesh" (NASB, NAB, NASB 95, ISV) or the more interpretive renderings "of *his* sensual body" (JB), "of *his* body" (REB), "of *his* sinful nature" (NLT), "*his* human weakness" (CEV) (italicization added to each). Most standard English translations favor a literal rendering for the genitive τῆς σαρκός ("of the flesh": KJV, ASV, RSV, NKJV, NRSV, NET, ESV, HCSB, LEB, NIV 2011). A minority of versions prefer more interpretive renderings: "of the body" (NEB), "of natural life" (NJB), "the sinful nature" (NIV 1984), "of the sinful nature" (TNIV).

46. Standard English translations almost invariably render τὸ πνεῦμα as "his spirit"; KJV and ASV, conversely, preferred "the spirit."

47. Barth Campbell, "Flesh and Spirit in 1 Cor 5:5: An Exercise in Rhetorical Criticism of the New Testament," *Journal of the Evangelical Theological Society* 36, no. 3 (1993): 331–42.

48. Thiselton, *First Epistle*, 396–97; cf. Paul A. Toseland, "Delivered to Satan: 1 Cor. 5:3–5 and 1 Tim. 1:18–20," *Testamentum Imperium* 1 (2005–2007), 1–19, accessed May 18, 2018, http://www.preciousheart.net/ti/2007/011_07_Toseland_Delivered_to_Satan.pdf.

49. The precise wording of the genitive expression ("in the name of the Lord [of us] Jesus") in the first prepositional phrase also involves a text-critical question. Here, however, it is enough to note that the referent is clearly the Lord Jesus, with some question as to whether the pronoun "our" is original or secondary. There is considerable variation in wording of the textual witnesses: "our Lord Jesus" (B D* 1175 1739 itb, d), "Lord Jesus Christ" (Aleph itar vgmss geo1), "Lord Jesus" (A Ψ 1852), "our Lord Jesus Christ" (P46 Dc F G P et al.), "our Lord" (*l* 1021), and even "Jesus Christ our Lord" (81). Standard contemporary English versions mildly favor "our Lord Jesus" (NASB, NJB, NASB 95, NET, HCSB, ISV, LEB, NIV 2011) over "the Lord Jesus" (RSV, NRSV, NLT, ESV), with the KJV and NKJV supporting the fuller "our Lord Jesus Christ."

50. Here, again, there is some degree of variation in the witnesses: "our Lord Jesus" (*P46* P Ψ 629 1505 *pc* vgst syh) vs. "our Lord" (630 1729 *pc*).

51. Hans Conzelmann identified six syntactical possibilities in 1 Cor 5:3–5 (*1 Corinthians: A Commentary*, Hermeneia [Philadelphia: Fortress, 1975], 97). Based on a survey of representative secondary literature, Keith Richard Krell delineates ten different punctuation options in this section ("Temporal Judgment and the Church: Paul's Remedial Agenda in 1 Corinthians" [PhD Diss., University of Bristol and Trinity College, 2010], 116 n. 750).

52. Most standard English translations convey a cognitive, juridical, or condemnatory nuance regarding κέκρικα: "I have judged" (NKJV, NASB 95, NET); "I have pronounced judgment" (RSV, NAB, NRSV, ESV; "I have condemned"—NJB) or "I have passed judgment" (NIV 1984, NLT, ISV, LEB, NIV 2011); "I have decided" (HCSB). Walter Bauer, Frederick W. Danker, William F. Arndt, and F. Wilbur Gingrich, *Greek-English Lexicon of the New Testament and Other Early Christian Literature*, 3rd ed. (Chicago: University of Chicago Press, 2000), favor a cognitive decision (s.v. κρίνω 4); cf. the similar use in Tit 3:12, "*I have decided* [κέκρικα] to spend the winter [in Nicopolis]." (References to Bauer's *Lexicon* will henceforth be identified as BDAG, plus the entry.)

53. Fee (*First Epistle* [1987 ed.], 207–208; [2014 ed.], 228) and Ciampa and Rosner (*First Letter*, 206) favor this. Fitzmyer considers it "too far removed" (*First Corinthians*, 237).

54. Thiselton (*First Epistle*, 384), Schnabel (*erste Brief*, 280), and Fitzmyer (*First Corinthians*, 228, 236–37) support this.

55. Archibald Robertson and Alfred Plummer preferred this construction (*A Critical and Exegetical Commentary on the First Epistle of Paul to the Corinthians*,

2nd ed. International Critical Commentary [Edinburgh: T. & T. Clark, 1914], 98). Fitzmyer considers it "not impossible" (*First Corinthians*, 237).

56. A strong advocate of this interpretation is Jérome Murphy-O'Connor, "1 Corinthians v, 3–5," Revue Biblique 84 (1977): 239–45, reprinted as "1 Corinthians 5:3–5," in idem, *Keys* (n. 1 above), 11–18. Additional scholars favoring this rendering include A. Yarbro Collins, "The Function of 'Excommunication' in Paul," *Harvard Theological Review* 73 (1980): 251–63; and Toseland, "Delivered to Satan," 4–5. Fee considers it "possible" (*First Epistle* [2014 ed.], 228).

57. Besides here in 1 Cor 5:4: 1 Cor 6:11; Eph 5:20; Phil 2:10; Col 3:17.

58. 1 Cor 6:11; Eph 5:20; Col 3:17. We have left 1 Cor 5:4 to the side, for the moment.

59. The one counter example is Phil 2:10, where ἐν τῷ ὀνόματι Ἰησοῦ is embedded in a subordinate ἵνα clause for emphasis: ἵνα ἐν τῷ ὀνόματι Ἰησοῦ πᾶν γόνυ κάμψῃ ("in order that at the name of Jesus every knee should bow").

60. 1 Cor 5:2a, "And you are arrogant! [καὶ ὑμεῖς πεφυσιωμένοι ἐστέ]."

61. 1 Cor 5:6a, "Your boasting is not good [Οὐ καλὸν τὸ καύχημα ὑμῶν]."

62. Ciampa and Rosner, *First Letter*, 202. Their response, however, is directed to an interpretation that explains vv. 2a, 6a, as an example of an abuse of Christian liberty. Against that interpretation they make three points (Ciampa and Rosner, *First Letter*, 202–3). However, none of their points—(1) Paul doesn't touch on the abuse of Christian liberty until 6:12–20, (2) Paul uses the particle δέ rather than the conjunction καί, and (3) Paul indicates that the Corinthians were already puffed up previously (e.g., 1:31; 3:21; 4:6, 18, 19)—is particularly persuasive, and none nullifies the larger point above.

63. καύχησις (noun: *boasting*): Rom 3:27; 15:17; 1 Cor 15:31; 2 Cor 1:12; 7:4, 14; 8:24; 11:10, 17; 1 Thess 2:19; καύχημα (noun: *boast*): Rom 4:2; 1 Cor 5:6; 9:15–16; 2 Cor 1:14; 5:12; 9:3; Gal 6:4; Phil 1:26; 2:16; καυχάομαι (verb: *boast*): Rom 2:17, 23; 5:2–3, 11; 1 Cor 1:29, 31; 3:21; 4:7; 13:3; 2 Cor 5:12; 7:14; 9:2; 10:8, 13, 15–17; 11:12, 16, 18, 30; 12:1, 5–6, 9; Gal 6:13–14; Eph 2:9; Phil 3:3.

64. If he were also a person of high social standing, as Clarke (*Secular and Christian Leadership in Corinth*, 95–99) and Winter (*After Paul Left Corinth*, 44–57) plausibly maintain, that would have provided additional plausibility to such a claim.

65. Fee, *First Epistle* (1987 ed.), 207; (2014 ed.), 227.

66. Murphy-O'Connor, *St. Paul's Corinth*, especially 55–57, 111, 144–46.

67. Less than five years, on common reckonings of Pauline chronology. Paul's initial eighteen-month ministry in Corinth (Acts 18:1–11), owing to the reference to Gallio (Acts 18:12), is commonly dated ca. AD 50–51 (cf. Loveday C. A. Alexander, "Chronology of Paul," in *Dictionary of Paul and His Letters*, ed. Gerald F. Hawthorne and Ralph P. Martin [Downers Grove, IL: InterVarsity, 1993], 123). His authoring of 1 Cor is no later than 54/55.

68. Murphy-O'Connor, "1 Corinthians 5:3–5," in *Keys*, 17.

69. Murphy-O'Connor, "1 Corinthians 5:3–5," in *Keys*, 17–18.

70. For example, KJV, ASV, RSV, NASB, NKJV, NIV 1984, NAB, NJB, NASB 95, NET, ESV, HCSB, CEV ("When you meet together in the name of our Lord Jesus, I'll be present in spirit with the power of our Lord Jesus"). Representative commentators

include Robertson and Plummer, *First Epistle*, 98; Thiselton, *First Epistle*, 384; Schnabel, *erste Brief*, 271–72, 280; and Fitzmyer, *First Corinthians*, 236–37.

71. Cf. notes 46–47 above.

72. Karl P. Donfried, "Justification and Last Judgment in Paul," *Interpretation* 30 (1976): 140–52, especially 150–51.

73. Campbell, "Flesh and Spirit," 331–42; Toseland, "Delivered to Satan," 1–19.

74. Campbell, "Flesh and Spirit in 1 Cor 5:5," 341.

75. Toseland understands that Paul is calling for expulsion of the offender, but he does not regard this as an irrevocable act. He additionally suggests that the expelled offender is the same one offered forgiveness in 2 Cor 2:5–11 following repentance ("Delivered to Satan," 17). This identification, while possible, is by no means as likely as adherents suggest.

76. Cf. Gordon D. Fee, *1 and 2 Timothy, Titus*, New International Bible Commentary, (Peabody, MA: Hendrickson, 1989), 59; and I. Howard Marshall, *A Critical and Exegetical Commentary on the Pastoral Epistles*, International Critical Commentaries (Edinburgh: T. & T. Clark, 1999), 415.

Tertullian (ca. AD 160–ca. 220), convinced that serious post-baptismal sins were irremissible, offered alternative ways of understanding the ἵνα clause in 1 Tim 1:20 (ἵνα παιδευθῶσιν μὴ βλασφημεῖν), including interpreting the third person pronoun implicit in the verb παιδευθῶσιν as a reference to "the rest, who, by *their* deliverance to Satan—that is, their projection outside the Church—had to be trained in the knowledge that there must be no blaspheming" ("On Modesty," 13, in *The Ante-Nicene Fathers: The Writings of the Fathers down to A.D. 325*, vol. 4, ed. and trans. Alexander Roberts and James Donaldson [Edinburgh: T. & T. Clark, 1885], 86–87).

77. Fitzmyer, *First Corinthians*, 239–40 (citation 239).

78. The infinitive could be taken as being in indirect discourse, here as an object of the previously expressed verb of communication κέκρικα (I have decided) (v. 3). If so, Paul's apostolic decision, before God, has already (ἤδη) been determined. It is up to the Corinthians to carry it out. If not connected back to v. 3, it could also be interpreted as a rare use of the imperatival infinitive (cf. Rom 12:15, χαίρειν μετὰ χαιρόντων, κλαίειν μετὰ κλαιόντων ["Rejoice with those who rejoice, weep with those who weep"]; Phil 3:16, πλὴν εἰς ὃ ἐφθάσαμεν, τῷ αὐτῷ στοιχεῖν ["Only, keep in step with that to which we have attained"]) or as a complement to an unexpressed but implied δεῖ ("it is necessary") (an explicit δεῖ appears in 1 Cor 8:2; 11:19; 15:25, 53; 2 Cor 5:10; 11:30; 12:1; elsewhere: 1 Thess 4:1; 2 Thess 3:7; Rom 8:26; 12:3; Eph 6:20; Col 4:4, 6; 1 Tim 3:2, 7, 15; 2 Tim 2:6, 24; Tit 1:7, 11).

79. In a discussion of "flesh" (σάρξ) Bultmann cited the language of ὄλεθρον τῆς σαρκός in 1 Cor 5:5 as an example of physical death: "death, as the end of physical life, is 'destruction of the flesh' (I Cor. 5:5)" (Rudolf Bultmann, *Theology of the New Testament*, 2 vols. [New York: Scribner's, 1951, 1955], 1:233). Two of his prominent students assumed this without any argument: E. Käsemann, "Sentences of Holy Law in the New Testament," in *New Testament Questions for Today* (Philadelphia: Fortress, 1968), 71 ("obviously"); similarly, Conzelmann, *1 Corinthians*, 97. Cf. too BDAG s.v. ὄλεθρος 2, citing the older works of Ernest von Dobschütz, *Die urchristlichen Gemeinden* (Leipzig: Sittengeschichtliche Bilder, 1902), 269–72;

and Hans Lietzmann, *An die Korinther I/II*, Handbuch zum Neuen Testament (Tübingen: Mohr-Siebeck, 1949), 28.

80. For example, M. Dods, *The First Epistle to the Corinthians* (New York: A. C. Armstrong, 1889), 118, who described the apostle's directive in terms of "bodily suffering" and "disciplinary suffering."

81. Robertson and Plummer, *First Epistle*, 99–100. Cf. A. T. Robertson, *Word Pictures in the New Testament* (Grand Rapids, MI: Baker reprint, n.d.), vol. 4, on 1 Cor 5:5: "Both for physical suffering as in the case of Job (Job 2:6) and for conquest of the fleshly sins, remedial punishment."

82. David Raymond Smith, "Hand This Man over to Satan: Curse, Exclusion and Salvation in 1 Corinthians 5" (PhD Diss., Durham University, 2005), v. Available at Durham E-Theses Online, http://etheses.dur.ac.uk/1789/. This dissertation has now been published as David Raymond Smith, *'Hand This man over to Satan': Curse, Exclusion and Salvation in 1 Corinthians 5*, The Library of New Testament Studies 386 (New York: Bloomsbury T & T Clark, 2009). Although I do not find Smith's interpretation fully persuasive, he offers very helpful background on the history of interpretation.

83. In Acts 13:11a Saul (Paul) pronounces an imprecation on a sorcerer, a Jewish false prophet named Bar-Jesus (also Elymas), who was seeking "seeking to turn the proconsul [sc. Sergius Paulus, v. 7] away from the faith" (13:8): "And now, behold, the hand of the Lord is upon you, and *you will be blind and unable to see the sun for a time*" (καὶ νῦν ἰδοὺ χεὶρ κυρίου ἐπὶ σὲ καὶ ἔσῃ τυφλὸς μὴ βλέπων τὸν ἥλιον ἄχρι καιροῦ). See similarly Gal 1:8–9, "But even if we or an angel from heaven should preach to you a gospel contrary to the one we preached to you, *let him be accursed* [ἤτω ἀνάθεμα]. [9] As we have said before, so now I say again: If anyone is preaching to you a gospel contrary to the one you received, *let him be accursed* [ἤτω ἀνάθεμα]"; and 1 Cor 16:22, "If anyone has no love for the Lord, *let him be accursed* [ἤτω ἀνάθεμα]. Our Lord, come!"

84. 1 Kgs 13:34; Hos 9:6; Obad 1:13; Jer 28:55; 31:3, 8, 32; 32:31; Ezek 6:14; 14:16; Prov 1:26–27; 21:7; Jdt 11:15; 2 Macc 6:12; 13:6; 3 Macc 6:30, 34; *4 Macc* 10:15; Wis 1:12, 14; 18:13; Sir 39:30; *Ps. Sol.* 8:1. Cf. Johan Lust, Erik Eynikel, and Katrin Hauspie, *A Greek-English Lexicon of the Septuagint* (Stuttgart: Deutsche Bibelgesellschaft, 1992, 1996), s.v. ὄλεθρος.

85. 1 Thess 5:3, 2 Thess 1:9, and 1 Tim 6:9.

86. 1 Thess 5:3, of sudden eschatological destruction (αἰφνίδιος . . . ὄλεθρος) that will come upon the unsuspecting; and 2 Thess 1:9, of the penalty of everlasting destruction (δίκην . . . ὄλεθρον αἰώνιον) that those who don't know God and on those who don't obey the gospel of Lord Jesus will pay (cf. v. 8).

87. 1 Tim 6:9, of the ruin and destruction (ὄλεθρον καὶ ἀπώλειαν) into (εἰς) that people are plunged who desire to be rich.

88. Fee, *First Epistle* (1987 ed.), 208–13 and (2014 ed.), 228–34; esp. James T. South, "A Critique of the 'Curse/Death Interpretation of 1 Corinthians 5:1–8," *New Testament Studies* 39 (1993): 539–61; Garland, *1 Corinthians*, 169–72 (largely indebted to South); and Ciampa and Rosner, *First Letter*, 208.

89. Thiselton, *First Epistle*, 384. For a full and convincing discussion that destruction of the σάρξ can refer to the particular aspects or qualities that σάρξ denotes, see Thiselton's earlier article, "The Meaning of Σάρξ in 1 Cor. 5:5: A Fresh Approach in the Light of Logical and Semantic Factors," *Scottish Journal of Theology* 26 (1973): 204–28, and, more briefly, *First Epistle*, 395–96.

90. For example, Gal 5:13, 16, 17 (*bis*), 19, 24; 6:8 (*bis*); Rom 7:5, 18, 25; 8:3, 4–6, 8–9, 12–13; 13:14; Eph 2:3; Col 2:11, 13. The NIV 1984, NLT, and TNIV translated σάρξ as "sinful nature" here; the NJB employed "natural life," a change from "his sensual body" (JB). (Cf. n. 46 above.) Robertson and Plummer observed: "As in 2 Cor. vii. 1, τὸ πνεῦμα is used in contrast to ἡ σάρξ and as the chief and distinctive factor in the constitution of man, but as not *per se* distinctive of a state of grace" (*First Epistle*, 100). See further 2 Cor 7:1, Col 2:5; cf. 1 Pet 4:6.

Elsewhere in 1 Cor σάρξ is used in 1 Cor 1:26 (κατὰ σάρκα—merely mortal standards), 29 (πᾶσα σάρξ of *every person, everyone*, a Hebraism for כׇּל־בָּשָׂר); 6:16 (in a citation of Gen 2:24, parallel in Paul's argument to "one body" [ἓν σῶμα]); 7:28 (of physical limitations); 10:18 (where κατὰ σάρκα is used of *earthly Israel*; cf. BDAG s.v. σάρξ 4); 15:39 (of the material forms of different kinds of creatures), 50 (flesh and blood—mere mortality; cf. BDAG s.v. σάρξ 3.a).

91. William Barclay, *Flesh and Spirit: An Examination of Galatians 5:19–21* (London: SCM, 1962; Grand Rapids, MI: Eerdmans reprint, 1976), 22; cf. Richard N. Longenecker, *Galatians*, Word Biblical Commentary 41 (Waco, TX: Word, 1990), 240. John M. G. Barclay contends that it designates "*what is merely human*, in contrast to the divine activity displayed on the cross and in the gift of the Spirit" (*Obeying the Truth: A Study of Paul's Ethics in Galatians* [Edinburgh: T. & T. Clark, 1988], 206; his italics). Gordon D. Fee argues that "when the usage is pejorative, it refers to what is 'human and over against God in deliberate fallenness'" (*God's Empowering Presence*, 385 n. 64). This contrasts with BDAG's suggestion that σάρξ in 1 Cor 5:5 refers to "the physical body as functioning entity, *body, physical body*" (s.v. σάρξ 2).

92. Fee, *First Epistle* (1987 ed.), 212; (2014 ed.), 233.

93. For example, ἀποθνῄσκω, *die* (1 Cor. 15:31); συνθάπτω εἰς τὸν θάνατον, *bury with in death* (Rom. 6:4); θανατόω, *put to death* (Rom 8:13); λογίσασθαι ἑαυτὸν [εἶναι] νεκρόν, *to consider oneself (to be) dead* (Rom 6:11); εἰς τὸν θάνατον βαπτισθῆναι, *to be baptized [or immersed] into death* (Rom 6:3); σταυρόω τὴν σάρκα, *crucify the flesh* (Gal. 5:24); συσταυρόω, *crucify (together) with* (Gal 2:20); νεκρόω, *put to death* (Col 3:5); θάνατος, *death* (2 Cor. 4:11).

94. This could be a reference either to the flesh or the Law itself.

95. Conzelmann, *1 Corinthians*, 97.

96. ἐναυάγησαν, from ναυαγέω, "suffer shipwreck" (ναῦς [*ship*] + ἄγνυμι '*break*') (cf. BDAG, s.v. ναυαγέω), used literally in 2 Cor 11:25, and employed figuratively here in 1 Tim 1:19. Paul's authorship of 1 Timothy is widely denied, but the case against it is not fully persuasive to all contemporary commentators: George W. Knight, III, *The Pastoral Epistles: A Commentary on the Greek Text*, New International Greek Testament Commentary (Grand Rapids, MI: Eerdmans, 1992); Gordon D. Fee, *1 & 2 Timothy, Titus* (n. 76 above); William D. Mounce, *Pastoral Epistles*, Word Biblical

Commentary 46 (Nashville, TN: Thomas Nelson, 2000); Luke Timothy Johnson, *The First and Second Letters to Timothy*, The Anchor Yale Bible Commentaries (New York: Doubleday, 2001); and Philip H. Towner, *The Letters to Timothy and Titus*, The New International Commentary on the New Testament, ed. Gordon D. Fee (Grand Rapids, MI: Eerdmans, 2006). For a helpful discussion of the subject of pseudonymity and the formation of the Pauline canon, see Porter, *The Apostle Paul*, chap. 6.

97. ὧν ἐστιν, οὓς [sc. Ὑμέναιος καὶ Ἀλέξανδρος] παρέδωκα τῷ σατανᾷ, ἵνα παιδευθῶσιν μὴ βλασφημεῖν (1 Tim. 1:20b)

98. So rightly Knight, *The Pastoral Epistles*, 111; Robertson, *Word Pictures*, vol. IV, on 1 Tim 1:20; Marshall, *Pastoral Epistles*, 415; and Towner, *Letters to Timothy and Titus*, 161.

99. Fee, *First Epistle* (1987 ed.), 209, and (2014 ed.), 230: "What the grammar suggests . . . is that the 'destruction of the flesh' is the anticipated result of the man's being put back into Satan's domain, while the express purpose of the action is his redemption." See the discussion below regarding Thiselton and Garland. Cf. also Ciampa and Rosner, *First Letter*, 209.

100. Fee, *First Epistle* (1987 ed.), 209; he repeats this observation in (2014 ed.), 230. An example of this understanding is reflected in Campbell's suggestion that the ἵνα clauses reflect proximate ("for the destruction of the flesh") and ultimate ("that the spirit may be saved") purposes ("Flesh and Spirit," 339).

101. Robertson comments regarding the ἵνα clause: "The ultimate purpose of the expulsion as discipline . . . . The final salvation of the man in the day of Christ is the goal and this is to be attained not by condoning his sin" (*Word Pictures*, vol. 4, on 1 Cor 5:5).

102. Fitzmyer, *First Corinthians*, 239–40.

103. Note, for example, NAB, NKJV, NRSV, NASB/NASB 95, NET, ESV, TNIV, HCSB, ISV, NIV 2011.

104. Thiselton renders it as follows: "we are to consign this man, such as he is, to Satan *with a view to* the destruction of the fleshly, *in order that* the spirit may be saved at the day of the Lord" (*First Epistle*, 384; italics added). Garland is similar: "hand over such a one to Satan *for* the destruction of the flesh *in order that* the spirit might be saved ʽin the day of the Lord'" (*1 Corinthians*, 155; italics added).

105. See BDAG s.v. εἰς 4.f (purpose) and BDAG s.v. εἰς 4.e (result).

106. See BDAG s.v. ἵνα 1 (purpose), BDAG s.v. ἵνα 3 (result), and BDAG s.v. ἵνα 3 (purpose-result); cf. also Daniel B. Wallace, *Greek Grammar beyond the Basics* (Grand Rapids, MI: Zondervan, 1996), 473–74.

107. Wallace, *Greek Grammar*, 473.

108. Wallace, *Greek Grammar*, 473, citing BDAG s.v. ἵνα 3.

109. This is perhaps a divine (or theological) passive, with God being understood as the implied, but unexpressed agent of the passive verb.

110. ἐκκαθάρατε τὴν παλαιὰν ζύμην, ἵνα ἦτε νέον φύραμα, καθώς ἐστε ἄζυμοι· (1 Cor 5:7a).

111. ἐξάρατε τὸν πονηρὸν ἐξ ὑμῶν αὐτῶν (1 Cor 5:13b). Cf. Deut 13:5; 17:7, 12; 21:21; 22:21.

112. This "day" evokes the "day of the LORD" in the Old Testament prophets and its connotations of punishment and vindication (Isa 2:12; 13:6, 9; Joel 3:14; Amos 5:18–20; Zeph 1:7, 14–16; Mal 3:17; 4:1, 3, 5).

113. 1:8 ("He [sc. God] will also confirm you to the end, blameless in the day of our Lord Jesus Christ"); 3:13 ("each one's work will become manifest, for the Day will disclose it"); 4:3 ("But with me it is a very small thing that I should be judged by you or by any human day").

114. 2 Cor 5:10; cf. Rom 14:10–12.

115. Fee, *First Epistle* (1987 ed.), 213 (2014 ed.), 233: "The intent of the action ... is the man's salvation"; cf. Bruce Winter: "The purpose of the community's action is the salvation of his soul at the judgment" ("1 Corinthians," in *New Bible Commentary: 21st Century Edition*, ed. D. A. Carson, 4th ed. [Downers Grove, IL: InterVarsity, 1994], comment on 1 Cor 5:5).

116. Craig L. Blomberg, *1 Corinthians*, The NIV Life Application Commentary Series, (Grand Rapids, MI: Zondervan, 1995), 111. Of course, the statement is anecdotal; however, accurate, social-scientific proportions would be difficult, if not impossible, to establish.

117. Brown, *Introduction*, 517–18. He further noted, "Responsible sexual behavior in and out of marriage is a major issue in life; and inevitably what belief in Christ meant for such behavior became a problem, especially since the Jews and Gentiles who came to faith did not always share the same presuppositions" (Brown, *Introduction*, 517–18.).

118. Winter, "1 Corinthians," comment on 1 Cor 5:13. See, too, the observations of Fee, *First Epistle* (1987 ed.), 213–14.

119. John Calvin, *Institutes of the Christian Religion*, trans. Henry Beveridge (Peabody, MA: Hendrickson, 2008), IV, 1.9: "Wherever we see the word of God sincerely preached and heard, wherever we see the sacraments administered according to the institution of Christ, there we cannot have any doubt that the Church of God has some existence, since his promise cannot fail, 'Where two or three are gathered together in my name, there am I in the midst of them'" (Matthew 18:20).

120. 1. The possession of the holy Word of God, 2. The holy sacrament of baptism, 3. The holy sacrament of the altar (i.e. Communion), 4. The office of the keys exercised publicly (i.e., Church discipline), 5. The public ministry (consecrates ministers), 6. Prayer, public praise, and thanksgiving to God, and 7. The Possession of the sacred cross (i.e., suffering for the sake of the Gospel). See Martin Luther, "On the Councils and the Church" (1539), in *Luther's Works*, vol. 41, *Church and Ministry* III, ed. Eric W. Gritsch (Philadelphia: Fortress Press, 1966).

121. Cf. Rom 7:11 (a highly rhetorical passage), "For sin, seizing an opportunity through the commandment, deceived me, and through it killed me." My own understanding of Romans 7:7–25 is very close to that of Michael F. Bird, who observes: "I am persuaded that this passage [sc. Romans 7:7–25] is not autobiographical of Paul either pre- or post-conversion, but underscores the plight of the Jew under the law and the dark vestiges of the 'Adamic self'" (*The Saving Righteousness of God: Studies on Paul, Justification and the New Perspective*, Paternoster Biblical Monographs [Waynesboro, GA: Paternoster, 2007], 147).

122. Mark A. Matson, "Sexual Sin as a Demonstration of Disunity: 1 Corinthians 5 in Context," *Leaven* 9, no. 3, article 3 (2001): 116–22, here 121–22, accessed May 18, 2018, http://digitalcommons.pepperdine.edu/leaven/vol9/iss3/3.

123. See esp. Ciampa and Rosner, *First Letter*, 221.

124. Blomberg, *1 Corinthians*, 114.

125. Heath W. Carter, "The Cautionary Tale of Jim and Tammy Faye Bakker," *Christianity Today* (September 19, 2017), accessed September 5, 2018, https://www.christianitytoday.com/ct/2017/september-web-only/cautionary-tale-of-jim-and-tammy-faye-bakker.html; Jean M. Bartunek, Mary Ann Hinsdale, James F. Keenan, eds., *Church Ethics and Its Organizational Context: Learning from the Sex Abuse Scandal in the Catholic Church*, Boston College Church in the 21st Century Series (Lanham, MD: Rowman & Littlefield, 2006); for recent news: "Roman Catholic Church Sex Abuse Cases," accessed Sept., 5, 2018, https://www.nytimes.com/topic/organization/roman-catholic-church-sex-abuse-cases.

126. To this end, see the challenging and provocative study of Linda L. Belleville, *Sex, Lies, and the Truth: Developing a Christian Ethic in a Post-Christian Society* (Eugene, OR: Wipf & Stock, 2010).

BIBLIOGRAPHY

Alexander, Loveday C. A. "Chronology of Paul." In *Dictionary of Paul and His Letters*. Edited by Gerald F. Hawthorne and Ralph P. Martin. Downers Grove, IL: InterVarsity, 1993.

Barclay, John M. G. *Obeying the Truth: A Study of Paul's Ethics in Galatians*. Edinburgh: T. & T. Clark, 1988.

Barclay, William. *Flesh and Spirit: An Examination of Galatians 5:19–21*. London: SCM, 1962. Grand Rapids, MI: Eerdmans reprint, 1976.

Bartunek, Jean M., Mary Ann Hinsdale, and James F. Keenan, eds. *Church Ethics and Its Organizational Context: Learning from the Sex Abuse Scandal in the Catholic Church*. Boston College Church in the 21st Century Series. Lanham, MD: Rowman & Littlefield, 2006.

Bauer, Walter, Frederick W. Danker, William F. Arndt, and F. Wilbur Gingrich. *Greek-English Lexicon of the New Testament and Other Early Christian Literature*, 3rd ed. Chicago: University of Chicago Press, 2000.

Belleville, Linda L. *Sex, Lies, and the Truth: Developing a Christian Ethic in a Post-Christian Society*. Eugene, OR: Wipf & Stock, 2010.

Bird, Michael F. *The Saving Righteousness of God: Studies on Paul, Justification and the New Perspective*. Paternoster Biblical Monographs. Waynesboro, GA: Paternoster, 2007.

Blomberg, Craig L. *1 Corinthians*. The NIV Life Application Commentary Series. Grand Rapids, MI: Zondervan, 1995.

Brown, Raymond E. *An Introduction to the New Testament*. Anchor Bible Reference Library. New York: Doubleday, 1997.

Buckland, W. W. *A Text-book of Roman Law from the Time of Cicero to the Time of Ulpian*. Rev. P. Stein. Oxford: Clarendon Press, 1991.

Bultmann, Rudolf. *Theology of the New Testament*, 2 vols. New York: Scribner, 1951, 1955.

Calvin, John. *Institutes of the Christian Religion*. Translated by Henry Beveridge. Peabody, MA: Hendrickson, 2008.

Campbell, Barth. "Flesh and Spirit in 1 Cor 5:5: An Exercise in Rhetorical Criticism of the New Testament." *Journal of the Evangelical Theological Society* 36, no. 3 (1993): 331–42.

Carter, Heath W. "The Cautionary Tale of Jim and Tammy Faye Bakker." *Christianity Today*, September 19, 2017. Accessed May 18, 2018. https://www.christianitytoday.com/ct/2017/september-web-only/cautionary-tale-of-jim-and-tammy-faye-bakker.html.

Chow, J. K. *Patronage and Power: A Study of Social Networks in Corinth*. Journal for the Study of the New Testament: Supplement Series 75. Sheffield: Sheffield Academic Press, 1992.

Ciampa, Roy E., and Brian S. Rosner. *The First Letter to the Corinthians*. Pillar New Testament Commentaries. Grand Rapids, MI: Eerdmans, 2010.

Cicero. *Pro Cluentio*. *The Orations of Marcus Tullius Cicero*, vol 2. Translated by C. D. Yonge. London: George Bell & Sons, 1902.

Clarke, Andrew D. *Secular and Christian Leadership in Corinth: A Socio-Historical and Exegetical Study of 1 Corinthians 1–6*. Leiden: Brill, 1993.

Conzelmann, Hans. *1 Corinthians: A Commentary*. Hermeneia. Philadelphia: Fortress, 1975.

Dobschütz, Ernest von. *Die urchristlichen Gemeinden*. Leipzig: Sittengeschichtliche Bilder, 1902.

Dods, M. *The First Epistle to the Corinthians*. New York: Armstrong, 1889.

Donfried, Karl P. "Justification and Last Judgment in Paul." *Interpretation* 30 (1976): 140–52.

Fee, Gordon D. The First Epistle to the Corinthians. The New International Commentary on the New Testament. Grand Rapids, MI: Eerdmans, 1987.

———. *1 and 2 Timothy, Titus*. New International Bible Commentary. Peabody, MA: Hendrickson, 1989.

———. *God's Empowering Spirit: The Holy Spirit in the Letters of Paul*. Peabody, MA: Hendrickson, 1994.

———. The First Epistle to the Corinthians. The New International Commentary on the New Testament, rev. ed. Grand Rapids, MI: Eerdmans, 2014.

Fitzmyer, Joseph A. *First Corinthians: A New Translation with Introduction and Commentary*. Anchor Yale Bible Commentary. New Haven, CT: Yale University Press, 2008.

Friesen, Steve, Daniel N. Schowalter, and James Walters, eds. *Corinth in Context: Comparative Studies on Religion and Society*. Supplements to Novum Testamentum 134. Leiden: Brill, 2010.

Gaius. *Gai Institutiones or Institutes of Roman Law*. Translated by Edward Poste. 4th ed. Oxford: Clarendon Press, 1904.

Gamble, Harry. "Letters in the New Testament and in the Greco-Roman World." In *The Biblical World*, vol. 1. Edited by John Barton. London and New York: Routledge, 2002.

Garland, David E. *1 Corinthians*. Baker Exegetical Commentary on the New Testament. Grand Rapids, MI: Baker Academic, 2003.

Hull, Michael F. *Baptism on Account of the Dead (1 Cor 15:29): An Act of Faith in the Resurrection*. Atlanta, GA: Society of Biblical Literature/Leiden: Brill, 2005.

Johnson, Luke Timothy. *The First and Second Letters to Timothy*. The Anchor Yale Bible Commentaries. New York: Doubleday, 2001.

Käsemann, Ernst. "Sentences of Holy Law in the New Testament." *New Testament Questions for Today*. Philadelphia: Fortress, 1968.

Knight, George W., III. *The Pastoral Epistles: A Commentary on the Greek Text*. New International Greek Testament Commentary. Grand Rapids, MI: Eerdmans, 1992.

Krell, Keith Richard. "Temporal Judgment and the Church: Paul's Remedial Agenda in 1 Corinthians." PhD Diss., University of Bristol and Trinity College, 2010.

Lake, Kirsopp. *The Earlier Epistles of St. Paul: Their Motive and Origin*, 2nd ed. London: Rivingtons, 1914.

Lietzmann, Hans. *An die Korinther I/II*. Handbuch zum Neuen Testament. Tübingen: Mohr-Siebeck, 1949.

Lim, Kar Yong. *Metaphors and Social Identity Formation in Paul's Letters to the Corinthians*. Eugene, OR: Pickwick, 2017.

Longenecker, Richard N. *Galatians*. Word Biblical Commentary 41. Waco, TX: Word, 1990.

Lust, Johan, Erik Eynikel, and Katrin Hauspie. *A Greek-English Lexicon of the Septuagint*, 2 vols. Stuttgart: Deutsche Bibelgesellschaft, 1992, 1996.

Luther, Martin. "On the Councils and the Church" (1539). Luther's Works, vol. 41. Church and Ministry III. Edited by Eric W. Gritsch. Philadelphia: Fortress Press, 1966.

Malcolm, Matthew R. *Paul and the Rhetoric of Reversal in 1 Corinthians: The Impact of Paul's Gospel on His Macro-Rhetoric*. Society for New Testament Studies Monograph Series 155. Cambridge: Cambridge University Press, 2013.

———. *The World of 1 Corinthians: An Exegetical Source Book of Literary and Visual Backgrounds*. Eugene, OR: Cascade, 2013.

Marshall, I. Howard. *A Critical and Exegetical Commentary on the Pastoral Epistles*. International Critical Commentaries. Edinburgh: T. & T. Clark, 1999.

Matson, Mark A. "Sexual Sin as a Demonstration of Disunity: 1 Corinthians 5 in Context." Leaven 9, no. 3. Article 3 (2001): 116–22. Accessed May 18, 2018. http://digitalcommons.pepperdine.edu/leaven/vol9/iss3/3.

Moffatt, James. *The First Epistle of Paul to the Corinthians*. Moffatt New Testament Commentary 7. London: Hodder & Stoughton, 1938.

Mounce, William D. *Pastoral Epistles*. Word Biblical Commentary 46. Nashville, TN: Thomas Nelson, 2000.

Muirhead, J. *The Institutes of Gaius and Rules of Ulpian*. Edinburgh: T. & T. Clark, 1880.

Murphy-O'Connor, Jérome. "1 Corinthians v, 3–5." Revue Biblique 84 (1977): 239–45.

———. *St. Paul's Corinth: Texts and Archaeology*. Good News Studies 6. Collegeville, MN: Glazier, 1983, 2002.

———. *Keys to First Corinthians: Revisiting the Major Issues*. Oxford: Oxford University Press, 2009.

———. *Keys to Second Corinthians: Revisiting the Major Issues*. Oxford: Oxford University Press, 2010.

Porter, Stanley E. *The Apostle Paul: His Life, Thought, and Letters*. Grand Rapids, MI: Eerdmans, 2016.

Richards, E. Randolph. *Paul and First-Century Letter Writing: Secretaries, Composition and Collection*. Downers Grove, IL: InterVarsity, 2004.

Robertson, Archibald, and Alfred Plummer. *A Critical and Exegetical Commentary on the First Epistle of Paul to the Corinthians*, 2nd ed. International Critical Commentary. Edinburgh: T. & T. Clark, 1914.

Robertson, A. T. *Word Pictures in the New Testament*, 6 vols. Originally 1930–1933. Grand Rapids, MI: Baker reprint, n.d.

Schnabel, Eckhard. *Early Christian Mission*, vol. 1. *Paul and the Early Church*. Downers Grove, IL: InterVarsity, 2004.

———. *Der erste Brief des Paulus an die Korinther*. Historisch Theologische Auslegung. Wuppertal: R. Brockhaus, 2006.

———. *Paul the Missionary: Realities, Strategies and Methods*. Downers Grove, IL: InterVarsity, 2008.

Smith, David Raymond. "Hand This Man over to Satan: Curse, Exclusion and Salvation in 1 Corinthians 5." PhD Diss., Durham University, 2005. Available at Durham E-Theses Online, http://etheses.dur.ac.uk/1789/.

———. *"Hand Tthis man over to Satan": Curse, Exclusion and Salvation in 1 Corinthians 5*. Library of New Testament Studies 386. New York: Bloomsbury T & T Clark, 2009.

South, James T. "A Critique of the 'Curse/Death Interpretation of 1 Corinthians 5:1–8." *New Testament Studies* 39 (1993): 539–61.

Stowers, Stanley K. *Letter Writing in Greco-Roman Antiquity*, Library of Early Christianity 5. Philadelphia: Westminster, 1986.

Sweeney, James P. "Review of Matthew R. Malcolm, *Paul and the Rhetoric of Reversal in 1 Corinthians: The Impact of Paul's Gospel on his Macro-Rhetoric.*" Society for New Testament Studies Monograph Series 155. Cambridge: Cambridge University Press, 2013. In *Bulletin of Biblical Research* 24, no. 4 (2014): 588–90.

Tate, W. Randolph. *Biblical Interpretation: An Integrated Approach*, 3rd ed. Peabody, MA: Hendrickson, 2008.

Tertullian. "On Modesty." *The Ante-Nicene Fathers: The Writings of the Fathers down to A.D.*, vol. 4, 325. Edited and translated by Alexander Roberts and James Donaldson. Edinburgh: T. & T. Clark, 1885.

Theissen, Gerd. *The Social Setting of Pauline Christianity: Essays on Corinth*. Philadelphia: Fortress, 1982.

Thiselton, Anthony C. "The Meaning of Σάρξ in 1 Cor. 5:5: A Fresh Approach in the Light of Logical and Semantic Factors." *Scottish Journal of Theology* 26 (1973): 204–28.

———. "1 Corinthians." *New Dictionary of Biblical Theology*. Edited by T. Desmond Alexander and Brian S. Rosner. Downers Grove, IL: InterVarsity, 2000.

———. *The First Epistle to the Corinthians*. New International Greek Testament Commentary. Grand Rapids, MI: Eerdmans, 2000.

Toseland, Paul A. "Delivered to Satan: 1 Cor. 5:3–5 and 1 Tim. 1:18–20." *Testamentum Imperium* 1 (2005–2007): 1–19. Accessed May 18, 2018. http://www.preciousheart.net/ti/2007/011_07_Toseland_Delivered_to_Satan.pdf.

Towner, Philip H. *The Letters to Timothy and Titus*. New International Commentary on the New Testament. Edited by Gordon D. Fee. Grand Rapids, MI: Eerdmans, 2006.

Wallace, Daniel B. *Greek Grammar beyond the Basics*. Grand Rapids, MI: Zondervan, 1996.

White, John L. "New Testament Epistolary Literature in the Framework of Ancient Epistolography." *Aufstieg und Niedergang der römischen Welt*. II.25.2. Berlin: de Gruyter, 1984.

Winter, Bruce W. "1 Corinthians." In *New Bible Commentary: 21st Century Edition*, 4th ed. Edited by D. A. Carson. Downers Grove, IL: InterVarsity, 1994.

———. *After Paul Left Corinth: The Influence of Secular Ethics and Social Change*. Grand Rapids, MI: Eerdmans, 2001.

Witherington, Ben, III. *Conflict and Community in Corinth: A Socio-Rhetorical Commentary on 1 and 2 Corinthians*. Grand Rapids, MI: Eerdmans, 1995.

Yarbro Collins, Adela. "The Function of 'Excommunication' in Paul." *Harvard Theological Review* 73 (1980): 251–63.

Chapter 8

Joy and Mercy

The Heart of Pope Francis's Rhetoric of Restoration and Reform

Dũng Q. Trần

INTRODUCTION

From the moment Pope Francis appeared on the balcony of Saint Peter's Square on March 13, 2013, the new "leader of the world's 1.2 billion Catholics"[1] demonstrated a desire to draw the Catholic Church into a "deeper and more positive dialogue with the world."[2] Francis visually distinguished himself from his predecessors by wearing a simple white cassock, without the traditional elbow-length red velvet cape and jewel-studded gold cross, and did not raise his arms in victory. Prior to imparting his first official blessing, the freshly minted pontiff sought a spiritual favor from the crowd: "I ask you to pray to the Lord that he will bless me."[3] In asking for their prayers, Francis was emphasizing his ministry as bishop of Rome, rather than supreme pontiff. Also illuminating was his rhetorical act of addressing the blessing "to all men and women of good will."[4]

For Italian theologian, Massimo Faggioli, these gestures concretized "the consequences of the choice of translating the theological centrality of the Gospel of Jesus Christ into the model of bishop and church."[5] In a few brief rhetorical moments, "packed with symbolism of so many kinds, Francis had set out a whole programme of governance in miniature and signaled that things were going to be rather different from now on."[6] As Robert Moynihan, the founder and editor in chief of *Inside the Vatican* magazine, concluded, "the world formed its first, and inevitably lasting, impression of the new bishop of Rome."[7]

In the years since Pope Francis's historic election as the first pontiff from the Americas and the first ever Jesuit, he has enjoyed (mostly) positive assessments and media coverage[8] for his inclusive leadership.[9] According to a January 2018 Pew Survey, 84 percent of Catholics in the United States held a "favorable opinion of the Argentinian pontiff" and approximately nine in ten U.S. Catholics found Francis to be "compassionate" and "humble."[10] However, a recent reemergence of the clergy sexual abuse scandal as a global crisis has undermined the pontiff's "once-soaring popularity."[11] Francis's image and reputation, which at one point seemed beyond reproach, have sustained significant damage and are in need of restoration and repair.

Since spring of 2018, a series of alarming developments involving Pope Francis and the abuse scandal have dominated international news headlines. This unprecedented period in contemporary church history is marked by the addition of several new chapters in the clergy abuse saga. The first is the forced resignations of Chilean bishops whom Francis initially defended against allegations of abuse cover-up. Second is the release of scathing letters from Italian Archbishop Carlo Maria Vigano, a former papal ambassador to the United States, accusing Vatican leaders, including Francis, of ignoring Vigano's requests to discipline Theodore McCarrick, archbishop emeritus of Washington, D.C., and Newark, New Jersey. Once a trusted adviser of Francis, McCarrick has been permanently suspended from public ministry for "credible"[12] allegations of sexual misconduct with minors and has resigned from the College of Cardinals. Compounding the latest phase of the crisis was the publication of a Pennsylvania grand jury report detailing the abuse of a thousand children by three hundred priests and the concealment efforts of Church leaders. Given these disconcerting developments, a more recent Pew Survey revealed that confidence in Francis's leadership had plummeted. As of September 2018, only 31 percent of U.S. Catholics rated Francis's management of the abuse scandal as good or excellent, down fourteen percentage points from earlier in 2018 and twenty-four points from a peak of 55 percent in June 2015.[13]

Needless to say, this scandal-plagued period weakened both Pope Francis and the Catholic Church's credibility, public image, and moral authority on the world stage. For image repair theorist, Joseph Blaney, "when negative publicity becomes associated with a represented group or person, practitioners must implement a communication strategy designed to salvage the images of their clients."[14] According to Natasa Govekar, a Vatican communications official, an essential element of the Vatican's media strategy is to "not be an obstacle to what this great communicator is already doing" and let the pope "be himself."[15] For instance, during an in-flight press conference following a visit to Ireland, Francis demonstrated his natural communication, political, and spiritual savvy with his responses. Leveraging his relatively positive relationship with reporters, Francis urged journalists to investigate Archbishop Vigano's claims and arrive at their own conclusions. Since then, Francis has only indirectly acknowledged Vigano's allegations by recommending "silence and prayer"[16] as prudent responses to those seeking scandal.

Contrary to Francis's approach, Vigano has since issued additional statements clarifying his initial accusations and further aligned himself with a campaign intended to disrupt and delegitimize Francis's reform-minded leadership.[17] For example, in his most recent missive, Vigano concluded that the "scourge of homosexuality" was the "root cause" of the clergy abuse crisis and cover-up.[18] As Faggioli observed, the depth and magnitude of the sex abuse crisis are "reacting explosively" with at least three rifts within the U.S. Catholic Church: 1) the long-standing rift between traditionalist and progressive interpretations of Catholic identity and culture, 2) the growing theological rift between Pope Francis and some of the more doctrinally oriented U.S. Catholic bishops, and 3) the development of a new rift between Francis and rank and file U.S. Catholics. "Even those who love him can't make out what his short-term strategy for dealing with the abuse crisis is—as opposed to the long-term fight against clericalism."[19]

Despite the emerging anti-Pope Francis[20] movements, some of which describe him as a dictator[21] and lost shepherd,[22] Francis has remained "relevant in a surprising diversity of places, where his unconventional style and speech, combined with his message of mercy [and joy], continue to draw wide attention and commentary. Even when embattled and under fire, Francis remains a magnet for the media."[23] As evidenced by magazine covers from *Time*,[24] *The Advocate*,[25] *Vanity Fair Italia*,[26] *Rolling Stone*,[27] and *Esquire*,[28] along with more than fifty million followers on Twitter,[29] and relatively strong approval ratings,[30] it is clear that Francis's message of joy and mercy has gone viral. For instance, during his first year Francis left "the global media swooning,"[31] as images of him paying his own hotel bill, washing the feet of prisoners, rescuing Muslim refugees, and embracing the physically disfigured circulated on the internet.[32] In short, despite his (mis)handling of the clergy abuse crisis, the Francis phenomenon continues to capture the world's imagination because of his compassion for the marginalized, message of joy and mercy, and openness to reform through a thoughtful process of discerning the world's complex realities.

As papal biographer Austin Ivereigh asserted, "Francis is a church leader who from an early age felt called to be a reformer and was given the authority to do so."[33] Whether it was the Argentine Jesuit province, the Church in Buenos Aires, or now the global Catholic Church, Francis has always been driven by a desire to unite humanity through "a radical reform that . . . leads them to holiness."[34] Vatican observer John Allen Jr. believes that Francis is a values-driven, community-oriented bridge builder who is on a mission to reform Catholicism in three ways: 1) shifting Catholicism toward the political and ecclesiastical center; 2) inspiring a deeper social commitment to defend the poor, oppose war, care for the environment, and protect people on the margins, especially immigrants, the elderly, and minorities; and 3) overhauling the Vatican's organizational bureaucracy.[35]

For Jesuit Thomas Reese, Pope Francis did such an incredible job of repairing the image of the Church in 2013 that "business schools could use him as a case study in rebranding."[36] As essays in *Forbes*[37] and *The Economist*[38] have noted, Francis initially functioned like a new CEO of a floundering corporation and *refocused* the company on its core mission of serving the poor; *restructured* the organization by soliciting feedback from internal and external stakeholders; and *reframed* Catholicism's support of traditional teachings on gay marriage and divorced Catholics by presenting them in a more nuanced and merciful manner.[39] Given the copious amounts of information available, Francis's eleven-year anniversary as pope is an appropriate moment to step back and scrutinize relevant visual and verbal artifacts from a rhetorical perspective. This theoretical approach involves "an imaginative critical lens, one that captures the rhetorical, aesthetic, and ideological implications of mediated images."[40]

With the aforementioned context in mind, this chapter examines Pope Francis's visual, verbal, and textual rhetoric of restoration and reform of Catholicism, as expressed through his joyful proclamation and embodiment of mercy in various addresses, documents, and images. This analysis includes a brief discussion of corporate crisis communication and scholarship applying image repair theory to Pope Francis's reform of style; reform of priorities; reform of the understanding and structure of the church; and reform of spiritual living. Particular attention will be paid to his apostolic exhortation, *Evangelii Gaudium*—The Joy of the Gospel, which has served as a vision statement of sorts for Francis's papacy. Namely, the spirit of poverty is at the heart of the church's identity, an identity that is "inextricably linked to the virtues of joy and mercy."[41]

CORPORATE CRISIS COMMUNICATION, IMAGE REPAIR THEORY, AND POPE FRANCIS

With a global flock of 1.3 billion, and pressures similar to that of a country's prime minister or president, the pope of the Roman Catholic Church and the image that person projects are often the subjects of intense scrutiny, especially during a corporate crisis. In crisis communication literature, several scholars have advanced the concepts of crisis communication by apology,[42] situational crisis communication theory,[43] and the rhetoric of renewal.[44] Because personal and organizational perception and reputation are so critical, any perceived or actual sign of crisis often triggers messaging aimed at controlling, minimizing, and/or eliminating damage. Given that crisis communication involves organizational and/or personal image repair or restoration efforts, this chapter now turns to that body of literature.

William Benoit, the intellectual parent of image restoration/repair studies, defined image as "the perception of a person (or group, or organization) held by the audience, shaped by the words and actions of that person, as well as by the discourse and behavior of other relevant actors."[45] In response to concerns raised by other scholars,[46] Benoit recognized that a corporation's image is constantly emerging and subject to the perceptions of diverse publics.[47] In a more recent image study, Jessica Furgerson and William Benoit acknowledged that "face, image, or reputation can be extremely important in human interaction, so when presented with a face threatening act, persuasive messages can help repair damaged reputations."[48] With regard to the fiscal implications of a tarnished image, Joseph Blaney estimated that "a damaged image can cost an individual or corporation millions of dollars, which is why it is imperative to understand key image repair strategies."[49]

Leveraging rhetorical scholarship[50] from various disciplinary[51] traditions,[52] Benoit advanced a theory of image restoration strategies. This theory rests on two assumptions: "First, communication is best conceptualized as a goal-directed activity. Second, maintaining a positive reputation is one of the central goals of communication."[53] For Benoit, image repair strategies attempt to address two key elements: "blame (responsibility) and offensiveness."[54] Image restoration theory consists of five rhetorical image repair strategies: denial, evading responsibility, reducing offensiveness, corrective action, and mortification.[55] In addition, three of the five strategies have further sub-strategies.

The first approach is denial. Simple denial involves repudiating the accusation or shifting the blame to another party who is "actually responsible for the offensive act."[56] Evading responsibility, the second strategy, is when "the accused does not deny committing the offense, but rather claims a lack of responsibility because the misdeed was a result of someone else's actions (provocation), a lack of information (defeasibility), an accident, or committed with good intentions."[57] A third method is corrective action, involving a pledge to correct the problem that caused the offensive act and prevent future recurrence.[58] Mortification, a fourth approach, is an admission of wrongdoing and plea for forgiveness.[59] The remaining image repair strategy, reducing offensiveness, includes six variants: minimization, attacking the accuser, compensation, bolstering, differentiation, and transcendence.[60]

Minimization is an effort to downplay "the extent of damage caused by the offensive act."[61] Attacking the accuser is a strategy aimed at reducing the credibility of the accuser by "tying the accusation to some unworthy source."[62] Compensation "offers something worthwhile to the victim in an attempt to redress the loss."[63] Bolstering involves emphasizing the positive qualities of the accused to offset negative feelings from the offensive act at hand. Differentiation is an attempt to situate the offensive act with similar but more reprehensible acts. Transcendence is an appeal to "higher values or more important ends"[64] to justify the offensive act.

Image restoration theory, the gold standard for scrutinizing image repair discourse,[65] has been applied to various contexts: political,[66] corporate,[67] civic,[68] athletic,[69] and other realms.[70]

With regard to religion, image repair studies have examined the discourse of figures such as Jesus[71] and American televangelist Jimmy Swaggart.[72] In terms of communication crises and controversies in the Catholic Church, previous scholarship has centered on the discourse surrounding governance at institutions of Catholic higher learning,[73] the revoked excommunication of a Holocaust denying bishop,[74] the clergy sexual abuse scandals,[75] and the abuse scandal responses of Pope John Paul II[76] and Cardinal Bernard Law.[77] Yet there remains a need for a more nuanced analysis of Pope Francis's rhetoric of reform and image repair efforts for the Catholic Church.

JOY AND MERCY: THE SPIRITUAL FOUNDATIONS OF FRANCIS'S IMAGE REPAIR EFFORTS

Given the embarrassing media coverage of the Vatican's organizational disarray and dysfunction during the waning days of Benedict XVI's pontificate,[78] the cardinal electors entered the 2013 papal conclave seeking change: "There was much talk of reform of governance—the need for a pope who was accessible, informed, and free to act—and for fluid contact between Rome and the local Church."[79] The cardinals recognized the need "to elect an outsider, someone not tainted by association with the recent Vatican regime,"[80] and someone who could be both task- and relationship-oriented enough to initiate the needed reform of the Roman curia and repair the Catholic Church's strained relationships with internal and external constituents.

According to image repair theorists Blaney and Benoit, religious rhetors tend to employ the transcendence strategy when attempting to restore images. They also claim that the very essence of religion "makes religious rhetoric subject to statements of transcendence."[81] This has certainly been the case with Pope Francis's visual and verbal rhetoric. Since 2013, Francis has contributed to the ongoing reform of the Catholic Church through his rhetorical efforts to reduce the offensiveness of past transgressions through a combination of transcendence, bolstering, differentiation, minimization, and mortification. All his image repair and reform activity to date can be classified into four categories—style, priorities, church understanding and structure, and the spiritual life.[82]

Before engaging with these four areas of reform further, this chapter explores the virtues of joy and mercy—the core values undergirding every (rhetorical) facet of Francis's papacy, especially his image repair efforts of transcendence, bolstering, differentiation, minimization, and mortification. Every word and gesture contribute to Francis's project of reforming Roman Catholicism's way of proceeding and repairing its image and reputation. As a July 2018 *Vogue* article asserted, "The tiny Fiats and Fords in which he rides, his humble Vatican residence, his simple white robes—all are designed to send a message."[83]

JOY TO THE WORLD

By taking the name Francis, the former Cardinal Jorge Mario Bergoglio of Argentina aligned his pontificate with the beloved Italian saint from Assisi who is revered for his humility, simplicity, concern for the poor, and joy.[84] Calling himself "God's court jester,"[85] the medieval friar felt that it was important for a servant of God to be joyful among others. The newly minted pontiff put this advice into action immediately after his historic election in 2013.

As the first pope from Latin America, the Argentinian jokingly remarked that the cardinal electors had "gone to the ends of the earth to get [him]."[86] Later that evening, at a celebratory dinner, the pontiff brought down the house by telling his brother cardinals, "May God forgive you for what you have done."[87] Those initial flashes of humor inaugurated joy as an important hermeneutic key to understanding Pope Francis's vision for restoring and reforming the Church.

In many ways, the importance of joy in the spiritual life was an idea to which Francis had given considerable consideration. In 2007, the bishops of Latin America and the Caribbean issued a document, which was initially drafted by then Cardinal Jorge Mario Bergoglio,[88] that urged readers to rediscover the beauty and joy of being Christian: "The first invitation that Jesus makes to every person who has lived an encounter with Him, is to be His disciple, so as to follow in His footsteps and to be part of His community. Our greatest joy is that of being His disciples!"[89] The document goes on to assert that being loved by God fills us with joy, which can serve as "a remedy for a world fearful of the future and overwhelmed by violence and hatred."[90] In addition, the document discussed the "joyful spirit of our peoples"—in a cultural sense, "the joyful spirit of our peoples who love music, dance, poetry, art, and sports, and cultivate firm hope in the midst of problems and struggles."[91] For moral theologian, Clemens Sedmak, this document presented joy "as a basic force in spirituality as well as cultural identity."[92] Joy was also presented as a pivotal component in the practice of pastoral leadership: "bishops must be joyful witnesses of Jesus Christ."[93] Ultimately, joy is a fundamental feature of a faith-filled life: "an authentic Christian journey fills the heart with joy and hope and moves believers to proclaim Christ continually in their life and environment."[94] Consequently, it would be difficult to make a case for a joyless faith life in light of this early document, which was drafted by the future Pope Francis.

Francis's understanding of joy was echoed in *Evangelii Gaudium*, the Joy of the Gospel, the first teaching document he issued in 2013. In addition to quoting extensively from the 2007 Concluding Document of the Fifth General Conference of the Bishops of Latin America and the Caribbean, Francis's first apostolic exhortation was notable for several reasons. Although important, Francis is concerned with more than ameliorating social injustice. In his view, the root of humanity's problems is "the lack of joy and lack of spark, the inner emptiness and the isolation of human persons closed up in themselves and the loneliness of hearts turned in on themselves."[95] Francis's analysis aligned with other thought leaders who arrived at similar conclusions. For example, both Søren Kierkegaard[96] and Martin Heidegger[97] identified anxiety as a basic human disposition.

With a firm grasp of humanity's challenges, another notable feature of *Evangelii Gaudium* was Francis's spirited invitation to consider the joy of the Gospel as an affirmation of reality, which can arouse a dormant passion to transform one's perspective. For theologian Walter Kasper, "the joy of the Gospel can awaken anew joy in life, in creation, in faith, and in the church."[98] According to Romans 14:17, joy is a gift of the Holy Spirit that can transform one's interior identity. For instance, in C. S. Lewis's partial autobiography, *Surprised by Joy*, he "sees his journey toward the Christian faith as a search for the joy he experienced as a young boy, when he was surprised—even overwhelmed—by the joy he found in Christianity."[99] Lewis's experiential encounters of joy transformed the way he perceived the world and his interior life.

For Francis, Christian joy can fill the heart and help people overcome an "inner emptiness,"[100] the fruits of a "complacent yet covetous heart,"[101] or a heart "gripped by fear and desperation."[102] As Sedmak posited, "the inner state of a person reflects her moral and spiritual condition. It is the place where attitudes and maturity levels are taken on board or abandoned, it is the place where dispositions, decisions to act, and ways of dealing with the social world are confronted and processed."[103] In Francis's view, an out-of-sync inner life renders us "incapable of feeling compassion at the outcry of the poor."[104] Moreover, "Whenever our interior life becomes caught up in its own interests and concerns, there is no longer room for others, no place for the poor,"[105] who often lurk in the shadows of society. As communication ethicist Ronald Arnett asserts, preoccupation with the self can result in missed opportunities, since we often encounter the profound and the sacred in the shadows.[106]

Ultimately, joy, for Pope Francis, as outlined in *Evangelii Gaudium*, has at least five characteristics: 1) It is a natural Christian state and available to persons of goodwill;[107] 2) joy is a Biblical motif—found in many instances in the Old and New Testaments;[108] 3) joy is nourished by a "certainty that when all is said and done, we are infinitely loved";[109] 4) joy inhabits our hearts alongside pain and suffering—"the pain of the cross is part of the joy of the Gospel";[110] 5) joy can be nourished by paying attention to small things in life[111] and remaining close to others, especially those who have very little.[112] By emphasizing joy in his first true teaching document,[113] Francis is demonstrating that Christian faith is a wellspring of hope[114] and a truth that never falls out of fashion.[115] As Walter Kasper concludes, Francis's "motive is to convince the faithful of the beauty of faith and encourage them to live joyfully the life of faith."[116]

Recognizing the importance of modeling joyful behavior, the pontiff recites Saint Thomas More's "Prayer for Good Humor" as part of his daily spiritual practice[117] and publicly presents a jovial orientation—as depicted in numerous images of Francis laughing with people from all walks of life. Even the tone of Francis's papal discourse reflects a dialogical accessibility—a willingness to engage in conversation with others about concrete matters. In *Laudato Si'*, his encyclical about caring for our common home, Francis reminded us that "the world is a joyful mystery to be contemplated with gladness and praise"[118] and that the difficulties of the world must not take away the joy of our hope.[119] For Francis, joy is both a "fundamental affirmation of the world where we also embrace the realities of life."[120] At the same time, Francis recognized that different people could interpret his message differently. He wrote, "If anyone feels offended by my words, I would respond that I speak to them with affection and the best of intentions."[121] By proceeding this way, Francis rhetorically demonstrated an openness to dialoguing with the wider world, which is complete "only with follow-up and substantial conversation carried out in a spirit of courage, generosity, and joy."[122]

A JOYFUL MESSAGE OF MERCY

In addition to joy, another critical component of Pope Francis's vision for restoration and reform is the biblical theme of mercy. The topic of mercy has served as a cornerstone of Francis's preaching, teaching, and leadership. Echoing the insights of his papal predecessors and Saint Augustine, Francis believes that mercy is an essential aspect of the spiritual life.[123] In *Evangelii Gaudium*, the word mercy appears thirty-two times. He calls for Church communities to become "islands of mercy in the midst of the sea of indifference."[124] Francis contends, "The Church must be a place of mercy freely given, where everyone can feel welcomed, loved, forgiven and encouraged to live the good life of the Gospel."[125] As he revealed in an interview, Francis is convinced that humanity's wounded nature has furnished "a kairos of mercy, an opportune time"[126] for renewal.

Francis's effort to recast the Church as place of mercy and inclusion was reflected in his reflections regarding the lesbian, gay, bisexual, transgender, and queer (LGBTQ) communities:

> when God looks at a gay person, does he endorse the existence of this person with love, or reject and condemn this person? We must always consider the person. Here we enter into the mystery of the human being. In life, God accompanies persons, and we must accompany them, starting from their situation. It is necessary to accompany them with mercy.[127]

Regardless of topic, the pope's plan to reform and restore the Church is anchored by the virtue of mercy. As longtime Vatican analyst John Allen Jr. asserts, "In all the ways that matter, mercy is the spiritual bedrock of this papacy."[128] Former U.S. president Barack Obama recognized this at Pope Francis's White House arrival ceremony:

> You remind us that "the Lord's most powerful message" is mercy. And that means welcoming the stranger with empathy and a truly open heart—from the refugee who flees war-torn lands to the immigrant who leaves home in search of a better life. It means showing compassion and love for the marginalized and the outcast, to those who have suffered, and those who have caused suffering and seek redemption.[129]

Pope Francis has sought to embody his mercy-filled message in his leadership practices and visual rhetoric: washing the feet of prisoners, embracing the physically disfigured, building shower and laundry facilities for homeless persons in Rome, and rescuing Muslim refugees. For leadership expert Chris Lowney, Francis is "doing what all good leaders do, jostling our imaginations when we become too complacent and stripping away the veneer of the familiar to expose the raw feel of a challenging truth."[130]

In addition to being a fundamental facet of Francis's papacy, the concept of mercy is a core concern of sacred texts and has been developed by thought leaders such as Thomas Aquinas, Catherine of Siena, Thomas Merton, John

Paul II, Benedict XVI, and Walter Kasper.[131] Drawing upon and developing Aristotelian and other classical sources, Thomas Aquinas conceptualized mercy as the "heartfelt sympathy for another's distress."[132] In his opening address at Vatican II, Pope John XXIII urged the church to engage contemporary culture and society with the "medicine of mercy."[133] More recently, James Keenan, a Jesuit theological ethicist, defined mercy as "the willingness to enter into the chaos of another so as to answer them in their need."[134] For Jesuit theologian Jon Sobrino, "Mercy is the primary and ultimate, the first and last of human reactions. It is that in terms of which all dimensions of the human being acquire meaning and without which nothing else attains to human status."[135] This robust understanding of mercy captures the underlying spirit of Francis's rhetoric and leadership, as it

> expresses his conviction that mercy is the fundamental reality that structures ... [divine activity], the perfection of the human person, and the mission of the church. It is the reality seen in ... [the] freeing of the oppressed and welcoming of the prodigal, and it is the demand placed upon all who seek to authentically love their neighbor.[136]

In gestures inspired by mercy, Pope Francis started reaching out to his spiritual neighbors immediately after his 2013 election. His papal installation was the first to be attended by the chief rabbi of Rome; Francis extended an invitation on his first full day in office. He also invited Bartholomew, the ecumenical patriarch of Constantinople, "who became the first head of the Greek Orthodox Church in nearly a thousand years to attend the installation of a pope."[137] Francis's proactive outreach has resulted in positive working relationships, joint appearances, and mutual respect. In *Laudato Si'*, Francis acknowledged Bartholomew as a vital voice in the ecological discourse.[138] Prior to a 2016 visit to Mexico, Francis became the first pope to meet with a patriarch of the Russian Orthodox Church in more than a millennium.[139] Then, during a 2017 trip to Egypt, Pope Francis and Coptic Orthodox Pope Tawadros II of Alexandria signed a historic declaration that mutually recognized the baptism of both faith traditions.[140] More recently, Francis hosted a daylong ecumenical gathering for most of the Middle East's Orthodox patriarchs to pray for peace and unity.[141]

To concretize his call for a poorer church for the poor, Pope Francis led by example. During Christmas 2013, he spent three hours visiting sick children and their families at a Roman hospital. More dramatically, during every Holy Thursday service since his election, Francis has washed and kissed the feet of twelve people forgotten by society (e.g., prisoners, the elderly, refugees, and the poor).

To help underscore the importance of mercy, Pope Francis also declared 2016 an Extraordinary Jubilee Year of Mercy. Francis's desire for the jubilee was for all people of good will to "enter more deeply into the heart of the Gospel where the poor have a special experience of God's mercy."[142] In *Misericordiae Vultus*, Francis's document convoking the jubilee of mercy, he began with the following acknowledgment: "Jesus Christ is the face of the Father's mercy. These words might well sum up the mystery of the Christian faith."[143] According to Francis, the motto of the jubilee year was "merciful like the Father."[144] Relying on scripture, the pontiff highlighted the invitation in Luke 6:37–38 to not judge or condemn others. For Francis, "To refrain from judgment and condemnation means, in a positive sense, to know how to accept the good in every person and to spare him any suffering that might be caused by our partial judgment, our presumption to know everything."[145] In Francis's view, contemplating the mystery of mercy can deepen one's understanding of mercy as "the fundamental law that dwells in the heart of every person who looks sincerely into the eyes of his brothers and sisters on the path of life" and as "the bridge that connects God and man, opening our hearts to the hope of being loved forever despite our sinfulness."[146]

Within this context, one can better understand why Pope Francis could utter his famous remark when asked about LGBTQ persons—"Who am I to judge?"[147] More concretely, Francis's rhetoric of mercy created the conditions for the funeral of a transgender homeless woman to be held at the mother church of the Jesuits—the Catholic religious community of which Francis is a member.[148] Through inclusive rhetoric and gestures, Francis has encouraged people to reflect on the corporal and spiritual works of mercy—activities that involve one's "obligations to the neighbor in need."[149] Although the tradition of the works of mercy is very rich, they are "considerably lost to the modern mind."[150]

According to theologian Charles Curran, "every pope or Christian leader should always have as the first priority the good news of God's gift of love and life to us."[151] However, given the need for greater emphasis on the proclamation of mercy in all facets of church life, Pope Francis chose to characterize this priority through the lens of mercy. Although every virtue or description cannot fully capture the totality of God's gift to humanity, "Francis chooses to see God's gracious gift in terms of mercy."[152] Curran offered two explanations for this choice: 1) Francis self-identifies as a sinner who has experienced God's gracious mercy and 2) he believes that "All that the church is and does must bear witness to God's mercy."[153]

ASSESSING POPE FRANCIS'S REFORM FROM AN IMAGE REPAIR PERSPECTIVE

For Brazilian liberation theologian Leonardo Boff, Pope Francis's leadership and rhetoric are best characterized by "the terms break and beginning anew."[154] With the virtues of joy and mercy theologically anchoring Francis's image repair and reform efforts, he has sought to reduce the offensiveness of past transgressions through a combination of transcendence, bolstering, differentiation, minimization, and mortification. In doing so he has attempted to reduce the negative media narrative of Catholicism in crisis. All his image restoration and reform activity to date can be classified in four categories—style, priorities, church understanding and structure, and the spiritual life. Using examples from each category as a case study, this chapter turns its attention to how Pope Francis's visual and verbal rhetorical acts of reform concretized the image repair strategies of transcendence, bolstering, differentiation, minimization, and mortification.

As soon as Pope Francis appeared on the loggia of Saint Peter's Basilica, he inaugurated a simpler, more humble style of being pope and of being church.[155] After leading the people in prayers for his predecessor, Francis then bowed his head, asking for the people's prayers prior to imparting his first official blessing. In Ivereigh's estimation, this "gesture of great humility" was also a "touching gesture of mutuality" that signaled a relational approach to rhetorical leadership that was "bent on implementing collegiality."[156]

After eleven years as pope, stories and anecdotes abound about Francis's simple lifestyle.[157]

He continues to dispense with the formal papal garb of his office by wearing a simple white cassock. Another early indication of Francis's reform of style was his decision to decline the spacious, yet isolating confines of the apostolic palace and live in a guesthouse, which is regularly inhabited by Vatican officials and other visitors. As often as possible, he dines in the common downstairs cafeteria and presides at the morning Mass for Vatican employees in the guesthouse's chapel. In other leadership practices, such as washing the feet of prisoners, rescuing Muslim refugees, opening laundry facilities for the poor, and hosting homeless persons for dinner and a private tour of the Sistine Chapel,[158] Francis has demonstrated an abiding awareness of attending to the task of repairing Catholicism's image by appealing to and bolstering the Church's social teaching of a preferential option for the poor and vulnerable.[159] He has even used social media to communicate this message: "A simple lifestyle is good for us, helping us to better share with those in need."[160] In both word and deed, Francis has focused on "valuing their uniqueness, and giving special attention to their personal needs."[161]

By making the poor the core social concern of his leadership agenda, Francis is rhetorically reforming the hierarchical priorities of Catholicism. Rooted in his emphasis on the virtues of joy and mercy as the paradigmatic logic undergirding Catholicism's standard operating procedures and processes, Francis has maintained,

> We cannot insist only on issues related to abortion, gay marriage and the use of contraceptive methods. . . . when we speak about these issues, we have to talk about them in a context. The teaching of the church, for that matter, is clear and I am a son of the church, but it is not necessary to talk about these issues all the time.[162]

Despite some criticism for his relative silence about Catholicism's teachings on sexual morality, Francis' visual and verbal rhetoric has focused on transcendent values of the Catholic tradition—prioritizing the joyful proclamation of God's mercy and the common good "before moral and religious imperatives."[163] In more recent apostolic exhortations, Francis contended that a consumerist culture "bloats the heart,"[164] thereby contributing to an impoverished sense of beauty and depreciation of joy.[165] Further, in *Laudato Si'*, Francis continued his critique of humanity's consumerist mentality and idolatry of market economies. He lamented how consumerism often only serves those wielding economic power rather than those on the peripheries.[166] For Francis, "unbridled consumerism combined with inequality"[167] can "offer occasional and passing pleasures, but not joy."[168] Time and time again, Francis has urged all people of good will to consider "a change of heart and attitudes as well as a change of structures."[169]

As noted in *Evangelii Gaudium*, Francis recognized the importance of serving as a good model of structural renewal and reform:

> Since I am called to put into practice what I ask of others, I too must think about a conversion of the papacy. It is my duty, as the Bishop of Rome, to be open to suggestions which can help make the exercise of my ministry more faithful to the meaning which Jesus Christ wished to give it and to the present needs of evangelization.[170]

Regarding discerning new ways of exercising his papal office, Francis has advocated for a more inclusive and collegial way of proceeding: "Excessive centralization, rather than proving helpful, complicates the Church's life and her missionary outreach."[171]

Given Pope Francis's reform of style and priorities, exactly one month after his election, Francis matched his reform rhetoric with action by creating a committee of eight (now nine) non-Vatican cardinals from all across the world to advise him on organizational change. According to Faggioli, "it was an unprecedented step in the history of attempts to reform the central government of the Church as it was created in the late sixteenth century."[172] In addition, during his first year, Francis hired consultants from McKinsey and KPMG to bring Vatican communications and finances in line with contemporary practice.[173]

In accordance with his vision to be more familiar with the global peripheries, Pope Francis has appointed approximately 75 percent of the 137 cardinals who will elect his successor.[174] Represented among the 121 Francis-appointed cardinals are fifteen countries that had never had one before, including Bangladesh, Cape Verde, Myanmar, Laos, Tonga, and the Central African Republic.[175] As Patsy McGarry concluded in a 2018 article in the *Irish Times*, "This is considered the most revolutionary thing Francis has done to date in terms of church governance, and with a view to ensuring that the legacy of his papacy is continued into the future."[176]

Another way Pope Francis has tried to account for the wisdom of local, national, and regional expressions of Catholicism is through the citations in his teaching documents. In *Evangelii Gaudium*, he cited from documents of international conferences of bishops nearly twenty times, establishing a new precedent in papal documents.[177] This rhetorical act acknowledged the doctrinal authority in these statements, but, more importantly, demonstrated that "the universal church can and should learn from the local conferences of bishops."[178] Prior to Francis, papal documents took a top-down approach. The pope was the primary authority in messages to churches throughout the world, but since his election, Francis has taken a more collegial and dialogical approach to the development of doctrine. Although some curial authorities[179] are uncomfortable with his openness to debate about disputed issues,[180] such as the treatment of divorced and remarried Catholics, female deacons, and married clergy,[181] this shift in organizational practice has created a space for dialogical discernment. As Curran claimed, "For the first since Vatican II, Catholics in the whole world have heard their bishops publicly discussing and disagreeing about what is good for the church."[182] However, two things that opponents and proponents of Francis can all agree upon concern his curious comments about women and their role in the church as well as the pontiff's stalled reform and image repair responses to the clergy abuse scandal and cover-up.

With regard to Pope Francis's understanding of women and their role in the church, he has noted the need to "investigate further the role of women in the church"[183] and "work harder to develop a profound theology of the woman"[184] because women are offering "new contributions to theological reflection."[185] At the same time, some of Francis's remarks about women have been perceived as reflecting a patriarchal perspective that subordinates women. For example, in an address to the International Theological

Commission, Francis referred to the increased number of female theologians as "icing on the cake"[186] but with a need for more women scholars. Francis made another strange comment during a speech to the European Parliament by characterizing Europe as a grandmother who was "no longer fertile and vibrant."[187] In a strongly worded response in the *Los Angeles Times*, New Testament scholar Candida Moss of the University of Birmingham and Yale Bible professor Joel Baden wrote that Francis's rhetorical decision to use the image of an aging woman and using her "natural loss of fertility and change in appearance that accompany aging to cast a moral judgment" was "nothing other than crass chauvinism."[188] While Francis certainly has room for improvement, to his credit, he has encouraged pastors and theologians to explore "the possible role of women in decision-making in different areas of the Church's life."[189]

Perhaps the most problematic aspect of Pope Francis's image repair and reform of church structure pertain to his (mis)handling of the priest abuse scandal. According to Faggioli, the widening clergy sexual abuse scandal in the Catholic Church is the most devastating crisis "since the Protestant Reformation, with still near-daily reminders of its scope, the fumbling nature of the institutional response, and the pain done to the victims and their families."[190] Even though Francis and his immediate predecessors have issued public apologies, met with survivors, and established a Pontifical Commission for the Protection of Minors (PCPM), victims and commentators have characterized these reconciliation efforts as inadequate. Although initially hopeful, Marie Collins, an Irish abuse survivor and former member of the PCPM, noted the following "stumbling blocks" for her resignation: "lack of resources, inadequate structures around support staff, slowness of forward movement and cultural resistance."[191] In addition, "The most significant problem has been the reluctance of some members of the Vatican Curia to implement the recommendations of the Commission despite their approval by the pope."[192]

Further damaging to Pope Francis's reputation were the following developments during the latter half of 2018: 1) his public defense of a Chilean bishop who embodied a systematic culture of abuse and cover-up, 2) a credible accusation of the sexual abuse of minors against a retired U.S. cardinal, 3) the release of a damning grand jury report about clergy abuse of minors in Pennsylvania, and 4) the publication of three scathing letters calling for Francis's resignation by a retired Vatican ambassador to the United States. After sending two experts to investigate the Chilean matter further, the pontiff admitted "serious errors in the assessment and perception of the situation"[193] and invited victims to the Vatican so Francis could personally apologize to them. With regard to the substantiated allegations of sexual misconduct against McCarrick, Francis promptly suspended McCarrick from any form of public ministry and subsequently accepted his resignation from the College of Cardinals.[194] In response to the Pennsylvania report, Francis penned a "blunt"[195] letter addressed to the "People of God"[196] that acknowledged the painful "experiences of at least a thousand survivors, victims of sexual abuse, the abuse of power and of conscience at the hands of priests over a period of approximately seventy years."[197]

Although both John Paul II and Benedict XVI had referred to clergy sex abuse as a sin and offered public apologies in the past, Francis was the first pope to characterize clergy sex abuse and its cover-up as a "crime."[198] Recognizing that any and all efforts to "beg pardon and to seek to repair the harm done"[199] would be insufficient, Francis promised to help create a clerical culture that would protect children and prevent further abuse and cover-up in the future. This commitment was concretized by the pontiff's meetings in Ireland with that country's survivors of abuse and the convening of emergency meetings in Rome with church leaders. Through repeated apologies to and meetings with Chilean and Irish abuse survivors, the summoning of church leaders from impacted regions to Rome, and accepting the resignations of bishops and cardinals credibly accused of sexual misconduct and cover-up, Francis employed image repair strategies of mortification and corrective action to acknowledge his role in the global scandal and demonstrate a commitment to preventing a recurrence of the sexual abuse of minors by clergy in the future. Finally, by keeping largely silent about Archbishop Vigano's accusations and suggesting prayer and silence as appropriate responses to scandal instigators, Francis sought to reduce the offensiveness of Vigano's allegations through minimization and transcendence.

The Jesuit cardinal formerly known as Jorge Mario Bergoglio was elected pope in 2013 with a mandate to reform the Roman Curia. Inspired by a desire to encourage everyone to bear witness to God's joy and mercy, Pope Francis has embodied these reforms through his style, priorities, and the understanding of the church and its structures. However, for Francis, the expression of any and all reforms ought to be preceded by a profound interior reform of heart and attitude. Francis's call to a more contemplative approach to human experiencing enables one to "be serenely present to each reality."[200] As he stated in *Laudato Si'*, becoming more mindfully present involves an "attitude of the heart, one which approaches life with serene attentiveness, which is capable of being fully present to someone without thinking of what comes next."[201] Francis believes that the development of a capacity for wonder inspires and impels people toward a "deeper understanding of life."[202] The cultivation of a deepening of spirituality can "foster a spirit of generous care, full of tenderness."[203] For Francis, this sense of compassionate mindfulness is grounded by two important insights:

First, it entails gratitude and gratuitousness, a recognition that the world is God's loving gift, and that we are called quietly to imitate his generosity in self-sacrifice and good works. . . . It also entails a loving awareness that we are not disconnected from the rest of creatures, but joined in a splendid universal communion.[204]

For the "ideal is not only to pass from the exterior to the interior to discover the action of God in the soul, but also to discover God in all things."[205]

CONCLUSION

Regardless of medium or occasion, Pope Francis's image repair activity has endeavored to renew public confidence in Catholicism and reform the way in which the Church is perceived by and engages with the contemporary world. In emphasizing the importance of the poor and appealing to Catholicism's positive virtues of joy and mercy in his rhetoric and reforms of style, priorities, church understanding and structure, and spirituality, Francis has situated offensive acts such as abuse of minors by clergy and its cover-up by church leaders with other dire acts such as the plundering of the planet and how ecological degradation harms the most vulnerable in our midst. According to one Francis biographer,

After two papacies of philosophically precise rigidity, Pope Francis . . . has legitimized an alternative. No one can say that the only way to be Catholic is to be dour and rules-based. He has shown that another kind of Christianity is possible. Those who have lived through his papacy will never forget it. Pope Francis has not just demonstrated a different way of being a pope. He has shown the world a different way of being a Catholic. And he has said to people of all faiths, and of none, that in our troubled times the Gospel is indeed good news which—if embraced with mercy, humility, and joy—really can make the world a better place.[206]

As evidenced in the preceding presentation, Pope Francis continues to encourage the entire global community with his image repair efforts. Unfolding across a series of reforms of style, priorities, church structure, and spirituality, Francis is inviting all people of goodwill to reflect, rediscover, and dialogue about how best to live and lead with joy and mercy—two essential human truths and compelling antidotes to the spiritual and social ills of our time.

NOTES

1. Christopher Hale, "Could Pope Francis Be a Feminist Pope?," *Washington Post*, April 13, 2016, https://www.washingtonpost.com/news/acts-of-faith/wp/2016/04/13/could-pope-francis-be-a-feminist-pope/.
2. John L. Allen Jr., *The Francis Miracle: Inside the Transformation of the Pope and the Church* (New York: Time Books, 2015), 2.
3. Francis, "First Greeting of the Holy Father Pope Francis," Vatican website, March 13, 2013, https://w2.vatican.va/content/francesco/en/speeches/2013/march/documents/papa-francesco_20130313_benedizione-urbi-et-orbi.html.
4. Francis, "First Greeting of the Holy Father Pope Francis."
5. Massimo Faggioli, *Pope Francis: Tradition in Transition* (Mahwah, NJ: Paulist Press, 2015), 13.
6. Paul Vallely, *Pope Francis: Untying the Knots: The Struggle for the Soul of Catholicism* (New York: Bloomsbury, 2015), 162.
7. Robert Moynihan, *Pray for Me: The Life and Spiritual Vision of Pope Francis, First Pope from the Americas* (New York: Image, 2013), 7.
8. James Carroll, "The Transformative Promise of Pope Francis, Five Years On," *New Yorker*, March 13, 2018, https://www.newyorker.com/news/daily-comment/the-transformative-promise-of-pope-francis-five-years-on.
9. Dung Q. Tran and Michael R. Carey, "Mercy within Mercy: The Heart of Pope Francis' Inclusive Leadership in a Broken World," in *Breaking the Zero Sum Game: Transforming Societies through Inclusive Leadership*, ed. Aldo Boitano, Raul Lagomarsino, and H. Eric Schockman (Bingley, UK: Emerald Publishing, 2017), 231–48.
10. Pew Research Center, "Pope Francis Still Highly Regarded in U.S., but Signs of Disenchantment Emerge," *Pew Research Center*, March 6, 2018, http://www.pewforum.org/2018/03/06/pope-francis-still-highly-regarded-in-u-s-but-signs-of-disenchantment-emerge/.
11. Laurie Goodstein, "Pope Francis' Once-Soaring Popularity Has Dropped Dramatically, New Poll Says," *New York Times*, October 2, 2018, https://www.nytimes.com/2018/10/02/us/pope-francis-popularity.html.
12. Jason Horowitz, "Pope Orders New Inquiry into Abuse Accusations against McCarrick," *New York Times*, October 6, 2018, https://www.nytimes.com/2018/10/06/world/europe/pope-francis-mccarrick.html.
13. Pew Research Center, "Confidence in Pope Francis Down Sharply in U.S.," *Pew Research Center*, October 2, 2018, http://www.pewforum.org/2018/10/02/confidence-in-pope-francis-down-sharply-in-u-s/.
14. Joseph R. Blaney, "Introduction: Why Sports Image Restoration and How Shall We Proceed?," in *Repairing the Athlete's Image: Studies in Sports Image Restoration*, ed. Joseph R. Blaney, Lance Lippert, and Scott J. Smith (Lanham, MD: Lexington, 2012), 1.
15. Cindy Wooden, "Official Explains Vatican Media Strategy: Let Pope Be Himself," *Crux*, June 14, 2018, https://cruxnow.com/vatican/2018/06/14/official-explains-vatican-media-strategy-let-the-pope-be-himself/.

16. Frances D'Emilio, "Pope's Remedy to Those Seeking Scandal: Prayer and Silence," *Associated Press*, September 3, 2018, https://www.apnews.com/c454f7fc66494d2ba62e2a3656d0524d.

17. Daniel Burke, "The Silent Popes: Why Francis and Benedict Won't Answer the Accusations Dividing Their Church," *CNN*, September 23, 2018, https://www.cnn.com/2018/09/23/europe/silent-popes/index.html.

18. Diane Montagna, "Archbishop Viganò Issues Third Testimony, Refutes Accusations of Cardinal Ouellet," *Life Site News*, October 19, 2018, https://www.lifesitenews.com/news/archbishop-viganos-third-testimony.

19. Massimo Faggioli, "Flirting with Schism: The Right-Wing Effort to Delegitimize Pope Francis," *Commonweal*, September 6, 2018, https://www.commonwealmagazine.org/flirting-schism.

20. George Neumayr, *The Political Pope: How Pope Francis Is Delighting the Liberal Left and Abandoning Conservatives* (New York: Hachette, 2017).

21. Marcantonio Colonna, *The Dictator Pope: The Inside Story of the Francis Papacy* (Washington, DC: Regnery Gateway, 2017).

22. Philip Lawler, *Lost Shepherd: How Pope Francis Is Misleading his Flock* (Washington, DC: Regnery Gateway, 2018).

23. John L. Allen Jr., "Francis at Five Years: Love Him or Hate Him, This Is One Relevant Pope," *Crux*, March 13, 2018, https://cruxnow.com/news-analysis/2018/03/13/francis-five-years-love-hate-one-relevant-pope/.

24. Howard Chua-Eoan and Elizabeth Dias, "Pope Francis, The People's Pope," *Time*, December 11, 2013, http://poy.time.com/2013/12/11/person-of-the-year-pope-francis-the-peoples-pope/?iid=poy-main-lead.

25. Lucas Grindley, "*The Advocate*'s Person of the Year: Pope Francis," *The Advocate*, December 16, 2013, https://www.advocate.com/year-review/2013/12/16/advocates-person-year-pope-francis.

26. Yasmine Hafiz, "Pope Francis Named Man of the Year by *Vanity Fair Italia*," *Huffington Post*, July 10, 2013, https://www.huffingtonpost.com/2013/07/10/pope-francis-man-of-the-year-vanity-fair-italia_n_3572939.html.

27. Mark Binelli, "Pope Francis: The Times They Are A-Changin," *Rolling Stone*, February 13, 2014, https://www.rollingstone.com/culture/culture-news/pope-francis-the-times-they-are-a-changin-49434/.

28. Max Berlinger, "The Best Dressed Man of 2013: Pope Francis," *Esquire*, December 27, 2013, https://www.esquire.com/style/mens-fashion/a26527/pope-francis-style-2013/.

29. Vatican News, "Tenth Anniversary of @Pontifex's First Tweet," *Vatican News*, December 12, 2022, https://www.vaticannews.va/en/pope/news/2022-12/twitter-pontifex-10th-anniversary.html.

30. Daniel Burke, "Pope Francis Still Popular, but Conservative Opposition Rises, Survey Shows," *CNN*, March 6, 2018, https://www.cnn.com/2018/03/06/us/pope-pew-survey/index.html.

31. Eric J. Lyman, "Analysis: Are the Media Giving Pope Francis a Pass?," *Religion News Service*, September 24, 2013, https://religionnews.com/2013/09/24/analysis-are-the-media-giving-pope-francis-a-pass/.

32. Tran and Carey, "Mercy within Mercy," 233.
33. Austin Ivereigh, *The Great Reformer: Francis and the Making of a Radical Pope* (New York: Henry Holt, 2014), xv.
34. Ivereigh, *The Great Reformer*, xv.
35. Allen, *The Francis Miracle*, 5–7.
36. Thomas Reese, "Pope Francis after a Year," *National Catholic Reporter*, March 14, 2014, https://www.ncronline.org/blogs/faith-and-justice/pope-francis-after-year.
37. Laura Rittenhouse, "Five Lessons for CEOs from Pope Francis I," *Forbes*, January 6, 2014, https://www.forbes.com/sites/laurarittenhouse/2014/01/06/five-lessons-for-ceos-from-pope-francis-i/#10d7396b1ab8.
38. *The Economist*, "The Francis Effect: The Pope as Turnaround CEO," April 16, 2014, https://www.economist.com/leaders/2014/04/16/the-francis-effect.
39. Mary Thompson, "What CEOs Can Learn from Pope Francis," *CNBC*, September 24, 2015, https://www.cnbc.com/2015/09/24/what-ceos-can-learn-from-pope-francis.html.
40. Keith V. Erickson, "Presidential Rhetoric's Visual Turn," in *Visual Rhetoric: A Reader in Communication and American Culture*, ed. Lester C. Olson, Care A. Finnegan, and Diane S. Hope (Thousand Oaks, CA: Sage, 2008), 358.
41. Clemens Sedmak, *A Church of the Poor: Pope Francis and the Transformation of Orthodoxy* (Maryknoll, NY: Orbis, 2016), 9.
42. Keith Michael Hearit, *Crisis Management by Apology: Corporate Response to Allegations of Wrong-Doing* (New York: Routledge, 2006).
43. W. Timothy Coombs, *Ongoing Crisis Communication: Planning, Managing, and Responding*, 4th ed. (Thousand Oaks, CA: Sage, 2015).
44. Timothy L. Sellnow and Matthew W. Seeger, *Theorizing Crisis Communication* (Malden, MA: Wiley-Blackwell, 2013).
45. William L. Benoit, "Hugh Grant's Image Restoration Discourse: An Actor Apologizes," *Communication Quarterly* 45, no. 3 (1997): 251.
46. Judith P. Burns and Michael S. Bruner, "Revisiting the Theory of Image Restoration Strategies," *Communication Quarterly* 48, no. 1 (2000): 27–39.
47. William L. Benoit, "Another Visit to the Theory of Image Restoration Strategies," *Communication Quarterly* 48, no. 1 (2000): 40–43.
48. Jessica L. Furgerson and William L. Benoit, "Limbaugh's Loose Lips: Rush Limbaugh's Image Repair after the Sandra Fluke Controversy," *Journal of Radio & Audio Media* 20, no. 2 (2013): 275.
49. Blaney, "Introduction," 2.
50. Kenneth Burke, *The Rhetoric of Religion* (Berkeley: University of California Press, 1970).
51. Marvin B. Scott and Stanford M. Lyman, "Accounts," *American Sociological Review* 33 (1968): 46–62.
52. B. L. Ware and Wil A. Linkugel, "They Spoke in Defense of Themselves: On the Generic Criticism of Apologia," *Quarterly Journal of Speech* 59 (1973): 273–83.
53. William L. Benoit, *Accounts, Excuses, and Apologies: A Theory of Image Restoration Strategies* (New York: State University of New York Press, 1995), 63.
54. Benoit, "Hugh Grant's Image," 252.

55. William L. Benoit, "*NPR*'s Image Repair Discourse on Firing Juan Williams," *Journal of Radio & Audio Media* 18, no. 1 (2011): 84–91.
56. Benoit, "Hugh Grant's Image," 180.
57. William L. Benoit and Susan L. Brinson, "AT&T: 'Apologies Are Not Enough,'" *Communication Quarterly* 42, no. 1 (1994): 77.
58. Blaney, "The Vatican's Response," 201.
59. William L. Benoit and Robert S. Hanczor, "The Tonya Harding Controversy: An Analysis of Image Restoration Strategies," *Communication Quarterly* 42, no. 4 (1994): 421.
60. Joseph R. Blaney and William L. Benoit, *The Clinton Scandals and the Politics of Image Restoration* (Westport, CT: Praeger, 2001).
61. Blaney, "Introduction," 2.
62. Blaney and Benoit, *The Clinton Scandals*, 18.
63. Benoit, "*NPR*'s Image Repair," 85.
64. Furgerson and Benoit, "Limbaugh's Loose Lips," 276.
65. Blaney, "Introduction," 2.
66. William L. Benoit and Jayne R. Henson, "President Bush's Image Repair Discourse on Hurricane Katrina," *Public Relations Review* 35, no. 1 (2009): 40–46.
67. Joseph R. Blaney, William L. Benoit, and LeAnn M. Brazeal, "Blowout!: Firestone's Image Restoration Campaign," *Public Relations Review* 28, no. 4 (2002): 379–92.
68. Ernest Zhang and William L. Benoit, "Former Minister Zhang's Discourse on SARS: Government's Image Restoration or Destruction?," *Public Relations Review* 35, no. 3 (2009): 240–46.
69. Joseph R. Blaney, Lance Lippert, and Scott J. Smith, eds., *Repairing the Athlete's Image: Studies in Sports Image Restoration* (Lanham, MD: Lexington Books, 2013).
70. Wei-Chun Wen, Tzu-hsiang Yu, and William L. Benoit, "The Failure of 'Scientific' Evidence in Taiwan: A Case Study of International Image Repair for American Beef," *Asian Journal of Communication* 22, no. 2 (2012): 121–39.
71. Joseph R. Blaney and William L. Benoit, "The Persuasive Defense of Jesus in the Gospel According to John," *Journal of Communication and Religion* 20, no. 2 (1997): 25–30.
72. Karen L. Legg, "Religious Celebrity: An Analysis of Image Repair Discourse," *Journal of Public Relations Research* 21, no. 2 (2009): 240–50.
73. Joseph R. Blaney, "Restoring the Juridical Image: Apologia for *Ex Corde Ecclesiae*," *Journal of Communication & Religion* 24, no. 1 (2001): 94–109.
74. Cesar Garcia, "Could It Happen Again? Catholic Church Image Repair Strategies in the Revocation of the Excommunication of the Four Lefebvrian Bishops," *Public Relations Review* 36, no. 1 (2010): 70–72.
75. C. T. Maier, "Weathering the Storm: Hauser's *Vernacular Voices*, Public Relations and the Roman Catholic Church's Sexual Abuse Scandal," *Public Relations Review* 31, no. 2 (2005): 219–27.

76. Maria A. Dixon, "Silencing the Lambs: The Catholic Church's Response to the 2002 Sexual Abuse Scandal," *Journal of Communication and Religion* 27, no. 1 (2004): 63–86.

77. James Kaufman, "When Sorry Is Not Enough: Archbishop Cardinal Bernard Law's Image Restoration Strategies in the Statement on Sexual Abuse of Minors by Clergy," *Public Relations Review* 34, no. 3 (2008): 258–62.

78. Nick Squires, "Pope Benedict XVI Resigns: A Papacy Marred by Crises and Controversies," *Telegraph*, February 11, 2013, https://www.telegraph.co.uk/news/worldnews/the-pope/9862461/Pope-Benedict-XVI-resigns-a-papacy-marred-by-crises-and-controversies.html.

79. Ivereigh, *The Great Reformer*, 353.

80. Allen, *The Francis Miracle*, 31.

81. Blaney, "The Vatican's Response," 206.

82. Charles E. Curran, *Tradition and Church Reform: Perspectives on Catholic Moral Teaching* (Maryknoll, NY: Orbis, 2016), 261–76.

83. Jason Horowitz, "How Pope Francis Is Changing the Church," *Vogue*, July 16, 2018, https://www.vogue.com/article/pope-francis-vogue-august-2018-issue.

84. Regis J. Armstrong and Ignatius C. Brady, eds., *Francis and Claire: The Complete Works* (Mahwah, NJ: Paulist Press, 1982).

85. Gina Loehr with Al Giambrone, *Saint Francis, Pope Francis: A Common Vision* (Cincinnati, OH: Servant Books, 2014), 94.

86. Francis, "First Greeting of the Holy Father Pope Francis."

87. Ivereigh, *The Great Reformer*, 366.

88. Sedmak, *A Church of the Poor*, 7.

89. Fifth General Conference of the Bishops of Latin America and Caribbean, "Concluding Document," June 29, 2007, http://www.celam.org/aparecida/Ingles.pdf, 144.

90. Bishops of Latin America and Caribbean, "Concluding Document," 9.

91. Bishops of Latin America and Caribbean, 29.

92. Sedmak, *A Church of the Poor*, 8.

93. Bishops of Latin America and Caribbean, "Concluding Document," 46.

94. Bishops of Latin America and Caribbean, 67.

95. Kasper, *Pope Francis' Revolution*, 24.

96. Søren Kierkegaard, *The Concept of Anxiety: A Simple Psychologically Orienting Deliberation on the Dogmatic Issue of Hereditary Sin*, trans. Reidar Thomte with Albert B. Anderson (Princeton, NJ: Princeton University Press, 1980).

97. Martin Heidegger, *Being and Time*, trans. John Macquarrie and Edward Robinson (New York: Harper & Row, 1962).

98. Kasper, *Pope Francis' Revolution*, 25.

99. Sedmak, *A Church of the Poor*, 10.

100. Francis, *Evangelii Gaudium*, apostolic exhortation, Vatican website, November 24, 2013, https://w2.vatican.va/content/francesco/en/apost_exhortations/documents/papa-francesco_esortazione-ap_20131124_evangelii-gaudium.html, 1.

101. Francis, *Evangelii Gaudium*, 2.

102. Francis, *Evangelii Gaudium*, 52.

103. Sedmak, *A Church of the Poor*, 10.
104. Francis, *Evangelii Gaudium*, 54.
105. Francis, *Evangelii Gaudium*, 2.
106. Ronald C. Arnett, "Temporal Light and Shadows: The Rhetoric of the Sacred," (keynote address, Sacred Rhetoric Conference, Findlay, Ohio, Winebrenner Theological Seminary, May 31, 2017).
107. Francis, *Evangelii Gaudium*, 3.
108. Francis, *Evangelii Gaudium*, 3.
109. Francis, *Evangelii Gaudium*, 6.
110. Sedmak, *A Church of the Poor*, 14.
111. Francis, *Evangelii Gaudium*, 4.
112. Francis, *Evangelii Gaudium*, 7.
113. While *Lumen Fidei* was technically Pope Francis's first major papal publication, it was initially drafted by Pope Benedict XVI. Francis, *Lumen Fidei*, encyclical letter, Vatican website, June 29, 2013, http://w2.vatican.va/content/francesco/en/encyclicals/documents/papa-francesco_20130629_enciclica-lumen-fidei.html, 7.
114. Francis, *Evangelii Gaudium*, 11.
115. Francis, *Evangelii Gaudium*, 265.
116. Kasper, *Pope Francis' Revolution*, 29.
117. Jon Wertheim, "Pope Francis Shares Candid Thoughts in New Documentary," *CBS News*, May 13, 2018, https://www.cbsnews.com/news/pope-francis-shares-candid-thoughts-in-new-documentary/.
118. Francis, *Laudato Si'*, encyclical letter, Vatican website, May 24, 2015, http://w2.vatican.va/content/francesco/en/encyclicals/documents/papa-francesco_20150524_enciclica-laudato-si.html, 12.
119. Francis, *Laudato Si'*, 244.
120. Sedmak, *A Church of the Poor*, 15.
121. Francis, *Evangelii Gaudium*, 208.
122. Francis, *Evangelii Gaudium*, 33.
123. Pope Francis, *The Name of God Is Mercy* (New York: Random House, 2016), 5–10.
124. Francis, "Message of His Holiness Pope Francis for Lent 2015," Vatican website, October 4, 2014, https://w2.vatican.va/content/francesco/en/messages/lent/documents/papa-francesco_20141004_messaggio-quaresima2015.html, 2.
125. Francis, *Evangelii Gaudium*, 114.
126. Pope Francis, *The Name of God*, 6.
127. Antonio Spadaro, "A Big Heart Open to God: An Interview with Pope Francis," *America: The Jesuit Review*, September 30, 2013, https://www.americamagazine.org/faith/2013/09/30/big-heart-open-god-interview-pope-francis.
128. Allen, *The Francis Miracle*, 10.
129. Barack H. Obama, "Remarks by President Obama and His Holiness Pope Francis at Arrival Ceremony," Obama White House website, September 23, 2015, https://obamawhitehouse.archives.gov/the-press-office/2015/09/23/remarks-president-obama-and-his-holiness-pope-francis-arrival-ceremony.

130. Chris Lowney, *Pope Francis: Why He Leads the Way He Leads* (Chicago: Loyola Press, 2013), 43.

131. Tran and Carey, "Mercy within Mercy," 241.

132. Thomas Aquinas, *Summa Theologica*, trans. Fathers of the English Dominican Province (New York: Cosimo, 1912), II–II q. 30 a. 1.

133. John XXIII, "Address on the Occasion of the Solemn Opening of the Most Holy Council," Vatican website, October 11, 1962, https://w2.vatican.va/content/john-xxiii/la/speeches/1962/documents/hf_j-xxiii_spe_19621011_opening-council.html, 7.

134. James F. Keenan, *Moral Wisdom: Lessons and Texts from the Catholic Tradition*, 3rd ed. (Lanham, MD: Rowman & Littlefield, 2017), 117.

135. Jon Sobrino, "Spirituality and the Following of Jesus," in *Mysterium Liberationis: Fundamental Concepts of Liberation Theology*, ed. Ignacio Ellacuria and Jon Sobrino (Maryknoll, NY: Orbis, 1993), 682.

136. Todd Walatka, "The Principle of Mercy: Jon Sobrino and the Catholic Theological Tradition," *Theological Studies* 77, no. 1 (2016): 97.

137. Vallely, *Pope Francis: Untying the Knots*, 170.

138. Francis, *Laudato Si'*, 8.

139. Jim Yardley, "Pope and Russian Orthodox Leader Meet in Historic Step," *New York Times*, February 12, 2016, https://www.nytimes.com/2016/02/13/world/americas/pope-arrives-in-cuba-for-historic-meeting-with-russian-orthodox-leader.html.

140. Francis and Tawadros II, "Common Declaration of His Holiness Francis and His Holiness Tawadros II," Vatican website, April 28, 2017, http://press.vatican.va/content/salastampa/it/bollettino/pubblico/2017/04/28/0279/00640.html#orig, 11.

141. Trisha Thomas and Nicole Winfield, "Pope Denounces 'Murderous Indifference' by Powers in Mideast," *Washington Post*, July 7, 2018, https://www.washingtonpost.com/world/europe/pope-and-orthodox-patriarchs-pray-for-mideast-christians/2018/07/07/5890567c-81b5-11e8-b3b5-b61896f90919_story.html.

142. Francis, "Message of His Holiness Pope Francis for Lent 2016," Vatican website, October 4, 2015, https://w2.vatican.va/content/francesco/en/messages/lent/documents/papa-francesco_20151004_messaggio-quaresima2016.html, 3.

143. Francis, *Misericordiae Vultus*, papal bull, Vatican website, April 11, 2015, https://w2.vatican.va/content/francesco/en/apost_letters/documents/papa-francesco_bolla_20150411_misericordiae-vultus.html, 1.

144. Francis, *Misericordiae Vultus*, 14.

145. Francis, *Misericordiae Vultus*, 14.

146. Francis, *Misericordiae Vultus*, 2.

147. Francis, "Press Conference of Pope Francis during the Return Flight," Vatican website, July 28, 2013, http://w2.vatican.va/content/francesco/en/speeches/2013/july/documents/papa-francesco_20130728_gmg-conferenza-stampa.html.

148. Tran and Carey, "Mercy within Mercy," 242–44.

149. Richard P. McBrien, *Catholicism* (New York: HarperCollins, 1994), 942.

150. James F. Keenan, *The Works of Mercy: The Heart of Catholicism*, 3rd ed. (Lanham, MD: Rowman & Littlefield, 2017), 4.

151. Curran, *Tradition and Church Reform*, 265.

152. Curran, *Tradition and Church Reform*, 265.
153. Curran, *Tradition and Church Reform*, 266.
154. Leonardo Boff, *Francis of Rome and Francis of Assisi: A New Springtime for the Church* (Maryknoll, NY: Orbis, 2014), 7.
155. Boff, *Francis of Rome*, 7.
156. Ivereigh, *The Great Reformer*, 365.
157. Curran, *Tradition and Church Reform*, 262.
158. Andrew Springer, "Pope Francis Surprises Homeless Visitors during Private Vatican Tour," *ABC News*, March 26, 2015, http://abcnews.go.com/International/pope-francis-surprises-homeless-vistors-private-vatican-tour/story?id=29923638.
159. "Option for the Poor and Vulnerable," United States Conference of Catholic Bishops, accessed July 20, 2018, http://www.usccb.org/beliefs-and-teachings/what-we-believe/catholic-social-teaching/option-for-the-poor-and-vulnerable.cfm.
160. Pope Francis, Twitter post, April 24, 2014, 1:24 a.m., https://twitter.com/pontifex/status/459246483930218497?lang=en.
161. Peter G. Northouse, *Introduction to Leadership: Concepts and Practice*, 4th ed. (Thousand Oaks, CA: Sage, 2018), 105.
162. Spadaro, "A Big Heart Open to God."
163. Curran, *Tradition and Church Reform*, 266.
164. Francis, *Gaudete et Exsultate*, apostolic exhortation, Vatican website, March 19, 2018, http://w2.vatican.va/content/francesco/en/apost_exhortations/documents/papa-francesco_esortazione-ap_20180319_gaudete-et-exsultate.html, 128.
165. Francis, *Amoris Laetitia*, apostolic exhortation, Vatican website, March 19, 2016, http://w2.vatican.va/content/dam/francesco/pdf/apost_exhortations/documents/papa-francesco_esortazione-ap_20160319_amoris-laetitia_en.pdf, 127.
166. Francis, *Laudato Si'*, 203–8.
167. Francis, *Evangelii Gaudium*, 60.
168. Francis, *Gaudete et Exsultate*, 128.
169. Curran, *Tradition and Church Reform*, 267.
170. Francis, *Evangelii Gaudium*, 32.
171. Francis, *Evangelii Gaudium*, 32.
172. Faggioli, *Pope Francis*, 33.
173. Liam Moloney, "Vatican Hires Global Firms to Modernize Communications, Accounting," *Wall Street Journal*, December 19, 2013, https://www.wsj.com/articles/vatican-hires-us-firms-to-modernize-communications-accounting-1387469598.
174. Elise Ann Allen, "Pope Names 21 New Cardinals, Including an American and His Envoy to The U.S.," *Crux*, July 9, 2023, https://cruxnow.com/vatican/2023/07/pope-names-21-new-cardinals-including-an-american-and-his-envoy-to-the-u-s.
175. John L. Allen Jr. and Ines San Martin, "As Cardinals Age, Looking Ahead to Pope Francis's Next Consistory," *Crux*, February 21, 2018, https://cruxnow.com/vatican/2018/02/21/cardinals-age-looking-ahead-pope-franciss-next-consistory/.
176. Patsy McGarry, "Five Years of Pope Francis: Lots of Style, Little Substance," *Irish Times*, March 10, 2018, https://www.irishtimes.com/news/social-affairs/religion-and-beliefs/five-years-of-pope-francis-lots-of-style-little-substance-1.3419878.
177. Curran, *Tradition and Church Reform*, 267.

178. Curran, *Tradition and Church Reform*, 270.

179. Catherine Pepinster, "Five Years on, Pope Francis Has Failed to Deliver on His Promises," *The Guardian*, March 12, 2018, https://www.theguardian.com/commentisfree/2018/mar/12/pope-francis-catholic-church-child.

180. Francis, "Greeting of Pope Francis to the Synod Fathers during the First General Congregation of the Third Extraordinary General Assembly of the Synod of Bishops," Vatican website, October 6, 2014, http://w2.vatican.va/content/francesco/en/speeches/2014/october/documents/papa-francesco_20141006_padri-sinodali.html.

181. Allen, "Francis at Five Years."

182. Curran, *Tradition and Church Reform*, 271.

183. Spadaro, "A Big Heart Open to God."

184. Spadaro, "A Big Heart Open to God."

185. Francis, *Evangelii Gaudium*, 103.

186. Francis, "Address of His Holiness Pope Francis to Members of the International Theological Commission," Vatican website, December 5, 2014, http://w2.vatican.va/content/francesco/en/speeches/2014/december/documents/papa-francesco_20141205_commissione-teologica-internazionale.html.

187. Francis, "Address Pope Francis to the European Parliament," Vatican website, November 25, 2014, http://w2.vatican.va/content/francesco/en/speeches/2014/november/documents/papa-francesco_20141125_strasburgo-parlamento-europeo.html.

188. Candida Moss and Joel Baden, "Pope Francis' Woman Problem, *Los Angeles Times*, December 7, 2014, http://www.latimes.com/opinion/la-oe-moss-pope-francis-women-20141208-story.html.

189. Francis, *Evangelii Gaudium*, 104.

190. Massimo Faggioli, "A Report with Ramifications: Australia's Findings on Clerical Sex Abuse," *Commonweal*, December 20, 2017, https://www.commonwealmagazine.org/report-ramifications.

191. Marie Collins, "Exclusive: Survivor Explains Decision to Leave Vatican's Abuse Commission," *National Catholic Reporter*, March 1, 2017, https://www.ncronline.org/news/people/exclusive-survivor-explains-decision-leave-vaticans-abuse-commission.

192. Collins, "Exclusive: Survivor Explains."

193. Francis, "Letter Sent by the Holy Father to the Bishops," Vatican website, April 8, 2018, http://w2.vatican.va/content/francesco/en/letters/2018/documents/papa-francesco_20180408_lettera-vescovi-cile.html.

194. Elisabetta Povoledo and Sharon Otterman, "Cardinal Theodore McCarrick Resigns amid Sexual Abuse Scandal," *New York Times*, July 28, 2018, https://www.nytimes.com/2018/07/28/world/europe/cardinal-theodore-mccarrick-resigns.html.

195. Sheena McKenzie, Barbie Nadeau, and Livia Borghese, "Pope on Pennsylvania Sex Abuse Report: We Abandoned the Little Ones," *CNN*, August 20, 2018, https://www.cnn.com/2018/08/20/europe/pope-francis-letter-sexual-abuse-intl/index.html.

196. Francis, "Letter of His Holiness Pope Francis to the People of God," Vatican website, August 20, 2018, http://w2.vatican.va/content/francesco/en/letters/2018/documents/papa-francesco_20180820_lettera-popolo-didio.html.

197. Francis, "Letter of His Holiness Pope Francis to the People of God."
198. Francis, "Letter of His Holiness Pope Francis to the People of God."
199. Francis, "Letter of His Holiness Pope Francis to the People of God."
200. Francis, *Laudato Si'*, 222.
201. Francis, *Laudato Si'*, 226.
202. Francis, *Laudato Si'*, 225.
203. Francis, *Laudato Si'*, 220.
204. Francis, *Laudato Si'*, 220.
205. Francis, *Laudato Si'*, 233.
206. Vallely, *Pope Francis: Untying the Knots*, 425.

REFERENCES

Allen, Elise Ann. "Pope Names 21 New Cardinals, Including an American and His Envoy to the U.S." *Crux*, July 9, 2023. https://cruxnow.com/vatican/2023/07/pope-names-21-new-cardinals-including-an-american-and-his-envoy-to-the-u-s.

Allen, John L., Jr. *The Francis Miracle: Inside the Transformation of the Pope and the Church*. New York: Time Books, 2015.

———. "Francis at Five Years: Love Him or Hate Him, This is One Relevant Pope." *Crux*, March 13, 2018. https://cruxnow.com/news-analysis/2018/03/13/francis-five-years-love-hate-one-relevant-pope/.

Allen, John L., Jr., and Ines San Martin. "As Cardinals Age, Looking Ahead to Pope Francis's Next Consistory." *Crux*, February 21, 2018. https://cruxnow.com/vatican/2018/02/21/cardinals-age-looking-ahead-pope-franciss-next-consistory/.

Aquinas, Thomas. *Summa Theologica*. Translated by Fathers of the English Dominican Province. New York: Cosimo, 1912.

Armstrong, Regis J., and Ignatius C. Brady, eds. *Francis and Claire: The Complete Works*. Mahwah, NJ: Paulist Press, 1982.

Arnett, Ronald C. "Temporal Light and Shadows: The Rhetoric of the Sacred." Keynote address delivered at the Sacred Rhetoric Conference, Winebrenner Theological Seminary, Findlay, OH, May 31, 2017.

Benoit, William L. *Accounts, Excuses, and Apologies: A Theory of Image Restoration Strategies*. New York: State University of New York Press, 1995.

———. "Hugh Grant's Image Restoration Discourse: An Actor Apologizes." *Communication Quarterly* 45, no. 3 (1997): 251–67.

———. "Another Visit to the Theory of Image Restoration Strategies." *Communication Quarterly* 48, no. 1 (2000): 40–43.

———. "*NPR*'s Image Repair Discourse on Firing Juan Williams." *Journal of Radio & Audio Media* 18, no. 1 (2011): 84–91.

Benoit, William L., and Susan L. Brinson. "AT&T: 'Apologies are Not Enough.'" *Communication Quarterly* 42, no. 1 (1994): 75–88.

Benoit, William L., and Robert S. Hanczor. "The Tonya Harding Controversy: An Analysis of Image Restoration Strategies." *Communication Quarterly* 42, no. 4 (1994): 416–433.

Benoit, William L., and Jayne R. Henson. "President Bush's Image Repair Discourse on Hurricane Katrina." *Public Relations Review* 35, no. 1 (2009): 40–46.

Berlinger, Max. "The Best Dressed Man of 2013: Pope Francis." *Esquire*, December 27, 2013. https://www.esquire.com/style/mens-fashion/a26527/pope-francis-style-2013/.

Binelli, Mark. "Pope Francis: The Times They Are A-Changin." *Rolling Stone*, February 13, 2014. https://www.rollingstone.com/culture/culture-news/pope-francis-the-times-they-are-a-changin-49434/.

Blaney, Joseph R. "Restoring the Juridical Image: Apologia for *Ex Corde Ecclesiae*." *Journal of Communication & Religion* 24, no. 1 (2001): 94–109.

———. "The Vatican's Response to the Sexual Abuse Crisis in America: An Image Restoration Study." In *The Rhetoric of Pope John Paul II*, edited by Joseph R. Blaney and Joseph P. Zompetti, 199–210. Lanham, MD: Lexington, 2009.

———. "Introduction: Why Sports Image Restoration and How Shall We Proceed?" In *Repairing the Athlete's Image: Studies in Sports Image Restoration*, edited by Joseph R. Blaney, Lance Lippert, and Scott J. Smith, 1–8. Lanham, MD: Lexington, 2012.

Blaney, Joseph R., and William L. Benoit. "The Persuasive Defense of Jesus in the Gospel According to John." *Journal of Communication and Religion* 20, no. 2 (1997): 25–30.

———. *The Clinton Scandals and the Politics of Image Restoration*. Westport, CT: Praeger, 2001.

Blaney, Joseph R., William L. Benoit, and LeAnn M. Brazeal. "Blowout!:Firestone's Image Restoration Campaign." *Public Relations Review* 28, no. 4 (2002): 379–92.

Blaney, Joseph R., Lance Lippert, and Scott J. Smith, eds. *Repairing the Athlete's Image: Studies in Sports Image Restoration*. Lanham, MD: Lexington, 2013.

Blasberg, Derek. "Katy Perry on her Career, Meeting the Pope and Protecting her Relationship with Orlando Bloom." *Vogue Australia*, July 18, 2018. https://www.vogue.com.au/celebrity/interviews/katy-perry-on-her-career-meeting-the-pope-and-protecting-her-relationship-with-orlando-bloom/news-story/4117bf5a899d32ce92fffc44f8f50c5b.

Boff, Leonardo. *Francis of Rome and Francis of Assisi: A New Springtime for the Church*. Maryknoll, NY: Orbis, 2014.

Burke, Daniel. "Pope Francis Still Popular, but Conservative Opposition Rises, Survey Shows." *CNN*, March 6, 2018. https://www.cnn.com/2018/03/06/us/pope-pew-survey/index.html.

———. "The Silent Popes: Why Francis and Benedict Won't Answer the Accusations Dividing Their Church." *CNN*, September 23, 2018. https://www.cnn.com/2018/09/23/europe/silent-popes/index.html.

Burke, Kenneth. *The Rhetoric of Religion*. Berkeley, CA: University of California Press, 1970.

Burns, Judith P., and Michael S. Bruner. "Revisiting the Theory of Image Restoration Strategies." *Communication Quarterly* 48, no. 1 (2000): 27–39.

Carroll, James. "The Transformative Promise of Pope Francis, Five Years On." *New Yorker*, March 13, 2018. https://www.newyorker.com/news/daily-comment/the-transformative-promise-of-pope-francis-five-years-on.

Chua-Eoan, Howard, and Elizabeth Dias. "Pope Francis, The People's Pope." *Time*, December 11, 2013. http://poy.time.com/2013/12/11/person-of-the-year-pope-francis-the-peoples-pope/?iid=poy-main-lead.

Collins, Marie. "Exclusive: Survivor Explains Decision to Leave Vatican's Abuse Commission." *National Catholic Reporter*, March 1, 2017. https://www.ncronline.org/news/people/exclusive-survivor-explains-decision-leave-vaticans-abuse-commission.

Colonna, Marcantonio. *The Dictator Pope: The Inside Story of the Francis Papacy.* Washington, DC: Regnery Gateway, 2017.

Coombs, W. Timothy. *Ongoing Crisis Communication: Planning, Managing, and Responding*, 4th ed. Thousand Oaks, CA: Sage, 2015.

Curran, Charles E. *Tradition and Church Reform: Perspectives on Catholic Moral Teaching.* Maryknoll, NY: Orbis Books, 2016.

D'Emilio, Frances. "Pope's Remedy to Those Seeking Scandal: Prayer and Silence." *Associated Press*, September 3, 2018. https://www.apnews.com/c454f7fc66494d2ba62e2a3656d0524d.

Dixon, Maria A. "Silencing the Lambs: The Catholic Church's Response to the 2002 Sexual Abuse Scandal." *Journal of Communication and Religion* 27, no. 1 (2004): 63–86.

The Economist. "The Francis Effect: The Pope as Turnaround CEO." April 16, 2014. https://www.economist.com/leaders/2014/04/16/the-francis-effect.

Erickson, Keith V. "Presidential Rhetoric's Visual Turn." In *Visual Rhetoric: A Reader in Communication and American Culture*, edited by Lester C. Olson, Care A. Finnegan, and Diane S. Hope, 357–74. Thousand Oaks, CA: Sage, 2008.

Faggioli, Massimo. *Pope Francis: Tradition in Transition.* Mahwah, NJ: Paulist Press, 2015.

———. "A Report with Ramifications: Australia's Findings on Clerical Sex Abuse." *Commonweal*, December 20, 2017. https://www.commonwealmagazine.org/report-ramifications.

———. "Flirting with Schism: The Right-Wing Effort to Delegitimize Pope Francis." *Commonweal*, September 6, 2018. https://www.commonwealmagazine.org/flirting-schism.

Fifth General Conference of the Bishops of Latin America and Caribbean. "Concluding Document." June 29, 2007. http://www.celam.org/aparecida/Ingles.pdf.

Francis. "First Greeting of the Holy Father Pope Francis." Vatican Website. March 13, 2013. https://w2.vatican.va/content/francesco/en/speeches/2013/march/documents/papa-francesco_20130313_benedizione-urbi-et-orbi.html.

———. *Lumen Fidei.* Encyclical Letter. Vatican Website. June 29, 2013. http://w2.vatican.va/content/francesco/en/encyclicals/documents/papa-francesco_20130629_enciclica-lumen-fidei.html, 7.

———. "Press Conference of Pope Francis during the Return Flight." Vatican Website. July 28, 2013. http://w2.vatican.va/content/francesco/en/speeches/2013/july/documents/papa-francesco_20130728_gmg-conferenza-stampa.html.

———. *Evangelii Gaudium*. Apostolic Exhortation. Vatican Website. November 24, 2013. https://w2.vatican.va/content/francesco/en/apost_exhortations/documents/papa-francesco_esortazione-ap_20131124_evangelii-gaudium.html.

———. Twitter post. April 24, 2014, 1:24 a.m. https://twitter.com/pontifex/status/459246483930218497?lang=en.

———. "Message of His Holiness Pope Francis for Lent 2015." Vatican Website. October 4, 2014. https://w2.vatican.va/content/francesco/en/messages/lent/documents/papa-francesco_20141004_messaggio-quaresima2015.html.

———. "Greeting of Pope Francis to the Synod Fathers during the First General Congregation of the Third Extraordinary General Assembly of the Synod of Bishops." Vatican Website. October 6, 2014. http://w2.vatican.va/content/francesco/en/speeches/2014/october/documents/papa-francesco_20141006_padri-sinodali.html.

———. "Address of Pope Francis to the European Parliament." Vatican Website. November 25, 2014. http://w2.vatican.va/content/francesco/en/speeches/2014/november/documents/papa-francesco_20141125_strasburgo-parlamento-europeo.html.

———. "Address of His Holiness Pope Francis to Members of the International Theological Commission." Vatican Website. December 5, 2014. http://w2.vatican.va/content/francesco/en/speeches/2014/december/documents/papa-francesco_20141205_commissione-teologica-internazionale.html.

———. *Misericordiae Vultus*. Papal Bull. Vatican Website. April 11, 2015. https://w2.vatican.va/content/francesco/en/apost_letters/documents/papa-francesco_bolla_20150411_misericordiae-vultus.html.

———. *Laudato Si'*. Encyclical Letter. Vatican Website. May 24, 2015. http://w2.vatican.va/content/francesco/en/encyclicals/documents/papa-francesco_20150524_enciclica-laudato-si.html, 12.

———. "Message of His Holiness Pope Francis for Lent 2016." Vatican Website. October 4, 2015. https://w2.vatican.va/content/francesco/en/messages/lent/documents/papa-francesco_20151004_messaggio-quaresima2016.html.

———. *The Name of God Is Mercy*. New York: Random House, 2016.

———. *Amoris Laetitia*. Apostolic Exhortation. Vatican Website. March 19, 2016. http://w2.vatican.va/content/dam/francesco/pdf/apost_exhortations/documents/papa-francesco_esortazione-ap_20160319_amoris-laetitia_en.pdf.

———. *Gaudete et Exsultate*. Apostolic Exhortation. Vatican Website. March 19, 2018. http://w2.vatican.va/content/francesco/en/apost_exhortations/documents/papa-francesco_esortazione-ap_20180319_gaudete-et-exsultate.html, 128.

———. "Letter Sent by the Holy Father to the Bishops." Vatican Website. April 8, 2018. http://w2.vatican.va/content/francesco/en/letters/2018/documents/papa-francesco_20180408_lettera-vescovi-cile.html.

———. "Letter of His Holiness Pope Francis to the People of God." Vatican Website. August 20, 2018. http://w2.vatican.va/content/francesco/en/letters/2018/documents/papa-francesco_20180820_lettera-popolo-didio.html.

Francis and Tawadros II. "Common Declaration of His Holiness Francis and His Holiness Tawadros II." Vatican Website. April 28, 2017. http://press.vatican.va/content/salastampa/it/bollettino/pubblico/2017/04/28/0279/00640.html#orig.

Furgerson, Jessica L., and William L. Benoit. "Limbaugh's Loose Lips: Rush Limbaugh's Image Repair after the Sandra Fluke Controversy." *Journal of Radio & Audio Media* 20, no. 2 (2013): 273–91.

Garcia, Cesar. "Could It Happen Again? Catholic Church Image Repair Strategies in the Revocation of the Excommunication of the Four Lefebvrian Bishops." *Public Relations Review* 36, no. 1 (2010): 70–72.

Goodstein, Laurie. "Pope Francis' Once-Soaring Popularity Has Dropped Dramatically, New Poll Says." *New York Times*, October 2, 2018. https://www.nytimes.com/2018/10/02/us/pope-francis-popularity.html.

Grindley, Lucas. "*The Advocate*'s Person of the Year: Pope Francis." *The Advocate*, December 16, 2013. https://www.advocate.com/year-review/2013/12/16/advocates-person-year-pope-francis.

Hafiz, Yasmine. "Pope Francis Named Man of the Year by *Vanity Fair Italia*." *Huffington Post*, July 10, 2013. https://www.huffingtonpost.com/2013/07/10/pope-francis-man-of-the-year-vanity-fair-italia_n_3572939.html.

Hale, Christopher. "Could Pope Francis Be a Feminist Pope?" *Washington Post*, April 13, 2016. https://www.washingtonpost.com/news/acts-of-faith/wp/2016/04/13/could-pope-francis-be-a-feminist-pope/.

Hearit, Keith Michael. *Crisis Management by Apology: Corporate Response to Allegations of Wrong-Doing*. New York: Routledge, 2006.

Heidegger, Martin. *Being and Time*. Translated by John Macquarrie and Edward Robinson. New York: Harper & Row, 1962.

Horowitz, Jason. "How Pope Francis Is Changing the Church." *Vogue*, July 16, 2018. https://www.vogue.com/article/pope-francis-vogue-august-2018-issue.

———. "Pope Orders New Inquiry into Abuse Accusations against McCarrick." *New York Times*, October 6, 2018. https://www.nytimes.com/2018/10/06/world/europe/pope-francis-mccarrick.html.

Ivereigh, Austin. *The Great Reformer: Francis and the Making of a Radical Pope*. New York: Henry Holt, 2014.

John XXIII. "Address on the Occasion of the Solemn Opening of the Most Holy Council." Vatican Website. October 11, 1962. https://w2.vatican.va/content/john-xxiii/la/speeches/1962/documents/hf_j-xxiii_spe_19621011_opening-council.html.

Kasper, Walter. *Pope Francis' Revolution of Tenderness and Love*. Mahwah, NJ: Paulist Press, 2015.

Kaufman, James. "When Sorry Is Not Enough: Archbishop Cardinal Bernard Law's Image Restoration Strategies in the Statement on Sexual Abuse of Minors by Clergy." *Public Relations Review* 34, no. 3 (2008): 258–62.

Keenan, James F. *Moral Wisdom: Lessons and Texts from the Catholic Tradition*, 3rd ed. Lanham, MD: Rowman & Littlefield, 2017.

———. *The Works of Mercy: The Heart of Catholicism*, 3rd ed. Lanham, MD: Rowman & Littlefield, 2017.

Kierkegaard, Søren. *The Concept of Anxiety: A Simple Psychologically Orienting Deliberation on the Dogmatic Issue of Hereditary Sin*. Translated by Reidar Thomte with Albert B. Anderson. Princeton, NJ: Princeton University Press, 1980.

Lawler, Philip. *Lost Shepherd: How Pope Francis Is Misleading his Flock*. Washington, DC: Regnery Gateway, 2018.

Legg, Karen L. "Religious Celebrity: An Analysis of Image Repair Discourse." *Journal of Public Relations Research* 21, no. 2 (2009): 240–50.

Loehr, Gina, with Al Giambrone. *Saint Francis, Pope Francis: A Common Vision*. Cincinnati, OH: Servant Books, 2014.

Lowney, Chris. *Pope Francis: Why He Leads the Way He Leads*. Chicago: Loyola Press, 2013.

Lyman, Eric J. "Analysis: Are the Media Giving Pope Francis a Pass?" *Religion News Service*, September 24, 2013. https://religionnews.com/2013/09/24/analysis-are-the-media-giving-pope-francis-a-pass/.

Maier, C. T. "Weathering the Storm: Hauser's *Vernacular Voices*, Public Relations and the Roman Catholic Church's Sexual Abuse Scandal." *Public Relations Review* 31, no. 2 (2005): 219–27.

McBrien, Richard P. *Catholicism*. New York: HarperCollins, 1994.

McGarry, Patsy. "Five Years of Pope Francis: Lots of Style, Little Substance." *Irish Times*, March 10, 2018. https://www.irishtimes.com/news/social-affairs/religion-and-beliefs/five-years-of-pope-francis-lots-of-style-little-substance-1.3419978.

McKenzie, Sheena, Barbie Nadeau, and Livia Borghese. "Pope on Pennsylvania Sex Abuse Report: We Abandoned the Little Ones." *CNN*, August 20, 2018. https://www.cnn.com/2018/08/20/europe/pope-francis-letter-sexual-abuse-intl/index.html.

Moloney, Liam. "Vatican Hires Global Firms to Modernize Communications, Accounting." *Wall Street Journal*, December 19, 2013. https://www.wsj.com/articles/vatican-hires-us-firms-to-modernize-communications-accounting-1387469598.

Montagna, Diane. "Archbishop Viganò Issues Third Testimony, Refutes Accusations of Cardinal Ouellet." *Life Site News*, October 19, 2018. https://www.lifesitenews.com/news/archbishop-viganos-third-testimony.

Moss, Candida, and Joel Baden. "Pope Francis' Woman Problem. *Los Angeles Times*, December 7, 2014. http://www.latimes.com/opinion/la-oe-moss-pope-francis-women-20141208-story.html.

Moynihan, Robert. *Pray for Me: The Life and Spiritual Vision of Pope Francis, First Pope from the Americas*. New York: Image, 2013.

Neumayr, George. *The Political Pope: How Pope Francis Is Delighting the Liberal Left and Abandoning Conservatives*. New York: Hachette, 2017.

Northouse, Peter G. *Introduction to Leadership: Concepts and Practice*, 4th ed. Thousand Oaks, CA: Sage, 2018.

Obama, Barack H. "Remarks by President Obama and His Holiness Pope Francis at Arrival Ceremony." Obama White House Website. September 23, 2015. https://obamawhitehouse.archives.gov/the-press-office/2015/09/23/remarks-president-obama-and-his-holiness-pope-francis-arrival-ceremony.

Pepinster, Catherine. "Five Years on, Pope Francis Has Failed to Deliver on His Promises." *The Guardian*, March 12, 2018. https://www.theguardian.com/commentisfree/2018/mar/12/pope-francis-catholic-church-child.

Pew Research Center. "Pope Francis Still Highly Regarded in U.S., but Signs of Disenchantment Emerge." *Pew Research Center*, March 6, 2018. http://www.pewforum.org/2018/03/06/pope-francis-still-highly-regarded-in-u-s-but-signs-of-disenchantment-emerge/.

———. "Confidence in Pope Francis Down Sharply in U.S." *Pew Research Center*, October 2, 2018. http://www.pewforum.org/2018/10/02/confidence-in-pope-francis-down-sharply-in-u-s/.

Povoledo, Elisabetta, and Sharon Otterman. "Cardinal Theodore McCarrick Resigns amid Sexual Abuse Scandal." *New York Times*, July 28, 2018. https://www.nytimes.com/2018/07/28/world/europe/cardinal-theodore-mccarrick-resigns.html.

Reese, Thomas. "Pope Francis after a Year." *National Catholic Reporter*, March 14, 2014. https://www.ncronline.org/blogs/faith-and-justice/pope-francis-after-year.

Rittenhouse, Laura. "Five Lessons for CEOs from Pope Francis I." *Forbes*, January 6, 2014. https://www.forbes.com/sites/laurarittenhouse/2014/01/06/five-lessons-for-ceos-from-pope-francis-i/#10d7396b1ab8.

Scott, Marvin B., and Stanford M. Lyman. "Accounts," *American Sociological Review* 33, (1968): 46–62.

Sedmak, Clemens. *A Church of the Poor: Pope Francis and the Transformation of Orthodoxy*. Maryknoll, NY: Orbis, 2016.

Sellnow, Timothy L., and Matthew W. Seeger. *Theorizing Crisis Communication*. Malden, MA: Wiley-Blackwell, 2013.

Sobrino, Jon. "Spirituality and the Following of Jesus." In *Mysterium Liberationis: Fundamental Concepts of Liberation Theology*, edited by Ignacio Ellacuria and Jon Sobrino, 677–701. Maryknoll, NY: Orbis, 1993.

Spadaro, Antonio. "A Big Heart Open to God: An Interview with Pope Francis." *America: The Jesuit Review*, September 30, 2013. https://www.americamagazine.org/faith/2013/09/30/big-heart-open-god-interview-pope-francis.

Springer, Andrew. "Pope Francis Surprises Homeless Visitors during Private Vatican Tour." *ABC News*, March 26, 2015. http://abcnews.go.com/International/pope-francis-surprises-homeless-vistors-private-vatican-tour/story?id=29923638.

Squires, Nick. "Pope Benedict XVI Resigns: A Papacy Marred by Crises and Controversies." *Telegraph*, February 11, 2013. https://www.telegraph.co.uk/news/worldnews/the-pope/9862461/Pope-Benedict-XVI-resigns-a-papacy-marred-by-crises-and-controversies.html.

Thomas, Trisha, and Nicole Winfield. "Pope Denounces 'Murderous Indifference' by Powers in Mideast." *Washington Post*, July 7, 2018. https://www.washingtonpost.com/world/europe/pope-and-orthodox-patriarchs-pray-for-mideast-christians/2018/07/07/5890567c-81b5-11e8-b3b5-b61896f90919_story.html.

Thompson, Mary. "What CEOs Can Learn from Pope Francis." *CNBC*, September 24, 2015. https://www.cnbc.com/2015/09/24/what-ceos-can-learn-from-pope-francis.html.

Tran, Dung Q., and Michael R. Carey. "Mercy within Mercy: The Heart of Pope Francis' Inclusive Leadership in a Broken World." In *Breaking the Zero Sum Game: Transforming Societies through Inclusive Leadership*, edited by Aldo Boitano, Raul Lagomarsino, and H. Eric Schockman, 231–48. Bingley, UK: Emerald Publishing, 2017.

United States Conference of Catholic Bishops. "Option for the Poor and Vulnerable." Accessed July 20, 2018. http://www.usccb.org/beliefs-and-teachings/what-we-believe/catholic-social-teaching/option-for-the-poor-and-vulnerable.cfm.

Vallely, Paul. *Pope Francis: Untying the Knots: The Struggle for the Soul of Catholicism*. New York: Bloomsbury, 2015.

Vatican News. "Tenth Anniversary of @Pontifex's First Tweet." *Vatican News*, December 12, 2022. https://www.vaticannews.va/en/pope/news/2022-12/twitter-pontifex-10th-anniversary.html.

Walatka, Todd. "The Principle of Mercy: Jon Sobrino and the Catholic Theological Tradition." *Theological Studies* 77, no. 1 (2016): 96–117.

Ware, B. L., and Wil A. Linkugel. "They Spoke in Defense of Themselves: On the Generic Criticism of Apologia." *Quarterly Journal of Speech* 59 (1973): 273–83.

Wedeman, Ben, and Michael Pearson. "Scandal Threatens to Overshadow Pope's Final Days." *CNN*, February 28, 2013. https://www.cnn.com/2013/02/25/world/europe/vatican-archbishop-resigns/.

Wen, Wei-Chun, Tzu-hsiang Yu, and William L. Benoit. "The Failure of 'Scientific' Evidence in Taiwan: A Case Study of International Image Repair for American Beef." *Asian Journal of Communication* 22, no. 2 (2012): 121–39.

Wertheim, Jon. "Pope Francis Shares Candid Thoughts in New Documentary." *CBS News*, May 13, 2018. https://www.cbsnews.com/news/pope-francis-shares-candid-thoughts-in-new-documentary/.

Wooden, Cindy. "Official Explains Vatican Media Strategy: Let Pope Be Himself." *Crux*, June 14, 2018. https://cruxnow.com/vatican/2018/06/14/official-explains-vatican-media-strategy-let-the-pope-be-himself/.

Yardley, Jim. "Pope and Russian Orthodox Leader Meet in Historic Step." *New York Times*, February 12, 2016. https://www.nytimes.com/2016/02/13/world/americas/pope-arrives-in-cuba-for-historic-meeting-with-russian-orthodox-leader.html.

Zhang, Ernest, and William L. Benoit. "Former Minister Zhang's Discourse on SARS: Government's Image Restoration or Destruction?" *Public Relations Review* 35, no. 3 (2009): 240–46.

Chapter 9

Leaning into Death
A Philosophy of Equanimity

Annette M. Holba

In contemporary Western cultures, the topic of death is often absent in public discourse; and when death becomes a topic in such arenas, it usually provokes fear, resistance, or grief (Duerringer 2013). Death has been capitalized as an industry; and the cost of final expenses such as funeral homes, probate actions, estate debt resolutions, and other such end-of-life necessities has stigmatized death as being very costly to families and survivors of the deceased. Stigmatization of this kind represents the negative implications of death in the minds of many (Duerringer 2013). It is common to see television commercials selling life insurance or final expense insurance after vilifying the government for only paying a $250 Social Security death benefit. Today's funerals with traditional burials including coffins, cemetery plots, viewings/visitations, masses, and graveside services can cost upwards of $15,000 for a basic burial. Historically, these costs were hidden or at least not spoken about in public settings (Copeland 2015). In fact, we avoid talking about death as a culture because we see it more as an end-of-life event (Kübler-Ross 1969; Carpentier and van Brussel 2012), so nothing is left to say other than to plan for death by purchasing something such as a coffin or grave site. It is rare to see a mainstream public advertisement of alternative modes of burial, such as cremation and green burials, which have smaller financial costs.

Contemporary Western cultures often do not embrace the idea of living with death as part of our future because we try to ward off death by fighting to conquer all types of terminal illnesses. Fighting terminal illness is not a bad thing and, in fact, researching terminal illnesses has provided many helpful ways of treating disease and making lives more comfortable in the face of pain and suffering that disease causes. But we fail to acknowledge that living—to be born—is the most significant terminal illness that all beings have in common. However, to acknowledge our own ontology, we must see ourselves as *being-toward-death* (Heidegger 1996, 241). We tend to avoid this eternal truth and fail to acknowledge its relevance in our everyday existence. Then, when death comes close to us—when our parents, children, or close friends die—we are not fully prepared for the absence we feel and the violence of the rupture that invades our interiority and daily existence. As responsible human beings, learning to understand death as part of life and to have a true contemplative knowing that death will come and suffering will accompany it, is the only way to be prepared for the violence of the rupture. Whether our own death or the death of another, coming to terms with the certainty of death in a healthy way eases the experience of the rupture for the individual and for society.

This essay explores what a philosophy of equanimity toward death would look like from a philosophy of communication perspective. A philosophy of equanimity grounded in a personal ontological truth about death could lead to a healing attitude of peace, acknowledgment, and understanding. The first section of this chapter explores Western rhetorics about death in popular culture seeking to illuminate the problematic nature of these rhetorics. Next is a discussion about how a philosophy of equanimity can provide an alternative perspective that disrupts the problematic rhetorics about death. Last, the notion of *leaning into death* opens sacred rhetorical ground from which the philosophy of equanimity serves as performative interplay that nourishes the existential rupture caused by experiencing the death of another, releasing one from incapacitation and grief and opening a pathway toward living despite that rupture. This is important because regardless of religious affiliation or coming from a perspective absent a religious affiliation, death naturally invites—and in some cases imposes—one to consider the sacred, either to seek it out or to think about what it means to be sacred, or to question the meaning of sacred.

By developing equanimity in our understandings and feelings about death, we engage in the inner work necessary for cultivating "empathetic knowing" (Zajonc 2009, 76) that allows one to not be incapacitated by the death of another. Instead, by leaning into death through equanimity and being able to sit with it, the absence becomes understood empathically, turning existential rupture into acknowledgment resistant of incapacitation. By considering various philosophical perspectives on death from Martin Heidegger (1996), Jacques Derrida (1993), Arthur Zajonc (2009), Mahatma Gandhi (2008), and Rudolf Steiner (1994), and illuminating the contemplative action of equanimity, this essay constructs a philosophy of equanimity that can balance those negative rhetorics about death and bring honor and humility to our very ontology as being-toward-death.

VARIOUS RHETORICS ON DEATH AND DYING

In the United States, we do not talk about death enough. When we do, we focus more on conquering it than about living well with it, but studies show that this might be changing in the twenty-first century (van Brussel and Carpentier 2014). Nevertheless, it is still difficult to talk about death, especially with children, in the United States. Death is more often associated with a bad act and punishment or retribution (Kübler-Ross 1969). At least in the public, death rarely receives adequate attention. From a psychological perspective, in our own unconscious mind we "can only be killed" because our mind will not allow us to die naturally (Kübler-Ross 1969, 16). However, if we look closer and seek out pockets of obscure locations, we find here and there, both in person and in digital communities, people who come together to create a space for conversation, sharing experiences, and exchanging positive ways people can experience death for both the dying person and those left behind.

For most Westerners living in the latter part of the twentieth century, the most familiar and accessible text on death was Elisabeth Kübler-Ross's book *On Death and Dying*. Kübler-Ross (1969) changed the way the medical community and popular culture understood death. Prior to this publication, understanding the dying person as a human being was not at the forefront of the medical community; disease was privileged and focused on so that it could be eliminated or attacked. Approaching death in this way would certainly aid medical practitioners in doing what needs to be done without emotions confusing them, but it also led practitioners to focus on the disease rather than on the patient (Kübler-Ross 1969). The human being was secondary, but the historical context can aid understanding that this was not an intentional negative practice in the medical community (Kübler-Ross 1969).

Medicine has an interesting history reaching as far back as ancient documents and hieroglyphs that reveal the practice of healing arts. Modern medicine has been organized by two distinct historical Eras beginning around the 1860s when, during the American Civil War, medicine became sophisticated and more scientific, which means the practices in medicine were supported with traditional research that followed the scientific method (Dossey 1999). Era I of medicine has been referred to as a mechanical period in which health and illness were perceived to be physically in nature and therefore, treatment and therapies should be physical (Dossey 1999). This meant that treatment was either surgical or pharmaceutical. The mind was set aside and the brain, because if its physicality, became primary.

Shortly after WWII, medicine evolved into Era II in which it was recognized that disease had a psychosomatic aspect, and doctors and researchers agreed that emotions and feelings could influence body functions, such as confirming that psychological stress could cause high blood pressure, heart palpitations, and other physiological, measurable indicators of bodily health (Dossey 1999). This does not mean that one day Western medicine intentionally moved from Era I to Era II in medicine. But it does mean that because medicine became measurable, mechanical, and scientific, specializations proliferated, pharmaceuticals became elaborate and complex, and researchers made discoveries by leaps and bounds to advance medical knowledge beyond what anyone could imagine. Kübler-Ross's book *On Death and Dying* was published in 1969, during the early part of Era II.

Larry Dossey (1999), world renowned medical doctor, researcher, and author, suggests that we are currently on the threshold (or perhaps already there) of a new era in medicine. Dossey (1999) argues that more and more medical professionals and medical researchers believe that consciousness is not confined to the physical body, and that the mind is "nonlocal" (25), meaning that it is boundless and infinite. As Dossey (1999) explains, the nonlocal mind refers to "the capacity of human consciousness to function outside of the confines of the individual brain and body" (37–38). Dossey (1999) stated that "the interknit web of life may be wider than we commonly imagine. It may be boundless, limitless, nonlocal" (69). Dossey (1999) suggests that non-locality is what leads to the transpersonal effects of the mind. This is a whole new way of understanding the human being, and these conversations have opened new fields of study in neuroscience and transpersonal psychology.

Kübler-Ross (1969) conducted hundreds of hours of interviews with people in the process of dying. This was the first study of its kind in which those dying were given a voice in the mass media to share their experiences and feelings about their diagnoses, prognoses, and experiences with those in the medical profession as well as their family members. As a result of her communication with these patients, Kübler-Ross identified, for the first time in the history of modern medicine, the five stages of death—of dying: denial, isolation, anger, bargaining, depression, and acceptance. Kübler-Ross (1969) realized that the medical professionals working with their patients had little understanding of how someone facing death, in imminent terms, felt about dying, and she believed that understanding these aspects of a dying patient's experience with his own death would be beneficial for medical professionals to know so that they can better know how to communicate with their patients and treat them. Kübler-Ross's perspectives on the death and dying of human beings was the first of its kind to arouse the attention of the modern scientific community toward learning from those who are in the process of dying. There are multiple cultural perspectives on death and dying; understanding how the medical community organized around the practice of medicine is helpful to see where we have come from related to a sociocultural perspective about death. Kübler-Ross broadened the conversation and prepared the Western world to move toward a kind of empathic knowing that can help to set the stage for a philosophy of equanimity.

The contributions by Kübler-Ross (1969) and Dossey (1999) have a very practical and pragmatic spirit that reflect a praxis engagement with death of the self or of others. In philosophical circles, Martin Heidegger and Jacques Derrida have very different conversations about the ontological truth of death. Martin Heidegger (1996), a premier philosopher of the mid-twentieth century, argues that death is the "possibility of an impossibility" and "the possibility of the absolute impossibility of Daesin" (232). In other words, Heidegger suggests that death possibilizes Dasein. In response to Heidegger's declaration of death as a possibility of an impossibility, Jacques Derrida (1995), a late-twentieth-century philosopher also known as the leading voice of reconstruction, questions how what is impossible (death) possibilizes being (Dasein). Derrida does not ask the question, what is death? Instead, he sought to understand death and its meaning. In Derrida's (1995) *Gift of Death*, he rethinks death not so much as a pure possibility but, instead, thinks of death as the "aporia" of the impossible (62). This means death is the impossibility of a passage to life or to be living. Aporia references a not-getting-thereness or a being without passage. Therefore, Derrida changes Heidegger's death as a "possibility of an impossibility" to an "impossibility" of passage, which means an impossibility cannot possibilize, the original problem Derrida saw in Heidegger's position.

The shift from the possibility (Heidegger) to the impossibility (Derrida) also shifts the ethical relation embedded in death. Heidegger's (1996) "call of conscience" discloses Dasein's essential ethical character as "being-in-the-world" built upon an a priori of care (255). Heidegger's ethicality of death resides within the ethic of care. However, Derrida does not situate the role of care in his perspective on death. According to Derrida, the aporia of the impossibility shifts our focus of attention to social ethics and our relation with those outside the self (Carel 2007). The difference between Heidegger and Derrida suggests that Heidegger's ethic of care is seen as an ontic absolute and not very specific within embedded contexts. For Derrida, death as a social ethic is embedded within the particular because it is intertwined with our social relations. Heidegger tries to resolve the notion of death by acknowledging that it is inherent in Dasein that is always-already in structure of Dasein, and death stands at the edges of the "thrownness" of Dasein. Derrida disagrees with this, suggesting that death is not a problem that has to be resolved; instead, it stands as a limit of truth—the truth of Being. It limits the passage into Being.

There is hope in Derrida's message of nonpassage in that it is an absolute waiting, where we stand and wait in a social relation with the other, for death, death of the other. We serve as an empathic witness for the other—the death of the other is the only death there is, because once it is our own turn toward the aporia of death, we no longer constitute Dasein, and we can no longer experience our own death. So, my individual death, since it is an aporia, is not primary or a priority. It is my social ethic in relation to the world, so the only death I experience is the death of the other. For Derrida (1993, 1995), death as an aporia is the biggest mystery of life; and it makes us quiver as we wait for nonpassage—we wait in anticipation of the impossibility of passage—we await our nonpassage.

The narrative of thanatology, in Derrida's *Gift of Death*, is an ethical act by witnessing. "It witnesses, in the manner of an ethical or political act, for today for tomorrow" (1995, 36). In witnessing the death of the other, we do become hostage to it; therein lies the ethicality—we serve it, and we are accountable to it. When Derrida (1995) explores the ethicality of death, he talks about a mask, "[t]he individualism of technological civilization relies precisely on a misunderstanding of the unique self. It is the individualism of a role and not of a person" (37). The role hides the person behind a mask. "And just as the role played hides behind the authenticity of the irreplaceable self behind a social mask, so the civilization of boredom produced by techno-scientific objectivity hides mystery" (37). Derrida is saying that we neutralize our thinking about death through a techno-scientific environment that hides the mystery of death/life, diverting our attention from the question of what it means to be here.

Our contemporary Western culture has an apprehension of death, "apprehension of death . . . refers as much to the anxious solicitude, care for the soul in the face of death, and the differing interpretive attitudes" we find about death in cultures and in particular moments, kairotic moments of "orgiastic mystery, platonic anabasis, and the mysterium tremendum" (Derrida 1995, 40). Derrida struggles with the sacrifice Jesus Christ made in Christian theology and the death he chose to take for the other. This is another death and announces another way of giving in death or of granting oneself death. The gift of this kind of death is a giving of goodness; it is the act of giving—a donation of goodness within a social relation.

The difference between Kübler-Ross and Dossey's perspectives and Heidegger and Derrida's perspectives is that both Heidegger and Derrida do what philosophers do; they contemplate, sometimes mechanistically, and delve deeply into hermeneutic expressions about existence as they try to make sense of the nonsensical. Kübler-Ross and Dossey dive deeply into human experience to understand it. Kübler-Ross, especially, focuses on listening to stories being told by people in their current experience of dying. Each of these perspectives is useful in pulling together an empathic understanding of death; they also provide starting places from which we can individually think about death on our own terms. However, this may still limit developing a broader perspective on death away from a traditional Western mechanistic perspective. Kübler-Ross and Dossey do more to resist this traditional mechanistic view of death because they attend to the human narratives of dying people through an empathic lens.

Rudolf Steiner (1861–1925) was an Austrian philosopher and an esoteric thinker. His philosophy on death was less mechanistic than most Western perspectives. Steiner (1994) believed death, as the Western world defines it, does signify a kind of change in the physical body in that it ceases to function physically. When the physical function of the body ends, it can no longer be a vehicle for the soul and spirit of the individual. This perspective does two things. First, it separates the soul from the spirit, identifying them as two separate entities or aspects of existence. In addition, Steiner argued that once the body can no longer be a vehicle for the soul and spirit, the body then becomes completely subject to the natural and physical world so that it disintegrates.

Steiner (1994) continued to explain that once the spirit and soul free themselves from the physical body, they remain linked. He suggested that similar to the way the physical body was bound to the physical world, the soul then binds itself to the soul world. The spirit remains bound to the soul in the soul world. They remain together in the soul world until the process of reincarnation occurs into another physical body, and they leave the soul world. Steiner (1994) suggested that the spirit's ultimate existence in the physical world is through being bound to a physical body—so until the binding of a new physical body, the spirit remains bound to the soul waiting to reach its potential, again.

Steiner (1994) advocated for reincarnation, and he identified karma as a reality and important to the experience of reincarnation. For Steiner (1994), compassion is a fundamental element in the soul life. Truthfulness and trustworthiness are necessary human actions in the physical world. Steiner (1994) also identified envy and falsehoods as negative elements that would attract negative karma and impact the reincarnation process as the soul and spirit move through existence in different worlds. Steiner's (1994) perspective on life and death was grounded in a philosophy of equanimity that is tied to the soul and the soul world so that each person has opportunities to expand this philosophy once reincarnated into the physical world. Although Steiner did not articulate his perspective on death as a philosophy of equanimity, the grounding of his perspective is situated within a framework of compassion toward the other—both physical and spiritual compassion. Having a philosophy of equanimity around the concept of death can provide an alternative understanding that opens to an expanded sensibility about death.

PHILOSOPHY OF EQUANIMITY

Equanimity has been described as a virtue of being calm amid a disruptive environment (Mathis 2018) and an inner calmness that joins with empathy to "create the possibility of a new forms of community life" (Zajonc 2009, 53). In the field of transpersonal psychology, equanimity is an outcome of "pure awareness" that is unconfined by any mind-state (Welwood 2002, 50) and being free or liberated from any kind of personal anxiety (Welwood 2002). It is an individual disposition that carries no presumption and no attachment, which creates inner harmony and peace (Welwood 2002). Buddhist thought also offers an enriching perspective on equanimity.

The Dalai Lama and Thupten Jinpa (2005) interpret Buddha's philosophy of equanimity as a genuine compassion toward the other, recognizing that all sentient beings are worthy of the ultimate sacrifice, the kind of unconditional compassion a mother has for her offspring. The Dalai Lama frames this sentiment in this way:

> Contemplation of beginningless lifetimes allows us to recognize that all sentient beings have acted in this very manner toward us, in some capacity and to some degree. Appreciating this, we develop a strong sense of empathy and gratitude toward other sentient beings, which in turn, enables us to feel a greater sense of closeness with them. Feeling this closeness, we are able to perceive their kindness to us, regardless of how they may behave at present. This is what is meant by genuine intimacy with all beings. (Lama and Jinpa 2005)

This kind of genuine intimacy takes time to cultivate. The first stage of cultivation is developing and living by a philosophy of equanimity (Lama and Jinpa 2005). Equanimity is one of the four qualities that cultivate the boundless heart; the other three qualities are immeasurable kindness, compassion, and joy (Feldman 2017). In Buddhist thought, these qualities are referred to as *Brahma Viharas*, which can be directly translated as "the noblest way of living in this world here and now" (Feldman 2017, 1). Developing a disposition of equanimity "allows us to act without becoming preoccupied with the results and outcomes of our actions. It is a quality of strength and inner poise that allows us to respond to the world of experience without fear and hesitation" (Feldman 2017, 3). Cultivating the qualities of the *Brahma Viharas* enables our communicative action to be grounded with intention shaped by the praxis of kindness, compassion, joy, and equanimity. The role of equanimity is to intend genuine openness toward the other—to be open, fair, tempered, and composed even when situations become tense, unruly, and challenge the very essence of our being. Cultivating an attitude of equanimity, especially toward our ontology, enables one to be open to the experience of death, especially the death of a loved one—one with whom we share a genuine intimacy.

A mind-set of equanimity as "an open, spacious, all-accepting, impartial attitude transcending such biases as good versus bad, self versus other" opens dialogue and resists devolving into incivility, rudeness, and coercion (Rinpoche 2015, 142). The other qualities in *Brahma Viharas*, kindness, compassion, and joy, ensure that this openness does not mutate into neutrality or a lack of interest in care for the other. Developing a mind-set, or a habit of mind, of equanimity to navigate a dialogic location enables movement toward understanding and reconciliation with the other (Zajonc 2009). In Zajonc's (2009) philosophy of contemplative inquiry, he suggests that cultivating a set of moods lays a foundation that opens to revelation. These moods are habits of mind that contribute to an ethos of communicative virtue; they are humility, reverence, devotion, and equanimity. Habits of mind such as these cultivate inner well-being that ultimately provides emotional distance and new perspectives that can shield the temptation to enter the communicative dark side when confronted by death.

Equanimity does more. Equanimity is the core of Zajonc's (2009) phenomenology of the meditative experience. Equanimity embedded in our feelings and experiences allows one to meet peace in moments of joy and moments of tumult. As death approaches our own self, or as a witness to the death of the other, this approximates to the experience of tumult and the fear of the unknown—standing on the edges of despair. It is in this moment or in these moments that unexpected possibilities emerge. Instead of feeling sadness, sorrow, or fear, leaning into these feelings, being hailed by these experiences, and seeing all of life's depths, equanimity invites our participation as helper, healer, or guide.

This is consistent, too, with Mahatma Gandhi's (1869–1948) perspective on human existence, which is to serve others: "We eat and drink, sleep and wake, for service alone" (Gandhi 2008, 92). In these moments, instead of being a spectator and watching suffering, we become, through equanimity, a partner and empathic witness—suffering with the other; and once death arrives, suffer for the other. The highest ethic one can live by is to be a partner and empathic witness with the other and to suffer for the other. Coming to terms with this ethic requires a leaning-into-death, not as a spectator but as an active participant. Leaning into our own death and leaning into the death with another requires a philosophy of equanimity to harness and guide our love, fear, and suffering for ourselves and for the other. Learning about how one might lean into death offers a philosophy of communication praxis perspective that informs and enriches individual understanding and action.

LEANING INTO DEATH

Philip Simmons leaned into his own death; his family and friends also leaned into his death in a final physical social relation. Simmons (2000), a New Hampshire resident at the time of his death, said it best when he stated, "life is a terminal condition" (14). This is an essential aspect for understanding existence; we must begin by accepting this as an ontological truth. Heidegger articulated this when he stated that human beings are "being-toward-death" (1969, 242). This next section first describes what it means to lean into death as a sacred experience. Then, sharing Simmons's story about how he leaned into death, exemplifies how leaning in enabled him and his family to develop a philosophy of equanimity.

Leaning into Death

Leaning into death requires removing those internal barriers that limit perspectives and understandings about death. The idea of "leaning in" refers to leaning into one's strengths and power in any environment, whether in the workplace or at home (Sandberg 2017). No matter how uncomfortable it feels, leaning into what comes before us is an enactment of truth. Adopting the metaphor of *leaning in* enables the development of a philosophy of equanimity toward death; one must lean into death, no matter how uncomfortable it feels and no matter how difficult it is. Leaning into death allows one to be familiar with it, to seek to understand it in some fashion, and to know fully well that death comes for every mortal being. When this is fully accepted, understanding with empathic knowing is cultivated.

By leaning into death and not avoiding thinking or talking about death, we prepare for death to come. Although it has been said that nobody can ever prepare or be fully prepared for death of the self or of the other, developing an empathic knowing about death and moving toward a philosophy of equanimity provides an empathic disposition for the suffering that follows with the one left behind. Leaning into death acknowledges fate, mortality, and the ontological truth of being. This does not mean one simply gives up and waits for death. Leaning into death means that one prepares for death by understanding its ontological truth and by embracing the suffering it brings. The mark of achieving a level of inner equanimity occurs when physical or emotional pain no longer creates turbulence in our existence; it is at this moment that human beings recognize that they can access "the supersensible world" (Steiner 1994). Inner equanimity shifts attention away from the physical and emotional pain of loss or rupture and shifts the focus of attention to beyond the physical—beyond the mechanistic. Simmons's story represents a shift away from the mechanistic understanding of death to a death surrounded by equanimity.

The Story of Philip Simmons

Learning to Fall: The Blessings of an Imperfect Life is an autobiographical account of Simmons's life as he faced his own death, which occurred July 27, 2002, from complications of amyotrophic lateral sclerosis (ALS), informally known as Lou Gehrig's disease, a disorder that affects the function of nerves and muscles in the physical body. ALS is a radically debilitating disease that attacks the body and bodily functions before impact on the mind or one's consciousness. Simmons was thirty-five years old when he was diagnosed with ALS and given the prognosis of five years to live. Simmons lived ten years after his diagnosis. During those ten years, he chronicled his process of dying by writing this book and making a documentary film of the progression of his disease and death. Similar to the impact that Kübler-Ross had on the medical community when she first published her studies about death and dying from patients' perspectives, Simmons's story has had a similar impact in the United States and around the world about how one learns to live with, by leaning in, the face of death confronting the self every day.

Simmons was associate professor of English at Lake Forest College in Illinois. After diagnosis of his disease, he continued teaching for nine years before he had to give it up when his disease debilitated him to the point where he could no longer navigate his surroundings. He moved to Sandwich, New Hampshire, with his wife and children until his passing in 2002. Here is his story from the edges.

Learning to Fall (2000) is about coming to terms with being fully human. The metaphor Simmons identified as capturing his story, learning to fall, is a practice that one does when he must learn to live richly in the face of loss—we do this by "letting go our grip on all that we ordinarily find most precious—our achievements, our plans, our loved ones, our very selves" (Simmons 2000, xi). Simmons identifies that the space of leaning in and letting go occurs at the edges of death, which is where we have a choice, either lean into death at the edges of existence, or turn from it in denial and fear and walk away from it. When we turn and walk, we miss the present moment of understanding life and death. Simmons (2000) also suggested that it is in standing against or leaning into those edges that we find meaning in our lives.

In Simmons's story, he recalls falling as a birthright, referencing Christian theology of the "fall," which is described as a fall from grace or a fall away from God (2000, 3). Simmons (2000) describes the fall as "falling into knowledge of pain, grief, and loss" (3). Life is a mystery that we are not intended to solve like we solve problems. If we consider life as mystery and not seek to solve it as if it is a problem, that is the only way we can experience it—life is truly mystical, and the only way to experience it is to let go of all solutions and notice the mystery—hand ourselves over to it, which is letting go of everything we think we know (Simmons 2000). The narrative Simmons (2000) weaves together is connected by "mystery points" (8) that reveal a philosophy of equanimity situated within mystery that suggests that only in falling and letting go to lean into death gives back one's life even when we physically lose it. The mystery points that are present in a philosophy of equanimity are acceptance, vulnerability, standing on the edges, and being present.

When we fall, we accept vulnerability. Whether or not falling is revealed through a debilitating diagnosis, every human being is falling since the moment of birth. When we avoid this acknowledgment, we avoid life and living. Simmons (2000) argued that when we fall toward death, we fall toward and experience life. Throughout Simmons's story, he discusses several *Meditations* of Marcus Aurelius that suggest death is merely part of life; it is a casual partner of life. One Meditation that Simmons does not quote resonates quite clearly with the overall message that Simmons seeks to impart on his readers: "[d]eath, however, is not only a work of nature, but it is also a thing that fulfills the purpose of nature" (Aurelius 1945, 23). In accepting this natural law, one accepts the present condition and simultaneously sets aside fear to discover love and compassion in the present condition. Simmons (2000) suggested that once this acceptance occurs, every moment of every day, regardless of physical condition, one persists within compassion and awareness standing on the edges at all times, regardless of physical challenges. Acceptance allows one to lean in and accept the present to see and fully experience it.

Acceptance and leaning in allow one to reconcile oneself with existence itself—absent any particular religious framework or attachment to God or other diety(ies). Brent Sleasman (2011) explains this in the context of his understanding of Albert Camus's philosophy, that one of Camus's frustrations with Christianity was the explicit need to rely upon God (or a god) to bring about justice. Camus's belief was that humans should not rely upon anything external to life or existence itself. Anything outside of human experience was not significant and could not be counted on as contributing to life's meaning. Sleasman (2011) argues, Camus was willing to "engage in an ever-changing historical moment on its own terms; for Camus, this meant rejecting a Christian faith that would have provided an objective position from which to judge the chaos experienced in life" (11). Leaning in allows one to engage and confront one's ever-changing historical moment on its own terms—the terms of existence itself, without leaning away toward that objective position. Simmons leaned into his existence every single day facing and confronting his life on his own terms at the edges of his own existence.

Simmons (2000) suggested that in the face of the challenges of his disease, it was his human duty to wake up every day and face the loss of his physical body, the grief in his family (his wife and children), and accept his evolving transition toward death. Acceptance allowed him to confront the challenges and intimately understand the suffering of life and of living. In his acceptance, Simmons (2000) stated that he lived in a dual mind-set, which meant that while he continued to strive everyday to do physical things and communicate physically with his friends and family, he also let go of everything amid this striving. He described his acceptance of the mystery of life as a mystical experience—a deeper experience of the present where one cannot be fooled into thinking life is permanent. He declared himself an ordinary mystic—someone accepting the unknown, letting go of what he used to think he knew about life, and living within ordinary mysticism.

Simmons (2000) believed that one's spiritual life involved an inner journey; however, for most people spirituality is expressed only in our relationships with other people, so the inner journey is forgotten or neglected. Simmons suggested that spirituality can be transformative only when the inner journey expression occurs together with others—for him it is a duty or obligation in the face of death to be with others as much as one is within the inner journey of the ending life. Dwelling in the present moment, standing at the edges "is our highest spiritual discipline" (Simmons 2000, 145). Simmons (2000) stated that "our very presentness [at the edges] is our salvation—entered fully—it is our gateway to eternal life" (145). There is no escape for any human being. We will all stand at the edge, an "evanescent sliver of time between past and future" (Simmons 2000, 145). The world around us constantly diverts our attention (Jackson, 2009), calling our attention away from the sense of equanimity to ignore the reality that life is a terminal condition even when it is slamming us in the face with reminders. The only way to meet our own death or to be with another in death is by leaning into it, sensing the vulnerability of the unknown or uncertainty and admitting that death is a part of our life without which we could not be truly alive.

A Philosophy of Equanimity: An Invitation to the Sacred

A philosophy of equanimity requires leaning into death through dispositions of genuine compassion, unconstrained responsiveness, openness absent of fear or judgment, cultivating a transcendent mind-set, openness to and in dialogue, a disposition of being-witness toward the self or other, and being open to revelation or transcendent knowing. These are absolute values of a philosophy of equanimity that situates communicative behavior evolving from a philosophy of equanimity as a form of the sacred—an exemplification of sacred rhetoric. There are competing understandings of sacred rhetoric; however, for the purpose of this discussion, sacred rhetoric is not confined to a religious paradigm, and it is not necessarily holy in the context of any religious framework (Marietta 2009).

Some scholars suggest that sacred rhetoric is a political expression of an absolute value or absolute principle that one is not open to adapting. The principle is simply nonnegotiable (Marietta 2012). In a philosophy of equanimity, leaning into death is nonnegotiable. Leaning into death is an absolute value that is unquestionable and the glue that holds the dispositions of genuine compassion, unconstrained responsiveness, openness absent of fear or judgment, a transcendent mind-set, openness to and in dialogue, being-witness toward the self or other, and being open to revelation. These dispositions are attuned with the absolute values of what makes rhetoric sacred: 1) having a protective status toward nonnegotiable values, 2) having a non-consequentialist framework and privileging values over consequences or outcomes, 3) rejecting calculated self-interest, 4) articulating a nonnegotiability and denial of compromise, 5) invoking a boundary, 6) invoking authority for the value or boundary, and 7) expressing moral outrage when the value is violated (Marietta 2009). Leaning into death through a philosophy of equanimity requires suspending the embedded ego so that communicative responses and actions are embedded within a disposition of equanimity. This is a significant commitment. Life is sacred. Death is sacred. In this essay, I intentionally use sacred to mean to honor and to value something beyond the ordinary. To be sacred has explicit religious traditions and connections; sacred can also be situated outside specific religious traditions and be promoted through the mystical, cosmological, or ontological.

The earlier interlocutors mentioned in this essay do not always attach the language of sacred to their thinking; however, it would be obvious to suggest that Zajonc, the Dalai Lama, and Steiner would certainly use the word sacred to describe both life and death because of their Buddhist alignments. Derrida (1995) would likely see both life and death as sacred because for him, both are mysteries, and he does refer to them as sacred mysteries because it is something we fully cannot grasp, yet it is omnipresent in our awareness, and we anticipate it. Heidegger might refer to Dasein as being sacred but not in a strictly theological sense. Heidegger's understanding and use of the sacred is tied to the holy, but as Adrian Mihai (2009) argues, "Heidegger has tried to explain the holy in itself without any recourse to its relations to society, psychology, or theology," (139) but he ultimately posits that the Holy is the Holy, and it basically precedes affectivity, utterance, and understanding. Mihai (2009) suggests that the Holy, to Heidegger, precedes existence and the fundamental existential that reveals itself by concealing itself. Heidegger, at once, separates the Holy from theology, but as this essay uses the term sacred, Heidegger's usage of The Holy and Sacred is honored and valued beyond the ordinary.

How we communicate about and around life and death should be considered sacred ground. Equanimity as a sacred value toward death could help to change the negative rhetoric around death. Some scholars suggest that a sacred value is something that one would rather die for than yield to or compromise the value (Marietta 2009). Cultivating a philosophy of equanimity can shift the rhetoric of fear about death toward a sacred rhetoric because death and life are the ultimate gift and the ultimate price.

CONCLUSION

This essay explored several perspectives on death to provide an alternative way of understanding something about death that is not tied to negative rhetoric relating to death. Changing the rhetoric about death in popular culture provides an alternative to becoming stuck in holding on to fear and grief. Moving beyond the mechanistic underpinnings of the rhetoric about death toward a philosophy of equanimity provides a deeper, inner perspective that liberates the individual from preconceived notions and other challenges or limitations caused by negative rhetorics. In *The Book of Equanimity*, Gerry Shishin Wick (2005) reminds readers that equanimity is cultivated when we contemplate deeper meanings in life. The key to equanimity is to "think not-thinking," and once this is achieved, preconceived ideas, thoughts, opinions go away and true revelation can occur. It is in this space of revelation where the ultimate equanimity emerges. In thinking this way, the ego is suspended, so one truly connects to the other within sacred dialogic space that shares compassion, openness, and empathy; thus, devolving into the space of negative rhetoric is no longer a possibility. Equanimity as a sacred value enables human beings to lean into death and teaches us how to be truly human.

REFERENCES

Aurelius, M. 1945. "Meditations." In Irwin Edman, *Marcus Aurelius and His Times: The Transition from Paganism to Christianity*, 11–133. Roslyn, NY: Walter J. Black.

Carel, H. 2007. Temporal Finitude and Finitude of Possibility: The Double Meaning of Death in Being and Time. *International Journal of Philosophical Studies* 15: 541–56.

Carpentier, N., and L. van Brussel. 2012. "On the Contingency of Death: A Discourse-Theoretical Perspective on the Construction of Death." *Critical Discourse Studies* 9, no. 2: 99–115.
Copeland, L. 2015. Who Owns the Dead? *New Republic* 7/8: 14–22.
Derrida, J. 1993. *Aporias*. Redwood City, CA: Stanford University Press.
———. 1995. *The Gift of Death*. Chicago: University of Chicago Press.
Dossey, L. 1999. *Reinventing Medicine: Beyond Mind-Body to a New Era of Healing*. New York: HarperCollins.
Duerringer, C. M. 2013. "Winking and Giggling at Creeping Death: Thanatophobia and the Rhetoric of Save the Ta-tas." *Journal of Communication Inquiry* 37: 344–63.
Feldman, C. 2017. *Boundless Heart: The Buddha's Path of Kindness, Compassion, Joy, and Equanimity*. Boulder, CO: Shambhala.
Gandhi, M. 2008. *Mahatma Gandhi: The Essential Writings*, ed. Judith M. Brown. New York: Oxford University Press.
Heidegger, M. 1996. *Being and Time*, trans. Joan Stambaugh. Albany: SUNY Press.
Jackson, M. 2009. *Distracted: The Erosion of Attention and the Coming Dark Age*. New York: Prometheus.
Kübler-Ross, E. 1969. *On Death and Dying: What the Dying Have to Teach Doctors, Nurses, Clergy, and Their Own Families*. New York: Touchstone.
Lama, D., and T. Jinpa. 2005. *The Essence of the Heart Sutra: The Dalai Lama's Heart of Wisdom Teachings*. Somerville, MA: Wisdom Publications.
Marietta, M. 2009. "The Absolutist Advantage: Sacred Rhetoric in Contemporary Presidential Debate." *Political Communication* 26: 388–411.
———. 2012. *The Politics of Sacred Rhetoric: Absolutist Appeals and Political Persuasion*. Waco, TX: Baylor University Press.
Mathis, R. 2018. *Developing Equanimity: Stay Calm*. n.p.
Mihai, A. 2009. "On the Essence of the Sacred in Heidegger's Philosophy." *Vox Philosophiae* 1: 139–48.
Neher, W., and P. Sandin. 2006. *Communicating Ethically: Virtue, Duties, Consequences, and Relationships*. New York: Routledge.
Rinpoche, D. K. 2015. *The Relaxed Mind: A Seven-Step Method for Deepening Meditation Practice*. Boulder, CO: Shambhala.
Sandberg. S. 2017. *Lean In: Women, Work, and the Will to Lead*. New York: Knopf.
Simmons, P. 2000. *Learning to Fall: The Blessings of an Imperfect Life*. New York: Bantam Dell.
Sleasman, B. C. 2011. *Albert Camus's Philosophy of Communication: Making Sense in an Age of Absurdity*. Amherst, NY: Cambria Press.
Steiner, R. 1994. *Theosophy: An Introduction to the Spiritual Processes at Work and in Human Life and in the Cosmos*. Hudson, NY: Anthroposophic Press.
van Brussel, L., and N. Carpenter. 2014. *The Social Construction of Death: Interdisciplinary Perspectives*. New York: Palgrave Martin.
Welwood, J. 2002. *Toward a Psychology of Awakening: Buddhism, Psychotherapy, and the Path of Personal and Spiritual Transformation*. Boulder, CO: Shambhala.

Wick, G. S. 2005. *The Book of Equanimity: Illuminating Classic Zen Koans*. Somerville, MA: Wisdom Publications.
Zajonc, A. 2008. *Contemplative Inquiry: When Knowing Becomes Love*. Great Barrington, MA: Lindisfarne Books.

Index

affordances, 21
Allen, John, Jr., 187, 194
Allen, Ronald, 147
anatheism, xiii
Anthropocene, 65
apophatic, 50, 51, 64
application or applicability, 151, 153, 166, 167
Apollo, 19, 23, 25–26
apologetics, 106, 107, 111, 117
Aquinas, Thomas, 65, 194
Aristotle, vii, viii, 48, 84
Asad, Talal, xii
Athens, 20, 23, 24, 25, 28, 30, 32
Augustine, vii, 5, 13, 85, 193

Bakhtin, Mikhail, 104, 106
Balkanized, 20
Barthes, Roland, ix
beatniks, 55
"being-toward-death," 222, 230
Benoit, William, 189–90
Berger, Peter, x, xii
Blaney, Joseph, 186, 189–90
blaspheme, blaspheming, or blasphemy, 159, 163, 164, 165, 175 n. 76
blues, 57, 58, 59
boast or boasting, 155, 157, 158, 174 nn. 61, 63

Boff, Leonardo, 196–97
boundaries, 19
Brahma Viharas, 228, 229
Brennus, 27–28
Brown, Brené, 81–83
Bruegemann, Walter, 146–47
Burke, Kenneth, xiii

Calvin, John, 85, 88, 166 179 n. 119, 181
canon, 21–22, 24, 27, 30
Catholicism, 54, 107, 188, 197, 199, 202
cellular/cell phone, 64, 67
chastening, 156, 160
church, Christian in Corinth, 154, 156, 159, 160, 166, 167, 168
Cicero, viii, 152, 170 nn. 11, 14, 181
community, Corinthian, 151–84
contemplation/contemplative, 48, 50, 63, 196, 201, 222, 228, 229
conviction-hesitancy dilemma, 135, 142–43
Corinth, 24, 30, 151–84
corporate crisis communication, 188–90
Crouch, Andy, 77
Curran, Charles, 196, 199

dance/dancing, 27, 66, 67

De las Casas, Bartolomé, xvii
death, 4, 10, 18, 54, 135, 137, 141, 145, 155, 156, 160, 161, 162, 221–36
Delphi, 23
Derrida, Jacques, 225, 226, 234
destroy or destruction, 156, 159, 160, 161, 162, 163, 164, 165, 166, 172 n. 44, 175 n. 79, 176 nn. 86–87, 177 n. 89, 178 n. 99, 100, 104
dialogue, xiii, xvii, 5, 55, 56, 79, 80, 102, 103–106, 107, 108, 110, 111, 113, 114, 115, 117, 119, 120
DiAngelo, Robin, 134
discipline, church, 166, 167, 168, 177 n. 101
disconnection, fear of as related to shame, 82
Dossey, Larry, 223, 224, 225, 226, 227

Eco, Umberto, ix, 113
Eliade, Mircea, x
empathic witness, 225, 229
equanimity, 222, 225, 227, 228, 229, 231, 232, 233, 234, 235
euphemia, 17
evil, xvii, 4, 5, 7, 8, 11, 14, 49, 56, 57, 58, 59, 63, 118, 155, 162, 165, 167
excommunicate or excommunication, 156, 160, 165, 174 n. 56, 184
exegesis, 8, 17, 21, 22, 27, 136, 158

Faggioli, Massimo, 185, 187, 198, 200
faith, as means to counter shame, 87–91
festival(s), 20, 23, 24, 25, 32, 67–68
"flesh," 159, 175–176 n. 79
Foucault, Michel, xiv, 33 n. 6

Gadamer, Hans-Georg, 67, 79–80, 82, 84, 91
Gallic invasion, 27–28
Gaonkar, Dilip, viii–ix
Geetz, Clifford, ix–x, xii, 34, n. 7
golden rule, 139–40, 142
Govekar, Natasa, 186

grace, Christian doctrine of as corrective for shame, 86–91
Gramsci, Antonio, xvii
Greek religion, 17

Habermas, Jürgen, xvii, 5, 79–80, 84
Hebrew Bible/scriptures, xiii, 49, 65, 87, 133
Heidegger, Martin, 192, 222, 225, 226, 230, 234, 235
hermeneutics,
    impact of white fragility upon, 138
    in relation to rhetoric, 79–80
    joy as hermeneutical key for understanding Pope Francis, 191
    Ricoeur's hermeneutics of proclamation, 6–7
Hesiod, 21
Hobson, Christopher, 134
Holy Spirit, 46, 59, 65, 152, 154, 156, 159, 160, 161, 162, 165, 166, 168, 172 n. 42, 173 n. 47, 175 nn. 73–74, 177 n. 91, 178 n. 100
Homer, 21
hyper-seriality, 31

ideal speech situation, 79
ideology-critique, 80, 84
image repair theory, 188–90
immanence, 49, 117, 118
imprecation, curse, or cursing, 156, 160–61, 176 n. 83
incest or incestuous, 152, 155, 165, 168
inspiration, 21, 62

Jesus, x, xi, 56, 58, 85, 91, 135, 136, 137, 138, 139, 140, 142, 143, 145, 151, 154, 156, 157, 158, 159, 161, 162, 166, 185, 190, 191, 192, 196, 198, 226
Johnson, Andre, 132–33, 145
justice,

Index

addressed by Pope Francis,
   197–98
addressed in preaching strategy,
   141–47
and love in Paul Ricoeur's
   thought, 4, 13
Christian understandings of,
   88–91
in Albert Camus, 232
in music, 57
justification,
   and justice, 87–90
   Christian doctrine of, 87–91

Kasper, Walter, 192–94
kataphatic, 50, 64
Kearney, Richard, xiii
Keenan, James, 195
Kosmos, 19–20
Krizek, Robert, 134
Kübler-Ross, Elisabeth, 221, 223, 224,
   225, 226, 227, 231

Lacan, Jacques, xv
Lewis, Amanda, 134
Lincoln, Bruce, xi
Lindbeck, George, xii–xiii
"linguistic turn," vii
Lowney, Chris, 194
LSD, 52, 53
Luckmann, Thomas, x
Luther, Martin, 85, 88, 166, 179 n.
   120, 182
Lyotard-Jean-François, x

McClure, John, 146
McMickle, Marvin, 146
Memphis Massacre of 1866, 141
Memphis Sanitation Strike, 132, 135
metaphor, 29, 52, 68, 107, 112, 119,
   136, 230, 231
metaphysics, xvii, 48, 49, 53
Moberg, Marcus, xii
Moynihan, Robert, 185
muse, 19, 59, 60, 61, 62, 63

music, xiv, 24, 26, 27, 45–75
mystery, 50, 60, 61, 65, 105, 111, 117,
   118, 193, 196, 226, 231, 232, 233
mysticism, xvi, 50, 51, 54, 55, 57, 58,
   59, 60, 61, 233
myth, 23, 31

Nakayama, Thomas, 134
narrative(s), viii, xi, xii, xv, 3, 4, 5, 6,
   8, 9, 10, 12, 13, 14, 18, 20, 22, 26,
   27, 29, 30, 31, 32, 102, 103, 106,
   107, 117
New Testament, xi, 64, 142, 167, 193

Obama, Barack, 194
Old Testament, 3, 10, 55, 132, 133, 193
Otto, Rudolf, x

paradigms, 23
pastoral rhetoric, 145, 147
Pattison, Stephen, 83
Percy, Walker, 101–29
Persian invasion, 28–29
Plutarch, 31
Pope Francis,
   controversy, 186–87, 199–201
   decentralization and inclusion in
      church offices, 198–99
   ecumenical efforts, 195
   Evangelii Gaudium, 188, 192–94,
      198–99
   image repair efforts, 190–96
   joy as repair strategy, 191–93
   Laudato Si,' 193, 195, 198, 201
   Misericordiae Vultus, 196
   mercy as repair strategy, 193–96
   positive public image, 185,
      187–88
   poverty and simplicity of life,
      197–98
   regarding LGBTQ community,
      194, 196
   views on women, 199–200
postmodern/postmodernity, x, xv, 12,
   57, 102, 103, 107, 108, 111, 117

prophetic rhetoric, 132, 145–46
Protestant, 64, 66, 85, 106, 117, 166, 200
Pseudo-Cicero, vii
purity, 151–84

religious definitions of self, xv–xvii
repentance, 164, 175 n. 75
restoration, 164
revelatory, 3, 4, 5, 6, 7, 8, 9, 12
rhetoric,
    as Christian doctrine, 84–87
    definition of, vii–x, 79–81
Richards, I. A., viii
Ricoeur, Paul, xiv–xv, 2, 3, 4, 5, 6, 7, 8, 9, 10, 11, 12, 13
Rorty, Richard, viii

sacred, definition of, x–xiii, 1–14
sacred rhetoric, definition of, xiii
Sedmak, Clemens, 191–92
semiotics, ix, 102, 108, 110, 111, 113, 117
Sensing, Tim, 147
sex or sexuality, 151–84
Scott, John A., Jr., 131
    "The Mind of Christ" sermon, 135–45
shame,
    in American culture, 77–78, 82–83
    rhetoric of, 77–83
Simmons, Philip, 230, 231–233
Sleasman, Brent C., 232
Sobrino, Jon, 195

Smart, Ninian, x–xi
spirit, human, 156–157, 159, 160, 161, 163, 164, 165, 166, 167, 172 n. 42, 173 n. 46. 175 n. 70, 178 nn. 100, 104
spirituals, 45, 57
Steiner, Rudolf, 222, 227, 230, 234
synecdoche, 29

Tamez, Elsa, 85
Tanner, Kathryn, 88–89
Taylor, Charles, xiv
Temenos (sanctuary), 18
Tertullian, 175 n. 76, 183
theology, 4, 10, 64, 65, 77, 83, 86, 88, 106, 118, 199, 226, 231, 234
"Think not-Think," 235
Thompson, Curt, 83
Tillich, Paul, xii
Tisdale, Leonora Tubbs, 146
triadic communication, 108, 110, 115, 116, 117, 118, 120
truth, xii, xiii, 10, 22, 30, 45, 46, 47, 50, 56, 57, 66, 79, 85, 87, 102, 107, 115, 147, 151, 155, 193, 194, 202, 222, 225, 227, 230

Vigano, Archbishop Carlo Maria, 186–87, 201
Volf, Miroslav, 85–86, 90–91

Ward, Keith, xv
White fragility, 134, 138, 141, 146
Wittgenstein, Ludwig, viii

About the Editors and Contributors

Ronald C. Arnett, PhD, is professor emeritus and former chair of the Department of Communication & Rhetorical Studies at Duquesne University.

David M. Barbee, PhD, is associate professor of Christian thought at Winebrenner Theological Seminary.

Steven Gaines, PhD, is professor of communication at Midland College.

Corey Hackworth, PhD, is visiting lecturer in classics at Baylor University.

Annette M. Holba, PhD, is professor of rhetoric in the Communication and Media Studies Department at Plymouth State University.

Michael R. Kearney is a PhD student in the Department of Communication & Rhetorical Studies at Duquesne University.

Aaron K. Kerr, PhD, is executive director of Groundwork Erie, an educational and environmental nonprofit in the city of Erie, Pennsylvania.

Sang-Il Kim, PhD, is staff chaplain at Long Beach VA Medical Center.

Brent C. Sleasman, PhD, is president of Winebrenner Theological Seminary in Findlay, Ohio.

James P. Sweeney, PhD, is the J. Russell Bucher Professor of New Testament Studies at Winebrenner Theological Seminary.

Dũng Q. Trần, PhD, is associate professor of organizational leadership in the School of Leadership Studies at Gonzaga University.